Growing
Vegetables

WEST OF THE CASCADES

Growing Vegetables
WEST OF THE CASCADES

THE COMPLETE GUIDE TO NATURAL GARDENING

5TH EDITION

Steve Solomon

SASQUATCH BOOKS
SEATTLE

First published in 1981 as *The Complete Guide to Organic Gardening West of the Cascades*.

Printed in the United States of America
Published by Sasquatch Books
Distributed by Publishers Group West
09 08 07 06 05 04 03   5 4 3

Cover illustration: ©Hokanson & Cichetti/Artville
Cover and interior design: Kate Basart
Interior illustrations: Muriel Chen
Copy editor: Rebecca Pepper

Library of Congress Cataloging in Publication Data
Solomon, Steve.
    Growing vegetables west of the Cascades : the complete guide to natural gardening,
5th edition.—[Updated and expanded].
    p.   cm.
    Includes bibliographical references.
    ISBN 1-57061-240-4 (alk. paper)
    Vegetable gardening—Northwest Coast of North America. 2. Organic gardening—
Northwest Coast of North America. I. Title.
    SB324.3 .S67 2000
    635'.0484'09795—dc21   99-047200

Sasquatch Books
119 South Main Street, Suite 400
Seattle, Washington 98104
(206) 467-4300
www.sasquatchbooks.com
books@sasquatchbooks.com

Contents

Introduction

There seems to be but three ways for a nation to acquire wealth.
The first is by war, as the Romans did in plundering their conquered neighbors.
This is robbery. The second is by commerce, which is generally cheating. The third
is by agriculture, the only honest way; wherein man receives a real increase of
the seed thrown into the ground in a kind of continual miracle.

—Benjamin Franklin

In your hands is a handbook for year-round vegetable growing in the maritime Northwest. It covers the at-home production of most types of garden food, with information on just about every regional aspect of vegetable gardening. It is as complete and as simple as I can make it.

Why I Write This Book

Please observe that I say "write," not "wrote." That's because I've been constantly writing this book since I began the first edition in 1979. This is the fifth edition. Each edition has demanded a complete rewrite, because each time I had learned too much to merely adjust the old structure. And even as I finish this edition, I know that I am still not done learning about how to grow vegetables.

However deep or shallow your interest in growing vegetables, my intention is that fresh, home-grown vegetables will become a major part of your family's food supply. You're about to learn how to grow a full array of vegetables, not only during the heat of midsummer, but all year round.

I homesteaded in Oregon twenty years ago because I believed in self-sufficient living. It is still my personal solution to a lot of the world's problems and many of my own. It seems to me that as people become more responsible for their physical survival—and there is nothing more essential to surviving than eating—they begin to have a more positive attitude about life in general. They're less dependent on a complex system that is entirely out of their control.

A self-sufficient person becomes "independence minded." The Oregon countryside is still dotted with homesteads on which vegetable gardens are grown; consequently, independence-minded is how many old-time Oregonians describe both themselves and the unique culture of the state. Washington State isn't much different.

Although independence-mindedness is a spiritual state, I'd also like my neighbors to enjoy a higher level of physical well-being, because I find it far more pleasant to be among healthy people. Having a feeling of well-being lets us throw back our shoulders, move confidently through life, and assert our independence. To enjoy solid health, we need to make a substantial part of our total food intake *fresh* vegetable food. But most North Americans have neither great vegetables nor strong health. The best way to change your diet in the direction of health is not to force yourself because someone told you to change, and certainly not to change by fighting your own bad habits and cravings. The best way to reform yourself is simple—experience the pleasures and wonderful tastes of fresh garden vegetables. Given a few years to work on a person, the garden will effortlessly change the gardener's preferences. I know this works because I've been through this change myself.

Growing Vegetables West of the Cascades has always been constructed a little differently than most other gardening guides. It strongly advocates thinking for oneself. It explains the basic processes that happen in growing food and then puts you in a position to decide for yourself exactly what to do. In that sense I see my book as being very Oregonian.

This book must, of economic necessity, be a regional book. My publisher believes that the cover price would far exceed the market's tolerance, and the book's size would scare away too many bookstore browsers, if I (I) tried to include all of the specialized information needed to succeed west of the Cascades and (2) also made this book into a complete, scientifically accurate general guide to gardening. As a result, I've had to concentrate on point 1 at the expense of point 2.

This restriction will mainly affect the novice. If you already know enough to succeed at growing vegetables in another climate, my book will be all you'll probably need. New gardeners, however, may want to find other sources of information about the general procedures for using raised beds, preparing the soil, making compost, and the many other gardening minutiae commonly called the techniques of gardening. Well, dear novice, the public library is full of national-distribution garden books. Following the varietal advice, soil management systems, and planting schedules in a book targeted at the East often won't reveal the potential of our climate and will often lead to failure, but the general information in them can be very valuable.

Why We Need a Regional Gardening Book

Most gardening books published in the United States and Canada are actually very regional, although this is often not directly mentioned. They maximize profit by addressing the area of greatest population—that part of North America east of the Cascade Range.

Gardening west of the Cascades is very different. Our winters are mild and rainy, and our summer days are rarely hot; even our midsummer nights are usually too cool for short-sleeved shirts. We also have a perverse pattern of rainfall. We get a lot of moisture in winter when our gardens don't need it, but it rains little or not at all in summer when they do.

If we adjust to our climate, we can grow fresh food year round. If we act as though we were gardening in the East, we will have fresh food for only a few months a year. The Americans who first settled the Oregon Territory gardened as though they were still living in Ohio. This seems ironic because the first colonial settlers were British gardeners from a maritime climate just like ours. But by the time these British had become Americans and then settled the continent, they'd forgotten not only that they were once British, but also how they used to farm and garden.

Had the native tribes of the Oregon Territory been gardeners like the natives of the East Coast, the first Anglo-Americans arriving here might have acquired appropriate agricultural technology, which is exactly what happened to the British in Massachusetts Bay Colony two centuries earlier. But the tribes on this coast were living quite comfortably by hunting and gathering, and gardening not at all. So the new arrivals continued to farm and garden here—especially garden—as though they were back in Ohio, which sort of worked but was far from optimal.

This situation persisted in Oregon and Washington until we started to smarten up in the late 1970s. Cascadia then resembled a Third World backwater, exporting lumber, livestock, and fruit to the rest of the United

States. Like other Third World countries, we depended on imported technology. We learned to garden from books describing techniques that worked in the East, and we bought our seeds from catalogs of eastern companies selling varieties that worked well where summers were hot and humid but that often did not grow as promised for us. And little in these catalogs helped us take advantage of the opportunities presented by our mild winters.

I do not know exactly how all of the diverse threads of change were woven together in Seattle or who to credit for what. Perhaps one reason that Seattle was the center of the new gardening movement was its proximity to *British* Columbia, where British seeds and British gardening books were available. The Canadians had done a much better job of adapting to their part of the Cascadia Biore-gion than the Americans had. I do know, though, that toward the end of the 1970s a group centered around an active community garden in Seattle began to experiment with winter cropping. One of their number, Binda Colebrook, then wrote what I found to be a mind-expanding book called *Winter Gardening in the Maritime Northwest.*

Since then things have become a lot easier for the region's vegetable gardeners. We now have the knowledge to make full use of the climate. We have regional seed companies whose ethics and quality are world-class. And you have this book and Binda's book to introduce you to all of the possibilities.

I have always made myself as available as I could to help people. If you wish to contact me, write to me care of Sasquatch Books, or send e-mail to ssolomon@soilandhealth.org.

Chapter 1 Basics

The agriculturalist is the servant of the plant.

—Louise Howard, wife and research partner of
Sir Albert Howard until her death in India in about 1932

Prior to 1870 most Americans grew up on family farms with a hoe and shovel in their hands. My generation grew up quite differently, knowing everything about automobiles. The next knew the television schedules; the current one knows computers.

My generation was guided toward a university education, which meant a healthy dollop of high school sciences, including plant biology and basic inorganic chemistry. These sciences and university-level geology did more to make me appreciate what was happening around me than anything I was taught about history or social life. I owe my teachers a debt of gratitude for this knowledge. But because we gardeners need to develop an even greater understanding than is found in a science class or textbook, I wrote this chapter to open your eyes, mind, and heart.

Please Be a Plant

The way to understand another being is to put on their boots and walk in them. So I'm going to ask you to assume the viewpoint of a wild plant and then the viewpoint of a garden vegetable.

Sure, plants have viewpoints! All living things do. Dogs and cats have dog and cat awarenesses. Some people are quite good at understanding animal awarenesses. Others lack this ability; these folks are the ones whom dogs growl at and cats scratch. Similarly, some people seem to have green thumbs. For others, every plant they tend sickens and dies.

I think, however, that most "brown-thumbedness" is caused by ignorance and can be cured by gaining a little insight. Rote instruction that offers steps to be followed blindly is not nearly as effective as insight. The Latinos have a few wonderful words that illustrate this concept. *Instruido*—often said with slight disdain—means someone who displays pride after having been well instructed. Those who are *instruido* can *seem* knowledgeable. They have learned the proper buzzwords and can parrot the trendy concepts, but they don't really have wisdom. The innately wise person is *educado.* And the best sort of educated being, the sort that gets the most respect in Latin America, is one who is *autodidactico,* meaning someone who is self-teaching, self-motivated, self-directed. Latinos also understand that most *autodidacticos* can barely stand being in a classroom.

I don't want my efforts to turn out *instruidos;* the universities and agricultural schools do more than enough of that already. So I am asking you to take the little bits of data and the strange and perhaps slightly funny viewpoints I provide about plants and try them on for size. Look around and see if what I suggest fits what you observe going on.

A plant has awareness and knows things, but it does not think. If you doubt this, I suggest you read *The Secret Life of Plants,* listed in the bibliography at the end of this book. Plants make an effort to survive just like we do, but unlike some animals, especially humans, plants seem to have no individual awareness. A plant is no more uniquely "one being" than a skin cell on your thumb is. Plants participate in a group consciousness composed of all of the same sort of plants in the area. Thus, all of the fir trees of the maritime Northwest might share one consciousness. To this group, enhanced survival of the whole is the common goal.

Plant awareness is so different from ours that to know it you have to just "see" it. One way to do this is by spending some time leaning on your hoe and just being with the plants in your garden. You can also get it by hugging trees in the forest or meditating on hillsides. I prefer hoe-leaning, though I've done some of the others too. I've come to some remarkable understandings while hoe-leaning; once I became the symphylans undermining my trial ground and saw in one flash of insight how to manage them. I share this with you in Chapter 4.

There's no shortage of books on how to meditate, but none as far as I know mention hoe-leaning. Here's how to do it. While working in the garden, when your muscles become a bit tired or sore, you put the working end of the hoe on the soil, hold the handle near the top with both hands for a bit of a prop, rest it against your shoulder and/or cheek, and, while supporting some of your weight on the tool and leaning slightly forward, stare off into space or at some part of your garden and *don't think*. Then, when you do resume thinking, don't try to force yourself to stop, which is what people who meditate do—just resume hoeing. Don't let anyone call this laziness; hoe-leaning is a vital gardening chore, equally as important as hoe sharpening.

What I've discovered from my own hoe-leaning is that plants are trying to be universal conquerors, engaged in a stiff competition for the control of light, soil resources, and space, in much the same way that people play a Japanese board game called Go. Plants attempt to own the space around them by getting there first and then by preventing their competitors from squeezing in around them. Because domination is their purpose, plants throw off a great deal of variations so that the one seedling with just the right stuff can succeed against all the others. Plants play this out by sowing dozens, hundreds, thousands of their own seeds in a small area and then letting their offspring have at the battle, competing with each other and with the progeny of other species. The victor's progeny will then be more likely to have the right stuff.

Most species are highly variable. To see this, take a close look at a patch of fir trees. Walk among them. Notice that one tree is bushy with long, well-developed side branches while another is taller and slender. One fir has dark green needles, another blue-green; one has long spaces between each whorl of side branches going up the trunk, another a short interstem. And although you can't see it, one has a deeply penetrating root system and another's roots are shallow and extend widely. The variations go on and on, in bark thickness and texture, in needle shape, and in the odor of, amount of, and thickness of sap. The closer you look the more differences you'll find. Yet all are Douglas firs. And all are competing with one another and with every other species for control of that forest.

There is very little "live and let live" in this game of competition by survival strategy. A thicket of firs starts out in a sunny spot. Gradually they shade out the grasses, berries, broom, and other herbs. Once the trees control all of the resources, their competition with one another makes the whole patch of trees grow taller faster. Those few that are able to overtop their competitors capture all of the light and thus kill off the shorter trees. A few end up owning all of the water and nutrition and get all of the light. Obviously, the game favors the taller-growing trees with fewer side branches.

So why do the firs keep on making trees that have a great deal of side-branch development? I imagine that it's because when trees with long and thick side branches grow at the edge of a forest (or alone in a clearing) they can shade a lot of ground, kill off the grasses and other low-growing herbs, and control that space better.

Similar battles go on in any site where a plant is capable of growing. In fact, in every natural setting, the plant already growing in a spot must be the one that is best suited to be there. This is proved by the fact that it is already there. If another plant were better suited to own that spot, it would already be there instead of the one that is there. How's that for logic?

Every kind of plant has a unique winning strategy. Young trees make no seeds for many years but first direct their energy to growing tall and strong. Once they have overtopped everything and control their space, they make jillions of seeds that can, because of the height at which they're released, travel long distances before sowing themselves. A fierce competitor like wild lettuce rapidly spreads a dense mulch of its own leaves over the low-growing competition, starving them for light, while it uses the light it collects to make and store up food in its fleshy, juicy core. Then the lettuce suddenly bolts, puts up a tall seed stalk that overtops any competition remaining around it, and, with that big reserve of food in storage, rapidly makes seeds that blow away in the wind.

Some vines can wriggle into any bit of light missed by a competitor or climb over the competition, while their big leaves rapidly fill in and dominate that spot. Biennials sprout in the cool of early autumn when other species can't grow, store up food during the sunnier days of winter and early spring, and use that food reserve to shoot up a tall seed stalk later in spring, way ahead of competitors that sprout in the spring. Biennials are especially well suited to our climate because their survival strategy matches the seasonal rains, starting out when the rains begin in autumn and mak-ing seed as the soil dries out the next summer.

Admiring the strategy each vegetable family uses allows the gardener to better assist them. In fact the word "cultivation" might be defined as creating a more ideal situation for a given sort of plant. And that's the whole of gardening in a nutshell. In Chapter 9, I categorize vegetables by their basic familial survival strategy because we cultivate (help) each group in its own unique way.

Weeding

Most wild plants are vigorous enough to dominate infertile soil and survive heavy competition. Wild plants develop tough stems and leaves. Bitter, unpalatable flavors and often spiny leaves and stalks discourage would-be grazing animals, as do assorted unpleasant or poisonous chemical contents. We can't eat many of them. Wild plants make large numbers of small, hard seeds that are broadcast widely, but people prefer to eat large, tender, fat seeds.

Vegetables once were wild plants too, but now have been changed by people. I understand plant domestication as an eternal contract whereby we humans promise to nurture a wild plant and protect it and its progeny from competition. In exchange the wild plant changes itself to suit us, the creators of its new environment. This contractual relationship was brilliantly exploited by a nineteenth-century American plant breeder named Luther Burbank—an *autodidactico* if ever there was one.

Burbank wrote that whenever he cultivated a wild plant in his garden it immediately grew to many times its wild size. We gardeners have all noticed this: Any weed that grows unhindered in our gardens becomes huge and wildly outdoes our weak and puny vegetables. Burbank also noticed that the wild plants he wanted to change seemed to "know" that they were being taken care of, because within a few generations, the plants would cooperate by trying to become what Burbank wanted them to be, even if that meant they became weak and unable to compete well. He said that this happened because the plant was trying to please its protector.

Burbank's system of plant breeding involved first studying all of the members of a potentially useful wild family to see what desirable characteristics already existed and then visualizing—strongly, clearly, and continuously—a recombination of those traits into exactly what he wanted that family to become. If Burbank kept his visualization in mind as he crossed and recrossed the various species that constituted the family, and in each generation propagated only those individual plants that contained ever more of the traits he wanted, the species would eventually become exactly what he envisioned.

Burbank's method sounds very primitive compared to the scientific mathematical procedures developed by his contemporary, Austrian botanist Gregor Mendel, and currently used by all plant breeders. Interestingly, Burbank said that he understood Mendelian genetics and believed that they worked, but that he personally preferred not to be a statistician. A more intuitive system better suited Burbank's genius.

Other changes inevitably occur over time when a wild plant is cultivated. Root systems become less extensive because crops are fertilized, perhaps watered, and certainly protected from competition by weeding and by thinning surrounding plants. A portion of the plant's energy can then be redirected away from making roots and toward producing thicker, juicier leaves, pods, or stems; larger flowers; bigger, sweeter fruit; and tastier seeds. Because vegetables don't have to compete, they can be inbred, which can emphasize desirable traits and uniformity, but at the expense of vigor.

Having become weak, vegetables cannot survive untended by a gardener. The successful gardener's unavoidable task must then be to create much better growing conditions than are found in wild fields.

PLANT SPACING AND WEEDING

The most popular and most widely taught gardening system uses raised beds laid out so that the vegetables are spaced as close together as possible. This method, known as intensive gardening, became standard practice during the 1970s, as population growth squeezed more and more gardeners into smaller and smaller backyards. It seemed the perfect solution to the postage stamp backyard. These days people look only at the pluses of intensive gardening, but some aspects of this method are not so desirable.

The intensive method's main promise is getting the most food possible from the least space. However, the wide raised beds it depends on are prepared and laid out so as to require a great deal of hand work, especially bent-over hand weeding. That's because it is possible to get quite a few more plants into a given space that has been laid out in beehive-like hexagons than into one patterned in traditional long rows. It is possible to increase the yield a bit more by placing plants so close together that a long-handled hoe can't work between them. And it is possible to harvest even a bit more if some seedlings are started in small pots and then transplanted into any gaps formed by the harvest of other plants. One plant comes out and plop, another goes in immediately. This technique seems very efficient. And while it is true that by harmoniously orchestrating your plantings you can increase your harvest by half, there is a price—and that is a lot more by-hand, with-fingers, bent-over work.

I started out gardening this way, and I know the system intimately. But when I began conducting a half-acre test plot for Territorial Seed Company in 1980, I set out not to grow food but to harvest information. The trial varieties had to be arranged in well-separated, far-apart rows so that careful observations could be made of each and every plant. Growing vegetables in this way turned out to have unexpected benefits. I discovered quicker ways to do garden work, and some of the species that I gave lots of elbow room became much larger, seemed healthier, and yielded longer and more. Consequently, a major theme that pops up in this book is a dialogue about "extensive versus intensive."

It is a lot less work to weed standing upright with a lightweight, sharp, long-handled hoe than it is to weed bent over with dull fingers.

But it is not possible to hoe between vegetable rows unless they are at least a foot apart. So for small-sized vegetables I lay out raised beds in short, straight rows at least 1 foot apart, the rows running across the width of the bed. I don't use hexagonal patterns. In this book you will not find any recommendations for spacing of less than a foot between rows. And I am sure that once you discover the joy of a sharp hoe, you will rarely pull a weed by hand.

Working humusy soil atop a raised bed with a sharp, light, well-designed hoe does not take much time or effort. My current vegetable garden is about 65 by 70 feet, more than four times the average-size garden. During late spring and early summer, when everything, including the weeds, is growing its fastest, I can keep rows, hills, beds, and paths virtually free of weeds in about two hours a week. Later in the summer, weeding takes even less time because growth rates for all plants slow down. Allowing the paths to get a bit weedy also stops winter erosion.

Types of Weeds

It is not necessary to get rid of every single weed in the garden—only most of them. I have a priority system, and I recommend it to you. One type of weed I do not allow to exist at all, anywhere, ever, is grasses.

GRASSES
Grasses have highly invasive, dense root systems. Although low-growing grasses may not

compete for light, their aggressive roots rob the soil of most of the available nutrients and water, stunting nearby vegetables. Grasses have a strong ability to grow rapidly in shade, and many types multiply through underground runners, forming big masses that are very hard to remove gently. Established clumps of grass neither hoe out nor pull out easily by hand, and getting them out by yanking or chopping can damage delicate vegetable roots nearby, so it is essential that you destroy grasses before they become established. Make a regular weekly patrol of the garden. In a single week no grass plant is going to grow very large. If, when hoeing, you try to expose the roots to the air and sun, the plant is almost certain to die. If it somehow reroots, this weakened plant is much less likely to survive when you hoe again. The only time I bother to pull grass by hand is when some has eluded me for a few weeks and formed a clump. If it is very close to a vegetable (and it usually is, because that is how I overlooked it in the previous weeding), I try to loosen it gradually and pull it gently by hand so as not to upset the vegetable the grass clump is trying to strangle.

Even grasses growing in paths should be removed. Otherwise, they'll form a tough sod and will soon be invading the beds.

Some people are terrified of grasses that propagate through underground runners, calling them witch grass or twitch or couch or cooch. Or worse names. This sort of grass isn't really so bad. If once a week you cut off twitch ½ inch below the soil line, getting every little bit of it that shows to the light, the food reserves stored below will gradually become depleted and the plant will eventually die. It might take you a couple of months of repeated weekly hoeing to accomplish this. You can also get rid of horseradish, blackberries (even wild ones), comfrey, and any other very persistent plant that puts up big, fast-growing sprouts from food-storing roots in exactly the same way. The key is a *sharp* hoe and enough room between your vegetables to wield it.

PERNICIOUS WEEDS

Certain weeds are very hard to eradicate because they grow quickly and/or spread through underground runners and/or make huge quantities of seeds that spread widely. Included in this group are thistles, morning glory, and nightshade. Sometimes I feel like including sheep's sorrel in this group, too. These weeds should not be permitted to make seed in or anywhere near the garden. It is wise to mow a swath 25 to 50 feet wide around country gardens once a month to reduce the number of weed seeds blown into the garden. Incidentally, thistle stalks store so much water that once the plant has flowered it can still make viable seeds after it has been cut down. So either cut them well before the blooms form or, if it is too late, chop the stalks into short pieces and make sure they're lying in the sun. Also be sure to cut off the stalk below the soil line to kill the growing point, or they'll resprout from the roots. Again, the key is a sharp hoe.

OTHER WEEDS

Even though your rows are at least a foot apart, a month or two after emergence the fast-growing vegetables form a leaf canopy that hinders hoeing. The shade of this canopy will strongly suppress any new weeds that sprout. But a few will sprout and grow anyway. Any weed in the garden that begins to peek through the crop leaf canopy should be pulled. There won't be many emerging, and they'll yank easily from the uncompacted soil.

I should also mention that toward the end of the summer I largely stop weeding except around overwintering crops (especially alliums). I stop fighting everything—everything, that is, but grasses. There are several reasons for this. One, the weeds growing at that time of year are not going to make seeds until next spring, and I will hoe them out before that happens. Two, weeds in fall and winter grow slowly, while in most cases the vegetables are way ahead of them. Three, I would like the garden to go through the winter covered with as much green as possible to reduce compaction from winter rains, prevent erosion, and leave the soil as loose as possible next spring. Weeds will do this job as well as any green manure I'd intentionally sow.

Thinning

It doesn't do much good to reduce weed competition if the vegetables compete among themselves. To grow properly, each vegetable needs a minimum of space. To grow its very best, each vegetable needs as much unoccupied space as it can possibly use at its full development. Crowded radishes will not bulb at all. Crowded carrots mostly develop tops. Densely packed bush beans set small, often tough, and frequently misshapen pods that take a long time to pick. Crowded tomatoes, zucchini, and cucumbers stop setting fruit.

I wish it were possible to produce a packet of seeds, every one of which would germinate and become a perfect plant. Then it would be possible to sow one seed where each mature plant was desired—and there would be no thinning. But alas, this is not the nature of vegetable seed. This brings to mind the old legend about Squanto teaching the Pilgrims how to grow corn: Make a hill of loose soil, dig a hole in it, put in a dead fish and cover it deeply, and plant four corn seeds well above the fish—one for the worm, one for the crow, one to rot, and one to grow. But if the one don't rot or the crow don't come, there's thinnin' to be done.

I've met gardeners who just cannot thin out crowded seedlings. It seems like murdering children to them. I entreat you, gentlest of persons, to reconsider the nature of plants. Thinning seedlings is not like drowning unwanted kittens. *Vegetables don't mind being thinned.* They actually like it. They know that you are helping them by thinning them out. They understand that the gardener has to plant several seeds to get a single plant established because they do the very same thing themselves on a much larger scale. Wild plants sow a hundred times more seeds than a gardener will sow to get a single plant that grows to maturity. And they thin themselves out in far less gentle ways than the gardener will do it.

Here are two examples from nature that

illustrate what I mean. Observe the natural propagation of any member of the cabbage family, collectively known as coles. Coles are mainly biennials. After overwintering, they shoot up flowering stalks covered with enormous sprays of yellow or white flowers; each flower then becomes a skinny seed pod an inch or two long containing half a dozen or so seeds. These pods mature and dry out in the heat and drought of midsummer. Some seeds fall to earth from pods that split quickly; these may sprout with the next rain and get a jump-start on the competition. But if the summer proves hot and dry, these early releases may well die off. Seeds held more securely within the pod are protected from the first rains of late summer; these sprout only after the whole pod falls to earth and gets thoroughly soaked, when soil conditions have become nice and moist in autumn. Often all of the seeds within a single pod sprout at once, splitting it open with their germination, and come up as a little cluster. All of this variation is good, just as Darwin says in Genesis.

Most likely, all of the seeds within a single pod are the result of a visit by a single bee, but each seed might be parented by a pollen grain from a different plant. Thus every seed in the pod may also be different. Brassica seeds are tiny and the seedlings weak and small, but coming up in a clump they combine their force to push through the soil on top of them, so a cluster of seedlings may emerge where a single seed would fail to grow. Each seedling in this clump competes for water, nutrients, and light. The single most vigorous one eventually dominates the space, and the others die off. The winner is best suited to reproduce. A wild cabbage may produce ten thousand seeds to have but one survive to produce seeds next year.

Or take a member of the cucurbit family. A wild cucumber or wild melon makes quite a few fruits, each full of seeds. After the fruit dries out, these all sprout in one huge cluster. Like the brassica pod, the seed within that single fruit was probably pollinated by a single bee bringing pollen from hither and yon. Consequently, the many seedlings are all different. The one that dominates the area is the one that grows to produce more seed next year. All the others die, mainly of starvation, and they die young.

I hope that's sufficient argument to convince you, gentle readers, that thinning agrees with nature's plan.

As a general rule it's wise to sow extra seeds and, after emergence, thin them in three gradual steps over three to five weeks. This ensures a stand even if germination is low, bad weather slows early growth, and you lose a lot of seedlings to insects, slugs, or diseases. Another general rule is that the bigger the seed, the more certain the germination and the fewer seeds you need to sow for each plant wanted. I always sow two to four large seeds (corn, beans, squash, melons, cucumbers, radishes) and four to six small seeds for every final plant I want. I make an exception for those very spendy hybrids that are priced by the seed; these are usually so vigorous and so uniform that it is enough to sow only two or three seeds for each plant desired.

Immediately after they emerge, the survivors should be thinned a bit, but only where so much seed was dropped that clusters of seedlings appear. During their first week some of the weaker seedlings will thin themselves out for you, by falling prey to damping-off diseases and insects. In most species the first true leaf should develop in another week. Then it's time to thin the stand to about ½ to 1 inch apart, with big seeds at least an inch apart.

With open-pollinated varieties, by the end of two weeks the more vigorous individuals will stand above the others. At this point, pull out the weakest seedlings to give the stronger ones more unencumbered growing room. Should a rare and remarkably vigorous plant appear, pull it out too. This one is probably an unintended intervariety cross-pollination. It'll grow like gangbusters, but what a cabbage-kale or zucchini-pumpkin cross finally produces may be very disappointing.

Guiding these thinning steps is the intention that vegetable seedlings should never, ever be allowed to compete with one another for light, water, and nutrients. I can't stress this enough. When you sowed those seeds, you undertook to maintain the terms of a contractual agreement we humans made with that species long ago when it agreed to become our vegetable and we agreed to prevent it from having to compete. If you don't fulfill your end of the bargain, the vegetables won't be able to do their best.

Once the little plants are "established" (by this I mean that they have three true leaves and are growing well), they are pretty immune to sudden loss from insect or disease, and they can be thinned to the desired final spacing.

The Facts of Light

Gardening with grace involves participating as vegetables respond to those things (factors) that control their behavior. Throughout the rest of this book, I use the scientific word "factor" to describe this. A "factor" is simply something that influences or determines what happens.

I've already discussed some of the factors that determine plant growth, such as competition and spacing. Eventually I go over most of them, and eventually you'll see how these factors interact. Then you'll be a pro.

To paraphrase Louise Howard, gardening consists mainly of being a servant to the plant. Our job as servant is to adjust plant growth factors toward the plant's ideal. We can do a great deal to improve soil moisture, soil nutrient levels, competition, the quantity of air, and organic matter in the soil. We usually cannot afford to change air temperature or overall light levels.

People living in temperate climates all notice that the "force" of the sun changes with the seasons. However, they may not notice how much these changes affect plant growth. Since my garden is my year-round produce counter, I have become as responsive to changes in light levels as my plants are. I feel the sun's force in my bones and on my skin; the sun's force tells me what do just as it does with the wild plants.

In about mid-February a bit of strength returns to the sun. After this date the hardiest of vegetables begin to grow slowly. Bulbs come up. And unless the spring seems unusually harsh, on around March first I begin sowing peas, radishes, broad beans, and other leafy greens like lettuce, mustards, and spinach. I also thoroughly weed and side-dress (fertilize) any overwintered onion family crops because just as their relatives the ornamental bulbs do, alliums resume growth at this time. Were I to sow or fertilize earlier, even if the weather cooperated with a few sunny, warm days, and they germinated, the little plants just couldn't grow. And although *I* may want to start gardening and *I* need to do some planting after a long winter of spending too much time indoors, if the weather of early March is not conducive to planting I have learned after many years of frustration and self-induced failures that there is little reason to rush out and put in seeds. The growth rates of early March are so slow that something started several weeks later will mature only a few days later.

By early April the sun has become forceful. Species that store sugar can now grow, so I sow beets, onions, and carrots. Even though these can often germinate under plastic five or six weeks sooner, they'll barely grow before April because there's not enough solar energy. By mid-April the sun begins to feel much stronger—when it shines. I can start those popular tropical vegetable species that in our temperate region must be started indoors. They'll be ready to put outside about mid-May. If I started them sooner indoors and set them out in a heated greenhouse when they were too big for an indoor environment they just would become spindly from low light levels, grow too slowly, and probably have disease problems. A few more weeks pass, and the sun feels extremely strong. I can begin to sow those semi-tropical vegetable species that we direct-seed outdoors, like beans and corn—unprotected if I live where there is no more frost danger, under plastic if there is still danger of frost.

I sow most autumn and winter crops before midsummer, while several months of strong sun remain. By August, I start species that will overwinter and be harvested in the spring, so they will gain some size but won't become too big before October's low light levels check their growth, because smaller (but still substantial) plants are more tolerant of frost and rain than are big ones.

About early September, while the juicer is cranking out "V-7" and real fresh prune juice by the gallon and I go into sugar shock every morning from the melons, my whole body begins to mourn the loss of summer. That may seem strange when the summer garden is at its peak. But not only does it become difficult to get a suntan after August, the flavor of our delicious garden fruit has already started to decline. Plants need strong solar energy to make the excess sugars and other flavoring substances that give garden fruit that special taste. Powered by less force, the tomatoes lose their richness, eggplants and peppers get smaller and become relatively tasteless, and melons aren't disgustingly sweet anymore, while their vines begin to look scruffy and soon succumb to powdery mildew. This leaf disease also affects the other cucurbits. First the cucumbers and melons go, and even if there is no rain or heavy dew, by the end of the month, the squash go too. The cause of powdery mildew *seems* to be rain or heavy morning dews, higher daytime humidity and chillier nights. The real cause is overall plant weakness from lack of light energy.

Since we eat mainly from the garden, these losses seem okay because by then we've had our fill of fruit anyway. I'm always glad to switch my diet away from sugars and toward more salads and other leafy greens, and starchy root crops.

Even if frost hasn't taken them yet, by the middle of October the tomatoes can no longer ripen fruit, and all of the tropicals and semitropicals succumb to molds and mildews. Putting a plastic tunnel over them will retard this by a few weeks, but not for long. There just isn't enough light energy for tropicals.

Under winter's weak light, only a very few ultravigorous species are able to grow any new leaves. A few more very hardy ones will barely maintain the leaves they've already made. Winter conditions don't provide enough light for accumulating surpluses, so plants cannot enlarge storage roots, form seed, or make and ripen fruit. Thus, winter gardens must of necessity consist largely of very hardy leafy greens and root crops that hold in cold storage under the soil.

West of the Cascades, where winters consist of day after day of cloudy skies and low light levels, protecting fruiting vegetables in greenhouses does not solve the problem of light deprivation. Even though they are warm and relieved of the stress of repairing the ravages of endless rain beating on their leaves, light-weakened greenhouse plants make flavorless fruit, set it very sparsely, and ripen it very slowly. The only way to have good-tasting tomatoes, peppers, zucchini, cucumbers, and the like from November through March is to provide intense artificial light.

LIGHT INTENSITY AND GROWTH RATES

If you want tender, sweet young lettuce salads every day, all summer, through the autumn, and as long into winter as possible, allow me to guide your thoughts for a few paragraphs.

The last section underlined the fact that as light intensity changes with the seasons, the speed at which plants grow changes. However, there's more to this concept, which when you grasp the idea, will give you a better supply of salad greens or radishes or whatever other fast-growing cut-once-and-be-finished-with-it vegetable you choose to grow.

At first glance it seems that many kinds of plants start out growing slowly and then pick up more and more speed as they get bigger. Actually, they often don't. From mid-April through August, the months when the sun's energy is quite strong, many plant species grow at a fairly uniform rate, but the amount gained in each period of time increases geometrically—1-2-4-8-16-32-64-128. Plants grow much as bacteria or yeasts do, by splitting their cells, two for one. A plant makes a leaf. That leaf gathers sunlight, water, and nutrients and makes enough food to support the leaf itself and some extra. The extra allows the plant to make new cells, which make food, which make extra. One leaf makes two, the two make two more each, or four; the four leaves double and make eight. This goes on as long as the plant is in a vegetative mode of growth, which simply means as long as it is producing new leaves and stems. Some plants, such as vines, would keep on doing this throughout their life cycle if they could. Others make vegetative growth for awhile and then, when large enough, do something different, like making seeds and then dying.

This growth by doubling every so often is easiest to see in a plant with a rosette growth habit, like a lettuce. A tiny lettuce seedling seems as though it will never grow but is actually doubling in size frequently. At emergence, the lettuce seedling is barely ⅛ inch in diameter. The amount of time it takes the plant to double in diameter is its rate of doubling. For most types of lettuce, doubling takes about one week during the four-plus months of high

The Relationship Between Solar Energy and Plant Growth

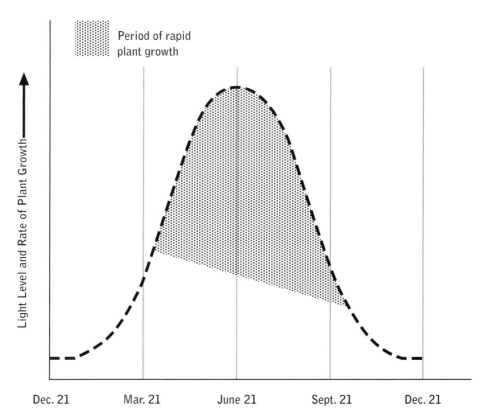

This chart takes into account both day length and climate. Above the clouds, exactly as much sun energy strikes the earth on March 21 as on September 21, while the peak energy occurs on June 21 and the minimum on December 21. But when you factor in our climate, the many cloudy days in spring lower the level of light received by plants.

Growth Rate of Two Different Sowings of Lettuce

Date	Doubling Rate	Diameter of Plants Emerging on March 1	Diameter of Plants Emerging on April 21
March 1	21 days	1/8 inch	
March 21	17 days	1/4 inch	
April 7	14 days	1/2 inch	
April 21	10 days	1 inch	1/8 inch
May 1	9 days	2 inches	1/4 inch
May 10	8 days	4 inches	1/2 inch
May 18	8 days	8 inches/harvest	1 inch
May 26	7 days		2 inches
June 2	7 days		4 inches
June 9	7 days		8 inches/harvest

light intensity. In the table above, the far right column illustrates this, showing how lettuce seedlings grow from 1/8 inch to a barely harvestable 8-inch size in about six weeks while hardly changing their growth rate.

If you waited six weeks (when the first planting had grown to half size) before sowing the next batch on May 10, the first sowing would already have completed six-sevenths of its vegetative growth. This would leave a huge gap in your lettuce supply or would have you eating a lot of tough, bitter lettuce. Since lettuce stays tender and sweet for only a few weeks from the time it is mostly grown, you have to begin a new patch every few weeks, when the earlier sowing is only an inch or two in diameter. The same strategy holds for radishes and turnips.

People try to avoid the trouble of starting a new salad patch every few weeks through the summer by growing one "cut and come again" patch and "mowing" some whenever they want a salad. In my opinion this is an unsatisfactory solution to not having enough time to tend the garden. Nothing tastes as good as the inner leaves of a three-quarters-developed, rapidly grown, tender head of loose-leaf lettuce. Nothing!

Growth rates change with the seasons as the amount of available light energy changes. Sown in the short days of early spring, lettuce takes two to three weeks to double. For this reason, early sowings don't result in quick harvests. As the season advances, the increasing light levels shorten doubling time. This is demonstrated in the table above, which shows that the second sowing, seven weeks after the first, results in a harvest only three weeks after the first. Sowing later also means better germination and less slug trouble. As you can see, there is very little advantage in being the first gardener to have some seeds sprout in spring.

If you want a continuous supply of top-quality lettuce, you have to make successive sowings, but at different intervals, depending on the growth rate. A sowing on March 1 will be ready only a few weeks before one made on April 21. But from mid-April through Mid-August, the growth rate hardly changes, so between those dates you'll have to sow every three weeks to have a continuous supply of lettuce. Then the pattern reverses, and with each passing week the growth rate slows. You have to sow even more frequently during August and September to enjoy continuous lettuce through the winter. I sow lettuce every ten days during these months. The last sowing, made toward the end of September, is a low-risk gamble. It may or may not gain enough size to be useful before freezing. Then again, it may not freeze at all during an unusually mild winter and be there to feed us in spring.

This pattern of changing growth rates applies to all crops grown for fall or winter harvest. They have to be approaching full size before their growth rate drops off greatly around the end of September. Started too early, they'll mature too soon—and who wants an unharvested patch of giant kohlrabi rapidly turning woody in September, especially while there are still tomatoes and zucchini? Who wants Brussels sprouts blowing up and getting aphidy in the heat of early September? But when started too late, the same plants will be disappointingly small when you do bring them into the kitchen.

In case all of this seems a bit overwhelming, take comfort: Chapters 4 and 9 provide you with the means to create a detailed year-round planting calendar that will work perfectly in the maritime Northwest.

Some Words About Tools

Many gardeners unnecessarily exhaust themselves chopping weeds. These unfortunates often become doubly unfortunate. They believe garden magazine propaganda and buy an engine-powered tool that allows them to weed "effortlessly." Actually, using a properly sharp hoe involves very little effort and is fast enough for almost any size garden. For many years I personally hand-hoed an immaculate three-quarter-acre trial ground, ten to twenty times larger than a good-sized home vegetable garden. The task took less than an hour a day during the peak period of light intensity, when the weeds and vegetables were growing fastest. Matthew, an employee with a good sense of humor who helped me, once quipped that he liked being a hoer in my garden because the beds were so soft. I think he more liked my sharp tools.

HOES

So how *do* you use a hoe? First, understand that a weeding hoe is primarily a slicing instrument, sliding just below the soil's surface with strokes like a sharp slicing knife. Occasionally a sharp hoe is used as a scraper, pressing down firmly on hard earth. Slicing and scraping won't tire you out, but chopping is exhausting and accomplishes little.

If you examine a common weeding hoe, you'll find that the blade is angled so that it will lie almost flat on the ground when you hold the handle comfortably, hands near your body. If it doesn't, it's because your height or arm length aren't what the hoe maker envisioned. The hoe blade is almost always attached to the handle with a curved rod (called a swansneck) of mild steel so that you can easily bend it in a vise to correct the blade angle for your body. The illustrations on this page and the next, showing a person hoeing, demonstrate the best angles of attack.

If that blade were very sharp, you could slice off weeds in long strokes by pulling the handle toward you, the blade very slightly angled so as to stay below the surface but not so angled as to pull itself deeper, the hoer sliding the knifelike edge just beneath the surface of the ground. It's very little effort when the weeds are small and the soil reasonably soft, as they should be if you cultivate every week or ten days without fail.

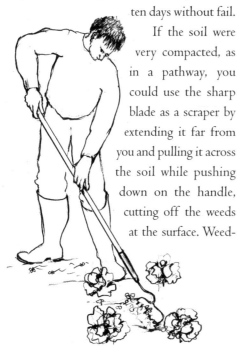

If the soil were very compacted, as in a pathway, you could use the sharp blade as a scraper by extending it far from you and pulling it across the soil while pushing down on the handle, cutting off the weeds at the surface. Weed-

Slicing weeds just below the surface.

ing this way is more effort than slicing but still much less effort than chopping.

When you use a sharp hoe in either of these ways, you develop strong wrists and hands, not a sore back and tired arms. Ah, but there's the rub! You can rarely buy a sharp hoe. The common hoe might have the suggestion of a bevel ground into the front of the blade, but rarely is it sharp. Using one of those so-called hoes as they come from the store forces the gardener to chop themselves into exhaustion. If I owned a garden center, I'd buy a bench grinder and presharpen every hoe and shovel that went out, and do this at the time of sale so that the customer knew it was being done at no charge. That would make some happy customers who would come back and spend more! I'd make a bit extra on the sale by selling every hoe or shovel customer a brand-new file with a sturdy handle attached to keep the tool sharp.

If you have access to an electric grinder, make sure you don't grind too fast; if you do, you can burn the blade and remove its temper. To sharpen a dull hoe by hand, clamp the blade in a stout vise and, with a *new, sharp* file, grind a 20-degree (very acute) angle on the outside edge. If you don't have a vise, hold the hoe securely on a porch step by having someone else stand on the handle while you file it. The hoe is sharpened like a chisel, on one side only (see the illustration on page 20). Once the bevel is perfectly ground, lightly file the burr off the back of the hoe blade by holding the file almost flat. When finished, you should be barely able to cut your finger on the edge if you press hard. I suggest using a 8- to 10-inch

Scraping weeds in compacted soil.

common mill file with a solid handle or a large and very coarse Carborundum stone.

I'm sorry to inform you that hand-sharpening a new tool for the first time can take awhile, and you'll probably sweat. And you have to concentrate on each and every stroke to ensure a uniform bevel. Don't forget that old files get dull and stop cutting after a few years' use. The only thing harder than working with a dull hoe is sharpening it with a dull file. And don't shortchange yourself by making the angle less acute; the extra effort it will take to use the tool will far exceed any effort you saved while grinding.

The steel of inexpensive hoe blades is not hardened (tempered)—perhaps so the blade isn't brittle and thus doesn't chip while chopping on stones (the charitable view), or perhaps because most home gardeners don't know a good hoe from a poor one (the cynical view). Soft steel is cheap and easy to shape and weld but will neither hold an edge long nor become knife-sharp no matter how long or carefully it

is worked. When hoeing with a cheap tool, the place for your file or sharpening stone is in your hip pocket, because the edge will appreciate being touched up every hundred feet or so. Prop the hoe against a sturdy garden post or the corner of your garage or toolshed to do this. Touch-ups take only a few strokes, but the time and effort spent honing the edge are saved manyfold during the next ten minutes of hoeing. Sharpening makes a nice break from hoeing. And a hoe that has just become dull offers a good occasion to practice a bit of hoe-leaning.

You can buy sharp hoes with quality steel blades. Some of these are called "weeder hoes" because they automatically make you lay a thin, sharp blade flat on the ground and slice off the plants at the root line. Weeder hoes that work on both the push and pull strokes are best; two common trade names for this sort of tool are "action hoe" and "hula hoe." Quality tools are often found in mail-order seed catalogs.

Here are a couple of designs for hoes you can make yourself (both illustrated on the bottom of page 20). For getting close to delicate plants, there's the onion hoe. The blade is a loop of ⅜-inch-wide spring steel, 2 inches in diameter, attached to a long, light handle by a metal ring or ferrule. Both edges of the spring-steel loop are sharpened. One of my favorites is what I call a thinning hoe. It has a 5-inch-long spear-point blade that can be

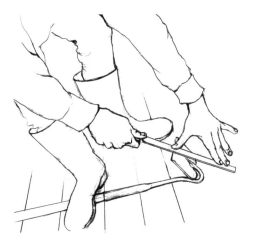

used like an ordinary hoe, one of the sharpened edges slicing sideways through the soil. Both edges are very sharp and come to an acute, stilettolike point. The back end of the blade is 1¾ inches wide. The blade's tip will slice close to a row of tiny seedlings, letting you hook out one seedling and leave another, which eliminates much thinning by hand.

One day I was visiting my uncle Geoff, an active vegetable gardener who lives along the Tamar River in northern Tasmania. We were chatting on the back stoop and admiring his garden. I described my hoe collection to him and especially praised the one with the stiletto-like blade. Good hoes are nearly impossible to buy in Australia, probably because Australians aren't as wealthy as Americans, and because many, like Geoff, are still handy, rarely thinking to buy something when they can make their own. Geoff lit up, and said he'd make one for himself. He began to buzz around at high velocity.

In the garden shed he grabbed an old pair of slightly rusty hand sheep shears, each blade already shaped like the one I described. To the workshop we went. In a flash he had cut off one of the blades with a cold chisel, ground a chisel edge into the backside with his bench grinder, drilled two holes about an inch apart right on the center line of the blade and about two-thirds of the way back from the point, made a swansneck to hold that blade out of a rusty foot-long ⅜-inch-diameter bolt that he rapidly "distempered" with his arc welder, pounded the bolt's end flat, drilled two holes in that flat end that matched the two he'd drilled in the scissor blade, and then amazed me by securely riveting the two pieces together with a couple of old nails cut off short and pounded flat on both sides using a heavy

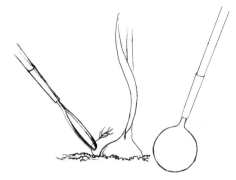

An onion hoe.

Hoe with a stilettolike blade.

hammer and anvil. He already had lots of long handles handy, a bundle of long, straight tree branches stacked in the corner reserved for exactly this sort of purpose. (Geoff already had a dozen other hoes he'd made of assorted bits of metal.) A fat hole was drilled into one end of the stick, the swansneck was pushed into the handle, and a metal collar (ferrule) to strengthen that weak point was cut from an old bit of chrome-plated under-sink drain-pipe and hammered down over the handle's end. Voila! Total time: about 30 minutes. And does Geoff love that hoe!

Now I'm thinking of making hoes myself using old kitchen knives and other odd bits of metal.

SHOVELS

Many gardeners do not realize how easy digging with a sharp shovel can be. Their blades are normally made of tempered springy steel, which will take and hold a much more acute edge than will common hoes. But, like hoes,

shovels are inevitably dull when purchased. For my stoneless garden, I sharpen the inside curve of shovels as acutely as possible (15 to 18 degrees), because a really sharp edge will cut into earth like a hot knife into butter. In one enjoyable hour while hearing the birds sing, I can loosen up a 100-square-foot raised bed 12 to 14 inches deep with a sharp "combination" shovel, use a heavy hoe to finely chop the top 4 or 5 inches while at the same time incorporating compost, lime, and complete organic fertilizer, and then rake it out to a fine seedbed. Yes, I could fluff up the top 5 inches of a bed with a rototiller in less time, but if I wanted the bed to grow right I'd still have to spade its depths by hand. And the time difference is not that great. After weighing how much trouble it is to get the tiller out, start it up, change its oil, put it away, and turn it around at the ends of the bed . . . I reckon that if more gardeners knew how to sharpen their tools, a lot fewer rototillers would be sold.

Chapter 2 Soil

. . . only after the supply of organic matter has been adequately provided for,
will the full benefit of artificials [chemical fertilizers] be realized. There appears
to be a great field for future experiment in the judicious use of artificials to
land already in a fair state of fertility.

—SIR ALBERT HOWARD,
The Waste Products of Agriculture

The soil in much of the United States is naturally fertile, and summertime soil temperatures are warm, this warmth accelerating the release of plant nutrients. Back east, all it takes to produce big, healthy vegetables of high nutritional content is a bit of properly made, reasonably potent compost—and some skill. Numerous eastern garden books explain exactly how to do so. Advocates of compost gardening say that your soil has become fertile enough when there are enough worms. Back east, they may be right.

The maritime Northwest is cantankerously different. Compost vegetable gardening frequently disappoints us because the fertilizing effect of compost happens from its decomposition (or, to use a fifty-cent word, nitrification). The speed of nitrification depends on how warm the soil gets. But compared to the sultry East, our summertime soil temperatures don't climb very high. So ordinary, average-quality compost provokes rapid growth only during a short month or so of midsummer when our soils warm up a bit.

Growing smaller, more thrifty-looking, compost-raised plants might be perfectly okay if they provided the kind of superlative nutrition we have read about in organic gardening books and magazines. But when raised on our ordinary composts, maritime Northwest vegetables usually aren't superlatively nutritious. In fact, by fertilizing exclusively with carelessly made compost, or by spreading and tilling in lots of our local horse/cow/sheep manure, we end up harvesting vegetables of low nutritional content.

The poor quality of our region's manures and composts is not the result of anything we can readily change. Nor do most of us realize how poor they are, because we rarely have anything to compare them with. Literature and propaganda in favor of compost gardening is so widespread that it rarely occurs to anyone that compost or animal manure could be variable—like wine. In one area the grapes grow world-class vintages, while in other regions the foxy-tasting wine is of very poor quality. That difference may be of little consequence so long as you're not stuck on tippling your own

skunky stuff. The Scots may not be able to grow a decent grape, but they can sure make fine whiskey from barley malt. And we mossbacks can grow huge, healthy, highly nutritious vegetables with complete organic fertilizer instead of compost, and use approaches other than massive additions of manure and compost to meet the soil's humus requirement.

The novice gardener will probably have an easier time accepting my suggestions than someone who has already read other organic gardening books and believed them. To those of you who already consider yourselves better informed, I apologize in advance; you may have to reconsider ideas you had depended on as being Truths. I know quite well that giving up valuable certainties can be difficult.

Grasping the explanations behind what is to come will be well worth the effort on your part, I assure you. But many of my readers will only want to know the essentials. So on pages 28–29 I lay out what to do, as simply as possible with minimum explanation.

Our Soil Is Poor

Millennia of heavy winter rains have leached all of our soils into a kind of chemical imbalance that won't grow highly nutritious food. Willamette Valley wheat, for example, is low-grade, low-protein soft white wheat used for noodles and starch. When I've tried to grow hard red bread wheat, it came out as soft red pastry wheat. My soil couldn't feed the wheat enough to produce the proteins required for bread-quality wheat. Maritime Northwest dairy farms have to truck in nutritious hay from the eastern side of the Cascades because the hay they grow won't keep their cows healthy. Our infertile soils do grow good trees, but what parts of Douglas fir can most animals eat?

Our soils have two sorts of liabilities. First, the overall amount of plant nutrients has been lowered because most of the minerals our soils started out with have, over geologic time, been washed away by rain water passing through them. Second, leaching does not remove all plant nutrients equally. It takes some more readily than others. If all of the minerals had been proportionately lowered, the situation would not be as serious. Unfortunately, the nutrients that provoke plants to become highly nutritious—calcium, magnesium, and phosphorus—are the ones most readily lost. I view this as a widespread regional mineral imbalance.

Our situation is not like that of other areas in the United States. In the East there are soil fertility profiles of all sorts in a complex checkerboard. Some soils have too much of one thing and too little of another. Others not far away are the opposite. It takes a wise agronomist to figure out how best to improve these soils; it takes a brilliant soils tester to back the agronomist up. The reason for this variability is the enormous variability of the underlying rocks in the East. However, west of the Cascades the leaching has eliminated most of the differences our soils started out with. In addition, the maritime Northwest has a rather simple geological history. With few exceptions,

our soils derived from rocks containing very similar mineral profiles.

There's only one positive aspect to this situation. Because our soils are so uniform, I can offer a generalized analysis of their nature and a single prescription to improve them that will work quite well for almost everyone gardening here.

Our Manures and Composts Are Low-Grade Too

Chemically unbalanced soils grow plants of lowered and unbalanced nutritional content. Unbalanced grasses fed to livestock produce poor manure. Chemically unbalanced plants combined with weak, unbalanced manures make unbalanced compost. Adding unbalanced manure or compost to already unbalanced soil makes the soil become even more unbalanced.

The essence of our region's soil imbalance hinges on an overly high level of an otherwise useful mineral, potassium. Our soils usually have lots of potassium—maybe too much. I've studied the results of hundreds of soil tests performed by Oregon State University and have never seen a test showing a marked potassium deficiency—lots of other deficiencies, yes, but not of K (for *kalium*, Latin for potassium).

Plants respond to high levels of soil potassium by having too much potassium in their systems. This shifts their entire chemistry around

Step-by-Step Soil Management System

If You Have Enough Land, Make a Two-Field Rotation

- Separate your growing area into two equal plots. If at all possible, separate the plots with a mowed but untilled barrier strip at least 15 feet wide. (This strip works far better if it is unwatered.) One plot grows vegetables; the other is unirrigated and grows pasture grass mix. The barrier strip is never tilled.

- Do not grow vegetables for more than three years on one plot, or problems will develop. It takes a couple of years in "healing grass" to restore the stability to soil after vegetables have been grown in it.

- Manage the pasture grass area by mowing it occasionally and allowing the clippings to lie and rot where they fall. Do not remove them or compost them. Fertilize the grass once a year in early October with complete organic fertilizer, using enough to make the grass grow strong until late spring. Spread 1 gallon per 100 square feet.

- Unless one of those plots is your front yard, never irrigate the grass in summer! And never add compost, manure, or other organic matter to the grass plot.

- Every two to three years, switch: Sow a pasture grass mixture on the well-used vegetable plot, and till up the established grass plot to make a new vegetable garden. If you don't switch, by the fourth year of growing vegetables on the same ground you will likely develop high levels of a nasty soil-dwelling pest called symphylans, and perhaps other serious diseases and insect problems. I know you city gardeners are having a very hard time with the instruction above to not irrigate your yard. Read Chapter 4, where I discuss the symphylan.

Break Ground for the New Vegetable Garden

- Separate your new vegetable garden into two equal parts, one half for summer crops and the other half for winter crops. If this space allocation seems unreasonable, read Chapter 4.

- For convenience and to greatly ease the task of eliminating the remains of the grass sod next spring, late in September or early in October (gardeners who are not religiously organic may thoroughly kill the grass with a spray of Roundup). Wait one week before proceeding to the next step, so the herbicide has a chance to work and decompose. This is the only occasion for which this book will advocate using a chemical herbicide or pesticide. Wear rubber boots when spraying, and do it on a windless morning.

- Cover the whole new vegetable garden area with no more than ½ inch of completely rotted compost or 1 inch of raw ruminant manure containing as little sawdust as possible (and absolutely no wood chips), and spread agricultural lime at 50 pounds per 1,000 square feet. Do this in early October. If your soil contains so much clay that it seems to demand more organic matter or more lime, read the section at the end of this chapter on clay soil.

- Scatter small-seeded fava bean seed at 6 to 8 pounds per 1,000 square feet.

- Rototill no more than 2 inches deep and relax. Wait for spring.

Growing the Vegetable Garden

- No spring garden is possible the first year.

- Rototill deeply (turn under the fava bean vegetation; there will be no seeds yet) and/or spade up the half of the garden allocated to summer crops in April (if spring rains allow), at the very least ten days before sowing. You'll have a beautiful seedbed.

- Rototill deeply and/or spade in the overwintered favas in the winter garden area in late May, at least ten days before sowing begins. You'll have a beautiful seedbed.

- Make a detailed garden layout plan. See Chapter 4.

- Grow your vegetables as directed in Chapter 9. Sow seeds as directed in Chapter 6. Irrigate as directed in Chapter 5. Weed and thin as directed in Chapter 1.

- If you follow these instructions, you'll almost certainly harvest a lot of food.

- At the end of the summer, clean up the vegetation left in the summer garden area and compost all of the trash (see Chapter 3). Make a couple of raised bed in this area for next year's spring garden. Scatter fava bean seed over all, and till it in shallowly (or hoe it in). Next summer this half of the garden will grow the spring and winter crops.

- In spring, pull the cabbage family stumps and clean up the winter garden area. Compost all of the trash. Cover with no more than $\frac{1}{4}$ inch of finished compost (this is where your compost pile is allocated to, but if the only source of this compost is vegetable garden waste, it won't be enough), and rototill or spade up. This will be your summer garden.

- After two or three years in vegetables, rotate and break sod for a new garden site!

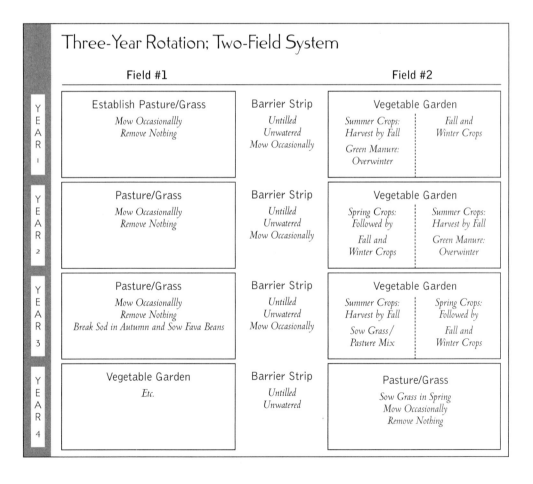

Three-Year Rotation; Two-Field System

	Field #1	Barrier Strip	Field #2	
YEAR 1	Establish Pasture/Grass *Mow Occasionallly* *Remove Nothing*	*Untilled* *Unwatered* *Mow Occasionally*	Vegetable Garden *Summer Crops:* *Harvest by Fall* *Green Manure:* *Overwinter*	*Fall and* *Winter Crops*
YEAR 2	Pasture/Grass *Mow Occasionallly* *Remove Nothing*	*Untilled* *Unwatered* *Mow Occasionally*	Vegetable Garden *Spring Crops:* *Followed by* *Fall and* *Winter Crops*	*Summer Crops:* *Harvest by Fall* *Green Manure:* *Overwinter*
YEAR 3	Pasture/Grass *Mow Occasionallly* *Remove Nothing* *Break Sod in Autumn and Sow Fava Beans*	*Untilled* *Unwatered* *Mow Occasionally*	Vegetable Garden *Summer Crops:* *Harvest by Fall* *Sow Grass /* *Pasture Mix*	*Spring Crops:* *Followed by* *Fall and* *Winter Crops*
YEAR 4	Vegetable Garden *Etc.*	*Untilled* *Unwatered*	Pasture/Grass *Sow Grass in Spring* *Mow Occasionally* *Remove Nothing*	

in such a way that their overall nutritional value—including proteins and vitamins—is lowered, and not just a little, but a lot.

Plants always concentrate potassium in their fiber and other woody parts. So local grass hay, sawdusty horse manure, and our vegetation in general is unbalanced in favor of potassium. Our grass hay and sawdusty horse manure contain a lot less calcium, magnesium, phosphorus, and proteins (nitrogen) than they otherwise might. Build a compost heap of that stuff and rot it down, and you concentrate all of the minerals in the vegetation and manure. Essentially, you end up further concentrating potassium. Spread this compost out and till it in, and you've added a great deal more potassium to a soil that probably already had too much to start with. You've also added too little of the other things plants need to balance out all that potassium.

Excesses of soil potassium can become so serious that some dairy farmers have had to restrict their own cows from grazing their own pastures because soil potassium levels, and consequently leaf potassium levels, have reached toxic proportions. If their farms had been what are called "closed systems," where nothing was brought in or out, returning their cows' manure to their own fields wouldn't have changed the fertility of their soils much at all. But shipments of milk from their farms took the soil's choicest mineral content with them—particularly calcium and magnesium and phosphorus, the good stuff people drink milk for. Cash farming like this depleted their land to the point that their soil produced hay that was too low in nutrients and protein to keep milk cattle healthy. Then dairy farmers began to feed their cows on better hay imported from more fertile places. Each time the farmers spread this hay out on their fields (after first passing it through their cows' guts and extracting the milk from it), they increased the potassium imbalance on their land.

Can you imagine what happens when a home garden receives heavy, regular additions of manure or compost made from vegetation brought in from outside? The same thing! The difference in health consequences to most home gardeners compared to the dairy cows is that only a portion of the gardeners' dietary intake comes from their own land. If the garden produces unbalanced food, it can be compensated for (somewhat) by the rest of the diet.

So if we're concerned with the nutritional content of our own produce, we should follow two closely related principles of wise soil management west of the Cascades:

- Minimize the amount of organic matter we incorporate into our gardens from off-site.

- When building soil fertility, avoid adding more than a minimum amount of potassium.

These principles do not apply everywhere in the world. They are generally true west of the Cascades and probably apply to many other soils that are heavily rained on or badly leached. In less leached soils that have a better chemical balance, the vegetation produced is also more balanced, and fair quantities of compost made from it can be put into a garden to increase both organic matter and plant nutrient levels. Parenthetically, some soils are very short of potassium, and so some potassium can be added as fertilizer with great benefit.

Why, then, do agronomists routinely advise farmers to add potassium to their fertilizer? I think it's because an overabundance of potassium makes plants change their growth habits, producing more bulk yield at the expense of overall nutritional content. A few hundred extra pounds of potassium per acre often will inexpensively increase crop volume and weight as much as 25 percent. That extra bulk, however, consists of fiber and sugar and starch, at the expense of protein and vitamins and minerals, which decrease proportionately as the bulk increases. But the farmer is usually paid for bulk, not for nutritional content. If you wish to pursue this line of thought further, I suggest starting with *The Albrecht Papers* (listed in the bibliography at the end of this book), particularly the second volume, and then subscribe to a monthly newsletter called *Acres, USA*, from the publisher of *The Albrecht Papers*.

What Our Soils Need to Grow Vegetables

The first idea I want to disabuse you of is that you need to pay for a soil test. Such tests are largely useless, as most soil testing does not provide information that a nutrition-minded gardener can really use. Your money would be better spent on buying soil amendments that you'll certainly need anyway. All of our regional soils are deficient in almost everything except potassium. These deficiencies range from moderate to extreme. It's best simply to assume that this is so and add to the soil what the vegetables need to grow well. Only if you were farming significant acreage and could, with soil testing, reduce your inputs by the amounts already present in the field, might a soil test save more than it would cost.

What all garden soils in this region need is pretty simple, actually: lime (two kinds), properly balanced organic fertilizer, and just enough organic matter to keep the soil ecology and growing plants healthy.

LIME

Your soil is acidic, deficient in calcium, and almost certainly deficient in magnesium. Repairing the deficiencies is far more useful than correcting the acidity. It might be better to say that the acidity happened *because* of the deficiencies. Unless you have a veritable clay pit for a garden, you can ignore what the average garden and soil book says about adjusting the pH to between 6.0 and 6.5. (I once recommended liming as a cure for acidity, so if you've made an icon of one of my earlier books, please don't fault me for disagreeing with myself; I learn and change.) Simply make sure your soil contains enough calcium and magnesium (in the right proportions) to nourish your vegetables (and your family). If you do that, and also make sure that the other needed nutrients are present, the pH will take care of itself.

Both of these minerals, calcium and magnesium, are equally important plant nutrients.

You'll come up with about the right proportion of calcium to magnesium by blending together more or less equal parts of the two kinds of agricultural lime commonly available: "agricultural lime," which is calcium carbonate, and dolomite lime, which varies a bit but usually is about half calcium carbonate and half magnesium carbonate.

Here's a rule of thumb:

When starting a brand-new garden or using one that has never been limed, or ending a years-long rebuilding period where an area was resting in grass, before doing anything else, spread an equal mixture of agricultural lime and dolomite lime at a combined rate of 50 pounds per 1,000 square feet.

This relatively heavy once-only application is enough for as long as you continue gardening on that site if you also use my formulation for a complete organic fertilizer (given later in this chapter) as an ongoing amendment. Fifty pounds of mixed lime per 1,000 square feet amounts to about one ton per acre. A ton of limestone contains about 1,000 pounds of combined calcium and magnesium.

Plants sorely need calcium and magnesium; when they get it they contain not only higher overall levels of calcium and magnesium, but also more and better-quality proteins and vitamins and higher levels of other needed minerals. All maritime Northwest soils can use more calcium. As far as I know, only one rare regional soil type has enough (or too much) magnesium. This soil is found only in the sparsely populated Klamath Mountains of southern Oregon. It is derived from a kind of rock called serpentine and needs very special

handling (and probably sage advice from the local extension agent). A few of the small islands off the mainland of British Columbia are composed of limestone. These soils may also take slightly different handling. Still, the advice in this book will serve over 98 percent of the gardeners in the maritime Northwest very well, a much greater number, in my opinion, than are helped by most other books. That's not because I'm so smart; it's because chemically, our region's soils are so similar.

Regular smaller additions of calcium and magnesium are also necessary to maintain the nutrients' availability. Every year our winter rains leach out as much as 500 pounds of calcium and somewhat less magnesium from each acre. This is roughly the amount you will have to replace on an ongoing basis. I've found that once the shortfall is made good with a ton of lime per acre, the best way to maintain calcium and magnesium levels is to blend the two sorts of ground limestone into the fertilizer you routinely use. Having calcium and magnesium in the fertilizer itself also places them close to growing plants and makes sure they are right there waiting for seedlings. The recipe I provide later for making your own complete organic fertilizer will maintain the availability of calcium and magnesium in your garden.

One final warning about lime. You can do a great deal of long-lasting damage by over-liming. If the soil becomes totally saturated with calcium and/or magnesium, it is incapable of holding other nutrients. Leaching may remove most other nutrients the first winter after soil is limed too heavily. It can take years to correct this situation. The amount of lime that soil can use is closely related to the amount of clay in it. For all but the heavier clay soils, one ton per acre will suffice to grow good vegetables without danger; adding more could be a serious, long-lasting error. Because growing vegetables on clay is such a dicey situation, I have included a special section at the end of this chapter to help those in that situation.

FERTILIZER

Vegetables need around twenty different mineral nutrients to grow well; if these are adequate and correctly balanced, the nutritional content of the vegetables will be much higher. Five or six minerals are needed in fairly large quantities—nitrate-nitrogen, phosphorus, potassium, calcium, magnesium, and sulfur. These are what are known as the major nutrients. Others, called trace minerals, are every bit as necessary but are needed in tiny amounts.

Chemical fertilizers do contain the major plant nutrients, but they also have major liabilities. However, toting up a balance sheet on chemical fertilizers and declaring them totally bad is beyond the scope of this book. Anyone who wishes to think of chemical fertilizers as being "of the devil" should first read Donald Hopkins's book *Chemicals, Humus, and the Soil*.

Here are some of the factors I considered when deciding generally not to use chemicals in vegetable gardening. Chemicals are too pure; consequently they often fail to provide needed trace minerals. Unless made at great expense into slow-release fertilizers, chemicals put into the soil go into solution much too fast and their effects are too short-lived for someone without a lot of experience or guid-

ance in using them. I've seen many gardeners do a lot of damage by overapplying chemicals. Chemicals are frequently too potent for the inexperienced; it's hard to use a small enough amount. People who come to depend on chemicals tend to forget that they need to maintain the soil's organic matter, which is primarily why the early organicists were so hostile to chemicals. Granular chemicals spread atop the soil often resist going into solution for a long time and, if nitrogen fertilizers, may volatilize atop the soil, going off as ammonia without helping the plants grow a bit. Being so potent and one-sided, unbalanced chemical fertilization can throw the soil's nutrient balances wildly out of whack.

Chemicals are said to harm soil microlife. This is untrue. It is even untrue of one common, very cheap, and frequently maligned chemical nitrogen fertilizer: ammonium sulfate. The evidence against ammonium sulfate is contradictory, and the people originally pushing the case against ammonium sulfate acted more like lawyers lying than like scientists deliberating. Actually, chemicals strongly encourage soil microorganisms, which build their bodies from the very same NPK (nitrogen, phosphorus, and potassium) from which plants build theirs. One of the quickest ways to rapidly increase the numbers of soil microorganisms is to add a bit of nitrogen from any source, chemical or natural. The undesirable consequence is that a lot less humus is present a few months later because the increased number of microorganisms decompose the humus at a faster rate. That's one of the reasons why nitrogen fertilizer makes plants grow so much better—for a while a lot more nutrients than were in the fertilizer itself are released due to the accelerated decomposition of organic matter. The creation of high fertility levels by any means, chemical or organic, accelerates the decomposition of soil humus.

We can create exactly the same decline in humus by using concentrated nitrogen sources in organic form as by using concentrated nitrogen sources in chemical form. Even fresh, uncomposted chicken manure will do this. We get into trouble with nitrogen-containing fertilizers only when we don't bother to restore the organic matter that is consumed.

One last item on this abbreviated organic-versus-chemicals balance sheet: Some artificial fertilizers are made by acid treatment of rock or are in themselves acidic. These will "chew up" the soil's lime supply a bit and, if used, need to be accompanied by more lime.

Vegetable gardeners will have far better results if they use complete and properly balanced organic fertilizers instead of chemical fertilizers. Sometimes you can buy an organic fertilizer like the one I describe later. However, you will save a great deal of money by making up your own blend. You can usually find the ingredients at a feed and grain dealer or farm supply. They are best purchased in 50-pound sacks. The dealer sells them as animal feed supplements and may be a bit surprised to hear that you want to fertilize a garden with them. If you buy these ingredients in tiny boxes at a garden center, you will pay far more than the vegetables will ever be worth. Do not be concerned if you don't immediately need a couple of hundred pounds of complete organic fertilizer for this year's garden. The stuff is entirely stable as long as it is kept dry. If you store the ingredients in a large, tightly lidded metal garbage can, your fertilizer will be safe from both mice and moisture until you are ready to use it.

My main consideration in developing this slow-release formula was to keep it simple. You can spade it into the soil before sowing or transplanting and use it to side-dress already-growing plants. It will not burn or shock anything unless hugely overused. This fertilizer blend will keep the potassium levels in your garden down, keep the trace minerals up, provide lots of nitrogen and nearly as much phosphorus (resulting in a much more robust and nutritious plant), and make sure that the plants don't want for calcium or magnesium—or anything else they might need, for that matter. That's why I call it a complete organic fertilizer. It is complete; you don't need anything else.

It is next to impossible to accomplish everything mentioned in the previous paragraph using most of the compost or manure we can make west of the Cascades. That's why you'll do much better by feeding your vegetables with fertilizer. And that's why you organic gardeners need to separate the word "fertilizer" from the word "chemical."

Complete Organic Fertilizer This is the best recipe I know for making a complete organic fertilizer. Other mixtures will end up costing more and will do no better job.

4 parts seed meal (cottonseed or canola meal is generally available in our region)

½ part lime (best is an equal mixture of agricultural lime and dolomite)

½ part phosphate rock or bone meal (steamed or raw)

½ part kelp meal (any kind of pure seaweed meal from anywhere)

All measurements in this formulation are by volume—by the scoop, bucket, jar, or sack. There is no need for more precision than this. It won't matter much if your particular blend comes up a bit stronger or weaker in one respect or another. If you are short of funds, the ingredients are listed in order of importance. In most cases seed meal and lime will grow a pretty good garden all by themselves.

I have accomplished the mixing in several ways. One way is to dump out whole sacks onto a concrete slab and, using a shovel, blend away. Then shovel the mixture back into the original sacks or into several metal garbage cans or other vermin-proof containers. Another method is to keep the ingredients separate and to mix smaller amounts of the fertilizer as needed. The advantage of the first method is speed and efficiency. The advantage of the second method is that it enables you to mix up a special blend for a unique purpose should you have a mind to do so.

Sometimes other kinds of oilseed meals can be obtained. I've had very good results with linseed meal and soybean meal. They cost more than cottonseed or canola west of the Cascades but would be cheaper in Iowa. Gardeners in Fiji have used coconut meal, a by-product of making coconut oil. All oilseed meals are similar in their fertilizing value per volume, and all are similarly safe and slow in terms of speed of release. Cottonseed meal is brought by rail from California's Central Valley. Canola meal is the residue from pressing canola oil from rapeseed, which is widely grown in Canada's prairie provinces. Assuming that whatever meal I found was dry and flowing, I would always use the cheapest.

If you want to verify that the price you're being quoted for a seed meal is reasonable, check the spot price commodities listings in any recent issue of the *Wall Street Journal*, where cottonseed meal is normally priced by the ton in rail hopper-car lots, freight not included. The price depends on the world cotton market and beef feedlot production conditions and doesn't change much from week to week. A ton makes forty 50-pound sacks, and you should add about a dollar a sack for bagging up and labeling 50-pound units from bulk material. Then add in the feed and grain dealer's profit, of course. Normal markups in the feed and grain business are around 20 percent. Other seed meals should cost about the same amount close to their source. A word of warning: If you buy these materials in attractive 5-pound boxes off the shelf in the garden supply section of a retail store, you'll pay enormously higher prices per unit of weight.

Most oilseed meals, when analyzed chemically, are in the vicinity of 6-4-2, or about 6 percent nitrogen, 4 percent phosphorus, and 2 percent potassium. A ratio more ideally suited to our soils would be about 5-5-1 plus trace minerals. My recipe attempts to optimize the values by blending in other potent nutrient sources.

Both sorts of phosphate rock (hard or soft) or bone meal (steamed or raw) will greatly increase the phosphorus content. Phosphate rock has the advantage of often containing significant and useful levels of trace minerals. Bone meal decomposes faster and is more readily available to the plants, giving it a different advantage. Each also has its negatives, however. Phosphate rock from some sources may contain traces of fluorine and/or cadmium, while bone meal may carry "mad cow" disease. For my part, I prefer a life fully lived, with a "no fear" attitude.

Kelp meal is a luxury soil amendment, one I indulge in for my own health and that of my plants. It may contain growth regulators that make vegetables a bit more winter hardy. The sea being the ultimate repository over geologic time of all soil nutrients, things that grow in the sea tend to be very high in all trace nutrients. Maritime Northwest soils are commonly a bit deficient in several: copper, zinc, boron, and cobalt. These may be present in sufficient quantity in the seed meal or the phosphate rock, but just in case, a bit of kelp meal won't hurt. Gardeners who are shocked at the cost of this product might consider bringing back a load of seaweed should they go to the beach and mixing it into their compost pile.

If I were a rich man I'd use two or three parts fish meal (fewer parts because it contains more NPK) in my blend instead of four parts seed meal. What I'd get for all that extra cost would be a very certain supply of trace minerals. The liabilities are that fish meal is a bit odorous even when dry and can rapidly get really rank and putrid if it gets wet. It may also draw the neighboring cats or other wildlife to scratch up your garden or to try to eat your fertilizer while it is still in the bag.

I am frequently asked at lectures if it's safe to use cottonseed meal, since cotton is heavily sprayed with herbicides and dangerously potent insecticides not approved for use on food crops. These chemicals tend to be oil soluble and become concentrated in the cotton plant's seed, so gardeners worry that the seed itself carries quantities of poisonous residues. Well, they're right—it does. But there's no need to worry about using seed meal for fertilizer. Fortunately for us gardeners, to make the meal, the seed is crushed, heated to a high temperature, and combined with a most efficient solvent that dissolves all of the oil. The cottonseed oil thus obtained probably contains virtually all of the pesticide and herbicide residues the cotton plant picked up. Thoroughly stripped of its oil content, the seed meal is now a fairly clean livestock food, sold as a protein supplement. I do consider cottonseed oil a suspect food. Because it is very inexpensive, it is sold in 5-gallon tins to fast-food and Asian restaurants for deep-frying and is also used extensively by makers of prepared salad dressings. Think about that the next time you go out to dinner, and read the label on your favorite salad dressing, mayonnaise, or tinned sardines. And ask yourself why, for the purpose of pesticide regulation, cotton is not considered a food crop!

How to Use Complete Organic Fertilizer

Short of dumping many times the recommended amount onto your plants, a bit too much complete organic fertilizer will not shock plants in the same way that a double dose of chemicals can, although with some delicate species it is wise to keep this fertilizer from coming into direct contact with growing leaves. Knowing how much fertility plants will be able to make use of requires a bit of experience and a bit of experimentation. The amounts recommended should be considered moderate guidelines for the inexperienced.

Regarding the amounts to use, the general principle is:

■ *Use as much complete organic fertilizer as the plants will respond to.*

And the guiding principle is:

■ *Plants mainly need nutrients to support vegetative growth. When light levels and temperatures let them grow fast, plants need to be fed; when they cannot grow fast, they need little.*

In early spring plants grow slowly. In this season they can't make use of heavy nutrition. However, in this season complete organic fertilizer releases its nutrients slowly; the rate of release equaling the rate at which it is decomposed by soil animals, worms, and microorganisms, which is determined by the soil's temperature. In March and April organic nutrients are released much more slowly than in May and June. So for early spring sowings in chilly ground, use a bit more than you might think necessary. To compensate for chilly spring soil, I at one time recommended adding one part blood meal to the mixture because blood meal is virtually water-soluble nitrogen. This works but is not necessary; simply use a bit extra of the ordinary blend.

Newly sprouted seedlings need no fertilizer at all. For a week or two after germination, seedlings supply their nutrient needs entirely from reserves held within the seed itself. Only after they have made a true leaf and are growing fast do seedlings use much nutrition brought through their roots. High levels of plant nutrients in the soil around sprouting seeds have several harmful effects: They can inhibit the sprouting and can also provoke massive increases in the sorts of pathogenic soil fungi that cause damping-off diseases and kill off seedlings wholesale. Very high levels of available soil nutrients will be taken up by small seedlings that can't yet use them but can't reject them either. Unable to build tissue with these nutrients, the seedling retains them in its circulatory system in the form of soluble salts. These salts can build up to toxic levels that may permanently stunt the seedling. It's better not to fertilize seedbeds too heavily until after the seeds are up and growing well.

Throughout the rest of this book I often recommend a range of fertilizer amounts, such as 1 to 2 gallons per 100 square feet or ¼ to ½ cup per plant. I intentionally create this uncertainty because I can't know how fertile your garden's soil already is, nor can I be sure how it will accept and release fertilizer. If you try the lesser amount and the plants seem to grow a bit too slowly, you can always side-dress them to provoke more growth and then begin using the larger amounts next time. If you use the larger amounts and the plants grow magnificently, seeming to need no more fertilization through their entire growth cycle, you might try a bit less next time.

Fertilizing Raised Beds: In raised beds, always rake in or shallowly hoe in 1 to 2 gallons of complete organic fertilizer uniformly spread atop each 100 square feet of growing area *before sowing or planting.* This amount is sufficient to supply very adequate background nutrition for all vegetables, and this single application can be enough by itself to grow less-demanding species like carrots.

Fertilizing Long Rows: When sowing seeds in long rows with paths between, two approaches work well. The first is to blend 1 to 2 gallons of complete organic fertilizer into each 100 row-feet of planting area. Concentrate the fertilizer in the top few inches of soil in an area about 12 inches wide toward the center of the row; there is less benefit from fertilizing the pathways. The second approach is to band the fertilizer. First deeply work the planting row with a shovel. Then with a large hoe make a sharp-sided furrow 4 to 5 inches deep down the center of the row. Sprinkle the fertilizer (again, 1 to 2 gallons per 100 row-feet) mostly in the bottom of this little trench. Then cover the banded fertilizer by pulling the soil back into the trench with the hoe. Sow the seed by making another shallow furrow an inch or two to the side of the subterranean band of fertility you have just created. As soon as the seedlings develop roots, they'll find a zone of super-fertile soil.

Fertilizing Transplanted Seedlings: At the site of each transplant, scoop out a small hole about 4 inches deep and 8 inches in diameter. Put ¼ to ½ cup of complete organic fertilizer into

the bottom of the hole. Blend well into a few inches of soil at the bottom of the hole. Then mud in the transplant atop this highly fertile spot. (For more information, see Chapter 7.)

Fertilizing Transplants Grown in Hills: To make soil fertile enough for those large, sprawly vegetable species usually cultured in hills (squash, pumpkins, melons, cucumbers, rambling indeterminate tomatoes, and, sometimes, when dry-gardening, the larger coles), remove a couple of large shovelfuls of soil from a spot and set them alongside the 6- to 8-inch-deep hole you just made. In the bottom of the hole, put 1 to 2 cups of complete organic fertilizer—that's a lot. Using the shovel, blend it in thoroughly and as deeply as possible into the bottom of the hole as you simultaneously dig up a 2-foot-diameter circle of earth around the hole. The result should be a low hill of fluffy soil dug 12 to 16 inches deep, with a concentration of fertility starting 6 to 8 inches down and located mainly below the hill's center. Because digging so deeply thoroughly destroys the soil's capillary water flow coming up from the subsoil, before sowing seeds or transplanting compress the soil directly below the planting spot somewhat to help subsoil moisture move up to that area. (This restoration of capillarity is discussed at length in Chapter 5.) Then sow seeds or set out a transplant atop this hill.

Side-Dressing: Fertilizing just before sowing or setting out seedlings will provide a sustained background level of plant nutrients for up to three months. During the time that plants are enlarging fast, they will respond to even more fertility by growing even faster and healthier. Remember that the overriding principle of using complete organic fertilizer is to give the plants all that they will positively respond to. Additional feedings should be side-dressed. This means thinly sprinkling a bit of fertilizer around the plant, mostly at the perimeter of its expanding root zone, where it is feeding actively. Across a 4-foot-wide raised bed I might sprinkle a small handful between each pair of 4-foot-long rows of five-week-old lettuce or spinach plants; I might sprinkle a small handful around each six-week-old broccoli or cabbage seedling a week or so after transplanting or six weeks or so after sowing seeds to really make the plant grow fast for the next month or so. I follow that with another, larger handful, side-dressed again, a month later, quite a bit farther out from the central stem. (See the illustration on this page.)

When side-dressing an irrigated garden where the surface layers are periodically remoistened, there is no need to cultivate in or water in the fertilizer. Remember that what you are using as fertilizer is animal feed. Just scatter it about. At night, microscopic soil-dwelling animals will emerge and eat the fertilizer, converting it into superpotent manure that is deposited under the soil an inch or two deep, right where the plant's active feeder roots are waiting for it. A few days after application, the fertilizer will seem to have vanished. With most chemical fertilizers, side-dressing by scattering them on the surface doesn't work so well because the hard granules resist dissolving unless they are in constant contact with moist soil.

Side-dressing complete organic fertilizer.

Some organic gardeners routinely side-dress with liquid manure tea, brewed in a barrel. Although this works, complete organic fertilizer is a far more balanced growth stimulant. The trouble with liquid organic fertilizers of every sort is that it is virtually impossible to get phosphorus, calcium, and magnesium into solution at the same time. Consequently, manure or compost tea, liquid fish emulsion, and liquid seaweed all contain mainly nitrogen and potassium, virtually no phosphorus, and next to no calcium or magnesium. If you are religiously organic and find a liquid fertilizer claiming to be derived from fish and/or seaweed but also claiming to provide more than a scant trace of phosphorus, beware! The source is most probably food-grade phosphoric acid—a chemical that is a very effective fertilizer. And while this particular chemical might grow great plants, the liquid fertilizer likely won't be organic according the definition promulgated by Rodale and assorted certification authorities.

High-Demand and Low-Demand Vegetables: During the 1940s and 1950s, devotees of organic gardening wrote how-to-farm books that still sow confusion in the minds of gardeners about the difference between what it takes to grow field crops and what it takes to grow vegetables.

Before the era of industrial/chemical farming, farmers increased yields by shifting fertility from field to field. Animals grazed one field; their manure was shifted to another field; the higher fertility thus created made hugely higher yields. Or a field was allowed to rest (lie fallow) in grass for a year or two, or a legume crop like alfalfa was grown, creating some nitrogen while allowing the organic matter to increase, and this accumulation of fertility was then plowed down and the next crop got both the annual release of nutrients that the soil would normally provide plus the nutrient and organic matter accumulated in the previous crop now decomposing on the site. The fertilization needs of farm crops in this era could be expressed as the difference between little and less.

When someone tells you that you can meaningfully increasing fertility by first growing a legume crop before growing another crop, they're talking about old-fashioned farming, not gardening. Yes, growing beans or peas might increase the nitrogen in the site a bit, but not enough to concern a home gardener.

The fertility needs of vegetables are usually several times greater than those of wheat, barley, oats, broad beans, the old low-yielding open-pollinated varieties of field corn (maize), rye, pasture grass, clover, and alfalfa. However, certain vegetables still resemble field crops. These include rutabagas, some kinds of turnips, carrots, parsley, parsley root, parsnip, many varieties of beets, Swiss chard, kale, collard greens, potatoes, and many sorts of field beans and garden peas Some of the chicory family—endive and the like—may also barely be included in this group. Sometimes these are called "low-demand" vegetables. They will usually do all right on soils that are fertile enough only for field crops, although they'll do much better with somewhat higher levels of nutrition.

To bring soil to a degree of fertility suitable for low-demand crops, it is often enough to add a small amount of compost and cultivate frequently enough to accelerate its decomposition. However, I gallon of complete organic fertilizer per 100 square feet of bed or per 100 row-feet will make these crops grow a great deal better. Generally, though, low-demand vegetables need no more than this.

Manures as Fertilizer The only kind of manure I have ever had good growing results with has been sold in sacks labeled "chicken manure compost." This stuff has been manufactured for many years in Canby, Oregon, and is widely available in both Oregon and Washington, commonly heaped into enormous stacks in front of supermarkets and garden centers. It is about 4 percent nitrogen and contains quite a bit of phosphorus as well. It is dry, granular, and, compared to fresh chicken manure, relatively odorless—at least the odor goes away after a day or two of its being spread.

I have tried this fertilizer on everything but

carrots and parsnips and have had great results. Although the label says that this particular chicken manure compost has about half the potency of complete organic fertilizer, I seem to need three or four times as much to create the same growth response. It must be even slower to release; perhaps it contains a lot of sawdust. I've used sacked chicken manure compost in exactly the same ways that I use complete organic fertilizer: broadcast and raked in, side-dressed, and banded. It might end up costing a bit less than the blend I make myself, but it's not as balanced and contains no lime.

Chicken manure makes such potent fertilizer because of its origins. When food passes through an animal's gut, it inevitably comes out containing somewhat less plant nutrients than when it started at the front end. Commercially raised chickens mainly eat seeds, so their manure is like weakened seed meal.

People usually think of compost as a way to increase the soil's organic matter. Sacked chicken manure compost—carrying 4 percent nitrogen—is too strong for that purpose. I speculate that if we took a test area and fertilized it with nothing but this compost, used enough to grow good plants, and grew only vegetables on that test plot, over the years the soil's level of organic matter would decrease rather rapidly.

There are two reasons that this particular chicken manure compost works more like a fertilizer than as a source of organic matter. First, I deduce it must be expertly made—during the composting process little of the high nitrogen content that chicken manure starts out with

can be lost, or it wouldn't carry an official analysis of 4 percent N. Second, from the look of it, this particular compost product is composed largely of chicken manure combined with just enough fine sawdust to stabilize the powerfully potent manure during composting and take the sting out of it.

I mentioned earlier that plants concentrate potassium in their woody structures. There's more to this story, however. Many sorts of plants grow vegetatively for a while and then expend everything in making seed in one fast rush before dying or going into dormancy. While preparing their vital inheritance for the next generation, seed-making plants translocate and concentrate into their seed most of the nutrition they accumulated during their entire growth process. The seed is packed with everything possible to get the embryo off to a fast and healthy start. The rest of the plant dries to strawlike stuff that contains little in the way of nutrients but potassium.

Proteins are built only to the degree that plants can acquire nutrient nitrogen and, to a lesser extent, phosphorus; plant proteins contain that N and P. Seed-eating animals get most of the proteins contained in plants, and they eat them in concentrated form. The one plant nutrient that seeds are relatively deficient in is potassium. To someone growing food in an area where the soils are already overly endowed with potassium, this makes ground-up seeds and other seed-based waste a great candidate for fertilizer.

I have seen other makers' versions of chicken manure compost with nutrient analyses that list nitrogen in the vicinity of 2 percent. I wouldn't use them, mainly for reasons of economy. Judging by feel and odor, these consist of chicken manure composted with larger quantities of low-potency organic substances. If someone with a small garden were buying all their compost, this fairly potent source of plant nutrition would be very useful. However, if I were using 2 percent nitrogen compost as my sole source of fertilizer *and* organic matter, and I wanted the vegetables to grow strongly as a result of using it, I'd have to literally use heaps of it. Buying heaps at several dollars a cubic foot is not cost-effective. Unless it could be obtained a lot cheaper by the ton or cubic yard, I'd not bother.

To gauge the fertilizing value of ordinary manures, it's helpful to know a few facts about haymaking and pasture grass in general. When making rapid vegetative growth, plants concentrate most of the phosphorus and nitrogen they take up into the vital protein called chlorophyll in their active leaves. If fodder is fed to animals at a tender, leafy stage (when it contains lots of chlorophyll), the animals respond to the high levels of protein and other nutrients by growing fast and being quite healthy. So green, leafy hay made while the grass is young and growing fast is highly valuable. So too is green hay made from alfalfa before it has begun to get seedy.

Anyone who is knowledgeable about feeding stock prefers (all things being equal) green, leafy hay. But it is impractical to make quality hay west of the Cascades. It's physically possible, yes; we do know various ways to preserve young grass both as hay and as silage when the weather is not conducive to low-cost haymaking. In terms of economic rationalism, however,

it's not possible. Quality grass hay from our side of the mountains would have to be mowed during early May, before any seed heads began to form in the field. May is also a time when it is still far too rainy to dry grass cheaply with a tractor-drawn rake. Other factors being equal (such as the soil fertility being high enough), leaves of our grasses contain about the same amount of protein as leaves of east-side alfalfa. But hand labor is too costly these days to dry the grass by spreading it over hundreds of hurdles in the field, like little thatched roofs, nor is it cost-effective to ferment the green grass into silage and store it wet.

From the moment that a flower stalk starts forming (hidden deep within the growing point of the grass), the nutritional value of the grass leaves begins to decline. Rapidly. Once seed heads emerge above the leaves, the leaves' protein (nitrogen) content has declined to about half of what it had been a few weeks earlier. By the time the seed begins forming in those heads, the nitrogen in the grass leaves has been halved again. And when there is mature seed in those heads, the brown leaves and stems holding the seed heads are little but strawy, virtually indigestible, nutritionless fiber. All of the minerals except the potassium have been translocated and deposited into the seed.

Usually, at about the time the seeds are well formed, our weather begins to settle down and get summery-dry. By then the grass has nearly turned to straw, and "hay" making begins. This is why local grass hay justifiably has a bad reputation. Horse fanciers prefer the much more costly alfalfa or grass hay made on the dry side, where stable spring weather allows the hay to be cut and field-dried at just the right moment to capture the highest nutritional content. Pity the poor livestock trying to derive adequate nutrition from the woody straw and empty seed heads that pass for hay around here.

When maritime Northwest home gardeners get a load of horse or cow manure, what quality of grass are they obtaining the residue of?

Two more pitfalls of manure should be mentioned here. The first is the main difference between chicken manure and other types—urine. The chicken has a single discharge for all food waste. All other farm animals make both feces and urine. What most overlook about this situation is that the urine contains a very large portion of the waste nitrogen and other soluble minerals. Wise farmers who wish to properly compost their barnyard waste and really build their farm's fertility make careful provision to capture every possible drop of urine and contribute it to their compost heaps. Farmers and stable owners who value manure so little that they are willing to sell it make no such arrangements. With chemical fertilizers so cheap, conservation of urine would not be economically rational either.

The second caution concerns the bedding most commonly used under barnyard animals and in horse stables—sawdust. This stuff needs to be avoided. Chapter 3 describes why. Until you read that far, consider this question: What portion of a truckload of horse manure is sawdust?

I hope you can now see why most vegetable gardeners in our region have such poor results when trying to make horse or cow or steer or sheep manure act like strong fertilizer.

Foliar Feeding Foliar feeding works as follows: A dilute solution of a liquid concentrate like fish emulsion or seaweed or of a rapidly soluble chemical intended for this purpose, like Rapid-Gro, is sprayed on the leaves. It is immediately absorbed and instantly prompts a growth spurt that lasts a few days to a week at most. The time to spray is early morning while the dew is still on the leaves, so as the plant dries off it will take in the nutrients. If the plants have waxy leaves that tend to make sprays bead up and drip off, a bit of spreader sticker softens the water and lets the fertilizer penetrate. (I've used a quarter teaspoonful of mild detergent to several gallons of spray to accomplish the same thing.)

This technique has certain advantages. You need less fertilizer to accomplish the same amount of growth because virtually all of it goes into the plant instead of feeding the soil bacteria. It also does not cause soil nutrient levels to become unbalanced, as can happen when fertilizers are amended there. And although soil chemistry can tend to make some elements unavailable shortly after they go into solution, this is not a problem when the same element is added by foliar spraying. Finally, if your fertilizing program has come up short for some reason, deficiencies can be instantly corrected with this technique. Even if you only suspect that there may be a nutrient deficiency, if one foliar feeding solves the problem you know it was a nutritional problem. If one foliar feeding does nothing positive, it will at least do no harm.

Foliar feeding does have disadvantages. Some leaves are very sensitive and will be burnt if the solution is very strong—spinach comes to mind here. Gardeners who use this technique have to patrol their gardens at least weekly with a sprayer to keep the growth going. And foliar feeding does not eliminate the need to maintain organic matter in soils.

THE VITAL IMPORTANCE OF SOIL ORGANIC MATTER

So far I have firmly directed your attention to the importance of soil minerals. Minerals, being inorganic, are relatively easy to understand. I suspect that's why chemical companies have such success getting farmers to pay attention to their fertilizers. And remember, even if you convince someone of the importance of soil organic matter, selling them a product based on compost or manure isn't nearly as profitable as selling them a load of chemicals.

But the decaying animal and vegetable matter in the soil, often called "humus," is every bit as vital to plant growth and plant/soil health as mineral nutrients are. Understanding what humus does and how to manage your relationship with it is not as simple as understanding the importance of a mineral, what it does, and how to handle it. The difference is very much like the difference in difficulty of learning inorganic chemistry compared to organic chemistry.

Many vegetable gardeners, especially those who consider themselves "organic," have already read heaps of information about compost and humus. But there is always the novice who needs

to learn. So first I want to list all the reasons why organic matter is so essential in our vegetable gardens.

One very interesting thing about humus is that we don't know much about it. No chemist can tell you precisely what it is. Humic substances have long defied chemical analysis, and this mysterious stuff has been the subject of some pretty fat books and scads of journal articles. The best of the lot was probably written by a soil microbiologist named Selman Waksman more than sixty years ago. Humus is not any one thing, but is a complex assortment of breakdown products that form when vegetation or manure rots down to a fairly stable material. All of the various sorts of humus are similar in that they're dark colored (brown or black) and spongy (hold a lot of moisture), and have some interesting and very helpful effects when mixed into mineral soil particles.

The name for the whole process of creating humus from plant material, from animal flesh, or from animal manure is *decomposition* or, when spoken plain, rotting. Most kinds of organic material incorporated into soil will initially rot rather rapidly, usually taking a matter of weeks or months to become humus. In comparison, humus in soil rots much more slowly, taking years to fully decompose (nitrify) to inorganic minerals.

Although we don't know what it is, we are quite certain about what humus does. If humus is not continually replaced, the entire soil structure and soil ecology falls apart. Organic matter usually starts decomposing by passing through the digestive tracts of animals— either large ones that deposit manure on the earth's surface or tiny soil-dwelling animals that eat leaves and stems, animal manure, and other plant residue. In the guts of these microanimals, organic matter first becomes microanimal manure. Then, after passing through one or more animal digestive systems, it is ultimately decomposed by soil bacteria and other soil microorganisms. It is the entire food supply of these essential organisms, and the whole chain of soil-dwelling life, from slugs to slime molds, depends on it.

Without a healthy and numerous ecology of microlife, soil becomes nothing but dead, lifeless grit blowing in the wind or, in the case of clay soils, cements itself into rock that water and air can't penetrate. With adequate organic matter, soil usually becomes sweet smelling and pleasant and functions like a creative organism. That's largely because of the many things accomplished by soil microlife.

N. A. Krasil'nikov, a brilliant Russian soil microbiologist of the 1950s (and one of my personal heroes), in his book *Soil Microorganisms and Higher Plants* (listed in the bibliography) very wisely defined soil fertility as "determined by biological factors, mainly by microorganisms. The development of life in soil endows it with the property of fertility. The notion of soil is inseparable from the notion of the development of living organisms in it. Soil is created by microorganisms. Were this life dead or stopped, the former soil would become an object of geology (not biology)." Krasil'nikov measured soil fertility by counting the number of microorganisms per gram of soil; there is always a very close match between this number and the productivity of the soil.

Of the many positive effects accomplished by soil microlife, the ones of most concern to gardeners are improved soil structure, suppression of soil-dwelling plant diseases, and enormously better plant nutrition through the bacterial creation of what Krasil'nikov called "phytamins."

Phytamins: Plant Vitamins It is possible to raise plants hydroponically, entirely on mineral nutrition. But hydroponic plants always look a bit "off" to me and are very susceptible to disease and insect attack. They are weak because they almost certainly lack phytamins, the plant's equivalent of vitamins. And plants need their phytamins just as animals and humans need their vitamins.

Judging by how they act, you might that think plants know they need phytamins in order to be healthy and grow right. They can't make these substances themselves, any more than humans can manufacture their own vitamin C, so plants create an external phytamin factory. Their roots secrete a large quantity of watery exudates that have several powerful effects; I describe only one here. (See Chapter 4 for another.) The exudate forms a chemical environment that strongly favors the multiplication and development of exactly those kinds of bacteria that the plants wish to have present in their root zone. The exudate also suppresses the growth of other sorts of bacteria that the plants do not wish to have in their proximity.

The favored and protected soil-dwelling bacteria multiply profusely around the plants' roots. It's a fair exchange; some of the bacteria's secretions are the very growth regulators and other phytamins that the plant needs to be healthy. The cultured microorganisms also create a chemical environment that suppresses competition from other forms of microlife, preventing soil-dwelling disease organisms from attacking the plant.

Keep in mind that the root exudates are not food for the bacteria; they only create a more favorable environment for some bacteria while suppressing others. The soil bacteria eat (decompose) organic matter. If there is enough bacteria food in the soil, the plants obtain their phytamins. If not, they go without.

Tilth Another group of soil microorganisms have no particular relationship with plant root zones; these create favorable soil structure by secreting slimy, gluey substances that cement soil particles and bits of humus into large, strong, irregularly shaped "crumbs." Without a crumb structure, the finer bits of silt and clay would fill in the gaps between the sand particles, and the soil would settle into a solid, airless mass. Air and water can freely enter into soil between irregularly shaped soil crumbs because crumbs won't pack tightly. A crumbly soil is said to have good *tilth*. It cultivates well and forms a finely textured, loose seedbed that stays loose. It doesn't slump or form a hard crust that prevents the emergence of sprouting seedlings. Few plants can make effective root systems in hard, compacted soil; tilth permits vegetables, which are generally very weak-rooting anyway, to extend their root systems very successfully.

Tilth lets the water flow into and through soil when it rains or when you irrigate. When you see long-lasting puddles on farm fields after a heavy rain, you are probably looking at humus-depleted soil. The water can't percolate into and through this soil because the crumb structure has broken down. (I say probably because there are areas of the Willamette Valley south of Albany and mainly west of Interstate 5 that are underlain by an impervious layer of clay not far below the surface. These fields inevitably become shallow lakes after a few days of heavy winter storms. Grass, being one of the few crops that can tolerate days of submergence in winter, is grown on this land for grass seed. Prior to the Second World War, this land grew flax, another crop that can tolerate wet feet.)

Humus has a very high ability to hold water, like bits of sponge. Soil crumbs, composed of mineral particles and humus cemented together, dry out slowly. Thus, having a lot of humus in a seedbed greatly enhances seed germination. Tilth also reduces crust formation atop the soil after rain or irrigation. Crusty soil can stop seedlings from emerging and greatly reduces the amount of air getting into the soil.

Air in soil is a lot more vital than most people know. The useful soil microorganisms are all oxygen breathers. Plant roots, too, need oxygen to live. If you fluff up humus-poor soil by tilling, a lot of air can be put there temporarily. But dead soil will soon slump back into an airless mass. Vegetables planted on freshly tilled soil may grow fairly well for a few weeks or a month, but after a few irrigations soil that lacks humus resumes its compacted condition. Only certain very coarse sand soils (containing next to no clay) permit the movement of enough air to satisfy the needs of plants without having a crumb structure. Naturally, these coarse, sandy (though very droughty) soils are very popular with commercial vegetable growers—if they have enough irrigation water to keep them moist.

To stay healthy, a plant must grow below the ground. If root growth ceases or even slows greatly, health is usually lost because plants obtain most of their nutrition from the tender young tips of actively growing roots and from the tiny hairs just behind those tips. The root's tip must constantly be re-created; new tip cells form ahead of the older ones as the tender young cells that used to be the tip toughen up, grow a bark, and change into ordinary root incapable of absorbing much nutrition.

Keep this fact in mind, because it has major implications for garden planning, plant spacing, companion planting, and so on. Much of our job as servants of the plant involves ensuring that its roots can continue expanding. For example, carrots, beets, and rutabagas will immediately begin getting woody and tasteless if they cannot expand their entire root system, but if the root system can continue to extend rapidly, these and certain other root vegetables are good eating no matter how large they get. Vines like melons and cucumbers will remain resistant to disease and be far more productive if they continue growing rapidly. And as soon as a heading brassica, such as a cabbage or a cauliflower, runs into a barrier to underground expansion, it becomes stunted aboveground no matter how much water and fertility there may be in the soil.

For a vegetable's root system to continue growing rapidly, it must, among other things, have enough oxygen in the soil. For that to occur the soil must remain loose and friable.

Having plenty of air in the soil also has another benefit: It causes soil-dwelling microorganisms to thrive and eat more, accelerating the decomposition of soil organic matter, releasing more of the nutrients contained in the organic matter and feeding the plants better. That's one reason, other than weeding, why farmers and gardeners cultivate the soil, breaking up the surface and introducing a fresh supply of air. For a week or so after each cultivation there's a lot more air in the soil, and the plants grow more rapidly. Jethro Tull, an eighteenth-century farm innovator, said of this, "Tillage is manure." Try gently sliding a sharp hoe through your soil more frequently; you may like the results. If you've concentrated all of the additions of organic matter into the soil's surface inch, you'll find that hoeing requires little effort. The more regularly you do this, the easier it is to do each time. I make it a regular weekly practice, during the main growing season, to shallowly cultivate and weed the entire garden.

How Much Organic Matter Does Soil Need, Anyway?

Decomposing (nitrifying) organic matter releases plant nutrients and becomes fertilizer. Decomposing organic matter feeds microorganisms and thus is essential to the health of plants and to the formation of good tilth. Thus it would seem that we could never get enough of it. Robert Parnes, author of *Fertile Soil: A Grower's Guide to Organic and Inorganic Fertilizers* (listed in the bibliography), says of this attitude, "A garden differs fundamentally from a farm. A farm is a source of nutrients, and a garden is a sink for nutrients. A farm produces hay and straw for mulch, and it produces animal manure, both of which contribute to the fertility of a garden. A garden takes all that fertility for producing a high intensity of valuable crops. Moreover, the tillage required to maintain a garden tends to destroy fertility, whereas the tillage on a farm, under ideal conditions, builds fertility."

I've noticed that a pair of related questions about organic matter in garden soils are rarely asked, much less answered, with understanding. One is, How much organic matter do we really need? The second, which is perhaps more important, is, Is it possible to have too much? Of the second question, I have already explained that compost and manure are heavy carriers of potassium because the leaf and stem vegetation that most manures and composts are made from is where the plant concentrates its uptake of potassium. West of the Cascades, we should avoid unnecessary additions of this mineral, in the interest of our own nutritional health. Still, we must maintain enough humus, and vegetable gardening is one of the most effective ways to accelerate the loss of soil organic matter I know of. What an interesting problem!

At this point I could simply give you a cast-in-stone rule that says that west of the Cascades we need to maintain 4 to 5 percent organic matter in our soils, which amounts to an annual addition of less than ¼ inch of compost. And it would essentially be true—4 or 5 percent is the target, and ¼ inch is essentially what has to be added each year to replace the losses once the garden has become a going concern. But clinging to these numbers in a stormy sea of uncertainty leaves you in the position of clinging to an Authority—me. It's better to understand how these figures were arrived at. However, if what follows is a bit too thick for your taste, you are invited to return to this paragraph and cast those figures in stone because they're pretty universally correct for our region. You can then skip ahead.

If you measured the organic matter content of various soils around the United States, there would be wide differences. Some low levels found on cropland are from bad farming. But even if you could measure virgin soils never used by humans, there still would be great differences. Hans Jenny, a brilliant soil scientist at the University of Missouri, noticed regional and climatic patterns in soil humus levels and explained how and why this occurs in a wonderfully readable book, *Factors in Soil Formation* (listed in the bibliography).

About organic matter in virgin soils, Jenny says, "Within regions of similar moisture conditions, the organic matter content of soil . . . decreases from north to south. For each fall of 10°C (18°F) in annual temperature the average organic matter content of soil increases two or three times, provided that [soil moisture] is kept constant."

Moist soil during the growing season encourages plant growth and thus increases the production of organic matter. So, all things being equal, wetter soils contain more organic matter than dryer ones. All organic matter eventually rots; it even rots in soil too dry to grow plants well. The higher the soil temperature, the faster the decomposition. But cool (not frozen) soils can still grow a lot of biomass. Thus, all things being equal, hot soils contain less humus than cold ones. Cool, wet soils have the highest levels; hot, dry soils are lowest in humus.

This model checks out in practice. If we were to measure organic matter in soils along the Mississippi River, where soil moisture conditions remain pretty similar, going from south to north we might find 2 percent in sultry Arkansas, 3 percent in Missouri, and more than 4 percent in Wisconsin. In scorching Arizona, unirrigated desert soils have virtually no organic matter because they grow next to nothing. Even Arizona soils that are irrigated and under cultivation don't have much because the high temperatures cause decomposition to occur at very rapid rates. In central and southern California, where skimpy and undependable winter rains peter out by March, it is hard to find an unirrigated soil containing as much as 1 percent organic matter, while in the cool maritime Northwest, reliable winter rains keep the soil damp into June or early July, and the more fertile farm pastures or natural prairies may develop as much as 5 percent organic matter.

Other factors, like the basic mineral content of the soil and its texture, influence the amount of organic matter that a spot will create and increase or decrease the humus content somewhat compared to neighboring locations experiencing the same climate. But the most powerfully controlling influences are soil moisture and temperature.

On native, unaltered (virgin) soils, the organic matter content naturally stabilizes at the highest possible level the site can create. At this peak, average annual additions of new organic material exactly match the average annual amount of decomposition. Let's envision that process for a moment. Imagine that we start out with a plot of finely ground rock particles containing no life and no organic matter but containing potential plant nutrients that are slowly released, if only by the moisture present in the rock dust. The rock dust is gradually colonized by life forms building their bodies from these dissolved nutrients, and it becomes soil. The organic matter created there stores up already released nutrients and then, when decomposing, releases them again, increasing nutrient availability. Weak organic acids created by microorganisms accelerate the breakdown of rock particles, increasing the release of new mineral nutrients and further increasing the creation of organic matter. Soil life—plant roots, microorganisms, and soil animals—breathe oxygen and exhale carbon dioxide gas. Some of this CO_2 dissolves in soil water and makes a weak acid—carbonic acid—that dissolves rock particles even more rapidly, releasing even more minerals. Humus steadily builds up, and with this increase the release of nutrients from newly decomposed rock also increases. Eventually a climax is achieved where the soil sustains as much humus as it can and the rock particles are dissolving as fast as they ever will, releasing plant nutrients at the highest possible rate.

The climax ecology that naturally lives on any site is usually very healthy and is inevitably just as abundant as the moisture and soil minerals that support it. Envisioning how such an ecology develops suggests to me how much organic matter it takes to grow a great vegetable garden. My theory is that, in terms of their organic matter requirement, vegetables will grow quite well at whatever level the humus would naturally climax at in that location. In arid areas I'd modify this theory to include greater biomass production from ongoing, regular irrigation. Expressed as a rough estimate, a mere 2 percent organic matter in hot, humid soils, increasing to 5 percent in cool ones, will support enough soil life to create good tilth and to grow totally healthy vegetables—if the mineral nutrient levels are high enough to suit vegetables.

What is most important about organic matter is not how much is present, but how much is lost each year through decomposition. For only by decomposing does organic matter release the nutrients it contains so that plants can take them up; only by being consumed does humus support the microecology that so markedly contributes phytamins to plant nutrition; only while consuming organic matter do soil microorganisms aggressively break down rock particles and release the plant nutrients they contain; and only by being eaten does soil organic matter support bacteria and earthworms that create better tilth. Having a high level of organic matter that does not rot makes a peat bog, not an agricultural soil.

I'm suggesting that in a maritime Northwest garden soil containing 4 to 5 percent organic matter, the amount of decomposition you'll get can support very satisfactory plant health and adequate tilth on all soil types except heavy clays, which are a special case to be discussed separately, a bit later and at some length.

That's how much organic matter our soils need. But how much do we have to add? The University of Missouri did a long-term study in soil management that answers this question. In 1888, a never-before-farmed field of native prairie grasses was converted into test plots. For fifty consecutive years each plot was managed in a different but consistent manner. They measured and recorded what happens to soil organic matter as a consequence of different farming practices. That virgin Missouri prairie had, probably for thousands of years, sustained an organic matter content of about 3.5 percent. The lines in the graph on page 51, "How Different Cropping Patterns Affect Soil Humus Over Long Periods of Time," show what happened to that organic matter over the period of the study.

Timothy grass is probably a slightly more efficient converter of solar energy into organic matter than was the original prairie. After fifty years of feeding livestock timothy hay cut from the field and returning all of the livestock's manure to the field, the organic matter in the soil had increased by about ½ percent. Obviously, green manuring has a very limited ability to increase soil humus above natural climax levels.

In another plot, growing oats and returning enough manure to represent the straw and grain fed to livestock held the level of organic matter relatively constant.

Growing small grain and removing everything but the stubble for fifty years greatly

How Different Cropping Patterns Affect Soil Humus
Over Long Periods of Time *(adapted from University of Missouri reports)*

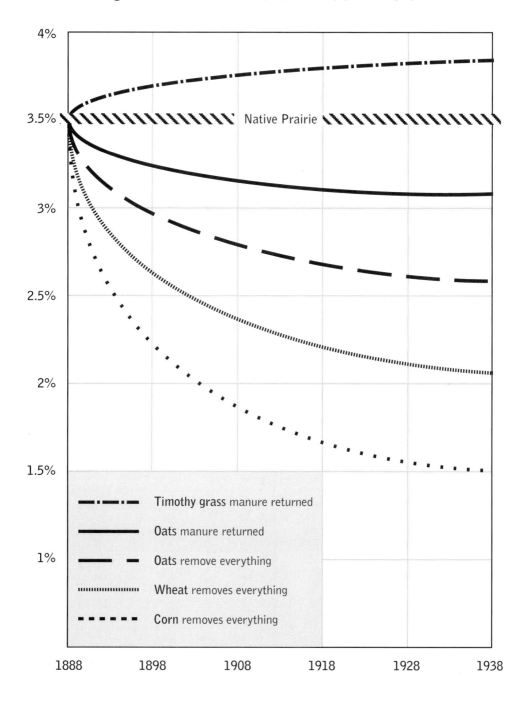

reduced the organic matter. Keep in mind that half of the biomass production in a field can't be removed because it happens belowground. And be aware that the chart doesn't reveal the sad appearance the crops probably had after a decade of so of this handling, once the organic matter had declined significantly. Nor does the chart show that the small, shriveled grain produced on those degenerated fields probably would no longer sprout well enough to be used as seed, so new seed would have been imported into the system each season, bringing with it new supplies of plant nutrients. Without importing the nutrients contained in that wheat seed each year, the curves would have been steeper and gone even lower.

Corn is the hardest of all the cereals on soil humus. The reason is fairly simple to understand. Wheat and other winter grains are closely broadcast in the fall and make an overwintering stand, forming a canopy that efficiently creates biomass from early spring until summer when the seed forms. Leafy oats create a little more biomass than wheat. Corn, on the other hand, is frost tender and can't be overwintered. It is also not closely planted but is sown in widely spaced rows. Corn takes quite a while to form a leaf canopy that uses all available solar energy. It stops making new biomass well before the frosts come. In farming lingo, corn is a row crop.

Vegetables are also row crops. Most types never form really dense leaf canopies that soak up every bit of received solar energy for the entire growing season. Like cornfields, vegetable ground is often relatively unvegetated for some of the best growing months of the

year. Vegetables also demand the highest levels of soil nitrogen and mineral fertility in general, so fertilizing them enormously boosts populations of humus-consuming soil microorganisms. Of all the crops that a person can grow, vegetables drain the most soil organic matter. Gardens are, as Parnes asserted, endless sinkholes for fertility.

When growing vegetables, we have to restore more organic matter to the soil than we could ever create by careful composting of all garden waste. The curves showing humus decline at the University of Missouri led me to a workable estimate of how much organic matter is lost from a vegetable garden. I pessimistically suppose that vegetable gardening is twice as hard on soil as growing corn.

With permanent corn culture, about 40 percent of the field's entire reserve of organic matter was depleted in the first ten years. Let's suppose that vegetables, being far more destructive of humus, might cause the loss of 10 percent each year. How much is that in practical terms?

The furrow slice, the normally plowed and tilled 7-inch-thick topsoil, is where most biological activity occurs and where virtually all of the soil's organic matter resides. Depending on soil type, the furrow slice weighs between one and two million pounds per acre or, at most, 1,000 tons. West of the Cascades as much as 5 percent of that 1,000 tons could be organic matter, 50 priceless tons that change 950 tons of dead dust into a fertile, productive acre. If, as a consequence of one year's vegetable gardening, 10 percent of that 50 tons is lost, the decrease amounts to 5 tons per acre, or about 25 pounds lost per 100 square feet.

Patience, dear reader! There is a very blunt and soon to be obvious point to all of this boring arithmetic. Visualize this: Lime is spread at a rate of from 1 to 2 tons per acre. Have you ever seen lime broadcast from the back of a spreader truck on a farm field, or have you yourself spread 1 ton per acre, by hand? That's 50 pounds of lime over a garden 33 feet square. It's mighty hard to accomplish! Even four times the amount of lime would barely whiten the ground. It is even harder to spread 250 pounds of compost uniformly on a 1,000-square-foot garden, because once done it seems as though nothing has changed: Most of the soil still shows, and there is no layer of compost, only a thin, random scattering.

For the purpose of maintaining an ongoing vegetable garden, however, this scant frosting once a year is a gracious plenty. Even if I were starting a new garden site on a totally depleted, dusty, absolutely humusless, completely mined-out old farm field that had no organic matter whatsoever, and I wanted to convert it quickly to a healthy vegetable garden, I would make a one-time amendment of only 50 tons of finished compost per acre, or 2,500 pounds per 1,000 square feet. A dose that big might cover the soil half an inch thick. Now 2,500 pounds of humus, even if not soaking wet, is still a groaning, spring-sagging, long-bed pickup load of compost heaped up above the cab's roof. A load that big will be sliding past the raised side boards like an honest cord of firewood. Spread over a small garden, that's enough to give one a sense of accomplishment.

Now you should appreciate what lies behind the point-by-point, made-simple instructions found at the beginning of this chapter.

- When starting a new garden, spread and till in no more than ½ inch of finished compost or 1 inch of ruminant manure containing a minimum of sawdust and absolutely no wood chips, because chips take forever to decompose.

- When maintaining an ongoing garden site, make no more than an annual addition of ¼ inch of finished compost. Use quite a bit less if you can bring yourself to do so.

- Keep all additions of compost to the surface inch or two of soil, where it will do you the most good.

If you can bring yourself to use this little compost, your vegetables may come out containing a lot more nutrition, and you may also reduce problems with a very nasty pest called the symphylan (discussed in Chapter 4). But if you don't keep the soil's organic matter above 4 percent, your garden soil and plant health will suffer.

Green Manuring and Cover Cropping

I hope the previous section made it clear that growing vegetables is very destructive to the level of soil organic matter and that occasional green manuring and cover cropping for short periods between vegetable crops will not replace the organic matter lost while growing vegetables. It seems that the only practice that will grow enough organic matter to maintain a high level of humus is to grow grass continuously for many years, with few or no removals.

Growing the right kinds of overwintered green crops between vegetable plantings does have several other advantages, however, and should be done wherever and whenever possible. The first benefit, obviously, is that when the soil is covered with actively growing green, it is at least producing some organic matter. Second, this organic matter is not imported, so creating it on-site does not risk unbalancing your garden's nutrient profile, as you would by bringing manure or compost in from off-site. These two benefits alone are worth the low cost and small effort of sowing a bit of seed. Third, a thick winter cover crop puts the soil in much better condition for spring planting. This will save you far more work later than you exerted to plant the crop, even if you have to mow the vegetation and compost it in heaps. Fourth, cover crops greatly reduce erosion from heavy winter rains on sloping sites. The last two points are probably the most important.

People who really mean to start planting as early as possible are usually frustrated by the seemingly endless rains of spring. The ground never seems to dry out enough to till. It won't work up into a fine seedbed, and unless you have very sandy soil, digging it wet risks making rocklike clods that won't break apart again until next winter. The right sort of winter green manure/cover crop handily remedies this. The green manure rapidly develops a dense leaf cover that stops the endless heavy rains from beating directly on the garden. As a consequence

the soil below the cover crop will be much softer in spring. During winter and early spring, the cover crop densely fills the earth with roots, drawing moisture out of the soil at every sunny opportunity and evaporating it rapidly through the leaves. Cover-cropped soil dries out much more quickly than bare earth. A spell of only two or three rainless days in March or April may be enough to allow the surface few inches of soil to be *gently* worked.

To sow or plant a cover-cropped bed after a brief spell of more-settled spring weather, first either pull the vegetation from the soil by hand, roots and all, or cut it off very close to the soil line with a hand sickle, corn knife, scythe, or lawn mower. The vegetation goes to the compost pile. Then work up a seed bed by chopping the soil an inch or two deep with the sort of ubiquitous and rather heavy hoe most people use and gently raking out most of the roots and stubble. Deeper tillage is not needed because the soil is entirely filled with fine, delicate roots that, if you used a legume green manure, will be entirely decomposed within ten days or so, probably about the time the seed you plant in that chilly soil has germinated. As the roots rot, the soil naturally fractures and welcomes the vegetables' invading roots.

It is essential to use the right green manures. Farming and gardening books are full of recommendations for cover crops that don't fit our climate or that could fit our climate but are suitable only to mechanized farming because they're far too tough for easy by-hand removal. So beware of green manuring with rye grain or many kinds of grasses and winter-hardy cereals. Also avoid red clover, a rather slow-growing perennial that is very hard to get rid of. I also strongly suggest avoiding any kinds of vetch, because vetch seeds can sit in the soil all winter and sprout the next summer, becoming a very undesirable and hard-to-eliminate weed. The two cover crops I recommend most highly are crimson clover and small-seeded fava beans. You'll find full cultural information for these in Chapter 9.

Finally, a word about the nitrate production of legume green manures. Does it help? Yes, it helps some, but not enough for a vegetable grower to be overjoyed about. Crimson clover and fava beans can produce nitrate-nitrogen in the soil while they are growing. However, virtually all of this nitrogen is used as fast as it is created by the growing plant itself, translocated mainly to the leaves. If the soil dries out enough in spring to permit you to till in all of the aboveground vegetation before it gets woody and tough, it will decompose rapidly and help fertilize the crops that follow. However, I have found that many springs are too rainy, and I end up putting the vegetation in the compost heap, where it does rapidly rot down to useful organic matter.

To Till or Not to Till
(and a Few Words on How to Till)

Gardeners are always looking for an easier way. In 1961 Ruth Stout, sister of the popular mystery fiction writer Rex Stout, wrote a revolutionary book called *Gardening Without Work.* Since then, enthu-siasts have kept Ruth's no-till system in prominent view, where it perennially attracts gardeners from all over—including those west of the Cascades. The trouble is, it doesn't work here. I tried it. Nor does permanent mulching work on vegetable gardens in California, which was the first place I tried it.

The way to garden without work is to live where it gets really hot in summer, so the mulch rots rapidly enough to fertilize the soil, and where it gets really cold in winter, so the bugs living in the mulch die off almost completely. In such a climate, you put down a mulch heavy enough to kill off the grass and other vegetation on the site. Wherever a weed manages to struggle through the mulch, it demonstrates that the mulch at that spot has become too thin, so you kill the weed by tossing a flake of hay on it. Easy. To set transplants, you pull the mulch back, exposing a bit of soil; as the seedling grows, you push the mulch back around it. To plant seeds, you expose a narrow row of soil by raking back the mulch and sowing the seeds; as they grow, you push the mulch back against them. And that's it. No tillage, no fertilizing, no manuring, no weeding. And not much watering either. The continuously rotting mulch gradually makes the soil very fertile and so soft that it never needs tilling. If the site was too infertile at the start to grow much of anything, you can accelerate the process of fertility building by putting down a one-time-only thin layer of chicken manure or cottonseed meal before you start mulching.

I do believe this works where Ruth did it— in Connecticut. But when I tried it in southern

California and again in Oregon, I ran into a catastrophe—the same catastrophe in both places. What happens in our climate is that the mulch provokes a steady and unstoppable increase in two kinds of insects—sow bugs (also known as pill bugs or wood lice) and earwigs (also known as pinchbugs). Both are present in all gardens and at their normal population levels are usually harmless, eating a bit of decomposing organic matter here and there. What happens under permanent mulch is that these insects encounter an unlimited supply of food and excellent cover to hide in. They also do not encounter what limited their population in Connecticut, which is real winter. West of the Cascades, by the second summer of permanent mulch their populations reach plague proportions. They start eating everything tender, including lettuce seedlings and ripening tomatoes. And there will be a heap more slugs, too.

If you've tried this gardening-without-work system to your dismay, and you have the soil mulched right now, it is easy to cure this insect plague. Simply rake up all the mulch, every bit of it, and make a compost pile with it, hopefully a bit away from the vegetable patch. In a few weeks there will be hardly a sow bug or earwig to be seen outside the compost heap, which, in my opinion, is where sow bugs and earwigs mainly belong—and where they do useful work by accelerating the breakdown of organic matter.

Perennial mulching does demonstrate one very useful principle, though—the importance of making all additions of organic matter at the surface, which imitates nature's method.

Nature generally has dead vegetation and manure begin their decomposition at the surface. This leads to a very marked humus profile in the soil, with the largest amount located in the top inch or so of soil and the humus content declining rapidly as you go deeper.

Here are some of the advantages of nature's method. The surface inch, by consisting of much more than 5 percent organic matter, has very little tendency to crust or get hard in any way. This keeps it open, better allowing in air and rain. The organisms that accomplish decomposition work near the surface and thus get a very good air supply. So organic matter near the surface decomposes more rapidly and functions more like fertilizer and less like a peat bog. Most minuscule soil animals that eat decomposing organic matter are light-shy. During the daytime they dig deeper into the earth, and at night they come up toward the surface to feed. Their daily up and down travel relocates predigested organic matter (insect manure) several inches deeper, where the plants' feeder roots are.

Your gardening should, as much as possible, imitate nature. When adding compost or manure and/or lime and/or complete organic fertilizer, rake or gently chop it into the surface. The tool to use is a bow rake or a hoe, not a spade or shovel. This is true of every kind of soil but heavy clay. Clay gardens are, as I've mentioned several times already, a special case and are discussed in their own section.

ELIMINATING SOD

Permanent mulchers get rid of sod by piling a thick-enough layer of hay flakes on it. Others have done it with a thick sheet of black plastic, left atop the grass until everything below dies. I once did it with a sharp shovel, painstakingly inverting 6-inch-thick chunks of sod for about a month and then reinverting them again. When they were turned back up, most of the grass had died and the soil then began to crumble. Still, cutting thick sod, even with the sharpest of shovels, and inverting it is a young person's work, and hard work at that.

I've also gotten rid of sod with a self-propelled rototiller. This is less work by far than removing it by hand. The first pass, made as slowly as possible, goes down only an inch or so. When you're done, most of the grass will still look intact. Wait a week or so and make a second pass; the tines will go down 2 inches or so, and the grass will look a bit damaged. A third pass over the plot a week later will go down 3 or 4 inches, and by this time most of the grass will be dead or will soon die. Then it gets much easier.

Gardeners who are not organic purists may wish to use glyphosate (Roundup). Spray one dose on grass and weeds anytime the grass is growing vigorously, and a week later, it is all yellowed and dying. Then spread the plot with lime and complete organic fertilizer. The increased fertility rapidly accelerates the sod's decomposition. A few weeks later, after the root masses have largely disintegrated, it becomes very easy to loosen up the soil with a rototiller or by hand with a shovel. Then you can sow a green manure crop to overwinter or, if it is spring, begin making seedbeds.

Here's how I justify the use of a chemical plant poison: The only occasion when it would ever be used is at the end of summer on a plot that is in permanent grass to be converted to a vegetable garden. The chemical rapidly disintegrates into harmless by-products shortly after it comes into contact with soil. (Glyphosate is actually a synthetic version of a natural hormone found in just about every plant. Given as an overdose, it makes the plant grow itself to death. Thus, spraying glyphosate on a plant is like giving an overdose of synthetic adrenaline to a human.) By the time you begin growing food on the plot, at least six months and an entire winter will have passed. This use of herbicide saves an enormous amount of effort. When applying glyphosate, you should take minimal precautions: Wear tall rubber boots when spraying, and do it on a windless morning. And stay out of the area for a few days after spraying.

TILLING DEEPLY

Deep digging helps plants grow roots better, although the help is only temporary in uncompacted soils because within a month or six weeks of digging, most soils will have slumped back to their native condition. However, many things may have occurred at your garden site that compacted the soil into a far denser state than its native condition. And it can take an awfully long time for some sorts of compaction to rectify themselves.

The most obvious compactor is our own feet. Hooves put far greater pressure on the soil than human feet; cattle or horses may well have been pastured on your land before it became yours. Allowed to graze during winter's wet, animals can do immense damage to the soil's structure. Other causes of compaction include the heavy machinery that may have converted a farm or forest into your house and lot. If your land was a farm before it was subdivided into homesteads, a century of plowing may have compressed the subsoil.

Perhaps the worst type of soil compaction is caused by the common plow. This farm implement is supposed to loosen up the soil and fit it for sowing seeds. It does that, but at the same time it seals off the subsoil in such a way that plants roots can barely access it. Moldboard plowing makes the crop grow almost entirely in the top 7 inches of the field. This damage is accomplished by the heavy weight of the plow resting on its bottom, or sole. The plow sole passes through the soil 7 inches below the surface; the weight of the plow compresses the layer of soil immediately beneath the sole. Each successive plowing further compacts the *plow pan.* If you have one it will be 2 or 3 inches thick and will start about 7 inches down. William Faulkner made himself famous in the 1940s by realizing this and suggesting no-plow farming after rehabilitating plowed land with subsoil tillage.

The easiest way I know of to test for a plow pan is to borrow a posthole auger and drill a few holes in moist soil. I suggest an auger because its speed and ease of penetration is much more telling of soil condition than a sharp shovel can be. The first inch of augering is always very difficult because surface roots and other vegetation tangle the cutters and because the surface of most pastures and lawns is quite compacted from being walked on. Then, as you get down into the soil a bit, bor-

ing gets much easier. But if, when you get down about 7 inches, the going becomes very slow, and then, when you get down another 3 inches or so the soil gets soft as hot butter, you'll be certain of what your problem is: plow pan.

Farmers shatter plow pans with a powerful tractor drawing an implement often shaped something like the tip of a shoe tree, which slides through the soil about 18 inches deep and pops the earth up an inch or two. When the task is done it looks as though a giant mole had been working through the field. In a home garden, all you need is a *very sharp* long-handled combination shovel of decent quality. Gradually wiggle the blade full length straight down into the soil, pressing down with one foot while you move the handle slightly back and forth. When the 12-inch-long blade is entirely buried (this does take a few wiggles and some foot pressure), lever the handle back to pop the soil loose. You won't be able to bite off more than a few inches at a time without breaking the handle, but it is not really very hard work when you nibble off little chunks in this way.

There is no benefit to turning the soil over. In fact, there is a good reason not to invert the soil: Most of the organic matter will naturally be in the surface few inches, and that's where you want to keep it. Merely wiggle in, pop loose, go back a few inches, and repeat over and over as you work your way down a raised bed or row. I enjoy this work; it is conducive to meditation and to breaking a light sweat.

Even if you own or rent a very powerful self-propelled, walk-behind rototiller or hire the work done by a big, tractor-sized rotovator,

Dig or rototill too early in spring when soil is too wet and you create rocklike clods that won't disintegrate until next spring. Getting seeds to germinate in cloddy soil is very tough. Here's how to work the soil without making clods.

■ If you want to work soil early, do it on a raised bed you made the previous autumn. Raised beds drain and dry faster than flat ground. The clods that will inevitably form after you work wet soil can be raked off a raised bed and down into the paths, where they'll gradually be broken up by your feet during the growing season.

■ If you want to work soil as early as possible, plant the raised bed you're going to use next spring to an overwintering cover crop in October. A dense cover crop will dry out the bed much more rapidly, while the thick root system of the cover crop will fracture the soil far deeper than you could dig, allowing a minimum-till planting next spring. All you'll have to do is yank out the vegetation, broadcast complete organic fertilizer, chop up the surface a bit with a sharp hoe, going no more than 1 inch deep, rake the bed out as fine as you can (pulling any clods down into the paths), and plant your seeds or set your transplants.

■ Here's how to determine whether soil is at the right level of moisture to be spaded up or rototilled without forming clods. Take a handful of soil and squeeze it together firmly between your palms to make a soil ball smaller than a tennis ball but larger than a golf ball. If the soil won't form a ball at all, it is too dry; tilling will make a dusty mess and will probably be extremely difficult because dry soil is hard soil. If it makes a ball that won't shatter when you press it firmly with your thumb, it is too wet. Tillage at this moisture content will make clods. If it makes a ball that falls apart when pressed with your thumb, the soil is just right.

the result will be soil worked no more than 5 or 6 inches deep. Rotary tillers will fool you. They introduce so much fluff into the soil that what seems like a foot of loose earth will slump back to 5 or 6 inches after the first good watering. Tillers do have one positive aspect. Because they loosen the first few inches and thoroughly break apart sod and root masses, subsequently spading a foot deep becomes much easier. If I were breaking a large new garden and a tiller were available, I'd use it for sure, but I'd only till deep enough to shatter the sod and root clumps. Then I'd do the rest with a spade. You'll have enormous productivity gains if you do likewise.

Once you've deeply loosened the ground, if you then don't recompact it by walking on it,

you'll find in subsequent years that digging is much easier than it was the first time. It may not even be necessary again. A hoe and rake on the surface may well be sufficient. That's one reason that semipermanent raised beds or semipermanent wide rows with semipermanent paths between make such sense. If we define this bit of soil as a "growing area" and that bit as a "path," our feet compress the paths and not the beds, greatly reducing the amount of work we have to do the next year to make that bed fit for seedlings.

DOUBLE-DIGGING AND MAKING RAISED BEDS

Alan Chadwick was a charismatic British gardening guru who brought the biodynamic

French intensive system to the States. While teaching at the University of California at Santa Cruz, he inspired John Jeavons, who went on to popularize the method through his very successful book *How to Grow More Vegetables Than You Ever Thought Possible on Less Land Than You Could Ever Imagine* (listed in the bibliography). Jeavons' book prompted numerous other intensive-gardening titles that still crowd the bookstore shelves.

The idea is to create a superfertile, continuously moist, highly aerated, never-stepped-on growing area at least 2 feet deep—which is the effective root zone of many kinds of vegetables. Not only do you dig 2 feet deep, but you also amend the soil that deep with heaps of compost and other natural fertilizers. You then take advantage of this high level of input by spacing vegetables as close as possible, while always having seedlings instantly ready to transplant into any vacancy.

Jeavons is now a successful gardening guru himself, operating out of a nonprofit called Ecology Action currently in Willits, California. His personal mission is ending world hunger by permitting small-scale, low-tech, highly intensive food production all over the Third World. Ecology Action publishes a newsletter and offers seminars and other educational opportunities.

If you are limited to a very tiny backyard, you may wish to produce every possible radish and head of lettuce regardless of the effort expended and the attention needed to get that last radish. However, I do not recommend this method for several reasons: (1) I am concerned about nutritional degradation caused by over-use of compost and manure. (2) Digging only 1 foot deep and using reasonable amounts of compost and complete organic fertilizer will result in a harvest nearly as large as double-digging 2 feet deep and using many times more compost. (3) Spacing plants as closely as generally recommended by intensivists makes plants overly competitive for light in the North, where we live. As you go south, there's a lot more light energy per square foot. (4) Establishing a double-dug raised bed initially involves so much effort that the gardener must consider it to be a permanent raised bed in a permanent garden. But growing vegetables in one place for more than three years in our climate results in a lot of trouble that obviously does not occur in the climates where the authors of books recommending this method practice it. (See the discussion of symphylans in Chapter 4.) Double-digging with a shorter time frame in mind becomes rather too much effort for what may be gained.

For a simple way to make an effective raised bed, see Chapter 4.

Clay Soil: Its Care and Special Handling

Soil is composed of minute mineral particles brought to life by organic matter. In the top 4 or 5 feet, soil can also contain a considerable amount of air; and filling some of the spaces and clinging to all of its surfaces you find moisture. The size and nature of those mineral particles are what concern us in this section. The size and nature of those particles are also the basis by which soils are classified and evaluated. Soil forms as rocks are weathered into little pieces—by running water, by wind, by freezing and thawing, and by time.

Rocks and gravel are too large to support plant growth, so we won't pay them any attention except to remove them from our gardens.

Sand particles are large enough to feel gritty when rubbed between the fingers. When looked at through a hand lens, sand appears to have sharp corners and flat surfaces, as though it has recently fractured out of rocks, which is just what happened. After sand has been exposed to soil acids and other weathering for a while, the particles get smaller. And smaller.

Eventually, the sand weathers down to silt. If you rubbed a sample of pure silt between your fingers, it would feel much like talcum powder, which consists of silt-sized particles ground from a very soft rock called talc. Viewed through a microscope, silt particles have lost the sharp edges they had when they were sand-sized because the edges of the particles have dissolved in weak soil acids. Eventually, silt particles are entirely dissolved.

As soil particles dissolve, the breakdown chemicals go through a complex molecular recombination and form clay, something altogether different from the original rocks it derived from. Clay is made up of thin, flat crystals that stack themselves in layers, like pages in a book. Clay crystals are so thin that seeing them takes the most powerful electron microscope, yet it is easy to visualize the nature of clays if you remember that slate and shale are two minerals formed when clay is subjected to high heat and pressure. These layered rocks fracture into thin sheets much like the microscopic crystals that formed them.

Being so fine, clay particles fit very tightly together, so clay soils tend to be heavy and airless. Clay particles also fill the gaps between larger particles of silt and sand, making these soils heavy and airless too, unless the biological process makes them aggregate with humus into stable crumbs.

Clay soils hold a lot more water than sandy or silty soils. Sand and silt particles are like books that are firmly closed, with water adhering only to their covers, but clay is like a book with the pages fanned open, exposing a great deal more surface area for moisture to cling to. If sand's ability to hold water were expressed numerically as 2, silt would be 4, clay 10, and, interestingly, humus might be 30.

Having some clay in soil is very desirable. Soils that are mainly clay, however, must be worked at exactly the right moisture content. If they are tilled when too wet, they form rock-hard clods, but they fall apart into dust if tilled when the slightest bit too dry. That dust then sags into a goo the first time it gets wet, and the goo becomes rock hard and airless once it dries. After irrigation or rain, the surface of a clay soil forms a hard crust, preventing the emergence of sprouting seeds and shutting out air. The root systems of most vegetable species are not adapted to such an environment.

Clay soils can make very acceptable permanent hay pastures because a pasture almost never needs tillage, while the dense sod keeps the surface open. Clay soils that also drain well (clay can become very compact and resist water's passage and thus have poor drainage) can make good orchards because some kinds of fruit trees have root systems adapted to the relative airlessness of clay, while the tree appreciates the higher moisture supply found in clay. The Salem hills, for example, are covered with 5 or more feet of well-drained clay soil. Before the suburbanization of the Willamette Valley, these grew productive orchards.

If you have the misfortune to have a clay soil for your vegetable patch, it is not a hopeless situation, but you had best apply some wisdom and be prepared to spend a bit of money, or you are bound to be disappointed.

TESTING YOUR SOIL

The first step is to make sure you really do have a clay soil. Any soil that is less than one-third clay is not, by definition, a clay soil. Your soil probably won't prove overly difficult until clay makes up half the volume. Someone with a bit of experience in classifying soil can simply feel a small sample of moist soil and know approximately what it is. There is, however, a very simple and amazingly accurate home test you can do on a bit of soil to determine what its percentages of sand, silt, and clay are. Here's how to perform this test.

Dry about a pint of soil (no roots or organic material), and grind it to as fine a powder as you can. Don't bother to dry it to rock hardness; just let it dry enough that you can pulverize it with a mortar and pestle or rolling pin. Do, however, break it up finely. Put that measured pint of ground soil into a quart mason jar with a good lid. Carefully mark a line on the side of the jar with a grease pencil or a bit of adhesive tape at the level the soil comes to; this mark may make all the difference in getting a result if your soil contains a lot of very fine clay. Then fill the jar with water, leaving about a ½-inch air gap at the top, and add ½ teaspoonful of low-sudsing liquid detergent to soften the water. Now start shaking, and keep on shaking. You want to make sure that every single soil particle has separated from every other. If you can, you might take the jar to the local hardware store and put it into their paint shaker for a couple of minutes and then take it home and reshake it a bit. When all of the particles are suspended in the water, put the jar down somewhere in very bright light where it won't have to be disturbed for two days.

Exactly two minutes after you stop agitating it, make a mark on the side of the jar at the top of the soil that has settled. You may need a powerful flashlight to determine this. That line is the amount of sand in the soil. Being larger particles, they settle out of suspension rapidly. Then wait exactly two hours and make another mark at the top of the soil that has settled out. That mark shows the amount of silt resting atop the sand. Now wait two days to get the final result. The water will probably clear as the clay settles out. Draw another line. This is the clay portion (the clay "fraction," in soil science jargon). Now measure the depth of each layer with a ruler. If you do a bit of arithmetic, you can express these amounts as the percentages of sand, silt, and clay. If the water doesn't ever seem to clear, your clay is extremely fine and may not settle out for a month or more. In that case, just assume that the line you made when you first filled the jar with dry, powdered soil is the line that the clay would come to.

If your soil is more than half clay, you've got troubles. I know of two solutions to your problem. One of them is a poor solution, but it's the one most gardeners attempt. Including me—once. The other is a good solution. Either solution will cost some money. The poor solution may cost you only some sweat and a little gasoline if you already have a pickup. For the good solution, you're probably going to have to buy some stuff.

THE POOR SOLUTION

The poor solution involves turning your clay pit into an organic Garden of Eatin' by incorporating heaps of organic matter and making it appear to become something like a loamy soil. This section describes what you'll need to do if you attempt to solve your problem that way.

Lime Because clay has a very high ability to chemically hold on to mineral nutrients, it tends to cling to any fertility you put in as though it were starving. Clay keeps nutrients from reaching the plants until you satisfy its hunger. The way clay has traditionally been "fed" is with lime. You saturate the clay's mineral-holding capacity with calcium, and then it will freely take on and let go of all the mineral nutrients. If you have a soil that is from half to two-thirds clay, make a one-time amendment of 2 tons of lime to the acre (50 pounds spread over 1,000 square feet equals 1 ton per acre). If your soil is from two-thirds

clay to all clay, make that 3 tons per acre. Regardless of how much lime you need, use one-half ordinary lime and one-half dolomite lime. Once you've done this, the lime you put into your complete organic fertilizer will maintain the improvement.

Organic Matter The very first time you rototill, make mighty sure that the soil is close to the right moisture. *Don't rush tilling.* Gardening is a year-round, many-years-long affair west of the Cascades. When it is time to till, spread lime atop the site, and then spread 2 or 3 inches of horse manure, cow manure, or compost. Get the biggest rototiller you can hire or rent. Dig as deep as you can with it, and mix the organic matter into the soil as far down as possible. It is best to have done this the previous October as preparation for the following summer.

You can now raise your garden like anyone else, except that you'll need a bit more fertilizer than most because all that organic matter will produce a giant bloom of microorganisms that, while decomposing it, will gobble up huge quantities of soil nitrogen and other nutrients for months. And your vegetables will never grow as large as they might have on more naturally suitable soil.

By the way, this solution involves a lot of ongoing work. The organic matter you've added will seem to disappear rapidly. Each year you'll have to put in a heap more. Where other soils might do fine with an annual compost addition of ¼ inch, clay gardens can require three or four times that amount. Clay gardens are very good candidates for raised beds because if you can religiously avoid stepping on the growing areas you'll avoid compacting them, making tillage much easier. In fact, with raised beds, green manures over the winter, and enough compost, you may never need to till deeply again.

THE BETTER WAY

Subsoils are naturally clayey. Soil scientists call the subsoil the "zone of deposition" because clay particles forming in the topsoil are deposited a foot or so down by rain water percolating through the earth. When you have a clay garden site, why not take the attitude that the clay is simply subsoil that happens to be missing its topsoil? Bring in the topsoil, put it atop the "subsoil," and off you go.

The cheapest and most certain way to obtain good, honest topsoil is to make it yourself. Buying topsoil as such is often an invitation to fraud. It may really be "top" soil from the surface layer of a field somewhere, but is it really loam that contains no more than one-third clay? Perhaps it is from a farm or industrial site where some heavy chemicals were used. Before buying, be sure to dig into its pedigree, because once you've got it, it'll be there for a long time.

Ideal vegetable soil is about 35 percent fine sand, 35 percent silt, 25 percent clay, and 5 percent humus. You can make this yourself with a little investigation. Find a gravel yard that sells genuine river alluvium, not glacial gravel or rock from a quarry crusher. One of its main products will be sharp sand, used to make concrete. To be strong, concrete must contain cement, some rounded gravel in assorted sizes, and *sharp* sand, with no small

particles mixed in. The name for the undesirable small stuff is "fines." The fines, consisting of smaller sand and silt particles, must be washed out or screened out of the sharp sand. These fines tend to accumulate in piles around the gravel yard and are exactly what make great vegetable soil, with the addition of a bit of clay.

You already have clay—too much of it. If you were to cover your garden site about 6 to 8 inches deep with fines and then spade it up so as to mix in about 3 inches of your "subsoil," you'd have just about a perfect mineral mix for vegetables. If you could rototill that "subsoil" first, it would mix in quite readily. If you couldn't till it first, it might take a few years and several spadings before it got thoroughly blended it. (And it would be a good idea to spread and till in lime (50 pounds per 1,000 square feet) and ½-inch of compost over the clay first.)

If you create this wonderful loam soil, you won't need excessive amounts of compost to make it workable. The suggestions made earlier in this chapter will hold perfectly. You'll have to spend a bit of money to haul in some big loads of fine sand and silt, but you won't have to haul in endless large loads of compost materials. Your vegetables may also come out much more nutrient-packed, and I guarantee they'll grow a lot bigger and lustier.

Soil Types

Earlier I mentioned that soils are classified according to particle size. Each type of soil behaves in its own unique way, so I can give you some general advice about your particular soil based on its type or classification if you know what you have.

How do you know what soil type you're dealing with? For garden purposes, it may not be necessary to do a soil fraction analysis, which is what a soils expert would correctly name the mason jar test I described previously. For home gardeners it is usually sufficient to rub some dry soil between your fingers and feel it. Sandy soils feel gritty, silts have a talcumlike smoothness to them, and clay soils can feel smooth too, but when dampened and kneaded, they get very gooey and sticky. But estimating how much clay there is can be dicey, so if you perceive much clay in your garden site, do the mason jar test.

Another solution for Americans is to pay a visit to the local Soil Conservation Service office. The SCS is a branch of the U.S. Department of Agriculture, whose job it is to map and classify all soils and to make and administer programs to preserve the nation's soils. They have offices in most counties and are paid well to be very helpful. Take them a cup of dry soil, and they'll be able to give you an immediate rough estimate of your soil type (not its pH or nutrient content). The SCS also has detailed air photo maps outlining soil types. It is very likely they'll be able to locate your land on their large-scale master map and give you a sheet containing general specifications of the exact soil you've got. (Canadian gardeners who feel in need of professional soil analysis have to go to private testing labs. Soil testing has not been available through the British Columbia Department of Agriculture since 1986. Check with the provincial Department of Agriculture of Agriculture Canada.)

For the best gardening results, you should tailor your soil management strategies to your soil type. Different soil types till differently and hold moisture differently, and some grow various species better than other soils. Some are natural vegetable producers and need only reasonable maintenance to stay in shape.

SANDY SOIL

Sandy soils contain more than 70 percent sand. They are very easy to till even when very wet, do not form clods no matter what, drain extremely well, and have very large air pores. When managed correctly, sandy soils grow great crops, especially roots and such heat lovers as melons. But they don't hold much water. Chemical fertilizers wash out very easily from sands; even with organic fertilizers great care must be taken not to overwater. Adding organic matter improves this situation somewhat. You often read that large quantities of compost increase the water-holding capacity of sandy soil and that humus has a high ability to hold on to plant nutrients. However, large quantities of organic matter are counterproductive in our climate. Instead, I suggest that you (1) try to keep the soil in green manure over the winter to hold nutrients there because the growing plants will capture some of what would otherwise be leached out; (2) add minimal amounts of organic matter and, to enhance seed germination, confine additions of manure or compost to the surface inch; (3) invest in very high-quality irrigation equipment that makes very frequent light watering easy and convenient. Because sandy soils usually have so little clay, not as much lime is needed. Assume that just about every bit of fertility you put in will wash out every winter. I suggest that you add lime (half agricultural, half dolomite) at 25 pounds per thousand square feet (1,000 pounds per acre) every year in spring before planting, also use the recommend amount in your complete organic fertilizer, and use fast-releasing bone meal as the phosphate portion of your complete organic fertilizer.

COARSE LOAM

Coarse loam is the most ideal stuff a gardener can have: It's mostly large soil particles. Being relatively unweathered, these particles often contain lots of potentially releasable nutrients, with just enough clay thrown into the mix to hold moisture and retain nutrients. Coarse loam is so soft that it seems able to grow any vegetable species magnificently. Drainage is excellent and pore spaces are large, so that even asparagus beds don't usually die out in an extra-rainy winter. Coarse loam tills easily when on the wet side without forming clods. It doesn't shrink or swell much when wet or dry, and it stays soft after tilling, so such roots as carrots and parsnips develop nicely. Crusts don't usually develop over emerging seeds.

Because coarse loams are relatively more fertile and growth promoting than other soil types, levels of organic matter start out natu-rally high enough for good soil health, especially if your garden began as a pasture or lawn. Growing row crops repetitively, however, will quickly deplete the organic matter. If this is happening, the soil may compact or puddle during a hard rain or while being irrigated.

FINE LOAM AND SILT SOIL

Fine loams and silt soils contain less sand and more silt and clay. The finer ones contain larger percentages of clay and may be formally classified as silty clay loams, clay loams, or clayey silt, although clay still is not the major soil fraction. Loams are properly defined as soils composed predominantly of sand and silt, with less than one-third clay; silt soils are mostly silt with minor fractions of sand and clay. The portion of unweathered soil particles in all loams and silts is high, and these types tend to be more fertile. However, clay crystals may fall between silt or sand particles, producing a soil of greater density with smaller pore spaces and slower drainage.

Cultural practices should be directed at increasing soil permeability through persistent additions of small amounts of organic matter, regular green manuring, and the use of raised beds and/or permanent paths to reduce soil compaction. Half an inch of compost or an inch of manure the first year is more than enough, followed by half that amount or less in subsequent years. Because fine soils tend to form surface crusts, which interfere with germination and movement of air into the soil, additions of organic matter are best confined to the surface inch or so of soil, raked in rather than tilled. There's plenty of clay to hold nutrients, so it makes sense to use slower-to-release nutrients like rock phosphate. Apply lime normally, 1 ton per acre for starters, and then maintain with the lime included in the complete organic fertilizer. These soils also contain enough clay to form clods fairly easily, so it's very important to wait until the soil has dried to the right point before tilling.

CLAY SOIL

Clay soils, as compared to fine clay soils, have not yet weathered fully to the finest particle sizes. Clay possesses many of the same liabilities as fine clays but has reasonably good drainage, more fertility and thus a higher organic matter content, better crumb formation, and (usually) a somewhat higher pH. Sandy clays tend to resemble concrete if not kept moist but are otherwise workable; silty clays are not bad to work at all if they're allowed to dry enough before tilling. I got reasonable results from silty clay for years at Lorane, Oregon, where I had my first Coast Range homestead, although it demanded three times the work a coarse loam would have taken. Clay's workability can be very fragile—it can fall apart and slump into an airless mass or become completely cloddy with the slightest mismanagement. I'd handle sandy and silty clays as though they were in the better silty soil category, with perhaps a bit more organic matter. Full-blown clays should be handled like fine clay soils.

Fine clay, sometimes called gumbo by its unfortunate users, is the most difficult of all types of soil to manage. It absorbs water only very slowly, becomes sticky when wet, takes forever to dry, and then turns into concrete.

Work clay when wet and it will form rock-hard clods; when dry, a shovel can't penetrate it. Fine clay can be tilled to a good seedbed only at exactly the right moisture, a condition that might exist for only a few days each season. Surface crusts form readily, preventing seedling emergence and shutting out air. Clay tends to shrink when drying, forming deep surface cracks. (The pattern of the cracks is similar to the shape of the clay crystals.)

Comprising very thoroughly leached soil particles that have fully decomposed, fine clays are old soils that, because of their age, tend to be mineral deficient in rainy climates like ours. Being nutrient poor and airless, these soils produce skimpy vegetation and so are low in organic matter and support few microrganisms. Without the action of microlife, clays don't aggregate, which accentuates their bad tendencies. Even when clay soil is heavily fertilized, plant growth can be very, very poor.

Fine clays can be temporarily improved by significantly upping organic matter content and thus causing soil aggregation. Although I do not recommend this practice, this technique and a better one I do recommend are discussed at length in the previous section.

Chapter 3 Composting

The soil solution represents a nutrient medium for the entire
population of the soil and especially for the microorganisms. In all
cases when the medium is favorable and there are no hindering factors,
the amount of organisms is abundant. The more nutrients in the solution, the
more intense the development and metabolism of soil microorganisms. Fertile
soils and soils fertilized with large amounts of humus have a high concentration
of nutrients in their solutions. Soils of low fertility, not containing humus,
have small concentrations of nutrients in their soil solutions and
the growth of microbes will be slight.

—N. A. KRASIL'NIKOV,
Soil Microorganisms and Higher Plants

Gardeners can make two sorts of compost—potent, effectively fertilizing compost or the average stuff. Most of us make low-grade compost, almost by default. I'm sure you would prefer to make the potent type. That's what this chapter is all about.

Four Little Words

It seems to me that the best way into the subject of compost is to clearly state the exact meaning of four essential words: organic matter, humus, compost, and composting.

Organic matter is created only by plants. As it says in the Book, "All flesh is grass," meaning that even flesh and animal waste started out as plant matter. We could just as well say that all flesh and all grass are rock, water, air, and sunshine organized by Life.

When Life departs, the organic matter immediately begins decomposing into the minerals it started out from. Dog feces, grass clippings, and leaves on lawns; fir needles and bark littering forest floors; a dead salmon on a stream bank—all these are forms of organic matter getting ready to be recycled.

Decomposing organic matter changes rapidly at first, and then more and more slowly, until it reaches a stable stage we call *humus*. When is that? What is that? The best definition of humus I can give will seem rather circular to someone used to rigorous logic: Organic matter has become humus when decomposition has slowed down a lot. I'd like to be able to define humus with some long chemical formula or be able to provide you with a single-reagent humus test kit like that used to check chlorine levels in swimming pools. But this is not possible, because we don't know what chemicals humus actually consists of. Scientists are pretty sure that there are about as many different chemicals named "humus" as there are things that decompose. Regardless of their molecular compositions,

however, all forms of humus act rather similarly.

My practical definition of humus is a very useful way to understand composting. When the composting process has pretty much stopped, we have changed organic matter into humus.

In nature, decomposing organic matter is eaten by animals; their feces are eaten by other, smaller animals; and their feces in turn are eaten by other even smaller animals. The smallest animals are microscopic in size and dwell in the soil. Enzymes present in this chain of animal digestive systems facilitate the breakdown of organic materials. Along the way bacteria and fungi grab on to this material and begin to consume it too. Before long the source of the original material can no longer be determined, because what you're basically looking at is insect feces and worm castings harboring large and active colonies of bacteria, thoroughly blended with clay and other soil particles into crumbs. This is another way to define *humus.*

The job of decomposing humus the rest of the way, back to the inorganic minerals it started out as, takes a lot longer than going from recently dead organic matter to humus, and is largely done by soil microorganisms. The last steps take so long because once organic matter has recombined into humus, everything that was easy to digest has already been digested; what remains is quite resistant.

When decomposition starts in a compost heap, there are only a few organisms and a lot of food for them to eat. The population of decomposers soon builds up, holds at a peak while consumption goes on steadily until most of the consumable organic matter has been "burned" as microbe fuel, and then declines catastrophically. During the fermentation, the microbes capture mineral nutrients that had been part of the organic matter they eat and use them to build microbe bodies. When the microbial population collapses, all this delicate protoplasm rapidly disintegrates; the nutrients with which they built their bodies are rapidly released into the heap and become available for growing plants to use. And this is how compost can become potent plant fertilizer.

Can you see how important it is to handle compost carefully once it is finished? If you don't need it immediately, you should store it under cover so that water won't pass through it, leaching out the soluble nutrients it contains.

Compost can be defined as humus that has been manufactured more rapidly than in nature, through a fermentation process we call composting. The main difference between compost and natural humus lies in the organisms that do most of the work. In nature the largest part of the task is done by soil animals, rather slowly at normal soil temperatures, with the final stages done by soil microbes. A compost heap is a high-speed, high-temperature decomposition "furnace." Although some soil animals are present in the outer, cooler layers, the greatest part of the task is handled by heat-loving microbes and fungi. These heat lovers are present only in small numbers in soil.

I call the heap a furnace because what essentially happens is that the carbon-based parts of the materials are "burned" as fuel for the digesting organisms. The heap starts out mostly as a mixture of carbohydrates—assorted forms of celluloses, lignins, and sugars—and some nitrogen compounds, largely in the form of proteins. When the fire goes out—if it burned right—what is left are all the nitrogen compounds, all the mineral nutrients, and much less of the carbon. As with any other form of burning, the carbon-hydrogen has gone up in "smoke" in the form of carbon dioxide gas and water vapor, which are the elements the plants made it from in the first place. In short, the fertilizing value of the material has become both concentrated and more available. And if the composter really knows his or her stuff, the finished heap can contain as much as 20 percent more nitrogen than there was in the raw materials. A properly done compost pile becomes a nitrate-nitrogen factory.

When you make alcohol, the fermentation is finished when the liquor stops bubbling; the same is true of making sauerkraut. While the microbes of composting are working, their activities generate a lot of heat. The central areas of a working compost heap can exceed 150°F. When, after some weeks or months, the pile will no longer heat up, even if it is still moist and even after it has been stirred up, aerated, and turned over, it is done.

Composting occurs when people enormously accelerate decomposition using controlled microbial ferments so that the end result—the compost—has become humus with qualities that suit us for the purpose of growing crops.

Ferments

Composting is similar to conducting other ferments—making beer, wine, sauerkraut, or yeast breads. If you're the sort of person who makes fermented or yeasted foods, you'll be a natural at composting, although in some ways it's very different. The home composter rarely gets the same materials to work with from batch to batch and cannot easily control the purity and nature of the organisms that do the actual work of humus formation. Nor do composters attempt to control ambient air temperatures.

Making compost may seem easier than brewing or baking because people don't eat or drink compost; the soil does. Within broad limits, soil will digest wide variations in compost quality without apparent complaint. And any time you heap up a mixture of vegetation and/or manure, keep it moist, and stir it up periodically, it will eventually rot down into humus, useful humus. Even if the heap is mostly sawdust, if you keep it moist and stir it up often enough, you'll eventually have a heap resembling humus. Eventually.

How long can "eventually" mean? A huge heap of nearly done humus is available near my home right now, free for the hauling. It started out as a sawdust heap beside a remote gyppo sawmill. The mill ceased working about thirty years ago; the scant remains of what was once thousands of cubic yards of sawdust have only recently become thoroughly black and crumbly and are beginning to resemble soil. New logging in the area has caused the road past the mill to be restored,

and this resource of old compost has been discovered. It might make fair mulch; I wouldn't use it on vegetables, though—it smells sour, like vinegar.

This example underscores the main difficulty of becoming a composting expert—time. Brewing a batch of beer takes only a few weeks from boiling the wort to bottling. Even though it has to age in the bottle awhile to get bubbly and smooth out, we home brewers pretty much know what we have as the caps go on. Bread usually takes only a few hours from start to finish. And we bakers are the consumers, too, so we experience the results. Bakers and brewers can readjust their procedures until they enjoy the result. But with compost, the results are not that heap of dark-colored soil-like materials, they are the vegetables grown with it. The heap can take from two to six months to finish working, and then the compost still has to grow something before we know whether it was any good.

This combination of the time involved to realize the results from a batch and the variability of the materials we have to start with makes mastering composting a lot more difficult than mastering other kinds of ferments. When I think back on all of the garden books and composting literature I've read, the few authors who really knew their subject were the ones who had the opportunity to make a huge number of batches of compost from fairly repeatable and high-quality ingredients and then could test their results, either in a laboratory or, better, on growing crops. Perhaps the best of the lot was Sir Albert Howard. If you really want to make the best possible compost, read his landmark book *The Waste Products of Agriculture.* A brief summary of Howard's book wouldn't do it justice.

Garden-Variety Compost and Strong Compost

Anyone who grows food almost has to make a bit of compost, if only to recycle vegetable trimmings, stumps, and stalks. Composting is not offensive; the heap doesn't smell bad as it gradually shrinks down and becomes something resembling soil. It's only logical to put these wastes into a tidy heap where they will rot. Because gardeners are composting anyway, we generally toss in the kitchen garbage, raked-up leaves, grass clippings, and so on. If we are homesteaders and have animals, their manure and the bedding materials we use around them also go into the heap, although in that case we'll probably have heaps of heaps.

Even if we do no more than pile up what we get as we get it and moisten the growing heap occasionally, and even if the pile doesn't heat up much, the stuff gradually rots, starting at the bottom. A passive heap, one that we never turn over or make any other effort to assist, eventually changes into something resembling sweet-smelling earth with worms in it, and we call it compost, whether or not it has decomposed far enough to properly be called humus.

To anyone who composts with their eyes wide open, the lessons are pretty obvious. Decomposition slows or stops if the heap dries out, so we water the pile occasionally. The core of the heap often gets hot, and this heat evaporates a lot of moisture, requiring that we somehow wet down the center of the heap. The hot core rots before the cool outsides. Most of us gardeners have noticed or been told that turning the heap over and mixing it up will also make it rot faster.

If we are short of space and need to get the heap done sooner, we casual composters may go to the effort of turning it. It can be watered at the same time. The object is to peel off the outer, insulating layers of the pile that did not get hot and make them into the core of the new heap, while pulling the inner parts of the old heap toward the exterior. The whole mass can be easily sprayed down at this time to restore essential moisture. When we do this the heap may heat up again for a while and then cool off again. After each turning, the heap heats less and cools more rapidly. Each turning reveals that more of the heap has turned into the black-brown crumbly stuff we are trying to make. During the winter, adding moisture is no problem; in fact, we in the maritime Northwest have the opposite problem—keeping rain from leaching out most of the nutrients in the heap. Covering the heap with an old sheet of plastic helps.

The product of these easy methods is, in almost every case, very average compost. And the results you'll get from using it to fertilize a vegetable garden will be rather unsatisfactory. I'm not denigrating the making of ordinary garden compost; I do it myself. I'm merely calling it what it usually is—low-grade. We should make it if only to responsibly recycle organic wastes. Besides, our gardens need organic matter.

What is low-grade compost good for? If spread under ornamentals and mixed into the surface a bit when hoeing weeds, it'll make bushes and shrubs grow much better. It makes a good mulch atop flower beds. It is useful in the vegetable garden too, as long as you don't expect that using it by itself will make a vegetable grow fast and big the way fertilizer will.

Composting in Containers

Composting containers are for people who highly value tidiness or whose backyard space is at a premium. Using containers has two disadvantages—the cost and the effort required to build them—and many advantages.

The compost fermentation needs to occur at high temperatures to work best, but if the pile is too small its core can't heat up enough. An unenclosed heap generally has to be at least 5 feet in diameter to heat up very much (and one that is 6 or even 7 feet around the base is better). A container will insulate the sides of the heap, retaining heat. Some barrel-shaped containers are as small as 3 feet across, and they still get hot inside. They'll fit conveniently into any shady backyard nook, often hidden from sight, while they digest each bit of organic matter as it is tossed in.

Small containers eliminate turning. This is especially advantageous in tight quarters. New stuff is continuously tossed on top, and as it decomposes it settles to the bottom. A door at the bottom allows you to periodically scrape out the soil-like finished material with a small shovel. About the only maintenance such a system needs is an occasional watering. The largest bin I've ever seen of this sort was around 4½ feet in diameter.

Another clever type of container semiautomatically turns the heap for you. These containers are also barrel-shaped, but the drum is supported horizontally on an elevated stand. The main advantage here is processing speed. Most of these are "batch composters," meaning that you fill the drum, make finished compost of the drum's entire contents (this takes a month or so), and then empty it and then make another batch. You'll have to store the next accumulation of vegetable matter elsewhere until the drum is ready to be loaded again. Every day you spin a crank for a few moments and roll the loaded drum once or twice around on its support. This mixing and aeration greatly accelerates the process. When the compost is finished, you rotate the drum until the door is facing down, open the door, and out falls the compost. This may sound like a good idea, but spinning the drum every day can get tiresome.

Backyard composters who make a lot of compost but who also wish to be tidy should construct a series of homemade bins. The wisest designs are rows of three-sided bins about

4 feet high or, if the bins have a fourth side for visual tidiness, the front side is removable to facilitate turning the heap from one bin into the next. Bins like this are also easy to roof over, keeping winter rains out.

In a row of four bins, the compost is cycled through as follows: The first and second bins are the largest ones and are usually about the same size. The first one holds the dry materials while they are being collected. When it has been filled, the material is turned into the next bin, mixed with soil and manure (if available) and/or seed meal, and watered down at the same time. A month later the second bin has heated, cooled, and settled a lot. Now the contents are turned into a third, smaller bin and again watered while being turned. After another month, the contents of this third bin are turned into the last, smallest one. Before you move material into a bin, the previous contents are moved to the next bin in line; when you empty bin number four, its contents go to the garden. You can find illustrations of these sorts of bin arrays in most gardening books.

People who build a series of bins like this are usually making compost all the time. Those who live in the country often don't bother with bins, but simply use less tidy heaps. That's what I always did.

Know Them by Their Works

Many have heard the marching song of the militant compost gardener. It goes, "There is no worry about fertilizing the plant, no need to even think about NPKCaMgS; merely feed the soil enough organic matter and the plant will find more than enough nutrition. You can tell when the soil has been fed enough—it'll be full of worms! And if the garden soil is worm filled, the vegetables will be huge and nutritious." I hope Chapter 2 has already disabused you of these notions. You can't just feed the soil any

Analysis of Various Composts

Source	N%	P%	K%	Ca%*	C/N Ratio**
Vegetable trimmings and paper	1.57	0.40	0.40		24:1
Municipal refuse	0.97	0.16	0.21		24:1
Johnson City refuse	0.91	0.22	0.91	1.91	36:1
Gainesville, FL, refuse	0.57	0.26	0.22	1.88	?
Garden Compost A	1.40	0.30	0.40		25:1
Garden Compost B	3.50	1.00	2.00		10:1

*Ca is calcium.
**C/N is the ratio of carbon to nitrogen.

kind of organic matter and get the most bountiful and most nutritious vegetables. What you feed the soil must be strong, and it must contain the right balance of nutrients.

The table on page 77, "Analysis of Various Composts," shows some typical compost analyses. The first one, "vegetable trimmings and paper," was an experimental effort by a municipal composting project to make compost strong enough that market gardeners would want to buy and use it. The city eliminated all decomposition-resistant tree trimmings that flow through the typical municipal waste stream. The result still wasn't potent enough; there was probably too much paper in the brew.

Garden Compost A is what you'll get from the casually made kind of heaps I describe in the preceding paragraphs. Garden Compost B closely resembles the chicken manure compost I praise in Chapter 2 as having strong fertilizing powers. What follows in this chapter are enough hints and suggestions to enable you to make backyard compost of a quality that approaches that of Garden B.

The ability of any organic soil amendment to grow plants is revealed by its C/N ratio—its ratio of carbon (C) to nitrogen (N). By carbon, I mean those plant substances largely composed of carbon—cellulose, sugar, lignin, and starch. By nitrogen, I mean nitrates or other readily decomposable materials that will release nitrates or ammonia. If a substance has a C/N ratio of 10:1, it means that for every ten parts of carbon-based material there is one part of (nitrate) nitrogen, usually combined in proteins. Humus in soil always has a carbon-to-nitrogen ratio of from 10:1 to about 12:1, similar to Garden Compost B.

AMENDMENTS WITH A LOW CARBON-TO-NITROGEN RATIO ACT LIKE FERTILIZER

Nitrate-nitrogen is the basic building block of all plant protein and of all protoplasm, animal and vegetable. When more of it becomes present in soil, microorganisms may quickly multiply to match that amount because their bodies are flesh too. To put it scientifically, nitrates are often the limiting factor on microbial population levels.

When organic material with a C/N ratio below 12:1 (strong enough to act like fertilizer) is amended into soil, nitrates are rapidly liberated by microbes eating it. The soil microbes respond to the increase in available nitrates by multiplying to the very limit of the available food supply. Their accelerated decomposition of humus and of organic matter that is not yet humus releases other plant nutrients, further enhancing the microbial population explosion. After consuming the more digestible portions of the humus and most of the carbon in the amendment, the microbes die off from starvation. Then the extra nitrate-nitrogen is converted to ammonia gas, escaping into the air, or is broken down completely by other microorganisms, and the soil returns to equilibrium, still with an overall C/N ratio of around 12:1—*but with less organic matter than it started with.* This loss of organic matter from low C/N (nitrate-nitrogen) fertilization is the basis for the organic farming and gardening movement's strong opposition to the use of

chemicals. However, the same loss can be produced by using organic materials with a low
C/N ratio like blood meal or chicken manure,
or even seed meal.

   Where the intensified release of nitrates
occurs in the soil has a lot to do with how
much organic matter is left after equilibrium
returns. If fertilizers are put close to the
actively feeding roots, many of the nitrates
will be withdrawn from the soil and used to
form more plant material. The soil ends up in
better shape than if nitrates had been dis-
persed throughout the field, where it would
feed hungry microbes outside actively feeding
plant root zones.

   How fast the release occurs is also important. I once experimentally side-dressed a large
raised bed of scallions with an assortment of
nitrate sources—complete organic fertilizer,
assorted chemical nitrate fertilizers, and blood
meal, which, though organic, is a very strong
source of nitrate that releases very rapidly. At
harvest time I carefully observed the soil
below each type of fertilizer. Where the scallions had been stimulated with fast-release fertilizers, the soil had lost a lot more humus
than in areas fertilized with slow-release materials. I assume from this experiment that
whenever fast-release sources of nitrate—
chemical fertilizer or blood meal—are used,
the soil nitrate levels become too high and the
resulting destruction of humus is greater. This
is one of the reasons I recommend repeatedly
side-dressing with smaller amounts of slow-
release organic fertilizer and placing it directly
above active plant feeder roots.

AMENDMENTS WITH A HIGH CARBON-TO-NITROGEN RATIO ARE COMPOSTED IN THE SOIL

When organic material with a C/N ratio
higher than 12:1 is mixed into soil, the soil
microorganisms find a carbohydrate banquet,
just as they do in a compost heap. Within days,
microorganisms will multiply to match the new
food supply. But to construct their bodies these
microorganisms need the very same nutrients
that plants need to grow—nitrogen, potassium,
phosphorus, calcium, magnesium, and so on.
Organic matter having a high C/N ratio rarely
contains enough of these nutrients—especially
nitrates—to match the potential needs of soil
bacteria, so soil microorganisms draw these
nutrients out of the soil.

   Digesting organic materials this way is
called "sheet composting." While sheet composting is happening, plants can't get adequate
nutrition; the microbes take it. Plant growth
will slow or cease. Initially, a great deal of carbon dioxide gas may be given off as huge
amounts of carbon are metabolically "burned."
However, carbon dioxide in high concentrations
lowers the amount of soil oxygen, lowering the
health of roots and further slowing growth.
Transplants put in right after amendments with
high C/N ratios are tilled in may fail to grow
for a while. High carbon dioxide levels can be
highly toxic to sprouting seeds, and consequently germination failures may occur.

   When I was in the seed business I'd get a
few complaints every year from irate gardeners
demanding to know why *every* seed packet they
sowed failed to come up well. There were two
usual causes. Either before sowing, all the

seeds were exposed to temperatures above 120°F for quite a few hours or days (they were left in a hot car with windows rolled up or put on a shelf very close to a woodstove, for example) or, more likely, a large quantity of manure had been tilled into the garden prior to sowing. If the "manure" contained a large quantity of sawdust, the soil would seem very infertile for a month or three. When I asked questions, I usually found that sheet-composting was the culprit.

Eventually the soil will digest its carbon meal, the overall C/N ratio of the soil will restabilize at 12:1, and the overall soil humus level will have increased. Having more humus will increase overall levels of available nutrients for a long while. The heavy microbial activity will also have released large quantities of assorted slimes and gums that create soil crumbs, meaning that the site will have acquired much better tilth and will enjoy increased soil air levels, which further enhance nitrification of the remaining humus. Put simply, plants will grow better overall for quite a while.

Sir Albert Howard had a unique and pithy way of expressing this reality. He said that soil was not capable of working two jobs at once. You could not expect it to grow plants while it was also being required to digest crude organic matter. That's one reason he saw heap composting as such a valuable process. The digestion of raw organic matter proceeds outside the soil; when the finished product, humus, is ready to act as fertilizer, it is tilled in. The field, meanwhile, can be used to grow a crop.

How long sheet-composting takes depends on how much material is involved, what the starting C/N ratio is, how fertile the soil was at the start, and what the soil temperatures were during the process. If much sawdust or conifer bark is involved, make sure that the process has the entire autumn, winter, and a lot of the following spring to proceed. If the site was very infertile to start with, sheet-composting will go slowly; if the soil is already fertile, it will go somewhat more rapidly.

One way to accelerate sheet-composting is to use fertilizer at the same time. Broadcasting 10 to 20 pounds of urea (a chemical fertilizer that is essentially a synthetic form of the main nitrogen-containing substance in urine) per 1,000 square feet is the cheapest way to accomplish this. Organic gardeners who shun all chemicals may top off a sheet compost having a high C/N ratio with a thin layer of fresh chicken manure or maybe 50 to 100 pounds of cottonseed or canola seed meal per 1,000 square feet.

If the garden soil is already pretty fertile, it is possible to sheet-compost *and* grow vegetables at the same time if you also fertilize, if you don't till in too much material with a high C/N ratio (say, a ½-inch layer at most), and if you work the material in only shallowly.

Making Better Compost

Take another look at the table on page 77, "Analysis of Various Composts." None of the municipal composts were even close to 12:1, the point at which enough of the material in the heap has been converted to humus that the compost will begin to act as an effective fertilizer. Low-grade compost does make good under-tree mulch and can be used to top-dress perennial ornamentals in parks and for land reclamation work. Used strictly as a surface mulch, compost with a high C/N ratio can slowly continue its decomposition without overly disordering the soil it rests upon. Commercial vegetable growers won't use amendments with a high C/N ratio for fertilizer, much less pay very much for them.

Municipal compost yards are forced to heap up and rot down whatever flows through the waste stream. A large part of this recycling is paper and tree trimmings. To make the kind of compost that will powerfully grow most sorts of vegetables all by itself, we have to carefully choose what goes into the heap, largely on the basis of its C/N ratio, and then closely manage the fermentation. Our goal is to start the heap with a C/N ratio that is not unduly high and then consume the carbon portion of organic matter at a rapid but controlled rate until the C/N ratio gets down to about 12:1. Ideally, we will accomplish this without losing any of the nutrients originally in the materials, instead concentrating them and having them become readily available to feed plants when we're finished. Ideally, we will increase the total amount of nitrogen in our compost to a level that is greater than what we started out with. This is the miracle of composting. A perfectly managed heap can increase the total amount of nitrogen.

We gardeners must of necessity make compost by the seat of our pants. We don't have a laboratory to test the final C/N ratio. The only way to know if we have accomplished our goal is if our product will make vegetables grow as we would hope. Many can do this successfully. It takes the same talents and intention that it takes to make great bread or dynamite home brew: You have to repeat a closely watched experiment a few times, and then you get the hang of it by intuition.

The rest of this chapter consists of a hodgepodge of suggestions and warnings that will help your compost come out better than just average. I explore in some detail the determining factors that control the heap. None of these factors is independent of the others; they all interact. To a beginner this complexity can seem incredibly confusing. If it gets to be too much, just follow the directions in "Making Your First Compost Heap" on page 83. Once you *do* composting, you'll acquire a hands-on feel for it. The whole thing will soon be as easy as making bread.

THE STARTING CARBON-TO-NITROGEN RATIO

Ideally, your compost heap should start out with an average C/N ratio of 25:1. When finished, about half the original volume will remain; the other half (carbohydrate) will have "burned" off as CO_2 and H_2O. The way you hit the target ratio of 25:1 is by blending some materials containing a higher proportion of carbon with some materials containing a lower proportion. (See the table on page 84, "Carbon-to-Nitrogen Ratio of Compostable Materials.")

Making Your First Compost Heap

These directions are for someone who has never had hands-on experience making compost in a heap. A warning: I assume that you have a flat space at least 10 feet by 10 feet available to do this work. If you do not have that much room, use a composting container: bins, a barrel, and so on. Some of these occupy as little as 3 or 4 feet of space.

■ When mowing the lawn, do not immediately bag the clippings. Allow them to dry atop the surface for a day before gathering them up, so you won't have soggy green grass to handle. In one sunny day they'll become more like hay.

■ All spring and summer, build a stack of dry, mixed vegetation—trash from the flower garden, leaves, grass clippings, almost everything vegetable that comes from your property. Spread the vegetation out to dry in the sun before you put the next layer on top. Do not include any tree prunings, twigs, sticks, or branches; these will not rot fast enough in the heap and can make turning it very difficult. If you have a dog, put its manure on top of the pile and let it dry. Spread out the kitchen garbage and let it dry if you can get away with it. If you can't do this, bury it in the pile.

■ After the first frost, clean up the vegetable garden. Lots of material will be ready for the heap. If there are cornstalks, chop them up into 6-inch lengths first or the heap will be hard to turn over. Rake autumn leaves while they are still dry; run the lawn mower over them several times to chop them up. Spread these out on the vegetation pile. If you have a lot of leaves, pile the chopped dry leaves separately next to the dry vegetation because you'll want to make sure they get thoroughly blended into the rest of the materials when you build the compost heap.

■ Now the leaves have fallen and the frost has come. The garden has been cleaned up, and it's time to make compost. Estimate the volume of the dry material you have. For every cubic yard of vegetable waste, you will need one 50-pound sack of cottonseed meal or canola seed meal or six 1-cubic-foot sacks of chicken manure compost of the potent sort I mentioned in Chapter 2. If the heap you make fails to heat up well, your particular mix of dried vegetation has a higher C/N ratio than I anticipated, so you needed twice as much seed meal. More can be blended in later, when you make the first turn.

■ For every cubic yard of dry waste, place about 2 cubic feet (2 feet by 1 foot by 1 foot) of loose garden soil next to the stack of dry vegetation.

You will now have two or three piles and a sack or two of organic fertilizer in close proximity. One pile is a layered stack of mostly dry mixed vegetation and kitchen garbage, one is a pile of chopped dry leaves, and one is a smaller pile of soil. Now it is time to make a compost heap.

■ If you have access to fresh manure unmixed with sawdust—horse, rabbit, pig, cow, chicken, or even elephant—this is the moment to get a load to uniformly mix into the blend. Though odorous, the smell will be gone within hours of making the heap. The fresh digestive enzymes in this manure will make better compost.

■ Get help! Have someone stand nearby with a hose fitted with a nozzle that puts out a fine spray.

■ With a manure fork or hay fork, put down a layer of dry vegetation 3 to 4 inches thick and large enough in diameter (6 to 7 feet) that once you've combined everything in all your piles it ends up as a heap 4 to 5 feet high. In no case should it be more 7 feet across. If you've got a huge amount of material to compost, you'll end up with a windrow instead of a circular mound. The minimum-size heap is 5 feet in diameter and 4 feet high. If you don't have enough for a heap this size, you should use a small composting container, inexpensively available from a garden center or hardware store. As you spear out forkfuls of dry vegetation, try to get a mixture of all the different things in the stack. Continuously wet down the heap as you build it.

- With a shovel, sprinkle the first 3-inch-thick vegetation layer with about 5 percent of your soil, 5 percent of your seed meal, and an inch or so of leaves. Then add another 3-inch-thick layer of dry vegetation and repeat with soil, seed meal, and leaves. All the while have someone spraying water back and forth across the heap—not so much water that rivers run out of it, but enough that the vegetation won't absorb any more and some does escape. Ideally you're going to put down 15 to 20 layers. If there's any soil left when you're done, thinly cover the outside of the heap with it.

- Every few days, push your hand into the heap and take its temperature. If it's moist enough, it will almost certainly be uncomfortably hot within a week. Take its temperature every week. After a while the temperature should begin to drop; it should be the end of October or early November.

- Get help again! You're going to turn the heap. Have someone stand nearby with a hose and nozzle set to put out a fairly hard, fine spray. With a manure or hay fork, move the entire heap over a few feet. Start with the outside of the existing heap, and put this material on the bottom of the new heap. Keep digging into the old heap and stacking the stuff atop the new one you're building, spraying water constantly.

- Every few days, push your arm into the heap and take its temperature. It'll be almost certain to be getting uncomfortably hot within a few days, but not as hot as the first time. After three weeks or so the temperature should begin to drop; it should be getting close to Thanksgiving.

- Turn the heap again. Moisten it again. Start protecting the heap against leaching. Get an old sheet of clear or black plastic and cover the top two-thirds of the heap; the bottom foot or so stays uncovered so air can flow in at the bottom. Make a half dozen holes 2 to 3 inches in diameter in the top so air can flow up and out. Most of the rain will be shed.

- Forget the whole business until a nice warm sunny day comes along in February or early March, the sort of day when you feel like getting some exercise in the sun. Then turn the heap one last time. It probably won't be necessary to water it down very much, if at all. By this time it'll resemble soil through and through. Put the plastic cover back on. Wait another three or four weeks and then begin using your finished compost. Any big resistant bits that failed to decompose can become the first deposit in the next year's accumulation of drying organic matter to compost next autumn.

You can't make decent compost if most of the materials you're composting are too "woody," even if you have blended a mix that comes to 25:1. Yes, theoretically you could take a dry-weight ton of sawdust with a C/N ratio of 500:1 and mix it with about 200 pounds of chemical urea (about 50 percent nitrate-nitrogen by weight) to bring the overall C/N ratio to about 25:1, add water and some soil, cover the heap to keep winter rains from passing through the pile and leaching out all the nitrogen over the next two or three years, and wait. But it won't make compost in reasonable time, and it'll never be very good compost.

A woody pile will not heat up much. Worse, the stuff may eventually seem to have

Carbon-to-Nitrogen Ratio of Compostable Materials

± 6:1	± 12:1	± 25:1	± 50:1	± 100:1
Bone meal	Vegetables	Summer grass	Cornstalks *(dry)*	Sawdust *(500:1)*
Meat scraps	Garden weeds	Seaweed	Straw *(grain)*	Paper *(175:1)*
Fish waste	Alfalfa hay	Legume hulls	Grass hay *(low quality)*	Tree bark
Rabbit manure	Horse manure*	Fruit waste	Cardboard *(corrugated)***	Tree needles *(conifer)*
Chicken manure	Sewage sludge	Grass hay *(top quality)*	Tree leaves *(deciduous)*	
Pig manure	Silage			
Seed meal	Cow manure*			
Tankage	Spring grass			
Hair/feathers	Garden soil			

Containing no bedding
**The glues used to make it are high-nitrogen chemicals.*

decomposed when it still is a long way from being humus. My father used to say to me that the cheapest advice you can get comes secondhand, so please just accept mine. I've paid my dues with respect to sawdust and bark. Don't use them. Use only limited amounts of grain straw or low-grade local grass hay, especially if it had become very stemmy and the ripe seeds had fallen from the heads before it was baled up. You can tell; just look closely. When June weather gets rainy and haymaking happens very late, spoiled hay is often available nearly free for the hauling. Even if the farmer paid you a few cents a bale to pick it up from the field and take it home, it still may be no bargain.

Although most kinds of leaves from deciduous tree have a fairly high C/N ratio, they contain lots of minerals and will decompose nicely. Beware, though: Leaves have a strong tendency to mat into airless, soggy clumps. They compost far better if you first grind them up by passing them through a power-driven shredder/grinder or by running an engine-powered lawn mower over them until they are well powdered. If they are not well ground up, be sure to blend them in so there are no thick clumps.

There are several good reasons for targeting 25:1 as a starting C/N ratio. If it is much higher than 25:1, the pile will take forever to finish and will not, within the time frame you'll be able to give it, get its C/N down low enough to act as fertilizer. If, on the other hand, the C/N is too low to start with, the microbial "fire" you will ignite will rage almost uncontrollably and burn out the carbon too fast. Its high heat will make it dry out too fast. Worse, extreme-heat-loving microbes will dominate, and these will tend to break down nitrate-nitrogen. You'll know this is happening because the heap will smell of ammonia, meaning that nitrates are escaping into the atmosphere.

Balancing Carbon and Nitrogen

Here's a simple arithmetic problem that illustrates how to balance carbon to nitrogen.

Question: I have 100 pounds of straw with a C/N ratio of 66:1. How much chicken manure (8:1) do I have to add to bring the average in the heap to 25:1?

Answer: Each 66 pounds of straw already contains 1 pound of nitrogen, so there are already about 1.5 pounds of N in 100 pounds of straw. A hundred pounds of strawy compost at 25:1 would have about 4 pounds of nitrogen, so I need to add about 2.5 more pounds of N. Eight pounds of chicken manure contain 1 pound of N; 16 pounds have 2. So if I add 32 pounds of chicken manure to 100 pounds of straw, I will have 132 pounds of material containing about 5.5 pounds of N, a C/N ratio of 132:5.5, or about 24:1.

What I'm gently suggesting here is that getting the materials to make extraordinarily good compost is actually rather difficult. Compostable materials that are inexpensively and readily available west of the Cascades have too high a ratio of carbon to nitrogen. They're either local grass hay, which, if rain-spoiled, can be very inexpensive; sawdust; or horse or cow "manure," which is usually mostly sawdust. Finding desirable materials can require some very careful and persistent investigation.

I recommend using high-quality green hay from youngish grass, or alfalfa hay. City gardeners can often get bags of grass clippings and of leaves in autumn from neighbors who do not compost. Some cities will deliver whole truckloads of autumn leaves free upon request. In any case, beware of snatching grass clippings from the curbside on trash pickup day—the batch you get may have been treated with herbicide from a "weed-and-feed" fertilizer. Although this potential contamination will probably disintegrate during the composting, you might not want to take the risk. I've known urban market gardeners who composted large amounts of grass clippings

obtained from a professional landscape gardener they know and trust to tell them if any herbicide was used by their client. This way the clippings are not concealed in plastic bags or contaminated with junk, trash, sticks, and what-have-you.

The arithmetic of arriving at a starting C/N of 25:1 is simple enough. If you combine a barrelful of 50:1 material with the same volume of 12:1 material, you get a combined C/N ratio of about 25:1. Or combining 50 pounds of 50:1 material with about 20 pounds of 6:1 material makes 70 pounds of material with a combined C/N ratio of about 25:1.

OPPORTUNITIES AND MANURE PITFALLS

Beware of bargains having a high C/N ratio, like nutshells. Sometimes these can be had very inexpensively, but they are so resistant to decomposition that they'll never rot. The same is true of tree chipper waste. It might be okay for mulch under trees or rhododendrons, but not for composting.

Don't use too many grass clippings in a heap; they compact to an airless green slime.

Without air in the heap, the heap won't work properly and may give off some pretty foul smells. If you're using very much grass, mix it in thoroughly with other materials, and be prepared to turn the heap over more frequently. The same is true of leaves.

Sometimes you can come up with wonderful materials with a low C/N ratio that are free or nearly so. One of the best is about as potent as chicken manure or seed meal—used coffee grounds. Coffee beans are seeds. Make friends with the staff at your local espresso shop and they'll probably be happy to swap a big bucket full of used coffee grounds for your clean, empty bucket, and make this swap almost every day. The paper filters that may be mixed in go right into the heap, where they'll decompose. I've also had very good results using okara, the soybean waste left after making soy milk and tofu. If there's a soy-foods factory in your area, see if you can get this stuff ahead of the local pig farmer. Another freebie can be alfalfa dust. Every bit as powerful as baled alfalfa (and maybe better because it has fewer stems than what's in the bales), this stuff collects on the ground around piles of alfalfa bales at feed and grain dealers. Often they're pleased if you ask to sweep up the dust and take it away. I've gone off with several feed sacks full, gathered from around a large bale stack.

Rural homesteaders living on the coast with no near neighbors can often obtain whole pickup loads of shrimp or other fish cannery wastes for nothing or next to nothing. This stuff is more potent than chicken manure or seed meal, with a C/N ratio of 4:1 or 5:1. The trouble is, the stuff stinks, and it decomposes really hot. If you contemplate using it, blend it immediately with a large volume of grass hay or other material having a rather high C/N ratio, doubling or tripling the amount you would normally use. After a couple of days in a properly made heap, this waste should stop being so powerfully odoriferous.

Another good source of very potent material for country gardeners who drive a pickup they're not too fussy about is roadkills. Opossums, raccoons, even whole deer can be buried in a building compost heap. It is amazing how rapidly their carcasses will disappear.

TOOLS

It isn't possible to move quantities of crude organic matter with a shovel until after it has formed a crumbly substance like soil. If you're going to make more than one heap in your lifetime, you'll want to own a *long-handled* manure fork or four-tined hay fork. Or maybe one of each.

SIZE OF PARTICLES

The stuff in your compost heap has to be consumed by bacteria, which start eating the chunks on the surfaces. If the heap is composed of large pieces, it'll have a very small total surface area. If the heap is composed of very fine material, there will be abundant surfaces for bacteria and fungi to work over. On the other hand, heaps of fine, soft material rapidly collapse and become airless. The best result comes from incorporating a broad mix of sizes, with the largest bits being things that are not too hard to decompose, like cabbage stumps.

It is true that you can greatly speed up

composting by grinding everything first and then turning the heap more often, but is the fastest possible speed of any particular advantage? I'd rather hear the birds and not burn the gas. In my opinion, buying a compost grinder causes you to consume more fuel and resources than the compost you're going to make will ever be worth.

TEMPERATURE

As soon as a moist heap is made, bacteria and fungi begin multiplying. Within days the core of the heap gets quite hot. As the temperature passes about 125°F, the microbial population shifts and heat-loving sorts predominate. These are the ones who can work the material over really fast. Keeping track of the heap's core temperature is what lets the composter know what to do and when to do it, so if you're serious about making good compost, invest in a long laboratory thermometer that reads at least between 100° and 170°F. Everything I say next about temperature assumes that the starting C/N was in the vicinity of 25:1, that the heap is not made of overly woody materials, and that the mix of particle sizes is reasonable.

The microbes you want working your heap are oxygen breathers, and when the heap gets hot they burn a lot of it. All things being equal, if the heap won't get to about 140°F, the microbes likely aren't getting enough air. Various techniques can be used to increase the oxygen supply. The simplest is to turn the heap. Turning fluffs it all up and introduces a lot of air. This improvement will last until the heap settles and compacts again. People trying to accelerate composting as much as possible will turn a heap every week. With each turn, the core temperature climbs back up rapidly but does not reach the same height as it did the previous time. During the time it takes to make four turns done three to four weeks apart, core temperature peaks might run something like 140°F, 130°, 110°, 95°, done.

The larger the heap, the more the outer layers can insulate the center and the less heat is lost from the core. Since we want to encourage a vigorous decomposition by heat-loving microorganisms, larger is hotter is better. On the other hand, the larger the heap, the harder it is to get air into the core. Generally, heaps about 6 to 7 feet across at the base and 4 to 5 feet high work nicely. A tidy heap could be formed within a 6-foot-diameter by a 3-foot-high cylinder of stiff fence wire; I always used 2-inch by 4-inch mesh "hogwire" for this purpose. The fencing can be removed after the pile has settled a bit and immediately filled again as you start a new pile.

You're better off with a colder, slower-working heap than one that is too hot. Fiery, hot heaps burn off too much carbon and, in the process, lose nitrogen too. You end up with too little compost that is not as potent as it might have been. One way to tell if your heap has exceeded about 150°F at the core is if it begins smelling like ammonia, a sure sign that nitrogen compounds are escaping into the air. Heaps with a starting C/N ratio that is too low get too hot. Heaps with too much air get too hot and dry out too rapidly. The way to cool a runaway heap down is to turn it and, while turning, add quite a bit of soil. This functions like the moderator rods controlling a nuclear reactor.

MOISTURE

Assuming that it gets hot, the heap will shrink, sag, settle, and dry out after a few weeks. When this happens it is an opportunity to turn and water the heap, introducing more air as well as more moisture and also bringing the outer parts of the heap, which haven't been exposed to high temperatures, to the center. How moist should a heap be? When you squeeze a handful hard, water should not drip out, but the stuff should be wet.

AERATION

Beware of too much air. True, the fermentation runs on air. But if it gets too vigorous the temperature will soar too high. The whole key to getting good compost is in regulating the temperature at around 140°F. Albert Howard, who made compost in the heat of India, where ambient daytime temperatures generally exceeded 90°F, dug trenches about 6 feet across, 2 feet deep, and about 20 feet long, and made his compost in them. Having earthen side walls restricted the air supply and slowed his heaps down, which was what he needed to accomplish in his situation.

SOIL IN THE HEAP

Rich garden soil is the vital and oft-overlooked ingredient in a compost heap. Because there is little carbon in soil to decompose, soil lowers the heap's temperature without changing the heap's C/N ratio. Soil is also the home of a type of microbe that specializes in cap-

turing ammonia, a gas often given off by composting bacteria, and converting it to water-soluble nitrates that are kept in the heap. Soil will also inoculate a new heap with an abundance of decomposers—microbial, fungal, and microscopic soil animals. If the materials being composted are a bit nutrient deficient, rich soil contains all the necessary nutrients to rapidly build a healthy population of decomposers. Finally, humus is well-decomposed organic matter combined with clay and soil mineral particles into soil crumbs. If there is no soil in the heap, humus cannot form properly. Generally, about 5 percent soil by starting volume is enough.

Soil should be mixed throughout the heap, but some can be used to thinly cover the outsides of a heap, especially to capture any ammonia given off.

When to Use Compost

Although there are reasons to cure a compost heap after it has cooled, the best time to use a heap is usually immediately after it has cooled. The longer it sits around, the greater the chance that nutrients will be lost. The huge population of microbes that had been working the stuff over dies off rapidly as the fermentation finishes. Microbial and fungal tissues are very fragile protoplasm that immediately go into solution like chemical fertilizer. In other words, a finished heap is filled with easily leachable plant nutrients. If you do have to store finished compost, keep it covered—in summer to retain moisture, in winter to prevent leaching.

CURING THE HEAP

The easiest and most sure-fire improver of compost quality is time. The C/N ratio of any compost heap will eventually decrease. The key word here is "eventually." The most dramatic decomposition occurs during the first few turns, when the heap is hot. But composting does not necessarily end when the pile has cooled and the material resembles soil. As long as a compost heap is kept moist and is turned occasionally, it will continue to decompose. "Curing" or "ripening" are terms used to describe what occurs once heating is over.

A different ecology of microorganisms predominates while a heap is ripening. After cooling, if the heap contains 5 to 10 percent soil, is kept moist, and is turned occasionally for some weeks or months after cooling so that it stays aerobic, a type of microorganisms called azotobacteria—soil dwellers that make nitrate-nitrogen—will be active. No special provision must be made to encourage azotobacteria. They slowly eat the carbon of the heap, steadily lowering the C/N ratio while making additional nitrate-nitrogen, raising the N component of the heap.

Feeding unripened compost to red worms is perhaps the quickest way to lower the C/N ratio and make a potent soil amendment. Once the high heat of decomposition has passed and the heap is cooling, it is commonly invaded by red worms, the same species used for vermi-composting kitchen garbage. These worms are not able to eat the high C/N material that went into the heap, but after heating and cooling, the average C/N ratio will probably have dropped enough to be suitable for them.

A municipal composting operation at Fallbrook, California, makes clever use of this method to produce a smaller amount of high-grade product out of a larger quantity of low-grade compost. Mixtures of sewage sludge and municipal solid waste are first composted. After cooling, the resulting compost, which has a high C/N ratio, is shallowly spread out over crude worm beds and kept moist. More crude compost is repeatedly added as the worms consume the waste, much like a household worm box. The lower portion of these mounds is pure castings, while the worm activity stays closer to the surface where food is available. When the beds have risen to about 3 feet tall, the surface few inches containing almost all the worms and undigested food are scraped off and used to form new vermicomposting beds. The castings below are considered finished compost. By laboratory analysis, the castings contain three or four times as much nitrogen as the crude compost being fed to the worms.

The marketplace gives an excellent indicator of the difference between their crude compost and the worm casts. Even though Fallbrook is surrounded by large acreages devoted to citrus orchards and row crop vegetables, the municipality has a difficult time disposing of the crude product. But its worm compost is in strong demand.

There can be pitfalls with buying worm

castings. I visited one extensive operation near Olympia, Washington, that was vermicomposting dairy manure. But the cattle were bedded on sawdust, and the worm composters did not thoroughly compost the manure and bedding in heaps first, but simply spread it out atop the worm beds. I observed the worms eating the cow manure but ignoring the sawdust. At least half the material was sawdust. The manure turned to humus/castings; these coated the sawdust and the product appeared to be "done." But the sawdust was virtually untouched. And the C/N ratio?

Anyone interested in vermicomposting should read Mary Appelhof's book *Worms Eat My Garbage* (listed in the bibliography).

Composting Manure

Sir Albert Howard found it impossible to make high-quality compost out of only manure, for several reasons. When a manure pile heats up, there is no solidity to the material, and it rapidly becomes an airless heap. Without sufficient oxygen present, the bacterial population releases ammonia gas into the air. Almost anyone who has visited a farmyard or an infrequently cleaned horse stable knows that smell. It means nitrogen is being lost. This type of heap also runs away with itself and gets too hot; as a result, too much of the carbon is burned out, and a huge heap of pure manure becomes a mighty small bit of compost. Fresh manure mixed with an equal quantity of bedding straw (not sawdust) that has absorbed a lot of the vital urine, and then leavened with about 5 percent soil, will make decent compost if turned frequently.

As I mentioned before, the main trouble with the kinds of "manure" most gardeners are able to get west of the Cascades is the kind of bedding used. Very little grain is produced in our region, so there is little or no straw available for bedding animals. Instead, farmers and horse owners use sawdust. The sawdust is highly absorbent, so the animals are usually allowed to walk on the same bedding for quite awhile before it gets too odoriferous for the comfort of humans. The droppings become broken up and thoroughly mixed into the sawdust; it is nearly impossible to rake out solid chunks of manure from the mix. The best you can say about this sort of "manure" is that most of the urine has been absorbed too.

When wetted down and heaped up, this type of manure will heat up a little, but it never gets very hot. If you believe you must use this stuff, make sure you keep the material moist, turn the heap every few months, keep it covered during the winter, and let it cure for at least two years.

A SHORT ESSAY ON MANURE

Liebig's invention of chemical fertilizers came before 1850. However, until the First World War, horses were everywhere. Most people lived on smallish farms with barnyard animals. City streets were littered with horse manure (street sweepings), so commercial vegetable crops were mainly grown with manures and composts. Yet potent manure was always in short supply and had well-recognized value.

Cow manure, of which there was a great deal, was considered weak, suitable only for field crops. Horse manure was much stronger, while the supreme and highly prized plant growth stimulant was poultry manure, always in short supply because preindustrial fowl weren't caged in factories or permanently locked in henhouses. Fertilizing with pure chicken manure is not very different from fertilizing with ground cereal grains or seed meals. It acts like fertilizer and is so concentrated that it can scorch plant leaves and must be applied sparingly to soil.

Since chicken manure was scarce, pretwentieth-century market gardeners depended on seemingly unlimited supplies of the next best thing, "short manure," from horses. The difference between "long" and "short" manure was bedding. Long manure contained straw from the stall, while short manure was pure street sweepings without adulterants.

People of that era knew the fine points of manure and hay quality as well as people today know their grades of gasoline. Horses of that era were expected to do a day's work, so they were fed on grass or grass/clover mixes that had been cut and dried while they still had a high protein content. Leafy hay was highly prized, while hay that upon close inspection revealed lots of stems and seed heads would be rejected by a smart buyer. The working horse's diet was supplemented with a daily ration of grain. Consequently, fresh nineteenth-century short manure probably started out with a C/N ratio of around 15:1.

Fertilizing with fresh horse manure gave many vegetables a harsh flavor, so it was first composted by mixing in some soil and a little lime (a good idea because otherwise a great deal of ammonia would escape the heap). Market gardeners raising highly demanding crops like cauliflower and celery incorporated composted short manure in layers that were inches thick. Crops that were less demanding of nutrients, like snap beans, lettuce, and roots, followed in succession without further compost. Long manures (horse or cow) containing lots of straw were considered useful only for field crops or, after composting, as being sufficiently potent to grow root vegetables, which are little more than field crops anyway.

Anyone interested in learning more about preindustrial market gardening might ask their interlibrary loan librarian to seek out a rare book called *French Gardening* by Thomas Smith, published in London about 1905. It was written to encourage British market gardeners to imitate the Parisian *marcier*, who skillfully earned top returns by growing out-of-season produce on intensive, double-dug raised beds, often under glass hot or cold frames. American biodynamic French intensive gurus obtained their inspiration from England through this tradition.

Inoculants

The only practical way to seed a compost heap with the right sorts of bacteria is to use a technique called mass inoculation. While building the new heap, you incorporate a small percentage of biologically active material from an older compost heap, or even with soil from beneath the last heap you made. Mass inoculation supplies large numbers of the most useful types of microorganisms, so they dominate the heap's ecology before other, less desirable types can establish significant populations. This speeds and directs decomposition.

I can't imagine how selling mass inoculants could be turned into a business. Suppose, however, that seeding a new heap with a tiny amount of superior microorganisms could speed initial decomposition and result in a much better product. Now that could be a profitable business. Such an approach is not without precedent. Brewers, vintners, and bread makers all do that. And ever since composting became interesting to twentieth-century farmers and gardeners, entrepreneurs have been concocting compost starters that are intended to be added by the ounce to the cubic yard.

But a small packet of inoculant is at very best a tiny population compared to the billions of microorganisms already present in any heap. In that respect, inoculating compost is very different from making beer, wine, or bread. These food products contain few or no microorganisms at the start. The inoculant, small as it might be, still introduces millions of times more desirable organisms than those few wild types that might already be present.

But the materials being assembled into a new compost heap are already loaded with microorganisms. As when making sauerkraut, what is needed is already present at the start. And the complex ecology of decomposition

will go through its inevitable changes as the microorganisms respond to variations in temperature, aeration, pH, and so on.

This topic is controversial, so I sought the advice of an expert—Clarence Golueke, who personally researched and developed U.C. fast composting in the early 1950s and who has been developing municipal composting systems ever since.

Golueke has run comparison tests of compost starters of all sorts because, in his business, entrepreneurs are constantly attempting to sell inoculants to municipal composting operations. Of these vendors, Golueke says, with thinly disguised contempt:

> *Most starter entrepreneurs include enzymes when listing the ingredients of their products. The background for this inclusion parallels the introduction of purportedly advanced versions of starters—i.e., "advanced" in terms of increased capacity, utility and versatility. Thus in the early 1950s (when [I made my] appearance on the compost scene), starters were primarily microbial and references to identities of constituent microbes were very vague. References to enzymes were extremely few and far between. As early ("pioneer") researchers began to issue formal and informal reports on microbial groups (e.g., actinomycetes) observed by them, they also began to conjecture on the roles of those microbial groups in the compost process. The conjectures frequently were accompanied by surmises about the part played by enzymes.*
>
> *Coincidentally, vendors of starters in vogue at the time began to claim that their products included the newly reported microbial groups as*

well as an array of enzymes. For some reason, hormones were attracting attention at the time, and so most starters were supposedly laced with hormones. In time, hormones began to disappear from the picture, whereas enzymes were given a billing parallel to that accorded to the microbial component.

Golueke has worked out methods of testing starters that eliminate any random effects and conclusively demonstrate their result, if any. Inevitably, and repeatedly, he has found that there is no difference between using a starter and not using one. And he says, "Although anecdotal accounts of success due to the use of particular inoculum are not unusual in the popular media, we have yet to come across unqualified accounts of successes in the refereed scientific and technical literature."

I use a variation of mass inoculation when making compost. While building a new heap, I periodically scrape up and toss in a few shovels of compost and soil from where the previous pile was made.

Last Words

If you apply all of the hints mentioned here and take control of every aspect of the composting process, you will soon come to know by "feel" what is happening in your heaps. Gradually your compost will come out better. If your efforts don't result in powerful, fertilizing compost, have no concerns. Go ahead and use it, but be sure to add fertilizer to the soil too.

One last word. There are dozens of books on the subject of composting, and most general garden books have at least a chapter on the subject. But the best of the lot was written by Sir Albert Howard. It is hard to find but at present is available on the World Wide Web. See the bibliography for publication information.

Chapter 4 **Planning**

The strip system [a crop rotation system widely used during
the Middle Ages that was very destructive to soil fertility] *has also
been adopted for the allotments round our towns and cities without any
provision whatsoever on the part of the authorities to maintain the land in good
heart by such obvious and simple expedients as subsoiling, followed by a rest
under grass grazed by sheep or cattle, ploughing up, and sheet composting the
vegetable residues. Land under allotments should not be under vegetables
for more than five years at a time: this should be followed by a
similar period under grass and livestock.*

—Sir Albert Howard,
The Soil and Health

I garden big, with passion, and measure in fractions of acres. I've grown half-acre and three-quarter-acre vegetable trial grounds; I've grown plots of cereal grains that were one-twelfth acre each. I've bred small-seeded fava bean varieties on plots that were one-twentieth of an acre. While learning to garden without irrigation, I

raised the same vegetables in two places at once—in the dry plot and in my regular irrigated garden; each was a sixth of an acre. Lately I am just vegetable gardening for two; a tenth of an acre, or about 4,000 square feet of growing space, produces a gracious plenty.

An acre is roughly 42,000 square feet; a suburban or small-town acre lot is typically about 200 by 200 feet or 100 by 400 feet. City lots in neighborhoods built between the 1930s and the 1960s seem to average 60 to 75 feet wide and 125 to 150 feet deep, roughly a quarter acre. Small-town lots of the same era were larger, often a half acre. As the country got more crowded, people's lots got smaller. Before moving to Oregon in 1978, I sold a San Fernando Valley acre lot to a developer, who demolished my old house and put six postage-stamp lots on the same land. No wonder more and more people are interested in intensive gardening.

Whenever I visit someone living in a city, I estimate the growth rate of neighbors' trees that soon will shade their yard. I gauge the amount of sunny area behind their house that could grow a vegetable garden, and I'm always asking myself, "Could I manage to live here?" So far the answer has been no. Maybe on a double lot, or maybe when I get old and can barely manage 1,000 square feet. Maybe then.

One thousand square feet is about what most urban gardeners use for vegetables. It's a plot 33 by 33 feet. Managing 1,000 square feet does not place too many demands on the time of a young family and leaves room in the shadier parts of the backyard for the kids and pets to play, plus room for a garage and a com-

post heap. And that much garden land can grow all the vegetables most people want. So together, let's design a year-round garden of this size and estimate what that 1,000 square feet producing food might mean to the economy of a family.

Since there'll be no surplus room, choose what to grow based on what makes the most value per square foot. True, value is not measured only in dollars; what value would you place on an ear of fresh sweet corn eaten raw, torn right off the plant and husked and munched in the cool of an August morning? That experience might be incredibly more valuable than a pound of yummy potatoes or three fresh heads of leaf lettuce. I sure have enjoyed raw corn myself. But corn yields very little cash value, considering the amount of space it occupies and the nearly three months it takes to reach maturity. And keep in mind that your corn matures at the same time that the local market gardener is selling it at ten ears for a dollar. So I've always decided to buy local corn in season and use my garden space for something more productive. Besides, as much pleasure as I get from the six ears of fresh corn I eat each summer, I get more from the huge bowl full of sweet lettuce I eat each day about nine months of the year.

The chart on page 100, "Scale of Relative Value of Garden Vegetables," shows vegetables ranked by their approximate economic value, based on what the vegetable would cost at the supermarket in the season you could grow it, while taking account of the yield you could produce per square foot and how long the vegetable will occupy that square foot before you can plant something else there. In a few cases I give more value to something than space and time would suggest because the ones you grow are so superior to the ones you can buy. If you are a novice gardener making a garden plan, I'd look this list over and first allocate space to those items toward the top half.

Many backyard gardeners conclude that the best economic use of garden space is to produce salad greens and tomatoes, because their freshness is so essential and because the gardener can grow varieties of unsurpassable quality that can rarely be found even in a gourmet or whole-foods market. Culinary herbs are also very expensive (and amazingly better) when used fresh. And the garden produces vine-ripened tomatoes the likes of which you can't buy at any price.

One year (1981), I actually kept close tabs on what I harvested out of my personal garden and compared it to the current retail supermarket price at the time I was harvesting. What I earned for my efforts was about a dollar a square foot per year after costs; this was the average gain from a whole range of garden vegetables. What are a thousand 1981 dollars worth now? And keep in mind, those are non-taxed dollars. The dollars you spend in the supermarket are after-tax dollars.

How to Achieve Fresh Garden Food Two and One-Half Months a Year

My goal for you is that you eat fresh food from your garden every single month of the year and come to depend on your garden for ever-increasing amounts of your family's nourishment. If you're a typical North American eater, you'll have to change a lot of habits and learn a lot to accomplish my goal for you. You'll probably learn to grow unfamiliar foods in ways that don't apply east of the Cascades or south of the Siskiyous. You'll learn to eat what may now seem unusual foods. A great deal about your life may change. It will take you many years.

Carl was my immediate neighbor when I first moved to Lorane, Oregon. Seeing the sad state of his family's garden and health every time I looked across my five acres motivated me to write the first edition of this book in 1979.

I don't think Carl ever did satisfactorily explain to himself how it was that in May I would be eating my usual daily garden salad. For Carl, late May was the very first chance he had to till his weed patch without making clods. I remember watching late in May as Carl walked his garden, broadcasting a few sacks of triple sixteen fertilizer and some years a sack or two of lime. Then a neighbor of ours who had a big, powerful tractor would rototill the whole plot, now very weedy after a long winter of neglect.

Scale of Relative Value of Garden Vegetables*

Fresh herbs *(basil, oregano, thyme, sage, rosemary, etc.)*	Tomatoes *(indeterminate, staked)*
Parsley	Cucumbers
Carrots	Peppers
Beets	Cantaloupes and other muskmelons
Parsnips	Snap (pole) beans
Loose-leaf lettuce	Broccoli
Most other leafy salad greens	Cauliflower
Scallions	Cabbage
Spinach *(for salad)*	Brussels sprouts
Kale	Bulb onions
Swiss chard	Winter squash
Leeks	Sweet corn
Kohlrabi	Watermelon
Potatoes	Pumpkin
Rutabagas	
Zucchini and other bush summer squash	

*The value drops from the top left column down to the bottom right column and is based on the approximate value per square foot of garden per the amount of time that area will be growing the crop.

The Lorane Valley was at about 900 feet elevation and prone to late frosts. But frost was highly unlikely after Memorial Day, so on that holiday weekend Carl and his wife ceremonially went out with packets of seeds and flats of transplants and "put in" the garden. It was a big garden, maybe the size of a city lot, 50 by 100 feet. At the expense of great effort the whole thing was planted at once: sweet corn, bush beans, several long rows of potatoes. There were beets, chard, and carrots in rows; many hills of zucchini and cucumbers; and lots of transplants for cabbages, broccoli, and tomatoes. Then little green lines of seedlings appeared, and the transplanted seedlings turned into little green circles that got larger as I watched. And Carl would come down in the evenings and proudly admire his handiwork.

Then, in about mid-June, the whole field speckled itself with green as jillions of weed seeds sprouted. Every few days I saw Carl working hard, chopping with a (dull) hoe (and sometimes setting a sprinkler) in the late afternoon. After the Fourth of July, other activities seemed to draw his attention from the garden, and gradually the weeds took over, but to give him credit the vegetables had gotten a solid six- or seven-week head start on the weeds.

By mid-August, the weeds and the vegetables were running neck and neck. About this time I'd see his wife and older kids out there in the weed patch picking countless buckets of stuff to can and freeze and dry. This harvesting and putting food by for winter continued into mid-September, by which time the garden looked like a big weed field with a few bursting cabbages left, a few broccoli covered with yellow flowers, and some chard plants sticking up. The weeds made seed and grew lustily through autumn and did it again in spring before he had the field tilled for next year. These weeds and the roots, trimmings, and unused parts of the vegetables were what kept any organic matter at all in the field. I tried to smile and say how beautiful the harvest looked when I walked over to visit, but it was actually pretty sad, pathetic-looking produce, most of it.

Carl and his family may as well have been living in Ohio or Utah for all the regionality of their garden. About the only concession they made to being in Cascadia was to use the varieties they found sold at the local garden center. They considered the garden a big success because they ate preserved food all winter. But their kids all had continuous bad colds and runny noses all winter and spring. The whole family could have been much healthier had a substantial portion of their diet been fresh.

One thing Carl couldn't seem to get a hook into was that it is less work to grow an extended harvest than to preserve while the garden is "on." He could have allocated a smaller area to summertime vegetables and used more space for autumn and winter harvests. Instead of some of that canning, he would have found it much less work to prepare a few raised beds in early autumn for early spring planting. Then instead of watching the overwintering weeds make mature seed while his soggy soil slowly dried down enough to till, he could have planted his pre-prepared beds in March.

He could have put some salad greens under inexpensive plastic coverings in early autumn and had fresh, tender salads all winter. There were so many things Carl could have done had he been able to plan and been able to execute that plan. I can hear him still, explaining to me with a little bit of a feel-sorry-for-himself whine, just why he couldn't. He couldn't get seeds to come up in the heat of summer, so he had to get his sowing all done before summer's main heat (but my seeds came up in July and August). And besides, his kids didn't like salads; they liked green beans and frozen corn. And lettuce wouldn't grow good for him anyway. And he couldn't rototill the soggy earth of early spring. And his soil got too hard to weed by midsummer (but my personal family garden was weedless and I spent less time by far than he did at it).

So the first time I wrote this book, it was Carl who was my audience, sitting in the invisible chair on the other side of the typewriter.

How to Achieve Fresh Garden Food Twelve Months a Year

Back east in northern latitudes like ours they have real winter with solidly frozen ground. To eat anything at all that came from the garden between November and June, it has to have been harvested between July and October and put into some sort of storage. So eastern at-home food producers can, freeze, dry, and maybe even have a

Year-Round Planting Calendar

■ February

Entire month   Transplant asparagus roots

15th   Sow peas, favas, spinach

■ March

Entire month   Sow peas, favas, spinach, asparagus seed, mustard and related Asian greens, radishes, parsley, bulb onions, scallions

15th   Transplant earliest broccoli and cabbage seedlings

17th   St. Patrick's Day ritual—sow potatoes

■ April

Entire month   Sow peas, scallions, spinach (summer varieties), beets, turnips, radishes, kohlrabi, chard, carrots, lettuce, broccoli, cabbage, parsley, sorrel, cauliflower, potatoes

1st   Transplant earliest cauliflower

after 15th   Transplant onion seedlings and early leeks. Sow celery and celeriac

■ May

Entire month   Sow cauliflower, cabbage, beets, radishes, chard, carrots, lettuce, broccoli, winter leek nursery bed, scallion, potatoes, lettuce

15th   Sow snap beans, squash (summer and winter), basil, dill, dry beans, sweet corn. Transplant tomato, celery, and celeriac seedlings

■ June

Entire month   Sow cucumbers, summer squash, melons, snap beans, beets, carrots, lettuce, broccoli, fall and winter cabbage, Brussels sprouts, cauliflower, scallions

15th   Transplant peppers and eggplant

■ July

Entire month   Sow lettuce. Transplant winter leeks

before 15th   Sow parsnips, carrots, summer beets, fall cauliflower, bush snap beans, scallions

after 15th   Sow rutabaga, kale, winter beets, spinach, overwintering broccoli

■ August

Entire month   Sow endive, spinach

before 15th   Sow overwintering cauliflower, loose-leaf lettuce

after 15th   Sow overwintering bulb onions

■ September

before 15th   Sow endive, corn salad, garlic and shallots, field turnips (as green manure)

■ October

Entire month   Sow green manures: favas, crimson clover, field peas

Note: This rough schedule is more or less right for the Willamette Valley garden. North of Longview, along the coast, and at higher elevations, spring dates might be too early while sowing dates after midsummer might be a bit too late. South of Drain, Oregon, spring dates might be a bit too late while dates after midsummer might be a bit early. Starting dates for transplants are found in a similar schedule in Chapter 7.

root cellar; it makes eastern sense to plan a huge patch of something that all comes to harvest at once. Then a big effort can be made to preserve a six- to nine-month supply of some food in just a day or two.

I wrote this book to help you do something more appropriate in our climate—create your own year-round backyard natural-foods-store produce counter. The idea is not to have huge quantities of a few things now and then some few others later and then none most of the year. It's far better to be able to pick and use the widest possible assortment of vegetables over the longest possible period of time—which, west of the Cascades, means just about all year, most years in most parts.

We vegetable gardeners have to focus on two things: getting our plants to grow well and arranging our efforts in space and time so we harvest the right amounts at the right times. That's what this garden planning chapter is all about. It's about negatives—avoiding common planning mistakes—and about doing things superlatively right.

Note from the "Year-Round Planting Calendar" on page 102 that planting can start almost before spring and can go on into autumn.

The calendar has to be adjusted a bit for the particular year. Some years, spring comes rather later than we gardeners might wish, and in those years, north of Longview, Washington, even the amazingly cold-tolerant fava (broad) beans can't even germinate until mid- to late March. Other years, early spring is mild and balmy and the garden starts a few weeks earlier. Either way it's a long season.

On anything but the most sandy soil, to be able to sow in early spring requires having already prepared raised beds for spring crops the previous autumn. Without this fore-thought you'll have to join the multitudes who will be waiting several more months for the ground to dry out enough to till. The difference is new food in May for those who went into the planting year prepared, versus the first food coming in July for those who didn't.

Also notice from the planting calendar that sowing dates for many kinds of vegetables have time overlaps; the same vegetable can often be sown over a long period. Not only can you do this, you should! If you want a continuous supply of lettuce heads, radishes, cabbages, cauliflower, or big central broccoli flowers, you'll make repeated small sowings a few weeks apart.

Other sorts of vegetables, the slower-growing heat lovers, are put outdoors during the one small window of opportunity we get, usually a few weeks before and after the last probable frost. That single planting will become the entire summer's supply of tomatoes, peppers, eggplant, melons, cucumbers, squash (winter and summer), snap beans, and sweet corn. With these crops, the earlier in, the better, so long as frost or cold-induced disease doesn't take them. Sometimes there's a surprise late frost and a second chance to sow, but there is almost never a good third chance. When heat lovers are sown much after mid-June, the small harvest seems hardly worth the effort.

Heat lovers are what most people envision when they hear the word "garden." Most novices naturally allocate most of their space to these crops. The result is usually a glut during August followed by a great scarcity of other vegetables later on. The mistake here is that midsummer is a period of strong sun, of extraordinarily rapid growth, and of very high production for the amount of space involved. Just a few healthy tomato plants will keep any kitchen counter covered while they're ripening. A short row of snap beans can't seem to be picked fast enough. In Chapter 9, you'll find information to help you estimate how much to plant of each vegetable.

What I'm getting to here is a strong suggestion that you make a garden plan. I mean it! Right now. Let's make one together as you read through the rest of this section. Get a large sheet of paper and a ruler, and make a scale drawing of your existing or proposed garden area. Do it even if you're in the same financial shape I was in when I first subscribed to *Organic Gardening and Farming* magazine back in 1972, when I was hard up, living in an inner-city Los Angeles cockroach apartment, and dreaming about my first house and garden. In that case make your imaginary garden 33 feet by 33 feet, that 1,000-square-foot space I described a few paragraphs earlier as being worth a lot to the family economy.

Now make a list of those vegetables you and your family like to eat, and rank that list from your stronger preferences to your least liked ones, and/or by what the item costs. Then compare your list with the list on page 100, "Scale of Relative Value of Garden Vegetables." I'm asking you to prioritize your list because almost no one has the room to grow everything they might imagine. And if they were able to grow all they wanted, the family couldn't begin to eat all that food.

If you are new to vegetable gardening, be sure your garden plan does not exceed 1,000 square feet. You have so much to learn that if you give yourself a bigger playpen than that, you'll likely make so many mistakes that you'll ruin the fun and may never garden again. Everything you attempt in the first year will be more difficult than it ever will be again. Accept in advance that you will make many mistakes. You can't avoid making them, but you can keep them small. The first year, give yourself a success.

Now skip ahead to Chapter 9, and begin reading up on the vegetable you ranked first on your list. Figure out how much space it'll take to produce as much as you'll want, and when it'll be planted and when harvested. Then allocate that amount of space on the plan to the vegetable, *with the dates of sowing and harvesting.* To get those dates to maturity right, you may need to consult a mail-order seed catalog. If you do that, I suggest you use a regional catalog so the maturity times honestly reflect what you'll experience. I bet that long before most of you get to the bottom of your lists, the garden plan you've drawn out will be filled up solid.

Please don't think you can be cleverer than I am and garden without one of these plans. I have been vegetable gardening for twenty-five years, and I still make one, every year. It goes down to the garden with me every day in the spring. By the time the plan has become smudged and dirty, it stays in the house, but that's because by then I've pretty much memorized it and have already changed it some too. And by that time I've also written down some planting dates with myself in my daily diary.

I make my own garden plan early in winter, while my mistakes of the previous year are still fresh and raw, and I use my plan when reading seed catalogs to compile my orders. I do confess, though, that in this respect having made a plan doesn't help me much. I've always been a sucker for seed catalogs. I just can't seem to resist buying an interesting variety, although I know from years of experience that many of these impulse purchases never even get planted.

A word about how much to grow: The first rule of abundant living is to produce twice what you'll need. If you overproduce in a garden, you don't have to fight insects or disease or fret if they take some. If the weather doesn't cooperate and your yield is smaller than anticipated, there'll still be enough and then some.

SUCCESSION AND YOUR GARDEN PLAN

Once you've made a garden plan, insert timing into it. Have one crop follow close on the heels of the last. Succession plantings allow a smaller garden to produce as much as a larger one, which means less compost, less fertilizer, less tillage, less watering, less overall effort. There are bound to be changes as you work this out, so make a rough draft of your plan in soft pencil and have a good eraser handy.

Suppose you're every bit as addicted to sweet lettuce salads as I am. A truly great salad can't be made from old, bitter leaves; for the garden gourmet the plants have to be cut at their prime. But even if you sow a half dozen varieties of staggered maturity all at one time, each sowing will only be harvestable in peak condition for three to four weeks. Suppose the first sowing is made early in April and will be past its best eating stage by the end of June. I then make another sowing of lettuce toward the end of April to harvest after the first one is done, and I make still more sowings, one every three weeks, more or less, until August. Then, because the growth rate drops off greatly in October, I make the August/September sowings a bit closer together so I can cut lettuce during autumn and into the winter until it is frozen out.

Indicate a sowing schedule on your plan. Suppose that each sowing will be a patch 4 feet by 4 feet. Nine sowings of lettuce—April 1, April 21, May 15, June 5, June 30, July 21, August 10, August 25, and September 10—would occupy a combined area of 4 feet by 36 feet. If we are planning a 1,000-square-foot garden of 33 by 33 feet, we could just about allocate a 4-foot-wide row across the whole width of the garden called "lettuce." (And don't forget when drawing the plan to allow for the paths on either side of each bed and row.) The first 4-by-4 patch is sown April 1 and is empty about 12 weeks later, July 1. Ah! We've got a vacant 4-by-4 space on July 1. What could we plant there? Check the Year-Round Planting Calendar (page 102). More lettuce? Yep. Why not put the June 30 sowing there? Or we could transplant winter leeks into that spot, or sow some root crops (such as parsnips, carrots, or beets). There are lots of options.

Now let's view the succession backward. We've already decided to use some areas for sowing lettuce during August. It makes no sense to have these do nothing from March through August. What could we plant there that would be harvested by the time we wanted to put in our fall/winter lettuce harvest? Peas? Spinach? There's no end of fairly fast-growing spring things that could go in during March or April and would be done by the time we want to put in lettuce.

Here are some successions I use over and over. The earliest sowing of peas is always completely picked by mid-June and can be immediately followed by the larger, slow-growing brassicas such as savoy cabbage, broccoli, or Brussels sprouts for fall or winter harvest. Later pea sowings can be followed by faster-growing brassicas like kale or rutabagas.

Generally, by the end of March there will be quite a few areas holding little but cabbage family stumps and the remains of winter crops. I often scatter these areas with garden pea seed, give them a light sprinkling of complete organic fertilizer and a bit of compost, chop it all in an inch deep with a hoe, and grow a pea crop, one I have no intention whatsoever of eating. In about mid-May, when the pea vines are blooming, I could use these areas for starting hot-weather crops. So I pull the pea vines by hand or with a rake (they come out very easily), toss them into the compost heap, and find that the pea roots have fractured the soil deeper than I could ever dig with a shovel. Peas leave the soil in magnificent, fine-textured condition, ready to rake out and sow seeds in, or ready to accept transplants.

Here's another succession scheme. Overwintered bulb onions and spring-sown spinach and other spring greens are all harvested before midsummer; they can be followed by beets, carrots, parsnips, or chard.

Overwintered broccoli is done by mid-April, and overwintered cauliflower is all cut by mid-May; their beds or rows, after a dressing of compost and fertilizer, are perfect for summer crops like tomatoes, peppers, and so forth.

For heat-loving vegetables no edible succession is possible; follow them with an overwintering green manure. This limitation actually makes planning much simpler. Summer heat lovers absolutely have to go in before mid-June, and May is better for most of them if you don't have late frosts. Early spring-sown crops would not be harvested in time from areas that will become heat lovers' beds, although heat lovers could follow our overwintered crops. So a big block of the garden must be kept empty all spring because it will be sown on about Memorial Day, just as my friend Carl did it, and will be done by the end of September. The main difference between you and Carl is that you're going to keep your summer garden weeded, and when the frost comes, you're going to clean up the space, put the trash into the compost pile, make raised beds of the area if you haven't already, and plant them to clover and/or fava beans. And in next year's garden plan, this probably will be the area for spring-sown vegetables. I'd like to see you eating your own salads and admiring your pea vines' flowers while your neighbors are still wondering when the weather will get settled down enough to till their gardens.

THE SEED BOX

I keep my seeds organized so that they act like a sowing appointment calendar. Before I knew much about seed storage I arranged my seeds in a shoebox with dividers saying March 1, March 15, April 1, April 15, May 1, May 15, June 1, June 15, July 1, July 15, August 1, August 15, September 1, September 15. Now I use widemouthed, airtight mason jars to hold the seeds I am going to plant that year; in each jar is a desiccant packet to remove moisture. After my new seed orders come in, all my seeds, new ones and carryovers, are sorted. The ones I plan to use are put into about a dozen mason jars that are labeled by those same sowing dates and kept in an old refrigerator. Around April 15 I open the April 15 jar. Some of the packets in this jar are used once and then are done for the year. As long as the sowing came up well, any remaining seed is left sealed in the refrigerator to be carried over for next year. Other April 15 packets are moved to a jar with a later date after sowing, if I plan to sow this variety again. Any time I'm in doubt about what to do that part of the month, I just open the jar and see what's waiting for me. I have a lot more to say about storing seed in Chapter 6.

THE FUNDAMENTAL VEGETABLE CROP ROTATION

As I plan my successions, I mentally group the vegetables into three general gardens: the spring garden, the summer garden, and the fall/winter garden. I try to keep all the vegetables in each "garden" physically close to one another. This doesn't always work, but it is my goal. The spring garden is sown during March and April and sometimes into May. It generally matures before things get hot. The summer garden goes in during May and the first half of June. It con-

sists of heat lovers or at least heat-tolerant species. The crucial requirement for membership in this garden group is that the crop must be finished with at or before the first frost, because this area will be sown to overwintering green manures. The fall/winter garden is mostly sown during June and July. A few fast-growing species and a few that overwinter for next spring may be started in August, and some gambler's salad greens go in during September. The fall garden is sown where the spring garden was. Doing it this way effortlessly creates a general rotation that tends to prevent the same vegetable species from following itself in the same place, while facilitating a winter green manure crop on about half the overall area. (See the diagram on page 29, "Three-Year Rotation; Two-Field System.")

Raised Beds: More of the Story

Let me briefly restate the pluses for raised beds. They are ideal for small-sized plants, especially when you have unlimited irrigation. Raised beds allow earlier spring planting. And they make tillage easier *if they're not stepped on.* So I treat a raised bed like a white living room carpet, never putting a shoe or boot on it. I do this mainly because of laziness. If a growing area is never compacted by my feet, and if it's kept busy growing vegetation, the space seldom (if ever) needs to be deeply worked again. Compost chopped into

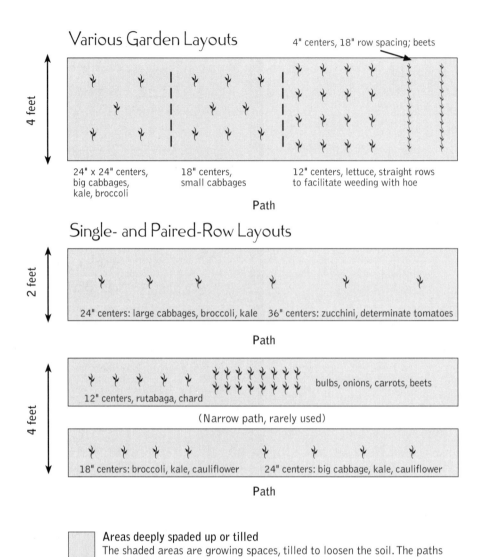

Various Garden Layouts

4" centers, 18" row spacing; beets

4 feet

24" x 24" centers,
big cabbages,
kale, broccoli

18" centers,
small cabbages

12" centers, lettuce, straight rows
to facilitate weeding with hoe

Path

Single- and Paired-Row Layouts

2 feet

24" centers: large cabbages, broccoli, kale   36" centers: zucchini, determinate tomatoes

Path

4 feet

12" centers, rutabaga, chard

bulbs, onions, carrots, beets

(Narrow path, rarely used)

18" centers: broccoli, kale, cauliflower   24" centers: big cabbage, kale, cauliflower

Path

Areas deeply spaded up or tilled
The shaded areas are growing spaces, tilled to loosen the soil. The paths
are not worked and are used to avoid compacting the growing areas.

the surface with a husky hoe keeps the surface so soft that weeding becomes almost effortless; this serendipitously puts the highest humus levels where the seeds are sprouting, greatly enhancing germination. Vegetable crops and green manure roots will penetrate the uncompacted soil 24 inches deep and more; as these roots rot they loosen the soil

further. The only time I feel any need to deeply work an established bed is when preparing to sow carrots or parsnips. And should I wish to loosen up the uncompacted soil with a shovel, the chore is hardly any effort.

As the size of the mature plants increases, the advantages of arranging them in raised beds decreases. At about 2 feet in diameter comes the break-even point, where you're just about as well off planting in a raised row or pairs of adjoining raised rows as in a wide raised bed. Sprawling vine crops are usually best grown atop well-spaced hills, but smaller vine-habit plants like cucumbers, melons, and indeterminate tomatoes that are allowed to sprawl can all be grown in raised beds if you wish; a single hill started in the center of a bed will more than cover the whole width of a 4-foot-wide bed, reach out into the paths, and cover 5 to 8 feet of its length as well. The diagram on page 108, "Various Garden Layouts," illustrates these possibilities.

Many gardeners, especially city gardeners, err by constructing permanent raised beds. Some think that beds raised higher are better than ones that are raised only a little and so will make strong retaining walls around each one. The biggest disadvantage to this is permanence. The permanent bed is too hard to rotate out of vegetables. Retaining walls also make it very difficult to work near the outside edges with a hoe, so you're always using your fingertips and hand-pulling the clumps of grass that anchor themselves in the crevices. If the walls are not really strong, it can be more difficult to spade the bed without disturbing them. Retaining walls made of railway ties or cinder blocks occupy valuable space that could otherwise be growing vegetables. And however you construct them, they cost a lot to build.

On the positive side, solidly contained raised beds can be attractive, and the retaining walls can function as unnecessarily strong and overly expensive but very convenient base supports for cloches. And for those with severe disabilities, a very high raised bed can be worked without bending or squatting. Beds surrounded by cinder block walls can be sat upon by someone sliding out of a wheelchair and perching. In areas where the land stays waterlogged most of the winter, a high raised bed allows vegetable roots to breathe. Finally, on hillsides with slopes in excess of 6 or 7 percent, a system of terraced raised beds and retaining walls is almost essential to hold the soil in place.

HOW TO MAKE AND MANAGE A SENSIBLE RAISED BED

The first step in planning a raised bed is to decide on its dimensions. The width is determined by how far you can reach while squatting in the path. I have fairly long arms, and though I'm nearly sixty years old I'm still flexible, so my beds are 4 feet wide. The length should be no more than twice as far as you can accurately toss compost from a wheelbarrow with a shovel; for me, that's about 12 feet, so my beds are 25 feet long. Besides, 4 by 25 feet makes a convenient 100 square feet.

There must be a path entirely around each bed. I make 3-foot-wide wheelbarrow/cart access paths along the narrow ends, and 18-inch-wide footpaths between the long sides.

The first time I make a bed I broadcast lime, complete organic fertilizer, and about ½ inch of compost over the bed area and then spade it up a foot deep. My focus is not to blend the compost in but to open the soil a foot deep while allowing some compost and fertilizer to fall in the cracks as the shovel works. Then I shovel up an inch of soil from the paths around the bed and toss it on top of the bed I'm making. This raises the bed a couple of inches above the paths. I then spread another ¼ inch of compost atop all and chop the surface inch or two with a hoe.

Using a bow rake, I then gently pull any clods or big chunks back off the bed and into the path. These come down with a bit of compost, too. When I'm done I have a fine seedbed ready to plant. Any resistant chunks from the surface of the bed are now in the paths, where my feet break them up and mix them with compost.

When it is time to plant the bed again, I go around the paths with a shovel and scrape up about ½ inch of soil to toss back into the bed. Then I add another thin sprinkling of compost and the usual complete organic fertilizer, hoe it up, and rake the clods back down into the path. It's mighty easy this way. The bed is raised, but only enough to proclaim that it is a bed rather than somewhere to step, and only enough that the surface inch or so dries out faster than the paths. I should also mention that with each succeeding year and each addition of compost, there'll be less clods.

Preparing long rows works in about the same way. Open the soil 18 to 24 inches (two to three shovel blades) wide and as long as the row will be; add a bit of compost and fertilizer on top, toss a bit of soil from the paths atop this, chop it all up with a hoe, and rake the clods back to the paths. What you end up with is a very slightly raised wide row. The paths between these wide rows should be as narrow as possible, say, 12 inches.

Short-Term Rotations

Some eastern garden writers expound on vegetable garden rotations at great length. Farmers also make rotations work—sensitive biological farming requires them. I usually can't make them work for me. Some eastern garden writers say they can organize their vegetable species into as many as seven groups and swap these groups among seven equal-sized plots over a seven-year-long rotation. They say that rotations prevent disease buildup and let them allocate scarce compost to that part of the rotation needing more fertility while growing the low-demand vegetables where the soil has intentionally been allowed to run down. They allege that a person can use the same garden in perpetuity if it is rotated correctly from one vegetable crop to another. Rotations also allow for companionate effects.

As I said, however, I can't make them work. The reason for this seems to have to do with our climate. Easterners enjoy a harsh winter during which their soil freezes for months, breaking all sorts of biological cycles very effectively. Our soil is alive and active year-round. After two or three years in vegetables, my troubles start. The only way I know to break the cycles of insects and other ill effects is to either accept that many kinds of vegetables have become hard to grow or to move the garden to a site that has been in grass for awhile.

The best advice I can give regarding short-term vegetable rotations west of the Cascades is to avoid planting the same species in the same place two years in a row and to plant green manure whenever possible. Cover crops at least rotate part of our gardens out of vegetables over the winter.

COMPANIONATE EFFECTS

I have noticed only a few of the so-called companionate effects that that are supposed to exist between plants, and I haven't been able to usefully sort out most of the effects I have noticed. Frankly, I am very confused about this. I'll share what I've discovered during my twenty-five years of vegetable gardening; maybe you can do better at figuring this out.

Briefly, some plants are supposed to "like" each other, and others are reputed to be "antagonistic." I'm sure you've seen articles about this in garden magazines, with titles like "Apples Love Peaches." The idea is that we should locate some plants among other plants because certain mixtures confuse and deter predatory insects (who hunt by smell), and because some plants help others grow better. Similarly, the gardener should locate some plants well away from others because when grown close together one species may grow fine but will hinder the other, or two species will be mutually antagonistic and neither will do well in proximity.

I once owned the original book on companion planting, written by mystical Steinerian biodynamic gardeners, the sort who interplant the whole garden with garlic and marigolds to keep the insects away. And it works for them. Naturally, I tried out all the relationships they wrote about. I confess that the only one that ever manifested in my garden was the antagonism between alliums and beans. I really did make my beans grow very poorly by planting alternating rows of bulb onions and bush beans across a raised bed. The others? Nothing happened. Everything grew well. Why is that?

I have a mystical, rather Steinerian explanation for all of this. When I interplanted marigolds, I had little problem with many insects. But when I didn't plant marigolds I also had little problem with many insects. That wasn't because marigolds won't chase away bugs. I believe they will chase bugs in your garden *if you believe they will.* Marigolds don't work in my garden because I don't need to believe in marigold magic. I have other protections already working to chase away the bugs. What I have working for me seems a lot easier than interplanting marigolds and lets me grow a lot more food without wasting space growing flowers I don't particularly want anyway. I'll explain my own technique in a bit.

Perhaps you love flowers as much as or more than vegetables. In that case, you should grow marigolds everywhere. Or perhaps you totally and completely love garlic and use it in just about every dish you prepare. In that case you should use garlic to deter insects by sticking a garlic bulb into every nook and cranny and gap in the garden and then, regardless of the difficulty you've created for yourself, carefully work your entire garden plan around this semipermanent vegetable that grows from October until July. And if you believe in garlic it'll probably work for you.

I do believe that there's magic in the garden, whether or not the gardener believes in it or is aware of it. The main magician in my garden is me; you're the magician in your garden. It would be terrific if I were a magician who made everyone's garden grow well. Maybe my desire to become that magician is why I still write these books and once sold seeds.

What is magic? Magic is affecting the physical universe by one's belief or action. We decide that something will be so, and it is. Creation by belief does happen just that simply—only we usually don't know we're doing it. Whatever we deeply believe usually is, but we prefer to also believe that we're the victim of circumstance rather than the creator of reality. So we pretend we can't create by belief.

The difficulty with magic is that to make it work by conscious intention we first have to overcome our disbelief in our own abilities. Magicians must not have any doubt whatsoever that their decision or intention will happen. None. So how do we overcome doubt? The usual way is by casting a spell. We decide that, once we've gone through some elaborate ritual or have obtained some magical object, the ritual or the object does the magic, not us. Underlying the ritual, however, is the certainty of the person. This is the real force at work. What you really believe, is.

I have a firm and unshakable belief that insects and diseases are entitled to their tithe. After all, I am using their space for my garden. Ten percent of what I grow would be cheap rent. Of course, because I am being so generous, they respond in kind and take only 5 percent. Really. I do not slap the wrists of the bugs except in the rare instances when they threaten to take more than 10 percent. So I don't often do much spraying, and I don't need

marigolds. And in those rare instances when I do have to fight for my crop, I prefer to spray something that is otherwise harmless than to give up a lot of valuable space to a bad-smelling flower.

I make yet another kind of magic in my garden, the sort that this book is teaching to you step by step. Honest, "good" magicians have to own what they are trying to affect, or their magic won't work. The reason for this is that ethical beings need to feel righteous about what they're going to do. That's why it's easy to make ourselves sick, but it's hard to heal someone else's body. After all, it's my body, and if anyone has a right to ruin it, it is me.

Let's reflect upon the magical side of making a garden. The first thing we do is take firm ownership of the space. We prove that ownership by changing it around a lot. We fluff up the soil, remove the existing vegetation, and put a fence around it to keep out the deer or the dog. Then we sprinkle the earth with magical powders like lime and complete organic fertilizer. These amount to magic spells, and just like any other spells, they have to be done just so. The right kind and amount of lime. The right powders in our fertilizer. We brew a cauldron of slimy awful stuff called compost and put that into the space, too. *And we decide that doing all of this will make the plants grow well.* So it does.

You may think I am kidding about all of this, running too far with a poetical fantasy. Let me give you a couple of real-life examples from the years I acted as an unpaid extension agent whose territory was the entire maritime

Northwest, which is a lot of what I used to do when I ran Territorial Seed Company.

An old guy from Douglas County, Oregon, once wrote me a long letter demanding that I recommend his favorite organic remedy for root maggots in radishes. He dissolved 1 heaping tablespoonful of genuine sea salt in a gallon of distilled water (it had to be distilled water or rain water, and it had to be sea salt, not mined salt, or it wouldn't work), and when his long row of radishes were at the point in their growth when the roots were just about to thicken and form bulbs (which is just when mother cabbage fly wisely decides to lay her eggs on the soil next to the just-about-to-appear food supply for her offspring), this guy would sprinkle this slightly sea-salty water on the soil around the base of his row of radishes. The result: no maggots, unless he failed to harvest the radishes soon enough. Eventually his insecticide stopped working, and old radishes would get maggoty.

I thanked him sincerely and told him I would try it out and tell others if it worked. Well, here I am, telling others. I am sure his method worked for him because he believed it would, but it didn't work for me. It might work for you, if you have enough faith in it. It's a little like getting into heaven. If you didn't find yourself there, your faith wasn't total enough. If you have any doubts about sea-salt water, I suggest you use parasitic nematodes, wood ashes, spun-fiber row covers, or any of the other more ordinary and sci-entific-sounding remedies I suggest later for radishes. Or try harvesting them promptly before the maggots get into them, which is what most gardeners do, and essentially what this old guy was doing, too.

Here's another example. When Dr. Jim Baggett would conduct eggplant trials in the Willamette Valley—and he always did grow eggplants at the Oregon State University research farm, mainly, I think, because he wanted some to take home—he would grow five or six varieties. All but one of these varie-ties were the earliest available, and they were usually hybrids. He chose early varieties because eggplants have a very hard time han-dling our cool nights. And he used hybrids because this species needs every possible bit of extra vigor to make it. Jim would do every-thing possible to encourage these early egg-plants, including putting black plastic mulch below them to heat their soil a bit. He always included one exception to the early and hybrid varieties: Black Beauty. Black Beauty has been *the* eastern open-pollinated eggplant for a cen-tury or more, sold by every seed house since we Americans started ordering seeds by mail. Black Beauty is a major heat lover. It rarely sets a single fruit in the Willamette Valley, although it will grow leaves. Baggett probably included it because if the summer was so unusually warm that Black Beauty *did* yield, he could throw out the rest of his results with the other eggplant varieties as anomalous.

One spring day I was giving a lecture in Seattle, and a lady in the audience demanded to know why I had such unpleasant things to say about Black Beauty as a varietal choice. She'd had good luck with it. She had just moved to Washington State from semitropical east Texas, and had brought along a family heirloom, treasured seeds of Black Beauty, saved from year to year in her family going back nearly to Noah. She had just transplanted a couple of her homegrown seedlings against the south-facing wall of her urban Seattle house, and they grew fine and yielded okay. And Black Beauty is cheap seed—open-pollinated—while the hybrid varieties I was selling in my seed catalog were mighty spendy in comparison.

Then I confess I did something a little mean. With all the pomp and authority I could muster as "gardener laureate of the maritime Northwest" (as I was known at the time), I informed her of Dr. Baggett's eggplants and of my own eggplant trials conducted at a higher elevation in an even more unfavorable location than Jim's warm, black, sandy loam beside the Willamette River at Corvallis. Then, feeling a little ashamed about having forever ruined her magic, I thought fast on my feet and told her that since she had had such good luck with Black Beauty she should continue to use it. But I wouldn't be at all surprised if she no longer could get any ripe fruit from it.

OTHER COMPANIONATE EFFECTS

Companion planters focus on what is happening *while* two plants are growing in close proximity, but they don't seem to pay attention to what happens *after* plants have grown somewhere. I believe that this aftereffect is one of the underlying reasons for many crop rotations.

In Chapter 2, I briefly mention a most interesting plant behavior—root exudates. Root secretions are a major plant activity.

Krasil'nikov tells of measuring exudates; for every bit of aboveground plant material grown, he found that the roots will secrete about 25 percent of that weight belowground. Root exudates are powerful chemical cocktails with many effects beyond influencing soil microbes. They also serve to help the plant win in its struggle for light, water, and resources, acting as very specific herbicides suppressing competing plants. Their effectiveness depends on the species involved; some species can really cripple certain others with their exudates. For example, onions will thoroughly stunt beans. Some exudates can be positive for another species; I suspect that Douglas fir's exudates facilitate the growth of nitrogen-fixing alder, because alders make firs grow better. Both relationships, cooperative and competitive, happen in the garden.

I believe that the reason I've never been able to observe positive companionate effects and almost never notice the negative ones is complete organic fertilizer. If you make the soil rich enough, the plants mainly respond to your actions. And keep in mind that antagonistic plants in adjoining rows don't necessarily grow *into* each other's root zones; they merely mingle a few roots at the fringes of the other's zone of control. Interplanted or closely planted species may have less subsurface interaction than you might think because their roots don't interpenetrate until both have already grown to substantial size.

There is, however, another, perhaps more important level of companionate effects that happen *after* the crop has grown to maturity and been removed from the space. After a vegetable has owned an area, that soil will be saturated with its exudates. If, for example, you harvest an overwintered onion crop in early June and then immediately follow it with a bush bean crop, the beans won't grow well.

I have observed, sometimes with dismay, that the suppressive effects of root exudates can go on a lot longer than most would think. If you grow onions one year and the next year plant beans there, the beans won't grow as well as they should. In fact, if you grow onions one year and two years later you grow beans there, the beans may still be stunted a bit. It is not difficult for a farmer to recall that a whole field grew onions two years ago, but it gets difficult to keep track of where things were even last year in a vegetable garden.

Realizing this has helped me understand those constant little mysteries. For example, on a 4-foot-wide raised bed, I would sow a 10-foot-long patch of bush beans and they would grow great—except for the last 3 feet of the planting. Digging out my prior year's plan, I would discover that I'd had a crop of scallions on that last 3 feet.

The best way I know of to eliminate most mysterious garden failures is not to grow vegetables for more than three years on any one plot, field, or garden site. Sir Albert Howard knew this. I suggest you reread the quotation that introduces this chapter. An allotment, by the way, is a community vegetable garden plot.

Long-Term Rotations

The usual reasons given for garden crop rotations have to do with stopping buildups of soil-borne diseases and predatory insects. Moving the garden a short distance may help with soil diseases, but it does little good with most insect predators, because the insects, overwintering or sheltering in the surrounding vegetation or in the old garden site's soil, merely move into the new site. What helps most with insect pests is making the plants so healthy that the bugs don't bug them.

When handling one widely found bug, however, the "healthy plant" strategy doesn't work so well. Most Oregonians and many Washingtonians are troubled by a minute soil animal called the symphylan. The biggest trouble the symphylan presents is that our region's gardeners rarely know what they're being troubled by and have no idea why their gardens grow so badly. I discuss this pest here, and not in Chapter 8, because the most practical and effective control I have found for this horrible pest is the long-term rotation, which basically is a form of garden planning.

Symphylans are given little more than a casual mention in even the most thorough eastern garden pest guides, but where you find them eating vegetable roots, these minuscule critters cause as much loss as all the other pests combined. The average gardener starts out with a few hugely successful years while, unnoticed, symphylan populations build up to plague levels. Problems then begin to show up, but they are usually misattributed to bad seed, poor soil, or mysterious diseases. Most gardeners come to think symphylan-susceptible species are hard to grow. Many with low failure tolerances give up gardening altogether. Few know what really happened.

Luckily, I was warned about symphylans from the beginning. In the late 1970s, there was a pretty good garden store in Cottage Grove, Oregon, where I bought supplies. The owner told this enthusiastic organic gardener who had just arrived in nearby Lorane, "You'll have a great garden over there for a year or two. Then things will start to go wrong. There's a little soil pest we have here in Oregon called the symphylan, and you won't be able to handle it with anything you organic gardeners know about. The only thing that will kill symphylans is Dyfonate."

He pointed out a large chemical sack on a high shelf above the window. "All the farmers around here use it before growing vegetables or strawberries. They couldn't harvest anything without it. Now, you can't legally buy Dyfonate—it takes a restricted pesticide applicator's license, and you've got to go to school for it. But I got one, and I'll be happy to supply you with Dyfonate and explain how to use it." (These days even farmers with restricted-use pesticide applicator's licenses can't use Dyfonate—it's been withdrawn from sale as too dangerous.)

"No thanks!" I said emphatically, with all my organic certainty (which I still had in those innocent days of foolish youth). "Any pest that comes along I can handle without chemicals!"

I eventually proved myself right, but not as right as I would have liked to have been. I did discover organic controls for symphylans, but I can't say I'm happy with what I've learned.

Imagine a $3/16$-inch-long, flattened, skinny tube of white or pale brownish-pink, flexible, hair-thin wire, multiply jointed like a crawdad's tail and fringed with twelve pairs of little legs, a pair coming out of each joint. The front joint is the head, with two long, thin antennae attached. That's the symphylan, shown at the beginning of Chapter 8, on page 213. This tiny, shy soil dweller moves fast and doesn't like light. Its speed and small size make it hard to spot. It lives for several years, breeds relatively slowly, and can move as deep as 5 feet into the soil or lurk near the surface. Like almost all other soil animals, the symphylan cannot survive in dry soil and must seek moisture. A single individual will generally confine itself to an area with a radius of only 15 or 20 feet. Symphylans are so small, so fast, and so well camouflaged that several dozen of them can be hiding in a shovelful of soil and yet only someone intently looking for them may ever realize their presence. To be sure you've got symphylan problems, put a shovelful of soil on a sheet of cardboard or newspaper and carefully pick through it. Another way is to put a recently cut potato into the soil an inch or so deep and dig it up the next day; the symphylans will be attracted to the potato and can be counted. An OSU entomologist I pestered during the early 1980s, when I was trying to figure out how to handle them, said ten or more symphylans per shovelful is about the level at which they become a pest.

A few predators somewhat limit their population, but not very effectively, and there's no easy management strategy I know of that both suits the home garden and can enhance predator populations enough to matter.

Symphylans eat two things: rotting organic matter and tender root tips, especially the roots emerging from sprouting seeds. Thus, their food is mainly found in the surface layers. That's why I believe their population is effectively reduced when unirrigated soils thoroughly dry out every summer, forcing the symphylans to seek moisture deep in the earth where there is little organic matter to feed them. Their greatest populations are found in clayey soils that hold more moisture through the summer and in which the solid soil structure maintains runways for them to disperse deeper into the soil. Just about the only soils up and down the West Coast where symphylans won't be found are very sandy ones that dry out thoroughly and deeply and then, once desiccated, sort of crumble internally instead of maintaining a runway structure.

Symphylans prefer the rootlets of some vegetables over others, and I've observed that they do the most stunting of plants, species, and varieties with the least vigorous root systems. One of the reasons that Territorial Seed Company was so successful when I ran the trials ground was that the variety trials were conducted on symphylan-infested ground, so I tended to choose varieties that were more resistant to this pest. The region's gardeners did not appreciate this aspect of why Territorial seeds grew better, but much of the reason was found in the nature of our varieties' root systems.

Symphylan problems show up after a new garden plot has been used for a few very successful years: All of a sudden, spinach, beets, strawberries, and cauliflower won't grow well. Cauliflower is stunted, spinach and beets germinate but fail to grow, and then much of the stand that did sprout disappears. What's happening is that the root-grazing symphylans are turning vegetables into bonsai miniatures, pruning their rootlets almost as fast as they appear. With heavier infestations, spinach and beets don't even seem to germinate because the symphylans consume the root tips as they emerge from the sprouting seeds. Once I broadcast an entire pound of highly vigorous beet seed into a heavily infested raised bed, and not a single seed emerged. Heavier infestations stunt even more vigorous brassicas, like broccoli and cabbage, and may affect peppers, beans, celery, and a wide range of other species. Tomatoes, carrots, corn, parsnips, parsley, lettuce, and members of the squash family seem relatively immune to all but the worst infestations. The more immune species are the ones regional gardeners widely consider easy to grow.

When I first discovered them wrecking things in my trial grounds, I spent a lot of time engaged in serious hoe-leaning, staring off into space while meditating on the symphylan. I imagined that a hundred years ago, when virtually all of the maritime Northwest was forest, symphylans lived in the moist, rotting forest duff, munching humus and occasional root tips. The woody humus wasn't very palatable and the root tips were few and not too tasty. There weren't many symphs. When homesteaders cleared the forest, planted fields, and made pastures, the level of organic matter in the soil dropped markedly, further reducing the symphylan population and somewhat increasing their appetite for root tips. However, most pasture grasses and weeds aren't particularly appealing to symphylans, and neither are the roots of most grains (which are also grasses). Nor are fava beans, as I found by experiment. (I describe a useful symphylan-suppressing rotation using fava beans in the "Green Manures and Field Crops" section of Chapter 9.) Another thing that probably depressed their population was that the now-grassy land may have dried out more thoroughly in summer than it had when covered with old-growth forest.

Common gardeners' lore about the symphylan goes, "They weren't in this place until I brought them in with that load of manure. Now they're a plague." That's probably not quite right: The symphylans weren't brought to the field with the manure; the manure fed them. Upping the level of decaying crude organic matter does feed the symphylan population and lets it increase somewhat. But it's when the farmer or gardener also begins to irrigate a piece of ground instead of allowing the top few feet to get thoroughly dried out that the soil ecology is really thrown out of whack; then the symphylan is permitted to feed and breed much more effectively. Which brings me to the first technique for handling symphylans that I worked out.

Leaning on my hoe, I was regarding a stunted cauliflower trial, maybe fifty eight-week-old transplants, six each of eight or nine different varieties. All of the varieties were alike in refusing to grow at all. (If only one of them *had* grown well while the others hadn't, I would have been seeing a rare and much-hoped-for event on a trials ground.) I dug up one seedling and found a dozen symphs working that single fragile rootball. So I imagined that field from a symphylan's viewpoint. The nasty gardener (that was me, folks) had tried to starve them all. He had recently tilled in all growing vegetation and then planted rows of seeds or set out rows of transplants, each row surrounded by much bare soil. Naturally, every symphylan from many feet away flocked to the few little growing plants and nibbled away, wreaking havoc. Maybe, I mused, if I fed them something else they would like instead of forcing them to eat my trials, they'd eat my vegetables less. How about buckwheat? That's sweet and tender, the seed is cheap and comes up fast, and, most important, buckwheat is a very easily removed weed—touch it with a sharp hoe and it's gone. So I grabbed a 5-pound bag of buckwheat seed from the seed room, scattered it thickly between the rows, rototilled it in shallowly, and sprinkler irrigated. Three days later the field was carpeted with buckwheat seedlings. One day after that all of the little stunted cauliflower plants started growing fast and lustily.

Thus came about symphylan solution number one: Sow buckwheat thickly. Wait five or six days. Once the field or bed is covered with little buckwheat plants, you can hoe out 4- or 5-inch-wide strips to plant seed in, or make foot-diameter holes in the ground cover to set out transplants. As the vegetables grow, the buckwheat can gradually be hoed back. As the vegetables develop large root systems and the buckwheat gradually disappears, the vegetables can withstand symphylan predation with only minor stunting. I used that solution on my trials ground for two years.

Three big problems make buckwheat an impractical symphylan solution: It does require very patient, precise, and thorough hoeing to prevent it from swamping the vegetables; it's not at all frost-tolerant; and it won't grow well after midsummer, when the days begin to shorten. Buckwheat is plantable only from the last frost until mid-July. For spring and late-summer symphylan trap crops, I suppose one could use cheap radish seed, the kind sold for sprouting in health food stores. Radish is also easy to hoe out, if you catch it before it bolts.

"Building up the soil" with heavy applications of manure or compost and then watering the garden begets a plague of symphylans in a few years. But average gardeners never realize the culprit. They figure that what's needed to cure their troubles is to further build up their soil. So they'll manure and manure and manure, hoping to build a high enough level of fertility and tilth and mistakenly coming to believe that their soil must be so bad it takes enormous building up to grow right. This handling works somewhat; some "easy-to-grow" vegetables (meaning those with symphylan-resistant root systems) do grow okay in this situation.

Building higher and higher levels of organic matter is an imperfect symphylan solution because it still leaves gardeners believing that some vegetables are nearly impossible for them to grow. It is also a harmful practice

in terms of the nutritional content of your vegetables. I've come to believe that in symphylan country, when it comes to manure or compost, least is best. If I add as little compost and manure as possible (while still incorporating enough to give the plants their needed phytamins and keep the soil in good heart) instead of as much as seems to do any good, I can use a plot for three and perhaps four years without building the symphlan population too high for comfort. And even when the organic matter is restricted, rotation out of vegetables and out of irrigation can eventually become essential—unless, that is, you consider a garden to be nothing but tomatoes, sweet corn, carrots, bush beans, and a bit of lettuce—all species the symphylans won't damage too much.

Perversely, dealing with symphylans is an area where the organic gardener has the edge over one habituated to chemicals, because garden centers can't sell home gardeners any chemical that is effective against symphylans. Diazinon, which we can buy, will not kill them, though one talented gardener told me it will make them unhappy enough to reduce predation a bit if used repeatedly in very high doses—but who would want to eat stuff that had been drenched in diazinon at levels far higher than recommended?

One organic control that does work effectively enough to permit growing even spinach in infested ground is finely ground diatomaceous earth, which is rock formed from the remains of single-celled marine algae. The natural unprocessed type, often sold under the brand name Perma Guard, is composed of microscopic needle-pointed diatom shells made of silica, a glasslike substance. When hard-shelled critters like the symphylan and other insects get these sharp particles caught in the folds of their joints, they are punctured, leak their vital fluids, and die.

There are two problems with working diatomaceous earth into the planting rows or around transplants. One is that the stuff is fairly spendy. It takes a big double handful to protect a transplant and a thick dusting raked in along a seed row, so it must be purchased in at least 50-pound quantities to even begin to be cost-effective. The other is that the clay in the soil immediately begins to coat the sharp points. Perma Guard will work for only several months before it is deactivated. Any gardener who even suspects the presence of symphylans should buy a small quantity of Perma Guard and blend a very liberal quantity of it into what will become the root system of one or two plants and see what happens. You may be amazed to discover how much symphylans have been thwarting your ambitions.

I know of only two general strategies to reduce symphylan problems in a cost-effective or effort-effective manner: (1) long rotations out of vegetables and (2) using a minimum of compost and manure instead of the maximum while using complete organic fertilizer to supply fertility. If several years of irrigation and composting have made symphylans a problem, the difficulty is easily cured by allowing the garden to return to unirrigated pasture grass for several years. This means a two-field rotation lasting about six years: three years in grass and three in vegetables. If you have enough ground, you could even have a three-field rotation: four years in grass and two years in vegetables. Rotating in this way also greatly reduces or virtually eliminates the need to make compost and import organic matter because the grass portion of the rotation will naturally and effortlessly rebuild the levels of organic matter. Importing less organic matter will also enhance the nutritional content of the food you raise. Unfortunately, long grass rotations are not acceptable to most urban gardeners working in very limited space unless they have a very large yard or are willing to garden the front yard for a couple of years and then the backyard—and then have a brown lawn in summer.

Locating the Perennials

Perennial vegetables don't adapt as easily to rotational schemes. However, if you are going to use a long fallow in grass, most of them will cope with, and some will actually benefit from, being transplanted into new soil every few years, and all of them will tolerate division or transplanting if it's done in mid-autumn or early in spring.

By perennials I mean globe artichokes, horseradish, and culinary herbs (most of them are perennials), as well as the small fruits typically grown in the vegetable garden—strawberries and the cane berries. Gooseberries don't move so well and need a permanent location.

Parsley is a biennial, and coriander (cilantro) and basil are annuals: These should be considered ordinary vegetables.

Think it over when planning your garden; you might prefer to set aside an area that is permanent, that doesn't form part of any rotation.

Mixing Varieties to Extend the Harvest

When I started doing variety trials, I quickly discovered that some varieties matured much faster than others. It occurred to me that since the greatest part of the cost of a small-sized seed packet was the handling and packeting, not the seed itself, I could save the customer a great deal of money if I sold lettuce, cauliflower, and broccoli variety mixtures. These proved to be quite popular.

Other seed companies around the nation saw what Territorial was doing and also began selling seed mixes. These days I never discard an old packet of lettuce, broccoli, cauliflower, or Brussels sprout seed unless I am absolutely certain the packet is quite dead. I keep a spring broccoli blend packet and a fall broccoli blend packet, the same for cauliflower, a Brussels sprout blend packet, and a spring lettuce blend packet plus a fall/winter lettuce packet. And, of course, the numerous overwintering cauliflower varieties with their very specific and tightly grouped heading dates work marvelously for the home gardener when sown as a mixture.

If you work with blends, you'll soon see why they're popular. Getting seeds to come up in hot weather often requires very close attention. If a single sowing will feed you for six to eight weeks instead of two to three weeks, you don't have to sow so often. Another reason for the success of varietal blends is that some are going to handle that season's unusual weather better than others. And some varieties will handle one soil type better than others—some like sandy soil, some actually prefer reasonably clayey ground, some will tolerate clay, and some won't at all. If you sow a blend, you are much more likely to have at least some of what you plant end up growing quite well.

One caution: There is a wide difference in vigor between varieties and between different production years and vintages of seed. So when thinning a blend, try to retain a mix of vigor levels, or you can may up with only the one remarkably vigorous variety. However, very weak seedlings should always be thinned out. It is much easier to thin lettuce blends, as the different varieties vary in color and leaf shape.

Increasing Plant Spacing to Extend the Harvest

Once an area of soil has been fully occupied by a plant's roots, it generally can't be used very well by another. In fact, a plant even has difficulty rooting more thickly into an area of soil where it has already put roots, as though one purpose of its own exudates is to encourage the plant to extend new roots into territory it hasn't yet occupied.

When vegetables stop growing, they stop producing new fruit. Edible roots like beets and carrots get woody, tough, and tasteless and soon aren't even worth harvesting. For most vegetables to continue growing vigorously, they must have room to expand their root systems. With species like ordinary kohlrabi or turnips, having a bit more growing space keeps them tender enough to eat a week or three longer than otherwise. With roots like carrots and beets, it seems that so long as they can continue to grow, no matter how large they've already gotten, they continue to be sweet and tender and worth eating. I've grown carrots a foot apart that reached a pound each and were still delicious.

Broccoli is another vegetable that really benefits from having more growing room. On 18-inch centers, broccoli usually makes one decent central flower and a few side shoots. On 24-inch centers, the same varieties make a much bigger central flower and many more side shoots of much larger size. On 30-inch centers, a given variety of broccoli won't make a main central flower any larger than it would at 24-inch spacing, but if side-dressed a few times most varieties will make many more big, tender, usable side shoots than they do at 24-inch spacing. They'll do this because they have the root room to continue to grow.

Winter gardeners should consider spacing their plants farther apart, because being able to keep growing through winter (should there be enough sun and warmth to allow it) can make all the difference in a crop's survival and/or edibility. Busy gardeners with nine-to-five jobs or without much spare gardening time should also consider using increased spacing to reduce the number of times they have to sow things. If you'd like to experiment with this technique, start with the spacings suggested in Chapter 9 and double the square footage I recommend for each plant. How much farther apart than that you can go depends on the variety, your soil, and too many other factors to make a solid list; you'll have to develop your own feel for this technique. To appreciate what it means to double growing room, consider that a plant on 18-inch centers has 18 by 18 inches of growing room, or 324 square inches. Double that would be about 650 square inches, or about 25½ by 25½ inches. There's no need to be that precise, however. The table on the next page, "Degree to Which Vegetables Can Benefit from Increased Spacing," will help you choose plants on which to try this technique.

Gardening Under Cover to Extend the Season

There are lots of books about cloches and cold frames. Most of them were written for the eastern gardener and do not take into account the facts of light and temperature in the maritime Northwest. One book that does is called *Gardening Under Cover*, by Bill

Degree to Which Vegetables Can Benefit from Increased Spacing

Great Benefit	Some Benefit	Likes Crowds
Carrots	Swiss chard	Bush peas
Beets	Onions, bulb	
Spinach	Radishes	
Kohlrabi	Turnips	
Broccoli	Arugula (rocket)	
Indeterminate tomatoes	Cauliflower	
Summer squash	Winter squash	
Rutabaga	Determinate tomatoes	
Corn salad	Peppers	
Scallions	Kale	
Pole beans	Bush beans	
Leeks		
Celery (celeriac)		
Pole peas		

Head (see the bibliography). I can't duplicate Bill's book in this one, nor can I provide construction details for cold frames and cloches in the allowable space. So if you need help with building or if the data that follows seems a bit vague, your best bet is Bill Head's book.

Let's first briefly look at and then dismiss solar greenhouses designed for the East. Where winter is really winter, cold frames and greenhouses demand maximum insulation; sometimes thermal masses are used to store heat accumulated during sunny periods. In the East the winter sun shines frequently, so heat loss can be minimized by putting glass only in the south wall and in the front half of the roof while heavily insulating the opaque north, east, and west walls and the rear part of the roof. Add a north wall full of black-painted water barrels to soak up extra heat when the sun shines and reradiate it at night or on cloudy days, and you've got the classic solar greenhouse.

Solar greenhouses designed this way are not workable in the maritime Northwest. I know several people who enthusiastically built one and then found it a better place to store stuff than to grow plants. To understand why, consider this: When the sun shines on a clear day, most light comes directly from the sun, and so a south-facing window allows virtually all available light to enter. In a snowy climate with an average of twenty sunny winter days a month, it's reasonable to sacrifice a little bit of light accumulation on cloudy days for insulation and heat retention. And where the sun shines regularly, bedding plants can be grown in a south or west window.

In the maritime Northwest, we're lucky even to see the winter sun a few days each month, much less have it shine all day. In fact, when I've traveled and people have asked me to describe the climate of western Oregon, I tell them that we see the sun on only five days during the months of January and February, ten days in March, fifteen in April, twenty in May, twenty-five in June, thirty in July and August, twenty-five in September, twenty in October, fifteen in November, and only ten in December. Isn't that so?

When it's heavily overcast, light comes to the earth with equal intensity from every direction at once, but the overall intensity of the light that does filter through the cloud cover is not nearly as strong as direct sunlight. Thus, west of the Cascades, a solar greenhouse that allows light to enter only through a south-facing window fails to grow plants during the crucial winter and early spring months. In our mild rainy region, we need a greenhouse that captures every bit of available light, not one that preserves heat at any cost.

Sometimes I dream of such a greenhouse. It would be a wonderful luxury, and someday when I'm rich I'm going to have one built for me. It will be 100 feet long and 12 or 14 feet wide, with a solar- and electric- or gas-heated competition lap pool the full length of one side of it and a gorgeous salad garden full of radishes and the most delicate lettuces, spinaches, and other cool-season greens down the other. And in the summer, I'll use that humid tropical environment to grow okra and peppers and other . . . well, back to reality.

Cloches and cold frames are compromise greenhouses, too short for a person to walk in but very inexpensive to build. And they have some advantages beyond low cost.

Although it's very relaxing to step through a door from a drizzly winter's day straight into the tropics, greenhouses have one serious liability: They don't retain much heat at night. During the worst of winter, much warmer nighttime temperatures can be had simply by shortening the greenhouse from 8 feet high to 1 foot high and walking around the outside of it instead of working inside of it. With only 1 foot of air to heat instead of 8, in this "green house" the soil becomes an effective heat sink. The greenhouse has become a cold frame.

My garden cold frames are constructed of Cuprinol-treated 2-by-10 fir planks with 4-by-4 corner braces and are about 10 feet long by 4 feet wide, covered with recycled glass windows in wooden sashes. (Warning: Some wood preservatives are toxic to plants, so use only a copper naphthenate–based treatment on cold frames and compost boxes.) If these frames ever rotted out, I'd make new ones out of 1-by-10 boards with 2-by-4 corners, because it takes two people to move my current frames. Like almost all carpenters, I tend to overbuild. But since they get a new Cuprinol treatment every three years or so, they're not likely to rot in my lifetime.

Nine inches of side height is sufficient for most winter greens. The frames should ideally slope slightly to the south, allowing in a bit more light and encouraging rain to run off the glass, but I'm a poor carpenter, so instead of sloping the boxes by cutting the side boards on a diagonal and doubling up two 8-inch boards

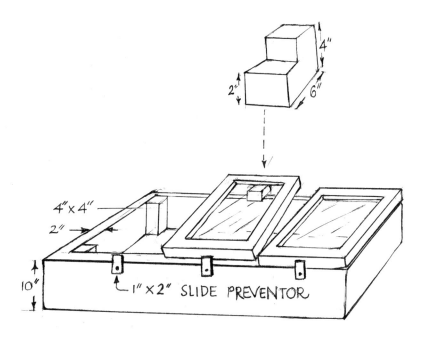

on the back side (which would have to become the north wall), I sloped the entire bed by raking the south side 2 inches lower than the north side. Opened sashes are prevented from sliding off by pieces of 1-by-2 nailed on the south side so that they stick up a few inches. The windows are held open by an adjustable block of 4-by-4 inserted opposite the "slide preventer." There is no weatherstripping, no crosspiece to rest the windows on for a tighter seal, no attempt whatsoever to fill the cracks. But the frames work, permitting maximum light entry while keeping off the rain and raising nighttime temperatures a few degrees. When the winter sun shines, I prop the windows up about 8 inches. On nights when frost threatens, I close them. During long rainy spells, I leave one window cracked open an inch or two to ventilate the box and prevent excess humidity and rot. Almost anyone could design unnecessarily better frames. (The illus-

tration above shows what I am describing.)

I mainly use these frames for extending the salad green season—two frames are sown in September and the other two in early to mid-October. The September-sown frames are harvested during December and January; the October-sown frames are cut in February and March. When the two September frames are empty, around the end of January, they are resown with another batch of salad greens that are ready to harvest in late April into late May, a good month earlier than would be possible from the earliest unprotected sowing. When the October-sown frames are through, it's mid-April and greens can be seeded directly outside without protection. It's that simple—quality lettuce, spinach, and endive salads all winter instead of an entire season spent exercising my jaw muscles chewing tough cabbage and kale.

In spring, the gardener can advance the

season by about six weeks by using a crude frame or cloche. What could not be safely planted outside until June 1 can be planted into a cloche on April 15. This little bit of effort can make a huge difference in how long one gets those hot-weather vegetables that make gardening gardening.

For example, at frosty Lorane, Oregon, I transplanted six-week-old tomato seedlings into the frost protection of a tunnel cloche around mid-April. These plants laughed at late frosts and chilly nights. By about mid-June the vines had sprawled so much that they were pushing against the walls of the cloche, but by then there was no frost danger, so I just removed the plastic and let them proceed. They begin ripening heavily by early July. At mild Elkton, where tomatoes, with some risk, can be set out without protection in mid-April, I've transplanted into a cloche on March 10 and had my first ripe tomatoes in early June. Summer squash, direct-seeded into a cloche on April 15, started yielding zucchini in mid-June.

Melons and cucumbers get a good early start in low wood-box cold frames like the ones I use in winter, but for forcing tomatoes and summer squash in spring, I switch to a taller and more fragile design. Low box frames have two liabilities. Although being closer to the ground with less air keeps them warm at night, wood-box frames heat up too much when the sun shines strongly, and they have to be opened wide. On very warm sunny days, the sashes may have to be removed entirely to avoid frying the plants. Also, some species I want to protect in spring need more head-room. So I make tunnel cloches (shown in the illustration on page 239, in Chapter 9).

The tunnel cloche is, if anything, simpler than a wooden box, though in certain ways it's less convenient to use. Basically it's a sheet of clear polyethylene stretched over supporting hoops bent to make a long half-cylinder. The edges of the plastic are held down with soil, and the ends may be open or closed. Tunnel cloches range from little tubes a foot high and a foot wide, supported by stout wire hoops stuck in the ground, to the kind I use, which are supported by 10-foot lengths of ½-inch galvanized thinwall conduit purchased from an electrical supply company and bent into giant croquet hoops with a borrowed pipe bender. The resulting arch is about 3½ feet tall in the center and matches my raised beds, being 4 feet wide at the bottom. Similar but short-lived supports can be made by twisting hoops of ½-inch or ¾-inch plastic pipe and sticking the ends in the ground; I prefer the greater initial expense because galvanized steel pipe will last as many years as I'm willing to keep the ends painted.

Every few years I buy a 100-foot-long roll of 10-foot-wide clear poly sheeting to skin the cloches. I erect the cloche by pushing both ends of each supporting arch about a foot into the ground, each arch about 4 feet apart down a 4-foot-wide raised bed. If your beds are wider or narrower, bend the hoops accordingly. Since the conduit comes in 10-foot lengths and the arches are pushed into the soil a foot, a 10-foot-wide sheet of plastic leaves about a foot of loose plastic along each side to anchor thoroughly with slabs of compacted earth shoveled up from the paths. I allow some plastic sheeting to drape over the ends and anchor it with a few 18- to 24-inch-long chunks of 4-by-4. The end plastic can be folded back over the top and anchored at the sides with those same 4-by-4s to keep the tube open on sunny days. Early in the season or when a late frost threatens, I close the ends in late afternoon. Otherwise, I leave them open all night. Even with both ends open, daytime temperatures inside the tunnel run 10° to 15°F higher than outside; nighttime temperatures hold 2° to 3°F higher. When it starts to be summery, the cloche tends to get too hot, so along the top I cut foot-diameter holes in the plastic, one between each pair of hoop supports. I leave the tunnel over the plants as long as possible—right up to the first harvest if I can. To keep the tunnel free of weeds, or to thin, you'll have to either crawl through on hands and knees a couple of times before the plants get too big or pull up the plastic on one side, tidy up the bed, and then reanchor the plastic. To water the tunnel, spray from the ends with hose and nozzle every few days, or install a line of microsprinklers in the cloche when it's first set up.

It's easy to grow in frames and cloches. Prepare the bed and fertilize as usual; if the soil gets too dry in winter, take off the sashes on a mild, drizzly day. You'll enjoy autumn salads all winter, spring crops a lot earlier, and summer vegetables four or five weeks longer each year. The table on page 128, "Year-Round Cloche/Frame Calendar," will help you know when it is best sow seeds under protection.

Winter Gardening

Surviving maritime winters can be tough for the hardiest of species and varieties. Low light levels and low temperatures, even if above freezing, slow or stop growth, while cellular damage caused by repetitive frosts and pounding rain mounts up. Most plants that winter over have food reserves stored in stem or root, and they'll use some of these reserves to get through January and February. A really dark, rainy winter, even one on the mild side, can gradually break down the plants' resistance, until they succumb to one of the many rots and molds that thrive under damp, cool conditions.

Overwintering endive provides a good example of how mild winter weather can be harder on the plant than clear, frosty weather. When the overall winter is dryish, or dry and cold, the hardier varieties of endive survive handily and tolerate freezes to 7°F (or lower sometimes) without damage. However, when the winter is rainy and mild, moisture is constantly trapped in the dense rosette of thin leaves, and the head slowly rots down to a nubbin. The plant may die before growing conditions improve. (This makes endive an excellent candidate for a cold frame, because merely keeping off the pounding rain permits it to overwinter reliably no matter how cold it gets some nights.) Winter cabbage varieties, on the other hand, have thick, waxy leaves that easily shed water, and the heads are wrapped in many protective outer layers that keep the rain away from the vital core. It doesn't really matter to the gardener (who just peels them

Year-Round Cloche/Frame Calendar

Planting Date	Crops	Harvest Period
September	Loose-leaf lettuce, mustard greens, spinach, endive	November to January
October	Loose-leaf lettuce, mustard greens, spinach, endive	February to April
February	Loose-leaf lettuce, mustard greens, spinach, peas	Mid-April to May
March	Lettuce, mustard greens, kohlrabi, spinach, broccoli, cauliflower, cabbage, beets, chard, carrots	Mid-May to June
April 15 to May 15	Tomato transplants, bush beans, squash	June to the end of summer
Late May	Pepper and eggplant transplants, melons, cucumbers	July to the end of summer

Note: This rough schedule is for the Willamette Valley, Oregon, garden. North of Longview, Washington, along the coast, and at higher Oregon elevations, spring dates might be too early, fall dates a bit late. South of Drain, Oregon, spring dates might be a bit too late, fall dates a bit early.

off before using) or to the cabbages if a few outer layers rot.

Plants deal with freezing by using a combination of two tricks. The first is to increase the amount of sugars and other substances in their cells. This sugar solution acts like antifreeze. It also makes many species taste much sweeter after they've been well frosted a few times. That's why California-grown kale and Brussels sprouts are pale imitations of the real thing. The second chill-handling mechanism is to actually pump water out of the cell as the temperature approaches freezing, so that when the cell does freeze it won't burst its walls. However, handling freezing and thawing takes work on the part of the plant; this intense effort depletes food reserves as the plant adjusts and readjusts.

The ability to handle frost is, to a degree, "learned": The plant's ability improves each time it is exposed to freezing. And the ability varies from variety to variety. For example, most varieties of succulent, tender, thin-leafed cabbage contain too much moisture to be really freeze-tolerant; their tender cell walls are weak. Tender varieties will die if they freeze solid. (It takes only a few hours of very intense cold [below 10°F] or a week or more of constant slightly subfreezing weather to freeze a big cabbage head solid.) Logically you'd expect freeze-hardy varieties to have tough, dry leaves, and they do.

The winter tolerance of each vegetable species varies, and the tolerance of each variety within each species varies. Because a number of factors are involved, it is not possible to state that any species or variety is hardy to any exact temperature. For example, the December 1983 freeze suddenly dropped temperatures to 7°F at Lorane, after a long, mild fall. Although conditions remained subfreezing for three and a half days, the soil was very warm going into the cold snap and did not freeze. Yet varieties that in previous years had survived lows of 3°F or that had only 50 percent losses at 6°F were totally destroyed. Why? Because in that frostless and sunny autumn, the plants had grown lushly and were tender right up into December. They were not nearly as hardened off as they would have been if they'd experienced a lot of chilly rain and frequent lighter overnight frosts. Only a few individuals of one extremely tough cabbage variety survived that freeze, and we ate supermarket salads the rest of the winter. That same year, the Vegetable Crops Research Station at Agassiz, British Columbia, experienced much frosty autumn weather and even a bit of snow during November. Most of its pre-toughened winter trials survived the December freeze, with somewhat colder temperatures than we had at Lorane.

Winters in a few maritime Northwest locations are usually so severe that year-round gardening is nearly impossible. For example, folks in the very northwestern corner of Washington State, in Whatcom County, can almost count on savage blasts of arctic air flowing down the Frasier Canyon, wiping out much of their garden most winters. Similarly, people gardening at elevations much higher than 1,000 feet may frequently experience low temperatures that will kill winter vegetables. At 900 feet, most of my Lorane garden was frozen out about once every three winters.

I calculate that Willamette Valley gardeners can count on winter survival about five years in six; from the Yoncalla Valley to the south, gardeners can pretty much assume successful

winter survival. It gets a lot more frosty in Washington State once you go north of Longview (the Columbia River). Proximity to the sea also changes one's odds greatly. Gardens close to the coast or to Puget Sound usually have milder winters, while farther inland or at a higher elevation, winter survival can be dicey. Washington microclimate differences are very pronounced: Only a few miles south of frigid Whatcom County, the very protected Skagit Valley offers excellent and generally safe winter gardening. That mildness, combined with cool summers that don't degrade the seed vigor of certain species, has caused many international vegetable seed companies to flock there.

Local soil conditions can make winter gardening difficult or impossible once the rains start up in earnest. When root systems remain waterlogged for days at a time, they are unable to take in oxygen. Plants then sicken and die. Large areas of the Willamette Valley have poor drainage, and I've noticed the same problem on the bottomlands between Monroe and Everett, Washington, and along the floodplains of various coastal rivers in both Oregon and Washington. In the Willamette Valley, the cause is a thin layer of gooey, fine clay 2 to 3 feet below the otherwise decent topsoil. When heavy winter rains fall for days on end, that clay layer in the southern Willamette Valley acts like the plug in a bathtub, and water fills pore spaces until the surface goes underwater. Huge, shallow lakes form and then take a day or two to disappear after the rains stop.

The only crop species that can tolerate waterlogged roots for days at a time have been flax and grass. The flax industry withered with the onset of synthetic fibers after World War II, and now farmers on these poorly drained soils grow grass seed instead. If you're considering the purchase of a rural homestead surrounded by grass seed farms, or even a city house in west Eugene or other areas where grass seed used to be produced, think twice if you're a serious year-round gardener. (After they dry out in spring, though, grass seed soils do grow good summer gardens.)

Poor winter drainage can sometimes be improved simply by making raised beds and using the surrounding paths as drainage ditches. Other situations may call for deep ditching and perforated drain pipes. Gardeners with severe problems can obtain a free consultation with the Soil Conservation Service.

Areas with high winds can also be difficult spots for gardens, winter or summer. Fencing and windbreaks can help; in fact, windbreaks aren't a bad idea for any garden, especially in winter. Lowering the wind speed raises the temperature considerably and may permit plants to make a little more growth, repairing the damage done by weeks of pounding rain and hard frost.

WINTER YIELDS

The simple fact that light makes plants grow means that if you wish to produce the same quantity of winter vegetables as you do of summer vegetables, the winter garden must occupy more space than the summer garden. From June through September, relatively small plots will totally overwhelm the kitchen: A 100-square-foot bed of summer squash fills a 5-gallon bucket just about every day; a bed half that size of mixed lettuce varieties yields a half dozen nice heads every other day for three or more weeks; and 100 square feet of bush beans produces 5 gallons every few days. A dozen pole-trained tomato vines on less than 50 square feet will keep a family supplied for months unless huge amounts are to be canned. In fact, unless a lot of summer food is to be preserved or the family is extremely fond of winter squash or space-wasting sweet corn, 1,000 square feet of well-grown, fertile summer garden will likely yield more than enough for even a totally vegetarian kitchen.

The winter garden is another matter, however. Since the vegetables don't grow much from mid-October until early April, what you've grown by the time winter arrives is essentially what you'll have for the whole winter—the static vegetables are in cold storage outside, awaiting harvest. Each winter, my family goes through a 100-square-foot bed of salad carrots (we could juice five times that amount if I were willing to grow that many) and 50 square feet or row-feet each of parsnips, rutabagas, and leeks. We use half a 100-square-foot bed of endive. One hundred square feet of lettuce is usually all cut between November and the time it freezes out in December. I grow 50 square feet of overwintering broccoli and at least 100 square feet of overwintering bulb onions (and scallions), plus 100 square feet each of kale (twenty-five big plants), Brussels sprouts (twenty-five big plants), fall and winter cabbage (twenty-five big cabbages), overwintering cauliflower (yielding maybe forty between March and

May if they all head nicely), and a whole bed of winter spinach. Add enough space for miscellaneous items like rocket, sorrel, parsley, Chinese cabbage, fennel, and so on, and a few cold frames to extend the use of lettuce in salads, and it amounts to another 2,000-plus square feet of growing bed, not considering paths. My family does not eat sweet corn or much winter squash, so the total vegetable portion of my personal garden approaches 4,000 square feet.

This section on winter gardening is located here in the garden planning chapter because winter gardening is not a special kind of gardening. Having a winter garden is mainly a matter of planning to have one and then putting in the right seeds at the right time. Most of the varieties needed *are* rather special; they're especially hardy and often not available in eastern seed catalogs. Besides our local seed companies, these varieties can be found in British catalogs. Chapter 9 contains full details on planting dates and varieties to use.

There are, however, a couple of general techniques that, if you keep them in mind, help the winter garden through.

AIR CIRCULATION

Earlier I mentioned that mold and mildew can be just as dangerous, if not more so, to winter survival as frost. If you spread your plants out just a bit farther than you might during the summer, so that when fully grown they do not quite touch, they'll dry off better and survive longer. In the same way, when tender, heading species like lettuce encounter an unusually warm winter and grow too much too soon, their leaves tend to wrap themselves into heads and trap humidity. I've lost more winter lettuce during warm, rainy autumns than during colder ones. For that reason, it is often a good idea to make that one extra, too-late sowing of loose-leaf lettuces. If it is a normally harsh year, your last planting won't yield much, if anything, before it freezes out. You're out a bit of seed and effort—no big deal. If it turns out to be a mild autumn, that last sowing may grow surprisingly large and end up feeding you after the one you started a few weeks prior to it either is all picked and gone or has rotted away. And every once in awhile, you'll have a winter mild enough not to freeze out lettuce but harsh enough that lettuce hardly grows during autumn. In that lucky circumstance, your last sowing may overwinter outdoors as very small plants that burst into rapid growth and feed you early the next spring before making seed early enough in the summer to actually ripen the seed.

FERTILIZATION FOR WINTER

It is generally a wise practice to slow the growth of winter crops after mid-August. Plants that aren't getting a lot of fertility tend to harden off and be more chill-tolerant than those that are still soft and tender as a result of being pushed into growing all they could. I generally stop side-dressing plants during August.

Some gardeners believe that kelp meal contains certain growth stimulants that make a plant more cold-tolerant. I don't know. I've not been able to do accurate comparisons of some with and some without kelp meal. My general response to information like that is to feed winter crops a bit more kelp meal when blending up their complete organic fertilizer. If they needed it, they got it. If they didn't, I'm not out a lot of money, and besides, it won't hurt.

Some gardeners like to spray liquid seaweed fertilizers every few weeks during autumn and even during warmer, sunny spells in winter. I haven't bothered. This seems to me like any other magical garden practice; I'm sure it works for some, but I wonder what would have happened had the gardener done nothing. If anyone has any "scientific" data on sprayed versus unsprayed winter survival under maritime Northwest conditions, please let me know.

Chapter 5 **Water**

Drouth is said to be the archenemy of the dry-farmer, but
few agree upon its meaning. For the purposes of this volume,
drouth may be defined as a condition under which crops fail to mature
because of an insufficient supply of water. Providence has generally been
charged with causing drouths, but under the above definition, man is usually
the cause. Occasionally, relatively dry years occur, but they are seldom dry
enough to cause crop failures if proper methods of farming have been practiced.
There are four chief causes of drouth: (1) Improper or careless preparation
of the soil; (2) failure to store the natural precipitation in the soil;
(3) failure to apply proper cultural methods for keeping the moisture
*in the soil until needed by plants, and (4) **sowing too much seed***
for the available soil-moisture. [emphasis mine]

—JOHN A. WIDTSOE,
Dry Farming

Watering gardens

seems essential! But I've never seen a thorough rundown on how to water in any garden book other than this one. I've also never seen a garden writer take a fresh look at the whole subject of irrigation and ask, "Do we *really* need to?" This chapter does both.

Many gardeners end up watering their vegetables the way they water their lawns. They use lawn sprinklers and run them long enough that the plants seem happy. Most gardeners doing that unintentionally overwater, which is nearly as destructive to plant growth as underwatering. Underwatering has effects you can quickly see—the plants look stressed, get "gnarly," and may wilt. Not wanting to underwater, gardeners water prolifically, which makes their soil act as if it were less fertile. Unfortunately, gardeners rarely realize that they're getting poorer growth, because they have no standard of comparison.

Almost no gardeners realize that by simply increasing plant spacing they can water less often. Closely packed raised beds are sucked dry in a day or two of summer heat. Keeping them moist can be experienced as a pleasant way to spend half an hour with the birds in the backyard or as a horrible responsibility you have to get someone else to handle should you want to get away for a few weeks. By adjusting plant spacing, you can control how long it takes for your plants to drain the soil of moisture. Conscious planning can shape a range of options— a high-yielding garden that during hot spells needs watering every day, or a garden that yields nearly as much but that needs a thorough watering only once a week, or a drought garden that yields a quarter as much as an intensive one but that almost never *needs* watering to survive and yield, although in our rainless summers it will benefit from occasional deep irrigation.

Even short periods of moisture stress will greatly reduce vegetable quality. Lettuce turns bitter; cauliflower "buttons up," which means that if it even makes a curd, it'll be the size of a silver dollar; summer squash may become dry and fibrous and small; winter squash

doesn't set many fruits; snap beans get small, stringy, and tough.

The most obvious example of moisture stress is when plants experience permanent wilting—and die. Temporary wilting is caused when the hot midday sun evaporates more moisture from plants' leaves than the dryish soil will yield up. Although the plants may recover in the evening and look healthy the next morning, temporary wilting is a severe shock to most vegetables—one they won't fully recover from for weeks, if at all.

The consequences of water stress are so obvious that all gardeners have watering equipment handy. However, very few have scientifically designed irrigation systems, nor do most water systematically. But they should become scientific and systematic. Underwatering may be subtle, and, if mild enough to cause low-grade stress, it may go unnoticed, with serious consequences; however, overwatering can be equally harmful.

Hand Watering

Many gardeners go out almost every day with hose and nozzle and wet down their garden, making sure intensively planted beds hold abundant moisture all the time. This method can be made to work quite well if it is done knowledgeably.

Even if the garden is watered daily, if it is done too lightly plants still can become water stressed. What can happen is that the surface soil (the top 5 to 8 inches) stays quite moist, while the gardener never discovers that the deeper soil has become bone dry. Under these conditions, vegetables that are watered daily will not show signs of moisture stress because they never suck the surface layer dry and so don't wilt, but they will be stunted from lack of root development. Water-stressed carrots, beets, parsley, and other root crops may not show any signs of wilting because the leaves can draw on stored water, but when harvested the roots will be poorly developed or woody.

Recognizing this possibility, John Jeavons, in his book *How to Grow More Vegetables Than You Ever Thought Possible on Less Land Than You Can Imagine* (listed in the bibliography), recommends watering with a fan nozzle daily until the entire surface becomes "shiny wet." This shiny appearance results from the water that has not yet flowed into the bed beading up on the surface. The shiny appearance lasts only a second or so initially, but as the soil becomes increasingly saturated, it lasts longer and longer. When the shine lasts long enough (one to ten seconds, according to Jeavons), the bed has been given enough water.

One to ten seconds is quite a range. Jeavons suggests trying different shiny times com-bined with digging some test holes to see how deeply the soil had become saturated. Without this check, gross overwatering or underwater-ing could result. Many clayey soils are slow to absorb moisture and could remain shiny for a long while, yet be quite dry a few inches down; on the other hand, very sandy soils take in water very rapidly and might be difficult to get shiny at all, no matter how much the gardener overwatered or how fast the water was put down, resulting in considerable overwatering.

I've hand-watered gardens and made the method work, but with a business to run I needed a less time-demanding way. And even with sprinklers I still hand-water sprouting seeds between gardenwide irrigations.

Water in Soil

When you irrigate, each soil parti-cle attracts to itself all the water it can hold against the pull of gravity before water can flow deeper into the ground. Thus, the surface inches of soil can quickly become saturated while deeper layers

A Wet to Dry Scale

Soil	Moisture Remaining
Totally dry	0%
Permanent wilting point	20% to 33%
Temporary wilting point	50%
Minimum moisture for intensive vegetable beds	70%
Field capacity	100%

remain dry. A layer of soil that has absorbed all the water it can hold against the force of gravity is said to be at *field capacity*. It's like a sponge holding all the water it can. Add any more and some starts dripping out of the bottom. Irrigation brings layer after layer to capacity and then seeps deeper. So every irrigation leaches plant nutrients from the surface layers down to the full depth that the water has reached.

The opposite of field capacity is totally dry soil. As soil particles dry out, the moisture film over the soil particles becomes increasingly thinner. The thinner the film, the more tightly the moisture is held, until it clings so tightly to soil particles that vegetable roots and even evaporation at normal temperatures cannot extract it. The point on a wet-to-dry scale where vegetables can no longer extract any soil moisture is called the *permanent wilting point*. Before the permanent wilting point is reached, the soil reaches a degree of dryness where the plants experience temporary wilting when hot sun increases their need for water beyond the ability of their roots to extract it. And well before the soil dries down to the temporary wilting point, most kinds of vegetables begin to experience moisture stress.

HOW MUCH TO WATER

Vegetables have always been less durable than field crops. In our century they've become even less so. To maximize profit in this age of handy irrigation, modern plant breeders have resculpted most vegetables. They produce ever larger edible portions ever more quickly, but often at the expense of root system development. High-yielding modern vegetable varieties don't deal as well with dry soil as the lower-yielding heirlooms once did.

For this reason, scientific farmers aim to keep moisture levels in vegetable fields close to field capacity from near the surface to the depth of the vegetables' root development (about 2 feet on average). Practically speaking, when growing closely spaced vegetables, once soil has dried out to about 70 percent of capacity to the depth of a foot, it should be watered up to capacity again. Certainly by the time the top foot has dried below 70 percent and the next foot has dried to close to 70 percent too, the vegetables *must* be watered.

If you contemplate the four tables about soil moisture appearing in this chapter, and do a little arithmetic, you'll see that during the heat of summer you will want to irrigate an

Available Moisture *(Inches of Water per Foot of Soil)**

Soil Type	Total Holding Capacity	Available Moisture
Sandy	1.25 inches per foot	1.0 inch per foot
Medium (loam)	2.5 inches per foot	2.0 inches per foot
Clayey	3.75 inches per foot	2.7 inches per foot

**After the soil has delivered its available moisture, it has dried to the permanent wilting point. Obviously, sandy soil has less ability to supply moisture than clay.*

intensive garden at least every two to four days—more frequently but more lightly on sandy soil, even more frequently in really hot spells or during the routine heat of southern Oregon, less often on clayey soils, and less often in the cooler northern microclimates.

Before you decide to avoid the dangers of moisture stress by watering your garden even more frequently and thoroughly than you do now, consider the consequence of overdoing it. The gardener goes to a lot of trouble and expense to increase the level of available nutrients dissolved in the water film clinging to soil particles. As irrigation water flows into soil, it leaches dissolved nutrients deeper into the earth. When water penetration exceeds the depth of feeder roots, available plant nutrients are beyond reach, where they largely remain until heavy winter rains take them even deeper—into the water table and eventually out to sea.

This brings to mind another plus for organic fertilizers. If water-soluble chemical fertilizers are used, a single overwatering may strip the root zone of available nutrients, and more fertilizer may have to be applied. If organic fertilizers are used, the root zone is only temporarily leached until the nutrient level builds back up from further decomposition of fertilizer and organic matter. Growth slows or stops only temporarily when the garden is watered too much. Judging by recommendations in garden books and magazines, and by the equipment most gardeners use for irrigation, gardeners grossly overwater more often than they underwater.

Lawn (and garden) sprinklers spread water thick and fast. Although buyers of home-garden sprinklers don't get performance specifications, as buyers of agricultural crop sprinklers do, it is easy to test any sprinkler for precipitation rate. Simply set out a few empty tin cans: one near the sprinkler, one near the outer limit of its reach, and a couple in between. Run the sprinkler for exactly one hour, measure the depth of water in each can, and average those amounts. That's the sprinkler's precipitation rate per hour.

You'll find that most lawn sprinklers spread more than 2 inches of water per hour. Oscillating sprinklers, the kinds that water in rectangular patterns, put down 2 to 4 inches per hour, depending on their design, on the water pressure, and on where their pattern

Amount of Water Needed to Bring One Foot of Soil from 70 Percent to Capacity

Soil Type	Irrigation in Inches
Sandy	¼ (0.25)
Medium (loam)	½ (0.50)
Clayey	¾ (0.75)

Peak Soil Moisture Loss in Various Climates*

Type of Climate	Inches per Day
Cool climate	0.2
Moderate climate	0.25
Hot climate	0.3
High desert	0.35
Low desert	0.45

*July and August moisture loss in the warmer areas of the maritime Northwest runs from 0.2 to 0.3 inch per sunny day. The amount of loss in this table assumes that the soil is covered by a dense leaf canopy, one that will draw up and evaporate (transpire) the maximum amount of water possible. This degree of leaf cover normally is the state of a raised-bed garden in midsummer.

adjustment knob is set. Soaker hoses and "spot" sprinklers designed to cover small areas usually put out an even higher rate. How much leaching do you suppose the average gardener causes by using one of these sprinklers?

Another benefit of running this test is that you'll see the uniformity of distribution (or lack of it) you're getting. You may be sadly disappointed in your current watering equipment. Actually, any sprinkler that wets the ground fairly uniformly, even the high-output ones just mentioned, can water a garden effectively without leaching if the gardener knows its precipitation rate and knows how much water the garden needs.

Soil moisture content is best gauged 4 to 6 inches under the surface. Once soil moisture has dropped from capacity, where it feels very wet, to 70 percent of capacity, where it feels nicely damp, apply the amount of water recommended in the table "Amount of Water Needed to Bring One Foot of Soil from 70 Percent to Capacity," on the preceding page. An accurate method for judging soil moisture

(unless you have very sandy soil, in which case this test won't work at all) is to take some soil from 5 to 6 inches down and firmly squeeze it into a ball—the classic "ready to till" test. If the ball feels gooey or sticks together solidly, the soil moisture is above 70 percent. If the ball sticks together but breaks apart fairly easily, the soil moisture is around 70 percent. If the soil won't form a ball no matter how hard it is squeezed, it is too dry for the comfort of vegetables.

Another way to determine when to water is to estimate the amount of water being lost from soil and periodically replace it. I do it this way myself. West of the Cascades, soils are kept close to or at capacity by rain much of the year and are strongly leached in winter. Our soils usually begin to dry out during April, but the surface layers of most soils aren't dry enough to be tilled—that critical point, 70 percent of capacity—until May. Sensitive vegetable crops have to be irrigated from then until the rains return in September or October. The daily amount that sun, wind, and heat remove from soil varies with the season and the amount of vegetation the soil supports, but not with the type of soil. Regardless of their texture, all soils lose water at the same rate because it is not the sun shining on the earth that dries it out; it is the sun evaporating moisture from plants' leaves that dries the earth out.

In June, soil supporting a dense crop canopy usually loses about 1 inch of water per week—except in southern Oregon, where June may already be very hot. During the intense light and heat of July and August, water loss will be around 1½ inches per week; during spells of really high heat, it can increase to slightly more than 2 inches per week. By mid-September, losses slow to an inch a week, and by October, hardly any moisture is being lost, even if it does not rain. Remember to adjust for cloudy days (when less evaporation occurs) and for any rain received. And remember that sandy soils should be irrigated after losing ¼ to ½ inch of water

to avoid leaching them. Clayey soils, on the other hand, if growing large-sized vegetables with 2-foot-deep root systems, can easily accept 1 to 1½ inches without danger of leaching nutrients below the root zone.

More frequent, lighter irrigations may be needed to keep the surface very moist while sprouting seed, when nursing small seedlings while they become established, or when growing certain species with unusually high moisture requirements, such as radishes, Chinese cabbage, and celery. These demanding crops are best supplemented with hand watering in between sprinkler irrigations.

DESIGNING SPRINKLER SYSTEMS

Agricultural-grade sprinklers can apply water fairly uniformly and at a known rate. The choice you make about the size of sprinkler to use can make quite a few differences. Although it takes more low-application-rate sprinkler

Comparison of High- Versus Low-Application-Rate Sprinklers

Nozzle Size in Inches	Operating Pressure (PSI)	Discharge GPM*	Radius in Feet	Spacing in Feet	Precipitation Rate in Inches per Hour
0.0039	15	0.15	13	13 x 13	0.10
0.0039	45	0.28	18	13 x 13	0.16
$\frac{1}{16}$	30	0.45	33	20 x 20	0.11
$\frac{1}{16}$	60	0.79	36	20 x 20	0.19
$\frac{7}{64}$	30	1.94	33	20 x 20	0.47
$\frac{7}{64}$	60	2.66	36	20 x 20	0.64
$\frac{13}{64}$	30	6.78	40	25 x 25	1.05
$\frac{13}{64}$	60	9.53	45	25 x 25	1.46
$\frac{5}{16}$	30	17.7	59	40 x 60	0.71
$\frac{5}{16}$	60	25.7	75	40 x 60	1.03

*GPM= gallons per minute.

heads (tiny nozzles with a smaller radius) to cover a given area, it is better to use this sort because they put out finer, lighter droplets. High-application-rate sprinklers (big nozzles that throw water farther) usually put out large, heavy droplets that cause soil compaction, reducing plant root development and making cultivation and weeding more difficult. Large droplets pounding on the surface mechanically float the fine silt and clay soil particles to the top, creating a crust in much the same way that a cement finisher does. Because crusts don't form on sod, most lawn sprinklers issue big droplets and produce high precipitation rates—apparently a time-saving convenience to busy home owners, even though sod leaches as easily as vegetable plots, with the same consequences. Think what can happen in the vegetable garden if one of these monster sprinklers runs forgotten for a few hours.

The smaller agricultural crop sprinklers can spread as little as $\frac{1}{10}$ inch per hour. This is great for avoiding compaction and crusting, but sprinkler systems applying less than $\frac{1}{2}$ inch per hour do have drawbacks. Sun, wind, and high air temperatures can combine to break up fine streams of water and evaporate them as fast as the sprinkler can put them out. That doesn't mean they are useless. At precipitation rates below 0.2 inch per hour, it is possible to water a clayey soil all night, from bedtime to breakfast, without leaching. For rural homesteaders with limited water supplies, night is also the time when there is no competition from showers, dishwashing, and so on. On light soils, you can spread $\frac{1}{2}$ inch at the rate of $\frac{1}{10}$ or $\frac{2}{10}$ inch per hour by sprinkling in the early morning

before breezes start and the sun gets strong.

Contrary to common gardening lore, with our low-humidity summers, all-night watering is not harmful to plants. It may even be the best time to water. Plants are naturally dampened by dew; during summer they quickly dry off in the morning. What can occasionally harm plants is being watered just before dark and then left damp all night—ideal conditions for the multiplication of disease organisms. Watering all night continuously washes bacteria and fungus spores off the plants before they can do any damage. This principle is well understood by nurseries, which propagate healthy plants by rooting cuttings under a continuous fine mist.

Designing a perfect sprinkler head seems like an impossible contradiction—make a single sprinkler uniformly spread water over a circle or a square while it sits in the middle of the space. To understand how difficult this problem is to solve, do the tin-can test described earlier, using any sprinkler you like—whether lawn, garden, agricultural, or commercial—made by any manufacturer. Almost no single sprinkler I know of can accomplish uniform coverage; most fail miserably. The reason: With a circular pattern, a single nozzle must deposit nearly ten times the amount of water on the perimeter as it does in the center, while every point in between the center and perimeter must get a different amount. The diagram on the next page, "Achieving Uniform Water Applications from a Single Sprinkler," illustrates this, for the mathematically inclined.

Many design tricks are used with agricultural sprinklers to approach the ideal of equal

Achieving Uniform Water Application from a Single Sprinkler

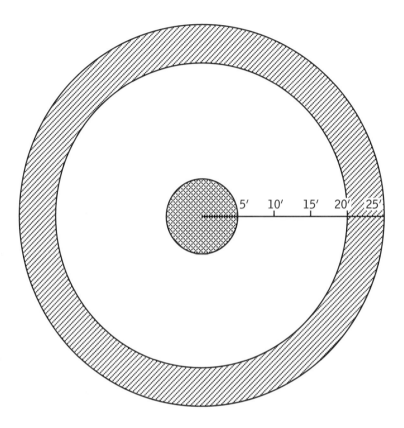

The formula for the area of a circle is: A=(pi) r². Imagine a sprinkler with a 25-foot radius. The innermost 5 feet of the sprinkler pattern occupy 78.5 square feet (3.14 x 5²). The area in the outer 5 feet of the pattern is 706.5 square feet ([3.14 x 25²] - [3.14 x 20²]). Thus, the nozzle must deposit nearly ten times as much water in the outermost 5 feet of the pattern to end up with the same application rate as the innermost 5 feet.

water distribution, but even the best puts twice as much water on the inner half of its coverage as on the outer half. Surprisingly, the one design that seems to so cleverly overcome this problem by watering squares and rectangles instead of circles—the oscillating sprinkler— is usually the worst culprit of all. The cam arrangement that moves the oscillating spray arm always seems to pause too long at the turnaround point, so this type of sprinkler errs by putting too much water at the ends of its rectangular pattern and too little above the sprinkler itself.

The impact sprinkler can't be uniform, because the spraying action of the rocker arm passing through the nozzle jet (its bouncing rotates the sprinkler head) dumps too much water close to the sprinkler while too little is thrown to the extremes. Most impact sprinklers sold for home use come with a diffuser paddle or an adjustable needle screw of some sort to shorten the water throw by diffusing the spray. But more than the slightest amount of diffusion increases the tendency to overwater the center while leaving the fringes too dry. The more the radius is shortened by breaking up the nozzle stream, the worse this effect becomes. Agricultural-quality impulse sprinklers do not use diffusers; instead, they have scientifically designed nozzles that, if used at the correct pressure, diffuse (spray) properly all by themselves and give fairly uniform coverage. The consequence of all this scientific design is that they end up putting only about twice as much water on the center half of the circle as they do on the outer half.

Test your sprinkler with some tin cans and see for yourself.

To compensate for the inherent limitations of sprinkler design, farmers use many at once, arranged in overlapping patterns so that one sprinkler's heavily watered area is overlapped by another sprinkler's deficiently watered area, and the differences cancel each other out. The diagrams on the next page illustrate some typical sprinkler patterns. Any multiple-sprinkler pattern still leaves a dryish fringe area where fewer overlaps occur. On the farm, these fringes are of no consequence; in the backyard, it may be essential to keep them within your own yard if only to keep overspray out of neighbors' yards or off windows.

The less-watered fringes can, however, be very useful for growing a dry garden or for locating deep-rooting and tall perennials like raspberries. Putting a row of raspberries or tall pole beans right along the more heavily watered edge of the dry fringe intercepts the overspray, and it all drips off the leaves onto their root zone. Thus the hedge gets about as much water as the middle of the sprinkler's patterns, and nothing much goes past it.

Sometimes sprinkler patterns are laid out in squares, sometimes in triangles. The triangular pattern spreads water slightly more uniformly, but the square pattern may lend itself better to a backyard situation. Agricultural crop sprinklers range from delicate little things that cover a 13-foot radius to firehose-nozzle monsters that will water several acres at a time. The closer the spacing and the shorter the designed radius of the sprinkler, the smaller the fringe area will be, making short-radius sprinklers preferable for backyard gardens.

The highest-quality all-brass impulse sprinklers are made by the Rain Bird Company. Their catalog is very informative and covers much of the same information found in this chapter. Other firms make impulse crop sprinklers too. The most interesting sprinklers come from Israel and Australia, which, because of their water situations, are world leaders in irrigation technology and design. The smallest nozzle I am aware of that will work with the rocker-arm impact design emits ¾ gallon per minute (gpm) from a $\frac{1}{16}$-inch-diameter nozzle bore, and has about a 25-foot radius. But I've found that this tiny nozzle needs very high pressure (over 55 pounds per square inch, or psi) to hit the impulse arm hard enough to

Sprinkler Patterns

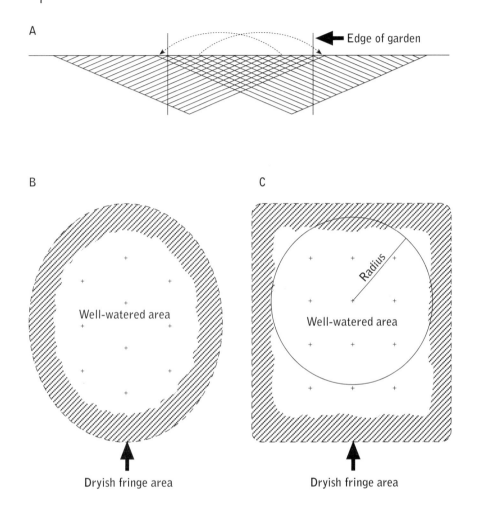

Using several sprinklers creates overlapping water patterns, permitting uniform coverage. The optimal spacing is about 60 percent of the sprinkler's throw radius. (A) A side view of correct sprinkler overlap. The shaded areas show the relative amount of water applied by an average impact sprinkler. (B) Sprinklers arranged in triangular patterns. (C) Sprinklers arranged in square patterns.

spin the head. The smallest impact sprinkler I've ever had work reliably is the next larger size, ⁵⁄₆₄ inch. An inexpensive yet durable line of low-output black plastic impulse sprinklers is made by Na'an (an Israeli company), work-

ing on a slightly different mechanism that can have emission rates as low as ⅓ gpm and a radius of 13 feet. You may have to consult a high-grade irrigation equipment seller to find Na'an sprinklers. And a visit to one may open your eyes to many other interesting possibilities.

Some gardeners use impact sprinklers with part-circle attachments to eliminate fringe areas, putting the sprinkler at the edge or corner of the area to be watered and reducing the sprinkler's arc to 180 or 90 degrees. Keep in mind that, with the usual impulse sprinkler, cutting the arc in half doubles the rate of application; reducing it to 90 degrees quadruples the rate of application. A simple way to prevent full-circle sprinklers from spraying where you don't want them to is to make a shield from a cut-out tin can attached directly behind the sprinkler. This is effective, though it does waste water by dumping the blocked spray at the sprinkler's base.

One of the best alternatives to the impact sprinkler has been developed by the Toro Company. Their designs use an internal water-powered turbine to rotate the sprinkler head. Toro's interchangeable nozzle heads provide the most uniform coverage possible and, most interestingly, the ability to cover reduced arcs without increasing the application rate. Turbine sprinklers were designed for watering lawns and ornamental plantings in institutional situations where sprinklers have to be located close to buildings and windows, and where precise coverages must be adjusted to avoid watering sidewalks, overspraying windows, and so forth. Gardeners who are really interested in optimum irrigation design should study Toro's catalog (but be prepared to pay more) before making any major decisions.

Agricultural-grade sprinkler heads are designed with different angles of throw. High-angle nozzles allow the stream of water to go its maximum distance, covering the largest area with the fewest number of sprinkler heads at the lowest rates of coverage while drawing the least number of gallons per minute. However, high-angle sprinklers are badly affected by wind, which can disperse the water stream, blow it off course, and cause high evaporation losses, especially if the sun is shining. High-angle sprinklers can be a wonderful solution for homesteaders with very limited water supplies who want large gardens—if they avoid the sun and wind by watering at night or early in the morning. Low-angle sprinklers are best for windier situations or midday use. Throwing water at an angle of about 6 degrees above horizontal makes their radius shorter and keeps the stream close to the ground, out of the strongest wind gusts. They're better in tight backyard situations, too. More low-angle sprinklers are needed to cover a given area, resulting in somewhat higher precipitation rates.

When gardeners go into an irrigation supply store for the first time and read over a commercial irrigation catalog, they sometimes leave confused. Sprinkler catalogs assume that buyers have sufficient understanding to lay out a proper system. Here are a few hints to make using them a little more successful.

Agricultural sprinklers come with manufacturer's recommendations for spacing and operating pressure. Operating a sprinkler outside its design limits results in poor performance. With crop-sprinkler nozzles, matching the shape of the bore to the water pressure is especially important. If the water stream jets from the nozzle at a pressure that is too low for the design, the water stream doesn't break up and "spray" or diffuse properly. When this occurs, the impulse arm, as expected, causes much water to be laid down near the sprinkler, and the tight, undiffused stream carries water to the fringes, but no droplets land in between the extremes, meaning that very little water is laid down in the middle. A doughnut pattern results, the doughnut being the dry middle. This is, naturally, called "doughnutting."

Run at excessively high pressure, the water jet mists and breaks up too much, or "sprays too much" as a farmer would say, shortening the throw of the water and greatly increasing the rate of application near the sprinkler, making the fringes much too dry. Diffuser arms that break up the stream do exactly the same thing—usually the opposite of what the user intended to achieve.

Different nozzles are designed to spray properly at pressures from 10 to 100 pounds psi, with most designed to work at from 30 to 60 psi. City household water supplies are usually between 30 and 45 psi. Homesteaders set their own water pressure at the well pump, within limits. Get something that matches your water pressure; when using lower-pressure nozzles, such as the ones made by Na'an, be sure to buy the proper pressure regulator if you need one. They don't cost much.

High-angle sprinklers should not be spaced at more than about 65 percent of their radius. This allows the right amount of overlap in the pattern and allows for wind blowing the spray a little without leaving areas dry. Low-angle sprinklers are less bothered by wind and are usually spaced at 75 percent of their radius.

The trickiest part of designing a multiple-head sprinkler system is improvising the risers that hold the sprinkler heads. Farmers use 20- to 30-foot-long lightweight aluminum quick-disconnect pipe systems; at each joint there is a riser to hold an impulse sprinkler. These pipes and risers are unnecessarily expensive for a garden. At times when I've had a lot of money to spend, I've constructed sprinkler system supply pipes and risers of ½- and ¾-inch galvanized pipe; this strong pipe has the advantage of not being damaged by an accidental hit with rototiller blade or hoe.

More and more interesting stuff is coming out using black plastic and quick-connect fittings. The trouble with most plastic watering equipment is that it is designed for lawn and ornamental edge gardens, so the height of the risers is insufficient for vegetables. To get above most crops, we vegetable gardeners need sprinkler heads that are 18 to 24 inches above the soil. One way to improvise risers is to glue a short plastic sprinkler spike into the end of a 30-inch-long piece of heavy ¾-inch white plastic pipe with its bottom end cut off at a sharp angle so that it can be pushed into the soil. The sprinkler spike is fed water through a barbed push-in connector fed into a black plastic supply line laid atop the soil; the white plastic pipe holding up the sprinkler spike carries no water. (See the illustration on page 148.)

If you know what you want to accomplish, you can reach your goal without ideal equipment. If a complete, permanent, multiheaded sprinkler system that turns on from a single valve is beyond your interest or budget, you can still have uniform irrigation with only one good sprinkler head on a tall stand supplied

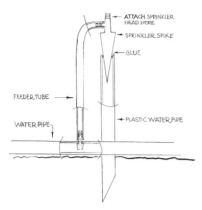

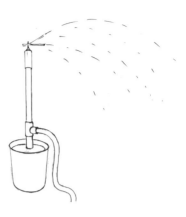

Two improvised sprinkler stands.

by an ordinary hose. It is moved around the garden and run for equal periods in carefully determined positions. I did it this way for the first years in my trials ground. I made the stand, shown in the illustration above right, with a sack of ready-mix concrete, a 5-gallon plastic bucket, and some pipe.

Lately, new advances in plastics manufacture have created a sort of hybrid between drip and sprinkling, called microirrigation. These systems use inexpensive low-pressure plastic tubing to carry water, cheap quick-disconnect fittings for corners and tees, cheap plastic spikes to hold sprinklers, and miniature short-radius sprinkler heads with emission rates so low they are measured in gallons per hour, not gallons per minute. Microirrigation systems provide an inexpensive and durable alternative for under-tree applications in orchards. They are also being used more and more by home owners to water ornamental beds around houses and are very useful in spring cloches to keep plants watered for a few weeks until the cloche is removed. Microirrigation equipment is sold prepackaged for the consumer in larger

garden centers and discount stores, but it is quite expensive purchased that way. Commercial irrigation suppliers have a much wider selection at a much lower cost. If you're considering a microirrigation system, be very wary about getting uniform water distribution from the heads. Sometimes microirrigation supply tubes and risers can handle ordinary crop sprinklers with nozzles that emit up to 1 gallon per minute.

How I Got Interested in Dry-Gardening

Irrigation is a bigger subject than most people think. It involves understanding the whole water-soil-plant relationship. When you grasp this, you attain a sort of liberation, because then you are freed to grow vegetables with or without irrigation, or anywhere in between. The whole mystery of plant spacing also becomes clear. That is the kind of expert mastery I'd like you to have. So this chapter covers the spectrum, from full irrigation with sprinklers like those used by commercial vegetable farmers all the way to dry-gardening like that done by the Papago Indians in the Arizona desert, and every point in between. Even if you have abundant water and no interest whatsoever in dry-gardening, this section still contains a lot of very valuable data that can save you work and trouble. I suggest that you don't skip it.

We bought our first five-acre homestead at Lorane, Oregon, in mid-March 1978. I'd come from Michigan by way of California, where I had spent seven years. It was mid-April when we moved in, so the Lorane Valley seemed a cool, showery green place of liquid sunshine and rainbows. Was that ever a misconception!

I intended to grow as much of my own food as possible, find a crop to raise for sale, live simply, and use as little cash as possible. Because I had agriculturalist ambitions, the homestead purchase agreement had been made subject to a well test; the well must deliver 15 gallons per minute. With 15 gpm I could keep an acre or two well irrigated. How foolish I was, thinking that I could earn our keep by raising crops on the homestead. As it turned out, the only crop I ever raised profitably at Lorane was the consciousness of other gardeners.

Homesteading. I dug a well, put in a driveway and a septic system, and got a power pole, meter service, and a smallish mobile home. I built a tin toolshed/woodshed. We paid for everything in cash, and then we were nearly

broke. While all of this settling in was happening, I also prepared the soil for our first garden, much like my neighbor Carl, who was putting in his summer-only plot. I spread a couple of pickup loads of sawdusty horse manure, a few sacks of lime, and a few more of seed meal; hired a big tiller; erected a 75-foot-by-75-foot deer fence; and constructed a very permanent ten-sprinkler-head irrigation system using ten 1 gpm sprinklers designed to put down about 0.2 inch per hour. The 15 gpm supply should be able to handle that 10-gallon-per-minute total water consumption quite comfortably, I thought. I intended to control the whole system from a single turn-on valve. I was so confident that I used galvanized pipes for supply lines and risers, because I knew I was going to be there for the rest of my life. Unfortunately, every time I've known that something would be "so" for the rest of my life, I've turned out to be wrong—usually painfully wrong.

Two months later, in mid-June, the seeds had sprouted and the transplants were growing fast. The days got hot. All the pasture grasses turned yellow-brown and my garden began needing water. So I fired up that fancy irrigation system for the first time and admired those ten little sprinklers putting out those thin, delicate streams of water, *psit, psit, psit.* Within about fifteen minutes, however, every one of those gallon-per-minute, scientifically designed, uniform-coverage, irrigate-the-whole-garden-with-a-single-turn-on-valve sprinkler heads had sucked the "tested" 15-gallon-per-minute well down to the very bottom. Not knowing much yet about pumps—

or Oregon wells—it took a while to get that figured out. Then I started improvising adjustments to the system as all through that summer I anxiously watched the well's flow fade and fade, wondering if it would completely dry out. By August the well delivered only 3 gallons per minute. Fortunately, I didn't end up with a completely dry hole or one that delivered less than 1 gallon per minute, as I discovered many of my neighbors were cursed with.

Three gallons per minute won't supply a fan nozzle (they need 8 to 10 gpm), so I could no longer do extensive hand-watering, except for a short few minutes with the watering hose to wet down some sprouting seeds. Nor will 3 gpm even power a common impulse sprinkler (which needs 5 gpm). But I could still sustain my big raised-bed garden by irrigating from bedtime to breakfast three or four nights a week, using a single, 2.5 gpm part-circle sprinkler that I moved from place to place. I well remember searching through a lot of irrigation catalogs to find that low-flow part-circle head. I also remember getting up at 2 A.M. a lot of nights to reset the sprinkler. At least there was enough extra to flush a toilet or draw a glass of water while the sprinkler was running.

At that time I never thought to abandon raised-bed gardening. John Jeavons, my first garden guru, had asserted with absolute certainty that gardening in raised beds was not only the most productive of all vegetable growing methods, and required the least work, it was also the most water-efficient system ever known (in terms of pounds of food harvested for gallons of water put in). I knew no other way.

Had my well delivered only 1 gallon per minute, I would have grown as many raised beds as I could have watered and might well have sadly concluded that first summer that food self-sufficiency on my homestead was not possible. Then again, I might have put a 1,500-gallon storage tank uphill of the garden and house and pumped 1 gallon per minute into it all day and night, drawing it all down daily in one two-hour-long rush of irrigation. I couldn't have moved very easily—we'd spent our wad, and five acres with a proven lousy well wasn't worth much. Fortunately, by late September the well could still supply a 2.5 gpm sprinkler, and supply it all night every night if I wished. What a relief it was to find out that at least one of the strata flowing into my well was a subterranean stream that didn't quit. I was not, as I had feared, pumping out a subterranean pond that would be sucked dry every summer. I had not invested every last cent in land that couldn't feed us.

For many succeeding years I gardened up lots of organically grown food on thoroughly watered, densely planted raised beds, but the realities of country life continued to remind me of how tenuous my whole survival system actually was. Without regular watering during high summer, closely packed stands of vegetables quickly become stressed and then stunted. Pump breakdowns had brought my garden close to that several times. Before my frantic efforts got the water flowing again, I could feel the struggling vegetables screaming like hungry babies.

I began to wonder how the early pioneers had irrigated their vegetables. There probably aren't more than a thousand homestead sites in the entire maritime Northwest with gravity water—or were there more dependably flowing springs before the forests were demolished? Hand-pumping into hand-carried buckets is impractical and seemed extremely tedious—and impossibly exhausting considering the amount of water I was using. Anyone who thinks they have the physical ability to carry buckets of water to a demanding garden should see a magnificent Gérard Depardieu movie called *Jean de Florette*, about a middle-aged man who works himself to death trying to grow food by carrying water to a dry garden. Or perhaps you should just try doing it for an hour or two. While learning to drygarden I did this, just to get a sense of reality about it; I got a yoke and hauled some water up from the Umpqua River. After a few trips I was sure grateful for my well, pump, and hose. I could have managed if I'd had to, but fortunately, I didn't have to.

The combination of dependably rainless summers, the realities of self-sufficient living, and my Lorane homestead's poor well turned out to be an opportunity. For I continued wondering about gardens and water and eventually discovered methods for growing a lush, productive vegetable garden with little or no irrigation in a climate that reliably provides eight to twelve virtually rainless weeks every summer, and usually another month on either side of that without adequate rainfall. If your situation is like mine was—not enough water—or if you'd like to garden in a style that lets you travel or vacation during the summer without worrying about your suffering veg-

etables, read on. It is possible to plan a garden that needs watering much less often than you might think, and in some cases not at all.

If you read any of the older back-east country garden books, those written prior to 1970, you'll notice that the gardens they show are laid out in widely spaced rows, not intensively planted raised beds. This is because back then, eastern country gardens were generally watered by rain, not irrigation, and gardeners who operated in that style knew they might have to deal with a long rainless spell. In a garden designed with wide spaces, drought did not equal a couple of days without watering. Drought was not a concern until the garden went several weeks without significant rain. Widtsoe, whose quote begins this chapter, wisely defines drought as occurring when the crop is damaged. This has nothing to do with how much time elapses between rains; it has to do with how wisely or foolishly the grower plans. It largely has to do with points 3 and 4 in Widtsoe's quote. Dry-farmed and dry-gardened crops can go for an incredibly long time without being watered—even an entire year in some cases!

Gardening with Less Irrigation

Being a garden writer and a seedsman, I am on the receiving end of quite a bit of local lore. I heard of an old mossback growing unirrigated carrots on sandy soil in the Applegate Valley. He sowed early and spaced the roots 1 foot apart in rows 4 feet apart. There's no hotter, drier place in western Oregon, yet the carrots grew to enormous sizes and the overall yield in pounds per square foot occupied by the crop was not as low as one might think. I read that Native Americans in the Southwest grew remarkable desert gardens with little or no water and that native South Americans in the highlands of Peru and Bolivia grew food crops in a cool land with 8 to 12 inches of annual rainfall.

The first summertime vegetable I grew entirely without irrigation happened by accident. I had sold the seed business and moved to an ideal homestead with a solidly productive year-round well and deep, rich soil, in the best microclimate Oregon had to offer. Having more free time at Elkton, I was working on growing more of my own seeds. I knew that the main destroyer of good seed germination is repeatedly moistening developing seed. So I transplanted six winter-surviving savoy cabbages far beyond the sprinkler-throw of my raised-bed vegetable garden, spacing them 4 feet apart because blooming brassicas make huge sprays of flower stalks. I did not plan to water these plants at all because cabbage seed forms during May and dries during June, just as the soil naturally dries out.

That is just what happened, except that one plant did something unusual, though not unheard of, as I later found out. Instead of going completely into bloom and then dying after setting a massive load of seed, this plant also threw a vegetative bud that grew a whole new head of cabbage among the seed stalks.

Amazed, I watched this head grow steadily larger through the hottest and driest summer I had ever experienced. Realizing I was being given what a conventionally religious person might call a revelation, I gave the plant absolutely no water, although I did hoe out the weeds around it after I cut the seed stalks. I harvested the unexpected lesson at the end of September. The head weighed in at 6 or 7 pounds and was as sweet and tender as any other of its type grown with all the water it could have asked for.

Until this point, all of my personal gardening had been on thoroughly watered raised beds. That cabbage said to me, "Elbow room might be the key to gardening with little or no irrigation." So I began looking for more information about dry-farming and soil/water physics. The next spring I rototilled four experimental 100-foot-long rows, their centers 5 feet apart, where I dry-gardened an assortment of vegetable species that I suspected might survive if they had more growing space than usual. Out of curiosity I decided to use absolutely no water at all, not even to sprinkle the seeds to get them germinating. I would pretend that I had no flowing water at all and sow everything before the hot weather came. This game is a little like what champion skeet shooters do when they use a .410 to give themselves a handicap.

I tried kale, savoy cabbage, Purple Sprouting broccoli, carrots, beets, parsnips, parsley, endive, dry beans, potatoes, French sorrel, and a couple of field corn seeds. I also tested one compact bush (determinate) and one sprawling (indeterminate) tomato plant. (The tomato seedlings got 1 cup of water each when I set them out.) Many of these vegetables grew surprisingly well. I ate unwatered tomatoes from July through September. Kale, cabbages, parsley, and root crops fed us during the winter. The Purple Sprouting broccoli looked gnarly by September but grew lushly all winter and bloomed abundantly the next March.

In terms of quality, all of the harvest was acceptable. The root vegetables were far larger but only a little bit tougher and quite a bit sweeter than usual. The potatoes yielded less than I'd been used to and had a thicker-than-usual skin, but they also had a better flavor and kept better than my irrigated spuds. I found out later, by the way, that potatoes grown dry often have up to 11 percent protein, while those given all the irrigation they can seem to use may contain as little as 8 percent protein. Protein and other nutritional elements are what we probably sense when we taste them.

The following year, I grew two parallel gardens. One, my insurance garden, was as always—6,000 square feet, thoroughly irrigated so that we would have plenty to eat no matter what. Another, an experimental garden of equal size, was entirely unirrigated. There I tried larger plots of species that I hoped could grow through a rainless summer.

By July, the growth on some of the unirrigated species had slowed to a crawl, and they looked stressed. I recalled having read in Widtsoe's book about an 1882 dry-farming experiment. It took 1,100 pounds of water to grow a pound of dry plant matter on infertile soil but only 575 pounds of water to produce

that same amount of plant matter on rich land. Wondering if the real cause behind what appeared to be moisture stress might actually be nutrient deficiencies, I tried spraying liquid fertilizer directly on these gnarly leaves, a practice called foliar feeding. Within days, I could see that it had helped greatly. I reasoned that this was because my fertilizer was located in the topsoil but when the topsoil gets dry, the plants draw on subsoil moisture containing relatively less plant nutrition.

Since foliar spraying had worked, I decided that some of these species might do even better if they had just a little fertilized water that I put into the subsoil. So I improvised a simple plastic-bucket drip system and metered out a 5-gallon dose of fertigation to some of the plants in late July and another bucketful in mid-August. I estimate the fertigation probably went down 4 or 5 feet and saturated a volume of soil about the size of a 50-gallon oil drum. (See the illustration below.)

Some species did fine with or without fertigation. But the unirrigated winter squash vines, which were small and scraggly, and

yielded about 15 pounds of food without it, grew far more lushly when given two 5-gallon fertilizer-fortified assists, and they yielded 50 pounds. Thirty-five pounds of squash for 10 extra gallons of water and a bit of extra nutrition is a pretty good exchange, in my view.

I tried two fertilizer approaches for both foliar spraying and fertigation. One method, organic, used an equal mixture of dilute liquid seaweed and liquid fish emulsion; the other used chemicals, in this case Rapid-Gro, the highest-quality complete and balanced soluble preparation, also very suitable for foliar spraying. Both approaches worked. I'm sorry to report to you organic gardeners that Rapid-Gro worked a little better for me, probably because liquid organic fertilizers are, of necessity, very low in phosphorus.

The next year I integrated both approaches into one garden. Water-loving species like lettuce, Chinese cabbage, and celery were grown through the summer on an adjoining pair of thoroughly irrigated intensive raised beds; each bed was 4 feet wide by 100 feet long. The watering that summer was done by hand with a fan nozzle, à la John Jeavons. This kept all of the water exactly where I wanted it. The rest of the garden was given either no irrigation at all or minimally measured-out fertigations. Some entirely unirrigated crops were foliar fed weekly.

Everything worked! And that summer I found still other species that I could grow surprisingly well on surprisingly small amounts of water—or none at all. So the next spring I set up a low-angle short-throw sprinkler system to water that parallel pair of intensive raised

beds and used the overspray (the inevitable dryish fringe area in the sprinkler's pattern) to support species that grew better with some moisture supplementation. (See the diagram on the next page, "Hypothetical Plan for a Dry Garden.") I continued using a bucket-drip fertigation system to help still others, while keeping a large section of the garden entirely unwatered. And at the end of that summer I wrote a little book called *Water-Wise Vegetables*. Sasquatch published it.

What I advise about dry gardening and about styles of irrigated gardening is not just theory, not something I've seen others do or have merely read about. Every one of these techniques is tested and workable. I can't reproduce the entire text of *Water-Wise Vegetables* in half of a single chapter here, but I can give the essentials.

The reason you can dry-garden is that you're planning on using the water naturally stored in the earth to grow your crops and supplementing stored soil moisture when it makes sense to do so. If you doubt that this is possible, take a slow country drive during late July and look closely at the wild vegetation around you. Notice especially the blackberries, which grow much better in some places than in others. Deep, open, moisture-retentive soil can be recognized immediately; it is found where blackberries grow huge and lush. You'll find blackberry patches 6 to 8 feet tall covered with big, sweet berries; you'll find patches 4 feet tall with smaller berries that may taste okay; and you'll find places where the berries will hardly grow. What you're seeing is mainly how much wintertime rain the soil has stored.

HOW SOIL LOSES MOISTURE

Suppose that we kept a good-sized area entirely bare of plants by rigorously hoeing it from April 1 through August, and then (assuming it had been a typical hot, rainless summer) measured the remaining soil moisture toward the center of the field, where plants surrounding it had no effect.

Let's also suppose that before the test started it had been a typical maritime Northwest rainy winter, so on April 1 the soil was at field capacity, holding all the moisture it could.

From early April on, the hot sun beat down on this bare plot. Any June-through-August summer rains generally came in insignificant installments and did not penetrate deeply; all of the rain quickly evaporated from the surface few inches without recharging deeper layers. Most would reason that unless we got an unusually heavy summer rain late in the season, a soil moisture measurement taken a foot down on September 1 would show very little water left. In fact, most gardeners would expect that very little water would be found in the soil

Hypothetical Plan for a Dry Garden

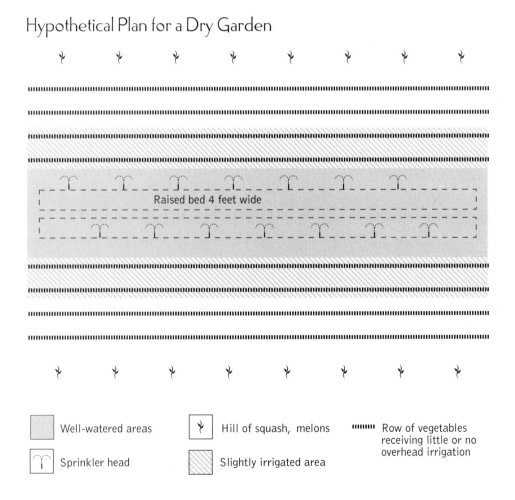

Raised bed 4 feet wide

Well-watered areas

Sprinkler head

Hill of squash, melons

Slightly irrigated area

Row of vegetables receiving little or no overhead irrigation

until we got down to Australia.

But that is not what happens! The hot sun does dry out the surface inches, but if we dug down 6 inches or so there would be almost as much water present in September as there was in April. Bare earth does not lose much water at all. Once a thin surface layer is completely desiccated, whether it be loose fluff or compacted, virtually no further loss of moisture can occur.

The only soils I know of that continue to dry out when bare of vegetation are certain kinds of clays that form deep cracks. These ever-deepening openings allow atmospheric air to freely evaporate additional moisture. But if the cracks are filled with dust by surface cultivation, even this soil type ceases to lose much water.

Soil functions as a moisture bank account, holding available water in storage. In our climate, soil is inevitably charged to capacity by winter rains, and then all summer growing plants make heavy withdrawals as hot sun and wind work on plant leaves, making them transpire soil moisture. Plants desiccate soil to the ultimate depth and lateral extent of their rooting ability, and then some. However, the amount of soil moisture potentially available to sustain vegetable growth is greater than most gardeners think. The amount of usable water "in the soil bank" at the beginning of summer depends on depth, soil type (moisture-holding capacity), and how open the soil is to root penetration. If you're really going to have to depend on this water bank for most of your garden's water supply, you'll simply have to run some performance tests and see how the vegetables grow. But I can assure you that

if the soil is open and deep, there's more water below your feet than you realize.

Rain and irrigation are not the only ways to restore soil moisture. If the soil body is deep enough, quite a bit of water will slowly rise toward the surface from below the root zone by a process called capillarity. Capillary flow works by the very same principle of adhesion that makes moisture stick to a soil particle—or to a coin, or to your finger. A column of water in a vertical tube (like a thin straw) adheres to the tube's inner surfaces in the same way. This adhesion tends to lift the edges of the column of water. In a straw, the amount of lift is less than 1 millimeter. As the tube's diameter becomes smaller, the amount of lift becomes greater. Trees use this principle to raise moisture through microscopic tubes to leaves several hundred feet above the earth. Soil particles form interconnected pore tubes that lift moisture from below to recharge drier soil above. However, the drier soil becomes, the less effective capillary flow becomes. That is why a thoroughly desiccated surface layer only a few inches thick acts as a powerfully effective mulch.

Industrial farming and modern gardening books downplay the significance of capillarity compared to the moisture needs of crops. But conventional agriculture focuses on maximized yields though high plant densities. Capillarity is too slow to support intensive crop stands where densely interpenetrated root systems are competing for soil moisture, but when a single plant can fully develop its root system without any competition, it will often find enough water in the soil bank to support it through the entire summer.

Plant density, the way you adjust your garden's water needs to your willingness or ability to irrigate, is the key. Spacing the plants farther apart gives them an ever-greater ability to find their own water. Spread-out plants can go a lot longer between irrigations too; you refill the soil's depleted moisture bank by watering, and it supplies the plants for weeks or even longer. Despite the efforts of plant breeders to make plants yield more at the expense of root system vigor, this technique still works with many vegetable species, especially with the old open-pollinated heirlooms. You'll find more vegetable-by-vegetable data about this in Chapter 9.

MULCHING

The common belief is that a thick vegetative mulch à la Ruth Stout will keep soil moist through a drought. This is both true and false. The fact is that mulched soil probably loses a bit more moisture than unmulched soil. However, under a vegetative mulch the surface inches, where most nutrients are located, stay moister longer, and growing plants may feed better and thus grow better for awhile. Stout never figured on getting a garden through droughts as long as we routinely get in the maritime Northwest.

Why do I assert that mulched soil loses more water than unmulched soil? Because bare earth, once it gets a thoroughly desiccated layer on top, loses virtually no moisture. Under a mulch, however, the soil remains moist right to the surface, and capillary flow continues to bring subsoil moisture up to the surface, where water is wicked up into the mulch and evaporates. I'm certain that if we did a careful experiment with two parallel plots, one mulched and one bare, each one growing no vegetation, and measured the soil moisture remaining after a long, hot Oregon summer without any irrigation or rain, a straw- or hay-mulched plot would have lost somewhat more moisture than one that had a dust mulch.

Mulching still might be a useful technique for dry-gardening vegetables with surface feeder roots, like squash. However, for species with deep taproots, like carrots or beets, no mulch would be better. In any case, if you mulch, avoid building up slugs, sow bugs, and earwigs during the rainy months to come by raking up the mulch and composting it when the crop is finished.

LOWERED PLANT DENSITY: THE KEY TO DRY-GARDENING

In the 1989 edition of this book, I recommended somewhat wider spacings on raised beds than I did in the 1980 edition because I've repeatedly noticed that once a leaf canopy forms, plant growth slows markedly. Adding a little more fertilizer helps plants keep growing fast after they "bump," but the rate of growth never equals that of younger plants. For years I assumed that crowded plants stopped producing as much because they were competing for light. But now I see that unseen competition for root room (probably through exudate wars) also slows them down. So allocating more elbow room allows vegetables to get larger and yield longer and also allows the gardener to reduce the frequency of irrigation.

The amount of water a growing crop will transpire through its leaves is determined first by the nature of the species itself and then by the amount of leaf it has produced. In these respects, the crop is like an automobile radiator. With radiators, the more metal surfaces there are, the colder the ambient air, and the higher the wind speed, the better the radiator can cool. In the garden, the more leaf surfaces, the faster, warmer, and drier the wind, and the brighter the sunlight, the more water is lost through transpiration.

If no plants are growing, most of the water will stay unused in the barren soil through the entire growing season. If a crop canopy is established midway through the growing season, the rate of water loss will approximate what I recommend adding through normal summer irrigation. (See the table "Peak Soil Moisture Loss in Various Climates" on page 140.) If by very close planting the crop canopy is established as early as possible and maintained by successive interplantings, as is recommended by most advocates of raised-bed gardening, water losses will slightly exceed this rate.

On very closely planted beds without irrigation, a crop can get into serious trouble in a matter of days. If that same crop were planted much less densely, it might grow for a few weeks without irrigation. And if that crop were planted far enough apart that no crop canopy ever developed and a considerable amount of bare, dry earth was showing, this apparent waste of growing space would result in an even slower rate of soil moisture depletion. On deep, open soil, the crop might yield a respectable amount without needing any irrigation at all. That is dry-gardening in a nutshell.

The biggest surprise to most gardeners is finding out that lowering plant density does not proportionally lower the yield. For most kinds of vegetables, having one-eighth as many plants reduces the yield by less than half. The main difference is not so much the final amount harvested but when it is harvested. Having more room to grow means that the plants just keep on getting bigger; most of the harvest from a plot with lowered plant density comes a bit later than in a more densely planted garden. Crowding plants together pushes them into yielding a bit sooner, but less per plant, while the final pick tends to be smaller and of lower quality.

CAN YOU DRY-GARDEN?

Everyone who can grow a vegetable garden can dry-garden to some extent. At the very least, you can give up the highest possible yields for the convenience of less watering and tending.

Vegetables That Must Be Heavily Irrigated

These vegetables are not suited to dry-gardening.

Bulb onions *(for fall harvest)*

Celeriac

Celery

Chinese cabbage

Lettuce *(summer and fall)*

Radishes *(spring radishes will grow on rainfall)*

Scallions *(for summer harvest)*

Spinach *(spring spinach will grow on rainfall)*

Imagine that you've got a total of 100 square feet in your garden. You could raise quite a bit of lettuce there by irrigating frequently. You could also grow three indeterminate tomato vines in the same area, giving each vine 33 square feet of room to eventually fill with its roots. A garden like this might go through an entire summer without any irrigation, while if you could give each vine 5 gallons of fertigation every two to three weeks during July and August, you might get five times as many tomatoes. The table on the preceding page, "Vegetables That Must Be Heavily Irrigated," shows those species that don't lend themselves to dry-gardening. All the other species can be dry-gardened.

If I were considering gardening with less irrigation at a site, the first thing I'd do would be to make sure the soil was deep enough. To find this out, you need to dig a deep hole. If there isn't at least 4 feet of soil, there can't be much water in the bank. Still, if there is at least 2 feet of soil below your garden, you can consider a wider spacing system that involves watering heavily enough to bring the top 2 or 3 feet of soil to capacity—maybe once every two weeks. If there is a plow pan, it'll stop the plant roots from accessing the subsoil; plow pans must be broken up by deep digging. If there is a layer of heavy, gooey, airless clay beneath a foot or so of topsoil, I can't advise you for sure. This might be a great site for dry-gardening, as capillarity from the incredibly large moisture bank in the subsoil will feed a spread-out garden for weeks and weeks. Then again, the site might not prove to be a good one. The only way to find out for sure is to conduct a test.

I mentioned earlier how wild blackberry growth will reveal the amount of soil moisture available. Homesteaders considering buying forest land and gardening a clearing in it might also look at the leaders of the surrounding conifers. Where Douglas fir grows 3 to 4 feet a year, you'll find lots of soil moisture; on droughty sites the trees make a lot less growth.

It's commonly believed that humus increases the moisture-holding ability of soils. This is true, but not enough for dry-gardening where it otherwise wouldn't be possible. To increase the water-holding capacity of a soil enough to matter, you'd have to heavily amend the site to a depth of 3 or 4 feet. This is not workable, nor is it wise in terms of nutritional consequences. This kind of advice often appears in eastern garden books because a large proportion of the moisture eastern gardens get comes from intense but brief rainstorms. Heavy rain will run off of land that is deficient in organic matter and not sink in. Having a garden with a humusy topsoil means that the rain that falls on the garden will tend to infiltrate the soil and stay there to help grow the vegetables.

DRIP SYSTEMS

Drip irrigation is more conserving of water than any other kind because there is no evaporation between the sprinkler head and the soil. Still, I do not recommend drip systems for the home garden if there is any other choice.

I used drip tubes on my Lorane trial grounds from 1982 until 1987 simply because drip was the only way to water extensive areas during daylight hours with my puny 3 gpm well. Drip tubes are expensive even when purchased in 2,500-foot rolls, and they are short-lived and troublesome, but at that time I did not care what it cost in money or effort to produce my trial grounds—I was growing information, not food. Drip tubes are easily cut with sharp hoes or shovels and, despite water filters, emitter holes tend to become plugged up at times. This means that the entire system has to be carefully inspected every time it is turned on. Drip lines also shift as they expand and contract, so they won't stay "spot-on" a new transplant and aren't good for germinating seeds. They are absolutely not suitable for sandy soils, because the water goes straight down through sand without spreading out horizontally, leaving large areas of totally dry soil that the plants can't root into. If the soil contains a fair amount of clay (even many loams are as much as one-third clay), the water spreads out horizontally as well as vertically. High-quality, durable drip lines might be very workable for permanent plantings, like rows of raspberries in heavier soils, but given any choice between drip systems and sprinklers, I'd always choose sprinklers.

Chapter 6 Seeds

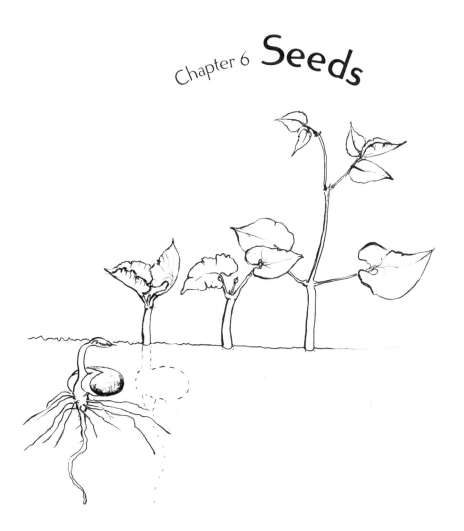

With all thy getting,
get understanding.

—ADVICE TO THE BUSINESSPERSON FROM
MALCOLM FORBES

You can sell the gardener the sweepings off the seed room floor.

—AN AGRIBUSINESS EXECUTIVE TRYING TO CONVINCE STEVE SOLOMON TO SELL HIS LOW-GRADE PRODUCT

Caveat emptor.
[Let the buyer beware.]

—ANCIENT ROMAN ADVICE ABOUT DEALING WITH THE BUSINESSPERSON

Home gardening

should be a matter of joining cooperatively with nature. Efficiency and economic rationalism are not required to be successful. While acquiring tools and fertilizers—simple goods, generally honestly sold—we don't have to be clever buyers in a difficult market. Should we get a poor tool, the only loss we may suffer is the expense of buying another. But when it comes to buying seeds, it is a very different matter.

Seeds are essentials used during brief windows of opportunity, a short time in each season when each vegetable can be started. If the seed fails us, we may miss our chance for that year. How do we prevent these kinds of losses? By choosing good seeds. But the contents of one packet look exactly like the contents of another. Other than differences in the price per gram or the picture on the packet, we really can't be sure about what we've bought until after the seed has germinated (or failed to). Sometimes we don't really know if the seed was any good until the crop approaches harvest. Thus, of all the aspects of gardening, buying and using seeds require the most cleverness.

Many gardeners have had such frequent failures using seeds that they avoid them whenever possible and buy seedling transplants. Doing this has its own pitfalls, as you'll see in Chapter 7. You're far better off starting with seed whenever you can. In this chapter, I explain how to get the best garden seed obtainable, how to sow it so it comes up reliably, how to store it so it will come up next year, and how not to spend any more on it than necessary.

Vigor

The most important characteristic of any seed is whether it will sprout and begin to grow vigorously. Everything else about what a seed might do is irrelevant if germination fails. The concept of vigor comes down to how likely the seed is to germinate and get started. Vigor is easy to recognize when you see it; vigorous seeds usually sprout quickly, ini-

tially grow fast, and have a husky appearance.

In a germination laboratory, if you test ten different varieties of the same species at the same time, you'll see obvious differences in vigor. You need no training, nor do you have to learn a bunch of Latin names for the parts of seedlings to spot it. Suppose, for example, that you germinate several lots of cabbage-family seeds. A few samples will sprout in three days, most in four or five, a few in six or seven days. The earlier sprouters will look much sturdier, with thicker shoots and bigger leaves, and will grow much faster. That's vigor. Seeds can vary in vigor from variety to variety of the same species, from year to year, and even from field to field in the same year.

Vigorous seeds usually germinate at very high percentages in sterile lab tests. In the field under real conditions, a high percentage of vigorous seedlings still emerge, and these seedlings rarely succumb to damping-off disease. They quickly develop into large, healthy plants if growing conditions permit. Slow-sprouting, nonvigorous seeds usually germinate at a lower rate in the laboratory. In the field they sprout much more poorly than they do in the laboratory, and they often will neither develop as rapidly nor achieve the same size or yield as a vigorous lot.

Vigorous seed is relatively denser (fatter, as we say in the trade)—a scoop of it is heavier—because it's equipped with large reserves of complete nutrition for the embryo within. It'll have a longer shelf life, too. So seed growers do their darnedest to ensure maximum seed vigor. They fertilize and irrigate carefully, spray pesticides to defeat any insects that might reduce parent plant vigor, and apply fungicides to eliminate any disease that could attack the forming seed or the next generation of sprouts.

In their quest for the best, seed growers flock to the most ideal production districts on the planet, places where weather conditions are most likely to be perfect for a particular species. Consequently, most of the world's cabbage seed (and a great portion of the beet seed) is produced in the Skagit Valley around Mount Vernon, Washington; growers in California's Central Valley north of Sacramento and around Rocky Ford, Colorado, see Dutch and Japanese technicians supervising squash seed fields; Italian hybrid broccoli seed from Japanese seed companies is grown in California's Imperial Valley; and Dutch seedsmen may grow their world-famous hybrid Brussels sprout seed in Italy. Not surprisingly, seeds arrive at the warehouse in reasonably vigorous condition most years.

Still, many efforts at growing seed do not turn out as hoped. Weather conditions are outside the growers' control. Sometimes a rented or leased field isn't as fertile as it might be. And I suspect that the vegetable seed–producing areas are overused; they would yeild much more vigorous seed if seed fields were put to pasture every few years. But the land probably seems too valuable to be rotated into relatively profitless grass pasture or cereals.

Vigor (and germination rate) is not a static condition—it goes down and down and down, relentlessly. Because the embryo is a living thing, slowly breathing and consuming its food reserve, it does age and die. Exposure to oxygen and the simple passage of time make the seed's food supply slowly deteriorate, and this too weakens the embryo. Eventually, vigor will decline to the point that the seed can no longer sprout successfully. To slow the inevitable decline, a whole technology of seed storage has evolved. Later in this chapter, I show how understanding seed storage can save you a lot of money.

You, the customer, have a right to expect vigorous seed that will come up and *grow*. To put it much too mildly, sowings that fail to come up, or spindly seedlings that, after taking a long time sprouting, grow very slowly or disappear are mighty disappointing. But gardeners are not expert horticulturalists and often are uncertain whether poor growth is their fault or the weather's fault. One way to recognize whether you've been sold low-vigor seed is when sowings of similar varieties or other similar species made at the same time do germinate and grow well.

Sprouting is exhausting, hard, and dangerous work. With the clock ticking fast from the moment the seed imbibes enough moisture to be activated, the embryo must build an entire functional plant before its limited food reserves run out. Even after emergence, the seedling must draw on its own food reserves because initially, with only one or two tiny leaves working, its ability to manufacture food by photosynthesis is insufficient for its needs. Only after the first true leaf has fully developed can the average seedling photosynthesize enough food to grow with. If cold, wet soil delays sprouting or if soil compaction resists the seed's effort to move root and shoot through it, the seedling may emerge with overly depleted reserves and be unable to build enough additional leaf from its own stores to take off and grow fast. Seedlings of average or low vigor that are weakened by a difficult sprouting often succumb to various environmental menaces shortly after emergence, growing very slowly and reeling like a beaten-up fighter from every insect and disease that comes along. Vigorous seed has enough food reserves to overcome a considerable number of environmental obstacles and still make a true leaf.

GERMINATION TESTS

Vigor is widely recognized but rarely mentioned by seed sellers. The last thing a seed company wants to do is suggest that any particular lot of seed possesses the certain ability to establish a stand in the field. There are just too many environmental risks. So seeds are bought and sold on the basis of their laboratory germination rate.

Laboratory germination rate is an absolute and repeatable result. Enough of a connection exists between vigor and laboratory germina-

Germinating seed.

tion rate that anyone sowing "high germ" seed can be hopeful that it will survive sprouting, emerge, and grow.

The custom in the seed trade is that the seller's legal responsibility is limited to providing seed that has a certain honestly stated ability to germinate in the laboratory. Period. What happens in the field is the buyer's problem. By law, every large bag of seed sold (containing much more than a garden-seed packet does) must be labeled with the results of a certified germination test performed within the past six months.

The seed law fails to protect the home gardener, however. Packets of less than one pound—meaning garden-seed packets—do not have to show recent germination test results as long as the results were above certain minimum standards. This sounds reasonable, avoiding an unnecessary packaging expense that would be passed on to the consumer. It also seems to protect the home gardener by keeping germination levels above a minimum. In reality, however, standard germination rates are so low that a commercial grower would never buy seed anywhere near the minimum level.

Under the Federal Seed Act, the minimum standard germination rate for cabbage seed is 75 percent. With virtually ideal field conditions—warm soil that is airy, loose, and moist but not soggy, no strong chemicals present, the seed perfectly placed on a firm seedbed and loosely covered to the right depth, no soil-dwelling insect predation, and minimal damping-off disease—cabbage seed that germinated at a rate of 75 percent in the lab might yield a 20 percent field emergence of

How Seeds Really Germinate in the Field

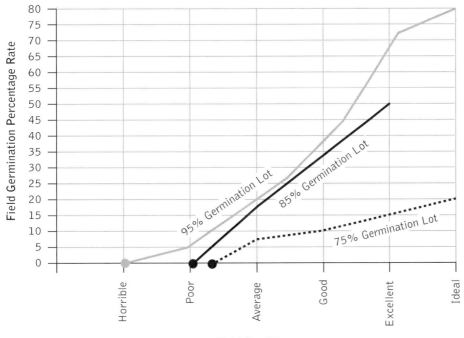

Shown in this graph are the actual field results of sowing three different lots of cabbage seed. One lot germinated at 95% in the laboratory; the next lot at 85%; the last at 75%, which is the legal minimum standard germination rate.

sickly seedlings. Under average field conditions, emergence would drop to below 10 percent; under poor field conditions, the cabbage seed probably would not come up at all—not one single seedling. However, cabbage seed with a germination rate of 85 percent might sprout in the field at a rate of 50 percent under excellent conditions and 20 percent under average ones. Cabbage seed having a laboratory germination rate of 95 percent might sprout at a rate of 80 percent under ideal field conditions, and a few seedlings from this super lot might even emerge under horrible field conditions. (See the graph "How Seeds Really Germinate in the Field" above.)

A knowledgeable farmer avoids a cabbage seed lot that has tested below 85 percent. (The farmer smiles when offered a 90 percent or better lot.) The home gardener, on the other hand, buys a small packet of cabbage seed that can have germinated at a rate of anywhere from 75 percent to 98 percent up to six months before it was packaged, and could possess anything from extremely low to extremely high vigor. What's a gardener to do?

After a few bad experiences, most gardeners decide to sow seed thickly because it's easier to thin out extra seedlings than to make up for lost time when the packet fails to sprout well enough. Some serious gardeners discover high-quality mail-order seed companies, such as Stokes and Johnny's, that do not depend on the gardener for the bulk of their business. They sell gardeners the same seed that they sell to farmers. There are also other very ethical seed merchants that sell commercial-quality seed to the home gardener. Fortunately for us, a pair of responsible mail-order businesses, Territorial Seed and West Coast, specialize in serving our region.

You can't count on each and every packet containing dynamite seed, even from the finest supplier. Occasionally, somewhat weaker lots must be sold, because growing seed is not like making screws and bolts—you get only one chance to produce it every year, and the weather doesn't always cooperate.

You can be reasonably sure you're getting seed with a very high germination rate when you buy hybrid seed by count instead of by weight. More and more these days, big growers are refining their seed production to a high art because the end users of their finest hybrid varieties are either commercial growers that raise transplant seedlings using automated seeding systems, or farmers using pelletized seed dropped from precision planters. These customers place a single seed at a time and expect almost every one to sprout, and they are willing to pay the price. But these labor-saving methods work only when germination is

extraordinarily good. So when you buy hybrid vegetable seed by the count at seemingly very high prices, you too can assume almost perfect germination—if your sprouting conditions are reasonably good.

Getting the Most Out of Your Seed

Even if you're willing to pay top prices to the best suppliers, you cannot count on every packet containing highly vigorous seeds. Therefore, it's wise to improve sprouting conditions so that seeds of only average vigor can come up and grow. You can do this by understanding how a seed germination lab coaxes the highest possible rate of sprouting out of a seed lot. In the lab, seeds are sprouted under perfect conditions: at an optimum moisture level, in an ideal medium, and at precisely controlled temperatures ideal for the species being tested. Those are the key factors: moisture, medium, and temperature. They control the rate of sprouting and its success or failure.

MOISTURE

Seed sprouts poorly when very moist. This fact surprises gardeners. Soggy soils are usually cold and certainly full of damping-off disease, a fungus that can kill seedlings even before they emerge into the light. Damping-off fungi will continue to pick seedlings off during their first two or three weeks after emergence. You can recognize damping-off disease when the seedling suddenly wilts or the stem forms a scaly collar at ground level and then pinches off at that point. Damping-off organisms don't thrive under dryish conditions.

Seed can absorb moisture and activate when soil is only slightly damp. Most testing labs get the highest possible percentage of germination by placing seed between or atop sheets of damp (not soaking wet) blotting paper sealed into a small, clear plastic container. Because the container is airtight, there is no risk that the seeds will dry out or that you will accidentally add too much moisture during sprouting by having to remoisten the medium. The very highest possible germination percentage being the goal, blotting paper, jar, and water are all sterile. The way the lab brings the blotting paper to the right moisture is to immerse it in water and then squeeze out as much water as possible by wadding the paper up in a very strong fist. This makes it tacky-damp, not wet.

When soil is used instead (some species germinate much better in soil), it is sterilized too. In preparation for a lab test, powdered sterile, dry, loamy earth is slowly moistened until a handful squeezed very hard into a ball will just barely stick together and will easily break apart into fine particles. (Note that this is similar to the test used to determine optimum tilling moisture.) To prevent dehydration, germination tests in soil, like blotting-paper tests, are done in airtight containers. In my own germination lab, I found that soil in covered containers with lowish but adequate moisture levels could sprout several times more

seedlings than soil exposed to open air that had to be watered every day or two. Consider the implications of this fact if you're in the habit of sprinkling your seeds every day. "But what do I do when it's hot and sunny?" you experienced gardeners ask. "I don't want my seeds dry out and die!" There are ways to prevent seeds from drying out so fast, so you can water them less often. I get to these shortly.

SPROUTING MEDIUM

First, consider how the sprouting medium itself affects germination. Emerging seedlings are capable of exerting only a small amount of force against surrounding soil particles as they push out roots and send up a shoot toward the light. In the lab, finely sieved, compost-rich vermiculite/perlite/sand mixes are used. These mixes permit even the most delicate seedling to develop. The delicacy of most sprouts is why we make friable seedbeds.

In the field, small seeds near the surface must be kept moist until they've put a root down into damper, deeper earth—or they die. However, frequent watering jeopardizes sprouting seeds, increasing damping-off and on many soil types creating crusts that can block emergence. And each time we water a germinating seedbed, the cold water lowers the soil temperature. By remembering that sprouting seeds prefer damp rather than wet soil, we can avoid unnecessarily watering the seeds on cloudy days.

The gardener can also enhance germination in ways that a farmer could never consider. Covering small, weakly sprouting seed with a light, moisture-retentive medium similar to that used in greenhouse mixes can greatly increase the sprouting rate, and it's not much trouble on a home-garden scale. Finely sifted compost, sifted very well-rotted horse manure, and potting mix (as recommended in the next chapter) are all materials that hold a lot of water, resist drying out, act as a mulch to conserve soil moisture, and do not form a crust. During warm, sunny weather, seed covered with sifted compost needs watering only every two days (except in the very hottest weather), while seed covered with soil has to be watered daily. I usually don't bother covering seed with a special soil mix in the spring or after mid-September, when moist soil tends to stay damp by itself, except when I am sowing very tiny seeds outdoors that are normally started indoors, such as celery and herbs like oregano and basil.

Another germination enhancer is next to no trouble at all. Instead of rototilling in compost or spading it in, we can rake it in. A thin layer of compost raked into the surface inch of soil of a bed will convert the whole surface into much the sort of germination medium delicate seedlings do best in.

The rule is to plant seed about three times the depth of its largest dimension. In the cool moistness of spring, I generally sow very fine seed (celery, basil) about ¼ inch deep. I do this by first raking in a bit of fine compost atop the bed, scratching a shallow furrow, and sprinkling the seed into that furrow without covering it. The minute seeds fall into little cracks and crevasses between soil particles and bury themselves at appropriate depths. Light watering with a fine spray will put the seed a

bit further into tiny soil pockets. I get very good emergence this way as long as I sow in spring, before the sun gets strong and the temperatures get high. I would never try to sow very fine seed during the hot, sunny summer unless I erected a temporary structure over the row to shade it until the seedlings emerged.

The deeper seed is placed, the slower it dries out. Loose, humusy soil atop seeds lets us bury them a bit deeper. I cover ordinary-sized small seed (cabbage family, carrot, lettuce) about ½ inch deep, huskier seed (spinach, radish, beet, Chinese cabbage) about ⅝ to ¾ inch deep, and large seed (squash, cucumber, melon, beans, peas) about 1½ inches deep.

One final technique is essential to reduce the need to water sprouting seeds: restoring capillarity. Most of us till the earth to make it fit for sprouting seeds. When we do this, however, we shatter and fracture the network of capillary connections that bring subsurface moisture up. If we sow in this loose earth, we'll have to sprinkle frequently. But have you ever seen what happens to footprints in a freshly rototilled field? Although the entire field may be dry at the end of the day, by the next morning, the footprints will be wet while the rest of the powdery field remains dry. The pressure of the foot has compacted the earth enough to restore capillarity. During the night, moisture came up to the surface there. When the sun shines on that footprint, it dries out in a few hours. The next morning it may be moist again.

Now imagine would happen if someone had dropped seeds atop that footprint and then covered them to the appropriate depth for that type of seed with a fine mulch of dryish soil or with a compost/soil mix that wouldn't crust over under any circumstances. The seeds would be lying on damp earth, exactly as they lie on damp blotter paper in a seed germination testing lab. The moisture would be protected from evaporation by the thin mulch above. Unless conditions got very hot and sunny, it would not be necessary to irrigate these seeds for several days, perhaps not until they sprouted. There's no need to beat the soil down to a brick to restore capillarity. Just firm pressure, enough to push the tilled earth down an inch or two, will do the trick.

This technique makes all the difference. I've used several methods to restore capillarity before sowing. I've run one wheel of my garden cart down the row I'm going to seed. You could similarly push a lightly loaded wheelbarrow down the just-tilled row. Either makes a furrow. Then place seed on that compacted tire track and rake a bit of loose soil over it. When sowing in short rows across a raised bed, after raking out the bed's surface I make furrows by compacting the soil with the narrow edge of a 5-foot-long piece of 1-by-4. The only species I'm reluctant to do this with are carrots and parsnips, which seem to demand the loosest, fluffiest soil to develop the nicest roots.

One reason many gardeners believe it is far easier to sprout big seeds—such as beans, peas, and corn—is that they're planted deeper, where the soil doesn't dry out so fast. Even for these seeds, it is wise to restore capillarity first. Then you won't have to sow them quite so far down,

and they'll emerge faster and at a higher rate.

One last capillarity-restoring technique I use I call "handmade footprints." To reduce thinning and avoid wasting seed, I start what will become large plants with clusters of seeds, a few seeds per cluster, carefully placed above a well-fertilized spot or hill. I'll arrange these a few feet apart down long rows, in 18- to 24-inch patterns atop raised beds (such as when starting brassicas), or in widely spaced hills for the cucurbit family. After mixing in some fertilizer well below where the seeds are to go, with my fist I gently push down a depression in the center of the fluffed-up mound. Sometimes my fist goes in so easily that I have to replace a bit more soil in the depression I just made and compress it again—gently. The purpose is not to make rammed earth or cement, only to make firm soil under a shallow, fist-sized depression. Then I place a few seeds atop the depression and cover them to the right depth with fine, humusy earth. Even if several hot, sunny days follow, I get good germination without watering.

This method is so effective that I can inevitably get two or three brassica seedlings to emerge from sowing four or five carefully counted out seeds. This seed economy matters when each seed costs a cent or more. When sowing outdoors, I would never start only two seeds to get one plant. There are too many risks to delicate seedlings, too many losses. Better to start five, get three to come up, and then thin gradually as they begin to compete.

TEMPERATURE

The last vital factor in successful germination is soil temperature. Cold seed sprouts slowly, if at all, and all the while the seed is struggling to get started it is prey to diseases and insects in the soil. Most vegetable seeds sprout at between 60° and 105°F, with the best germination at 75° to 85°F. For most species, sprouting stops at temperatures under 60°F; over 100°F, the seedling may die. Some tropical species like peppers, eggplants, and melons won't sprout at all if soil temperatures fall below 70°F for very long.

A few types of seeds sprout better at slightly cooler temperatures. Spinach, for example, will sprout at from 45° to 85°F, although it's best at about 55° to 60°F, and it seldom sprouts well over 70°F, so it's hard to get spinach going in July. The germination lab makes the optimum temperature for the species under test. In the garden during spring, 60°F is the critical minimum soil temperature for getting most summer crop seeds to sprout.

Planting by soil temperature usually works better than planting by the calendar. In February, when spring soil warm-up begins, soil temperatures may be below 40°F. Different soils warm up at different rates. Dark-colored, well-drained, light-textured loams heat faster than moisture-retentive clayey soils. Southern exposures warm up much more rapidly than eastern or northern ones. Many of our region's soils don't reach a stable 60°F until May. At Lorane, Oregon, I worked a northeast-sloping, light-brown silty clay (subsoil—the topsoil had long since washed away) at an elevation of 900 feet, and it wouldn't sprout bean seed until late May at best. At Elkton, Oregon, I gardened on rich, black, bottomland loam alongside the Umpqua River, less

than 100 feet above sea level, and beans would sprout easily in early April most springs.

Using a soil thermometer for a few years helps novice gardeners intuitively connect weather with soil temperature. (A soil thermometer can also help you track how cloches and cold frames respond to changes in weather and season.) Experienced gardeners often tune into nature's own soil thermometer—the procession of bloom and the appearance of new plants each spring. For example, at Elkton when the crocuses came up, it was time to fertilize overwintered onions; when Japanese plums bloomed, it was time to sow radishes; apple blossoms signified the beginning of lettuce sowing season; and when the cow parsnips were in full bloom, it was safe to transplant tomatoes without protection. You'll have to observe the indicators around your own garden.

Weather changes rapidly affect soil temperature several inches down. When the spring sun shines strongly, dark-colored soils heat up fast and can reach 80°F or more near the surface. At night, these same soils can drop to 60°F an inch below the surface but will warm again quickly the next morning if the sun comes out. However, if the weather becomes cloudy or, worse, rainy, soils can drop into the mid- to low 50s in a flash and stay that way until the weather improves. Watering the seeds has exactly the same effect on soil temperature, so I try hard to avoid it. When watering is essential, I do it midmorning, just before the sun starts heating up the soil. That way the soil will be warm again by midday and will stay reasonably warm all night.

Planting during spring's unstable weather

chances either a germination failure or the retarded emergence of a bunch of badly weakened seedlings on their way to becoming permanently stunted by further chilly, cloudy conditions. But not planting early can result in a late harvest, or none at all. That's the sort of dilemma we have with growing all food crops. If we miss our chance that year, there won't be another. And that's the main reason selling weak seeds seems such a crime to me. Gardeners have only a short time to make up for seeds that don't germinate and rarely can make up for a weak germination that won't ever grow right.

It would be good if we gardeners could determine the weather and then sow just before the onset of a long sunny spell. Or, as Will Rogers used to say about investing, "To make money in the markets, buy a stock that goes up. If it don't go up, don't buy it." If your precognition fails, or if the weather turns poor, replant as soon as conditions improve, even before you know the fate of the first sowing. If both sowings come up, you're only out a bit of seed, but you haven't lost your window of opportunity. In that case, choose the group of seedlings that does best over the next three to six weeks. In those lousy springs called "cabbage years," I'll cheerfully make three or more subsequent sowings of the same thing a week apart if necessary.

SOWING IN SUMMER'S HEAT

Mid-June until mid-August, when most of the winter garden is started, is the most difficult sowing period. When it gets really hot, it makes sense to presprout seeds. First give them an overnight soaking in water. At bedtime, place the seeds in a half-pint mason jar, cover the jar with a square of plastic window screen held on with a strong rubber band, barely cover the seeds with a few drops of tepid water, and soak them overnight. Drain them first thing in the morning. *Do not submerge them any longer than eight hours, or you may suffocate them.* Then gently rinse the seeds with tepid water two or three times daily, draining them carefully afterward and placing the jar on its side. Do this until the root tips begin to emerge. As soon as this sign of sprouting appears, the seed must be sown immediately because the emerging roots are easily broken and, worse, will soon form tangled masses. Presprouted seeds can be gingerly blended into a crumbly mix of moist soil and compost, and then gently sprinkled into a capillarity-restored furrow and covered to the correct depth. They'll emerge in a surprisingly short time.

GETTING A UNIFORM STAND

If the sprouts are particularly delicate or spendy, or if, as in the case of carrots, you want a very uniformly spaced stand, you can blend the sprouting seeds into a starch gelatin and, with a few cents' worth of jerry-rigged equipment, imitate what commercial vegetable growers call fluid drilling. Heat 1 pint of water to the boiling point. Dissolve in it 2 to 3 tablespoons of ordinary cornstarch. Place the mixture in the refrigerator to cool rapidly. Soon the liquid will set into a starch gelatin, about as viscous as very thick soup. You may have to fiddle about a bit until you find the correct ratio of water to cornstarch. If it's too thick, the mixture will not spread well and you won't be able to blend in the sprouting seeds uniformly without damaging them. If it's too thin, it won't protect the sprouts and may flow too fast when you're sowing.

Gently and uniformly blend the sprouting seeds into the gel soup. Pour the mixture into a cup and spoon a bit of it into each planting spot. Or put it into a 1-quart plastic reclosable bag and, scissors in hand, go out to the garden. After a furrow has been made, cut a small hole (slightly less than ¼ inch in diameter) in the lower corner of the bag. Walk quickly down the row, dribbling a mixture of gel and seeds into the furrow as though you were squeezing toothpaste out of a tube. It may take you a few experiments using gel without seeds to get the hole size and gel thickness right. But once you've mastered this technique, I think you'll really like it. After fluid drilling a few times, you'll realize that you need quite a bit less seed per row-foot than you previously thought.

Farmers use some very spendy and complicated seeding equipment to avoid wasting seed and reduce hand-thinning. Garden magazines and seed catalogs sell various planting machines that aren't all that expensive but that don't work very well for the most part. Here's one technique that does work well and that costs nothing. When sowing small seed in rows, either long rows or short ones across raised beds, put a pinch of seed into a quart or two of sifted compost or fine composty soil on the dry side, and thoroughly blend it in. Then distribute this mixture down the furrow. You may be amazed at how much thinning and seed waste you'll prevent.

I know, for example, that a heaping ¼ teaspoon of carrot seed mixed into a gallon of compost will start about one carrot per inch along about 50 feet of row. There's no way to be exact about this, however, because the size of the seed and the germination rate varies from lot to lot as well as from species to species. The same volume of lettuce seed would be more than enough for twice that length of row.

An Insider Tells About the Garden Seed Business

We toss two packets of cabbage seed through a window of opportunity, and hope. One packet explodes into life and grows lovely, dense, sweet heads, uniform as peas in a pod; the other, with identical-looking black specks inside, perhaps even with the same varietal name, sprouts much less vigorously and yields misshapen heads that burst open long before they get really hard. At ten weeks old, many of the more energetic plants in this sleazy lot begin to resemble kale and don't make heads at all. But how can you tell the difference before you plant the seed when all seed catalogs and most picture packets are designed to impress?

First, understand some things about the seed trade. Few gardeners realize that retail seed companies are merchants, buying and repackaging seeds, although some of these merchants grow a small percentage of their varieties themselves. Companies that actually produce vegetable seed (called primary growers) are virtually unknown to the gardening public. If they would speak frankly, they'd admit that the home gardener is relatively unimportant to their profit picture. Many primary growers also consider home gardeners to be an "uncritical trade," meaning that gardeners aren't very savvy. So primary growers treat retail garden-seed merchants differently than they treat their network of farm-seed dealers. Farmers account for the largest portion of the primary growers' profits. Farmers demand the best seed, and they can tell when they haven't been sold what they wanted. They're critical buyers, and their business is critical to the primary growers' bottom lines.

Home gardeners, amateurs, tend to blame disappointments on uncooperative weather or their own lack of ability. We may not even hold the seed merchant responsible for a packet that fails to sprout when field conditions are favorable. If we do blame the seed, we merely growl to ourselves about the inexpensive packet. We haven't lost enough to sue or demand a refund. Gardeners are such pushovers that a few sleazier primary growers more interested in supplying garden-seed merchants have a saying: "The gardener gets the sweepings off the seed room floor."

Few garden-seed merchants have buying clout. A California broccoli grower planting 160 acres may spend $25, 000 to $50,000 on a single seed purchase. That's buying clout. And this farmer knows broccoli, knows precisely how broccoli germination is affected by weather and seedbed conditions, and knows why a stand emerges slowly or thinly. The farmer knows how much the first week's growth is affected by environmental conditions and how much by seed vigor. The farmer often knows the variety from past years and has seen it grow at different seasons. So the big farmer demands, and gets, the best commercial-quality seed available. Or he gets another supplier.

A small to medium-sized garden-seed company supplying 25,000 home gardeners each year spends $50,000 to $100,000 each year on seed, if they're selling top-quality seed (much less if they're selling mainly cheap stuff). But that expenditure pays for some 300 to 500 separate items purchased from a dozen or so primary growers. Beyond the fragile and often illusory bonds of friendship and the force of moral suasion (which often has little impact on the corporate mentality), a small garden-seed company has little or no buying clout.

I suspect that being a garden-seed merchant trying to buy quality seed was easier a generation ago, when primary growers were smaller, far more numerous and thus more competitive, and family owned. The number of varieties to choose from was several times greater. In fact, the quality-minded garden-seed merchant of that era could build a business reputation on uniquely chosen superior varieties. I know that's how it was because in the early 1980s, when I was in the trade, there were still many independent primary growers. After a decade of heavy consolidation, about half of the remaining primary producers are now owned by foreign conglomerates—Swiss, Dutch, French, Japanese, Danish, British. The other half are owned by American conglomerates. Only a few are still family firms.

Occasionally, divisions of multibillion-dollar international corporations operate with compassion and a highly developed sense of ethics. Occasionally. But it's harder for the little customer to develop genuine personal relationships with high-volume job-hopping sales executives who are mainly concerned with the progress of their own career and the size of next year's salary increase. Garden-seed merchants trying to buy high-quality seed in this environment have to work especially hard at developing and maintaining their lines and keeping their suppliers honest. One indication of this hard work is when their catalogs talk about results in their own variety trials. If you are familiar with which primary grower produces which variety, and which varieties are the ones currently in commercial favor, quality also shows in the names of the varieties they sell.

The few surviving primary growers, having much less competition, do make much juicier profits. I suppose that over the past decade the cost of quality vegetable seed has increased several times faster than the official inflation rate. Still, seed cost is small compared with the value it can create, while it takes the same amount of fertilizer, water, tillage, and work to grow vegetables using poor seed as it does using the best. Small-space gardeners, who cannot afford to waste space with low-yielding plants, should never consider using anything but the best.

Give the big outfits some credit, too. Creating great new varieties is expensive. It takes talented plant breeders with an intuitive knack

that isn't guaranteed by their university degree; and it takes a lot of time. Beyond the cost of research and development, keeping existing varieties pure and uniform is also expensive.

A handful of primary growers intentionally produce the cheapest possible seed, grown with little quality control. Their customers are seed rack jobbers, some mail-order houses, and Third World seed merchants servicing market gardeners (and home gardeners) who cannot afford top-quality commercial varieties. Their cheap seed may be quite vigorous if it is fresh, but off-type and low-yielding plants are common in these sorts of lots. Usually sold from picture-packet displays in discount-store garden departments, this third-rate seed is what many home gardeners end up using.

Cheap seed is not always undesirable. A high percentage of off-type plants may not be significant when a gardener is growing unrefined species like chives, chard, parsley, scallions, or kale. Assuming that the germination is adequate and the variety is well adapted to the climate and soil, variations may not matter that much in the leaf shape of kale and parsley, or in the stalk width or color of chard, or in the shaft length of scallions. But a high percentage of quick-bolting off-types in a batch of head lettuce can matter. With refined vegetables like salad radishes, munching carrots, bulbing onions, heading lettuce, Brussels sprouts, cabbage, broccoli, or cauliflower, individual plants that vary too much from the ideal may produce little or no edible or marketable food.

For example, open-pollinated red radish seed grown exclusively for the home garden trade that costs the packeter a mere $2 per pound yields, at best, one or two near-perfect roots per ten plants. Skin colors in this cheap lot may vary widely, from pale pink to crimson or purple. Many of the bulbs will have thick, roughened skins, coarse and/or multiple taproots, and huge crowns, and more than half the plants will fail to make a roundish bulb at all. An average-grade commercial-quality radish seed lot, sold to the farmer at less than $10 per pound, gives five to seven decent bulbs and a couple of rougher but still acceptable ones for every ten plants. Extra-fancy radish varieties are sold by the seed instead of by weight, at a retail price that can reach $200 per pound, but such seed can produce between nine and ten absolutely perfect bulbs per ten plants if expertly grown.

These huge price differences don't make much actual difference in the price of garden-seed packets, because most of the cost when you're buying only a gram or two is in the packaging and distribution, not in the contents. A few grams of the cheapest radish seed sells for around a dollar, while Johnny's Selected Seeds sells a mini-packet of 'Sora', the most uniform and refined variety I know right now, for $2.35. My point is that you're far better off buying the good stuff.

Another way to recognize cheap seed produced exclusively for home gardens is by varietal names. In any species that lends itself to efficient mass hybridization, the old open-pollinated varieties vanish from the quality trade. Hybrid varieties have virtually taken over in the commercial production of broccoli, cabbages, cauliflower, cucumbers, corn,

summer squash, Chinese cabbage, Brussels sprouts, onions, and many carrots. I expect that soon most decent winter squash will also be hybrid.

In species like tomato, pepper, beet, radish, and melon, both hybrid and open-pollinated varieties will probably exist side by side for quite some time because hybrids are far more expensive to produce and often don't show sufficient advantages to justify the extra cost. When it comes to lettuce, endive, peas, or beans—species virtually impossible to mass hybridize—hybrid varieties are unlikely for the foreseeable future. Even with these species, however, the cheap old standards don't predominate in the quality trade, because commercial companies are always introducing interesting and superior patented varieties.

When I see a garden-seed company primarily selling old open-pollinated varieties long ago dropped from commercial trade—cabbage varieties like Golden Acre, Danish Ballhead, Chieftain Savoy, or Flat Dutch; carrots like plain Scarlet Nantes, Danvers, or Red-Cored Chantenay; Snowball cauliflower strains, often followed by a letter like A or T or a number; broccoli varieties like Waltham 29, Italian Green Sprouting, Calabrese, or De Cieco; Brussels sprouts like Catskill or Long Island Improved; onions named Early Yellow Globe or open-pollinated Yellow Sweet Spanish—I'm pretty sure I'm being offered cheap garden seed.

Rather than accepting the representations of the primary grower's salesperson or catalog or choosing varieties by hearsay or the reports of research institutions, responsible garden-seed merchants make decisions about what goes into their catalogs by performing their own variety trials. Doing this also gives their catalogs a decidedly regional bent, as the varieties offered will suit the climate where the merchant is. This regionality is not as pronounced as it used to be, because there are far fewer primary growers and far fewer choices available. These days the mail-order seed merchant really has to scratch around to find something to sell that is different from what everyone else has. The biggest difference between suppliers often is the point at which they'll throw out a weak lot with fast-declining germination (or refuse to buy it).

The best garden-seed firms grow out many of the new seed lots they purchase. Should the lot prove disappointing, they'll discard any carryover and/or demand a refund from the primary grower who supplied it, and get new and better seed for the coming year. Of course, thousands of their customers will also have discovered, right along with the seed merchant, that the "Siberian" kale was really some kind of field collard suitable only for cattle feed. This actually happened to me once when I ran Territorial Seed.

Growing variety trials, doing grow-outs to confirm that new seed lots they purchase are what they expected to be buying, and complaining and demanding refunds for unsold seed when they've been "had" or when an honest labeling mistake was made (you can't tell which)—these steps help, but nothing can guarantee perfect quality control. Allowing for errors, misfortunes, pitfalls, and mischief, how good a job can a garden-seed companies

do? If they try hard, all but a small percentage of the seed they sell will perform as expected.

If you really want to have your garden come out as expected, pick seed retailers with an emphasis on quality varieties who operate substantial trial gardens in a climate similar to our own. If possible, I'd lean toward companies that also supply a commercial clientele. Those are the companies that buy seed only when it is well in excess of minimum germination standards, that test germination levels of all new arrivals, and that discard any seed lot in their warehouses should its germination level decline appreciably.

If a high degree of uniformity and peak yield is important to you, avoid the old, generic, varietal names and go for the latest and best the catalog has to offer. From a quality-conscious company, gardeners should expect decent field germination and uniform results from 95 percent of their seed packets—but not from 100 percent of them. Not every attempt to grow seed yields a vigorous product with a high germination rate. Seed is a living entity. It occasionally deteriorates, mysteriously and suddenly.

We mostly get what we demand. To improve the garden-seed trade, become a responsible customer. Always take advantage of the company's offer of a replacement or refund when a packet fails to perform satisfactorily. Save up the disappointments all summer with a record of what didn't happen, and send the empty packets back when planting season is over with a refund demand. Complaints let the better suppliers know that something has slipped past quality control, and they let the cut-rate companies know that some gardeners out there are a critical trade. And don't give up on a company that sells you an occasional poor performer—that can happen even with the best.

Who to Buy From

I have been out of the seed trade for 15 years, so I am not able to give you an up-to-date insider's evaluation of specific seed companies. Still, I remain acquainted with the owners of several packet-seed businesses and am friends with two. And the basic nature of the trade today is not that different from what it was a couple of decades ago. With those disclaimers in mind, I leave it to the reader to judge what I have to say about individual companies in the garden-seed trade.

Consider first the seed rack business. Picture packets are conveniently available at supermarkets, garden centers, and discount stores; the larger seed racks even offer a wide range of varieties. But I have a lot of misgivings about picture-packet seed to share with you.

Some rack jobbers serve a larger territory than the maritime Northwest. Far fewer than 10 million people live in our bioregion—not a big enough market to satisfy some ambitious entrepreneurs. Supplying gardeners both east and west of the Cascades means making compromises in varietal choice—compromises that make profits but often work to the disadvantage of the maritime gardener who trusts that anything sold on the rack will grow okay. When I see a Willamette Valley rack selling ordinary open-pollinated okra or Hale's Best Jumbo melons—both heat-demanding crops suitable to the East or California—I am saddened. In our cool climate they rarely grow well.

Sometimes rack seed is not fresh and vigorous enough—not always, but too often. Picture-packet rack companies are in a highly competitive business with severe profit restrictions. After sharing 50 to 70 percent of the gross proceeds with the store the rack sits in, and then deducting their own overhead and distribution costs—not to mention the minuscule cost of the cheap seed in those pretty packets—there is not much left to cover the large number of unsold dated packets that must be returned, accounted for, and then discarded once a year. Credit collections are frequently a big and expensive problem because the usual accepted terms of the trade force the rack jobber to consign racks in January and often render no billing until the end of summer. Many garden-center owners with dollar signs for hearts take every possible advantage and will not pay for last year's seed until threatened with the refusal of next year's rack—and some won't pay even then. Or by then they've gone out of business.

Tight profit margins in this cutthroat business seem to force rack jobbers to save every possible penny. So these companies do no more than grudgingly follow the letter of the seed law, keeping enough of their packets above minimum standard germination to fend off the wrath of the state agriculture department seed cop. A high percentage of rack packets are filled with the most inexpensive seed obtainable, or with very small quantities of more costly stuff. Uncritical home gardeners rarely realize why a third of their kohlrabi isn't round but tapers to a point like a Cambodian temple and gets woody so rapidly, or why the loosely budded side shoots on their broccoli are larger than the central heads. They blame their fertilizing, or their watering, or the weather that season. But it's the seed that's really at fault.

This is not to imply that you never get good-quality, high-germination seed from an ordinary picture-packet seed rack. You do—sometimes. And I would not hesitate to buy a picture packet of parsley seed or pea seed or some other nonrefined variety if I needed some in a hurry.

Buying mail-order garden seed doesn't guarantee top-quality or better-adapted varieties, either. Even more than rack jobbers, almost every mail-order garden-seed company is trying to serve the whole of North America through a single catalog. Many do not tell the reader which variety is adapted to which location, if they even know. The more responsible companies describe how the variety grows on their own trial ground.

Mail-order companies range widely in quality and business ethics. The gardener sometimes has no certain way of knowing whether the company actually has much of a trial ground or what its in-house germination standards are like. Perhaps the company merely sends out an attractive catalog filled with old-fashioned, well-known varieties (most of them grown by those cheap producers for the home garden trade), spiced with a few recent All America selections that currently are being heavily promoted in gardening magazines.

Here's the story, as I see it, on a few prominent mail-order companies I can recommend. Some otherwise fine businesses are not mentioned because their catalog offerings have less relevance to the maritime garden; some I'm simply not currently acquainted with—no slight is intended.

Johnny's Selected Seeds:

Founder Robert Johnston, Jr., set out to focus his business on serving gardeners in the northernmost tier of states, high-elevation short-season sites, and southern Canada where summers are cooler and winter is severe—just like on his Albion, Maine, trial ground. Johnny's has grown enormously since it started about twenty-five years ago, has developed a large market-gardener trade, and breeds a few of its own varieties. Johnny's runs a thorough trial ground. Rob realized early on that the federally prescribed minimum germination standards were too low for a person of conscience, and so the company maintains higher in-house minimums, plainly published in the informative catalog that also shows soil temperature/germination response curves. Cultural information is quite complete and truly without overstatement or sales puffs, describing precisely how each vegetable grows at Albion, Maine.

Maritime Northwest gardeners will not be pleased by the performance of some of Johnny's varieties. Many of the tomatoes, for instance, seem to require warmer nights than are found west of the Cascades, and so are later and less prolific here than they are in Maine. Crops for fall harvest, typical of what is needed in the

East, tend to mature quickly and don't withstand maritime winter weather, though some are good here. If Territorial and West Coast did not exist, I'd be a happy but selective customer. *Contact Johnny's Selected Seeds, Foss Hill Road, Albion, ME 04910. www.johnnyseeds.com*

Stokes Seeds: Before I went into the business myself, I used to buy a lot of my seed from Stokes. Located in St. Catharines, Ontario, Stokes has a northern trial ground that tends to select for varieties that adapt fairly well to our summers. The company is also a big supplier to large vegetable growers in southern Canada and the northern United States. Most of the seeds in its catalog are commercial quality. The Stokes catalog also contains detailed cultural information and makes great wintertime reading if you've good enough eyes for the fine print. I've never been disappointed by Stokes. *Americans: Stokes maintains a U.S. warehouse to avoid customs hassles. Contact Stokes Seeds, Inc., P.O. Box 548, Buffalo, NY 14240. Canadians: Contact Stokes Seeds Ltd., Box 10, St. Catharines, ON L2R 6R6. www.stokeseeds.com*

Territorial Seed Company: I started Territorial in 1979 to be a Johnny's for the gardener west of the Cascades. In 1985 I sold the business to Tom and Julie Johns, a gardening couple with better heads (and hearts) than I have for business. We are still friends. Tom and Julie make every effort to purchase high-quality seed with germination levels at acceptable commercial levels. The seed is warehoused under climate-controlled storage to slow the otherwise rapid deterioration that occurs

when seed is held at high humidity—which is what we have in this temperate rain forest for half the year. Unsold seed is tested twice a year and discarded if it falls below commercial standards. Territorial runs large-scale grow-outs and variety trials evaluated strictly on the potential for success in the home garden.

The catalog offers a complete assortment of vegetable varieties for the maritime Northwest garden. It also contains herbs and flowers. Territorial custom-grows some locally renowned or especially well-adapted noncommercial vegetable varieties itself. It spends a great deal more on its trial grounds and breeding work than a company of its size needs to. Territorial also has about 200 seed rack locations throughout the maritime Northwest and a couple in Alaska, offering the very same seed sold through the catalog; rack locations are listed in the catalog. *Contact Territorial Seed Company, P.O. Box 157, Cottage Grove, OR 97424. www.territorial-seed.com*

Thompson & Morgan: Some of the varieties most crucial to our successful year-round gardening are big commercial crops in England and Holland. Thompson & Morgan (T&M) is a major English garden-seed company whose colorful catalog is filled with many interesting items that are common in the British garden, as well as unusual European gourmet specialties such as chicory and sea kale. Where Territorial offers two varieties of favas, T&M may have a dozen. T&M also has an amazing selection of flower seed. Unlike other British mail-order companies such as Suttons, Thompson & Morgan accepts U.S. dollars and ships to

American customers from a New Jersey warehouse, so gardeners get fast, reliable service. *Contact Thompson & Morgan, Inc., P.O. Box 1308, Jackson, NJ 08527. www.thompson-morgan.com*

West Coast Seeds. A year or so after I started Territorial Seed, a Vancouverite, Mary Ballon, came up my driveway demanding I that provide a seed rack for her garden store. Mary was so intent on having the best seeds obtainable that she brushed aside all the cross-border obstacles and succeeded. Then she started placing other Territorial Seed racks around southwestern British Columbia. This subsidiary arrangement went on until very recently, when Mary outgrew it and struck out on her own. West Coast Seeds now imports, buys, and packages its own. Mary also runs a very serious and helpful variety trials ground located just south of Vancouver, British Columbia. If there was ever anything gardeners in northwestern Washington State and British Columbia could fault Territorial for, it was having a trials ground toward the southern end of the bioregion. West Coast is an honest and proper seed source, and I try to divide the bulk of my seed purchases between them and Territorial. *Contact West Coast Seeds, 8475 Ontario Street, Unit 206, Vancouver, BC V5X 3E8, Canada. www.westcoastseeds.com*

OTHER MAIL ORDER SEED COMPANIES

The companies I just described have always made up the core of my seed buying; you can't go wrong with them. However, others offer interesting varieties. This section lists companies I consider worthy of acknowledging. A few words of advice and a warning: Many vegetable species are not all that critical in terms of regional adaptation, and it doesn't make much difference who you buy them from so long as you're getting a delicious variety and good germination. Beware of buying heat lovers from nonregional seed houses—species like tomatoes, melons, and cucumbers. And get your winter varieties from Territorial, West Coast, or Thompson & Morgan. A few other sources specializing in seed potatoes are listed under "potato" in Chapter 9.

Bountiful Gardens, 18001 Schafer Ranch Road, Willits, CA 95490. Of interest to us is that this company imports and repackages seed from an old-time British seed house, much of it well adapted to the warmer parts of the maritime Northwest. The company is closely allied with John Jeavons' Ecology Action, also in Willits. *www.bountifulgardens.org*

The Cook's Garden, P.O. Box 535, Londonderry, VT 05148. Like Shepherd's, a good source for the unusual of gourmet interest, especially salads. *www.cooksgarden.com*

Nichols Garden Nursery, 1190 North Pacific Highway, Albany, OR 97321. Though a local company, not a regional one. Nichols sells across the United States.

Richters, P.O. Box 26, Goodwood, ON L0C 1A0, Canada. No one compares to Richters when it comes to herb seeds. No one. *www.richters.com*

Seeds Blüm, Idaho City Stage, Boise, ID 83706. A broad list of mainly open-pollinated varieties, supported by an honest germination lab and an honest attitude.

Seeds of Change, P.O. Box 15700, Santa Fe, NM 87506. Fifteen hundred varieties of 100 percent open-pollinated, 100 percent organically grown seed. And a beautiful full-color glossy catalog. All seeds are grown by Seeds of Change or by their network of small producers. Beware of two things: (1) Their orientation is the Southwest, which is hot, and so some varieties are too heat-demanding for our region; (2) their small producers are amateurs, so don't expect their bee- and wind-pollinated varieties to have commercial uniformity. *www.seedsofchange.com*

Shepherd's Garden Seeds, 30 Irene Street, Torrington, CT 06790. Especially good for gourmet and unusual varieties. *www.shepherdseed.com*

Vesey's Seeds, Ltd., York, PE C0A 1P0, Canada. Has conducted variety trials on its five-acre trials ground for sixty-odd years. Prince Edward Island can count on chilly summers, so most of Vesey's summertime varieties will adapt well to our climate. *www.veseys.com*

Saving on Seed Purchases

Most gardeners are fearful of saving leftover seed, so they purchase all new packets each year and throw out the old ones. Except in the case of a few species whose seed has a very short shelf life, this is a false economy. If the seed sprouted strongly and started growing well, if the variety pleased you enough to want to grow it again, and if there's some left, you should keep it for next season. If the seed sprouted weakly, or if you didn't much like what it grew, then by all means throw it out. Even if you've had a packet for several years, if it sprouted strongly this year, it'll very likely carry over.

If there's a chance that you'll grow a variety more than once, buy a larger-sized packet. Most of the expense of a small packet is not the seed itself, but the handling—the envelope, the catalog, and everything that went into filling and delivering it to you may well cost as much as or more than its contents. The only time you won't save much with a bigger packet is with very expensive hybrid varieties, where the seed costs much more than the handling. (Some hybrid seeds cost more than a dollar a gram wholesale—and there are 454 grams in a pound.)

Seed for most vegetable species usually has a vigorous shelf life of three to four years after harvest when held under ordinary ambient room conditions. Many species will last five to seven years if you make only a small effort to improve their storage environment. I wish I could give you a believable chart of anticipated seed life by species, but much sad and costly experience in buying seed for Territorial taught me that there is simply no way for a gardener to determine how intrinsically vigorous any seed lot is at the time it is purchased, how much it had already deteriorated, and how much longer it might last. Despite the uncertainty, however, it still pays to buy in bulk. You won't throw out nearly the value you'll save. Besides, the seed you buy "new" this year might turn out to be older or less vigorous than the seed you threw away last year. With the exception of very expensive hybrids, the only species I'd hesitate to stock up on would be the alliums (onion, leek, scallion), parsnip, spinach, and hybrid sweet corn, because they're known for having a very short shelf life.

To prevent germination failure with carried-over seed, you merely note the vigor of your seed supply each year when you sow it in the garden. To make a fair vigor test, always try to sow more than one variety of the same species at the same time so you have a chance to see differences in vigor. This is a wise practice in any event, because it insures you against a total crop failure. If a packet sprouts fast and produces husky seedlings, you can safely assume that it will retain sufficient vigor for another year. If it does not seem vigorous, discard it that season. Each year you might also mark on the packet the number of days it takes to sprout. The next year, if the time increases by several days and the weather has not been highly unfavorable, take that as a cue to discard the packet.

SEED STORAGE

With virtually no effort at all, you can make seed last four times longer than usual. For the purposes of this book, I define normal storage as being in a cardboard box on a shelf in a closet away from the woodstove, where humidity isn't excessively high and the air temperature tends to be stable. More precisely, let's call normal storage 70°F and 70 percent relative humidity (RH). The rule of thumb used in the seed trade is that for every 10°F drop in temperature from normal, combined with a corresponding reduction in humidity that lowers the seed's moisture content by 1 percent, the life of the seed doubles. It takes roughly a 10 percent drop in relative humidity to lower seed moisture by about 1 percent. So at 60°F/RH60%, the seed life is more or less double the normal span. At 50°F/RH50%, it doubles again, to four times normal.

Creating something like 50°F/RH50% at home is a piece of cake. Just get a big, freshly recharged silica-gel desiccant packet and seal it with your seed in a tightly lidded gallon jar or other airtight container. That handles the RH part. Territorial sells hefty desiccant packs, each large enough for a gallon jar, for a little more than a dollar. You can also purchase silica gel in larger quantities at hobby/craft suppliers, where it is used to make dried flower arrangements. It's also found at chemical supply shops, and sometimes a bag comes free when you buy new electronic equipment. The desiccant lowers humidity in an airtight container until it has either sucked all the moisture it can out of the air or has saturated itself. I recharge my silica gel once a year by putting it in the oven at 250°F for a few hours. If silica gel is not handy, an inch of fresh, dry, powdered milk on the bottom of the jar will do almost as well.

To keep the seeds cool, store the jar under the house or in the cellar, or keep it in a spare refrigerator. Even airtight desiccated storage in a cool closet along a north wall is enormously better than holding your seeds on a shelf in the furnace room or just tossing them into a damp cardboard box outdoors in the shed.

Seed life responds to increases in temperature and humidity, too. Temperatures above 70°F and relative humidity above 70 percent age seed faster than normal. Seed at 80°F/RH80% lasts half as long as normal; seed at 90°F/RH90% lasts one-fourth as long. Keeping your seed in a damp place where it can get hot is sure to lead to germination failures.

Growing Your Own

Although raising seeds of high uniformity is a specialist's art, quite acceptable garden seed for most species can be grown in the maritime Northwest. I do a lot of it in my own garden and find it's fun—and I'm really proud to use my own. I hope all my readers will, at least once, transplant a few surviving overwintered kale, endive, lettuce, or beet plants to the dry fringe of their garden and let them have at it. Six big kale plants will make a lot of seed!

In Chapter 9, I run down seed making, vegetable by vegetable. Here are some general hints that apply to almost all at-home production.

In the vegetable-seed industry, seed is divided into two general sorts: dry and wet. Wet seed forms and matures inside a moist fruit. After separation from the pulp, the seed has to be dried. This describes tomato, pepper, egg-

plant, squash, cucumber, melon, and so on. The other sort, dry seed, dries in the field on stalks or in other sorts of little pods or containers.

The biggest problem facing the gardener who wants to produce vigorous dry seed is how to avoid moistening the forming or drying seed when irrigating the rest of the garden. Accomplishing that is mostly a matter of careful layout to establish a seed-growing area. Many species that make dry seed are biennials; those that survive the winter can be dug early in spring and transplanted. When saving dry seed from annuals like beans or peas in a generally irrigated garden, you may have to take special pains to pick the seed pods one at a time a few days before they've completely dried out. This isn't much trouble; a few dozen pods will provide plenty of seed for next year.

Only fully mature seed will be vigorous, so the home seed grower should take great care to allow dry seed to dry out fully (or at least form to the point that the plant is no longer putting nutrients inside the seed coat) before harvest. Remember that seed needs to be harvested as soon as it dries out or, with species that tend to lose a lot of seed to birds or shattering seed pods, just before it completely dries out. Repeated dampening by the heavy dews of late summer greatly lowers vigor and germination percentage, and rain is worse. (If the late-season weather doesn't cooperate, dry the nearly mature seed under cover before threshing; it won't be quite as vigorous, but it still may sprout okay for some years. It all depends on how close to ripe the seed was when cut.) When raising wet seed, let the fruit get completely ripe, even beginning to rot a bit, before you pick it off the plant and extract the seed.

Raising your own seed means being an amateur plant breeder. There is no avoiding this. You must decide which plants to propagate. Even if you choose to make seed from all the plants you started, you are making a choice not to choose. As John David Garcia, the great philosopher of ethics and my neighbor at Elkton, Oregon, said, "Not to decide is to decide. Not to decide is unethical."

Your goal will probably be to have a variety that is both reasonably uniform and vigorous. If you're going to get serious about producing your own, you'll probably search the libraries and find other books on the subject. And you'll probably have a lot of fun at it. Here are enough concepts to get you started as an amateur breeder.

Some species exchange pollen from plant to plant; some are self-fertile. Self-pollinating species include beans, peas, tomatoes, peppers, eggplant, lettuce, and chicory. Occasionally one flower of a self-fertile species will outcross (be fertilized by pollen from another plant) because an unusually aggressive bee will manage to transfer pollen from one plant to another at just the right moment. Occasionally one flower will mutate and throw a sport. Either way a whole bunch of potential new varieties are created. Occasionally a plant breeder will play the role of an aggressive insect and force a cross between two plants that otherwise would never outcross. Every variety you grow of a self-pollinating species once started out as a single desirable and unusual plant.

Most self-pollinated species will not cross even if grown in close proximity, or will rarely cross. Growing seed for several varieties of tomatoes or beans is mainly a problem of keeping the collected seeds organized and separated. Unwanted crosses are rare. If one shows up among plants started from your own seed and you just weed it from the garden, there's no problem. But an unanticipated outcross might prove interesting, and you might want to make it a new variety. Getting a first-year cross to become a uniform and true-to-type variety can take several years and involves growing out "lines" where the seeds from each single fruit or pod on the plant are planted out separately in a line; those lines that are uniform are retained; those that are raggedy are discarded. If you decide to do this, you'll want to read further about backyard plant breeding.

Other species make seed with pollen transferred from other plants, brought by insects or wind. These also have the ability to self-pollinate, or "self." Vigor among these species is kept up by the exchange of genes; selfed plants become inbred and the progeny get weak and lose vigor. Professional breeders play many tricks with open-pollinated varieties that outcross, far more than this book can begin to even mention. But I can give you some general guidelines that will allow you to preserve your favorite bee- or wind-pollinated variety so that it will not become too raggedy or inbred.

By far the most important single thing when making seed of these sorts—beet, cabbage family, spinach, parsley, and so on—is to use many plants. If the whole gene pool of a seed crop consists of one plant, then the seed is, of necessity, all self-fertilized unless pollen comes from a distant garden somehow. Inbred seed will become weak. After a few generations of this inbreeding, you'll lose the variety completely. I would not ever make seed of an outcrossing species unless I had at least ten or, better, twenty-five plants. Ideally I would have at least a hundred plants. This fact alone means that you'll have to make a pretty large amount of seed (from a home gardener's viewpoint) when you do make it. Seed-saver clubs soon see the sense of specializing. One person raises enough of one variety to supply dozens of other gardeners.

The next thing to keep in mind is that vigor comes from variation. The more uniform the genes are, the less vigorous the variety. So when selecting parent plants, allow as much variety as possible in unimportant aspects. Slight differences in the bead size or color of broccoli flowers or in the amount that the leaves are cut and frilled are not important, while having large, tightly beaded flowers is important. With a root crop like rutabagas, it is the root you're concerned with; variations in leaf shape or color are usually not relevant unless they are linked to some aspect of root quality. And you can't find out whether there are such linkages without years of patient observation.

One last piece of advice: When growing a seed crop, start by planting a great many seeds, and thin gradually. Once the row is a few weeks old and solidly established, remove all seedlings that stand head and shoulders above the rest. These are the most vigorous because they contain the most genetic diversity; if used for your parent plants, they will produce seed that is wildly variable. Then remove all the weak plants; these are the ones that are most genetically uniform or that possess poorly adapted traits. You're seeking to make seed from the middle range of vigor, using plants that are only somewhat diverse. Then as they grow, start removing plants that are very different from what you desire, as best you can tell by close observation. You'll get even better results by growing thirty to fifty mature plants and then making seeds from the best dozen or so.

Chapter 7 Transplants

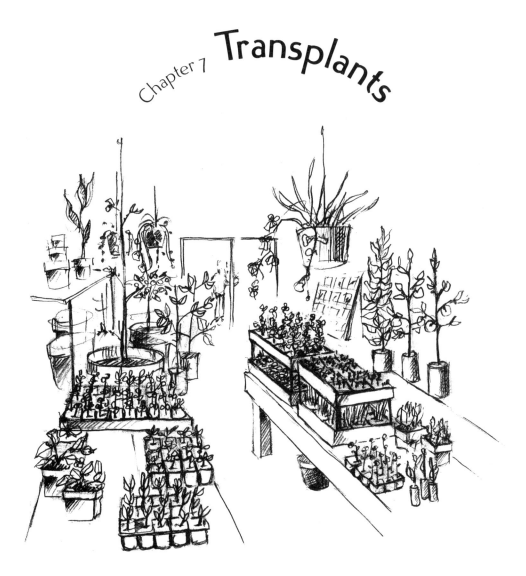

My well-beloved had a vineyard in a very fruitful hill;
And he digged it, and cleared it of stones,
And planted it with the choicest of vine,
And he looked that it should bring forth grapes,
And it brought forth wild grapes.'

5 ISAIAH, THE HOLY SCRIPTURES
(MASORETIC TEXT)

In spring, eager vegetable transplants are available almost everywhere. Supermarkets, drugstores, garden centers—even bookstores—have displays. Some of these seedlings are nearly as good as the best homegrown transplants; others are weak specimens, almost certain to die when set out in the garden. How do you tell them apart?

A transplant should look sturdy—thick stemmed and stocky—rather than fragile—tall, spindly, and thin stemmed. The seedlings should have at least three completely developed pairs of true leaves, be dark green (unless the variety is naturally purple or some other color), and be well rooted but not pot-bound. It's easy to see whether a transplant is stocky, strong, and dark green, but to inspect the root system, you must carefully invert the pot or cell tray and discreetly take a look.

Supporting the soil by placing as many fingers as possible around or between the stem, fingertips facing the soil, invert the pot and firmly tap the bottom with a loose finger until the seedling, roots, and soil drop ½ inch down into your waiting hand. Then slowly ease the pot up so you can inspect the soil ball. If roots have not yet filled the pot, few or none will be visible and the soil will tend to crumble and fall apart. In that case, carefully pack the seedling back into its pot and put it down for someone else to buy. Unless it is a small seedling in a big pot, it has too much top for the amount of "bottom," and it is almost sure to wilt and will probably go into shock when set out. It probably was grown too warm and too fast with excessive nitrogen, which over-stimulates top growth. If you're set on having the plant, take it home and harden it off for a week or ten days before transplanting it.

If the roots are wrapped around the outside of the soil ball, the plant has become pot-bound. In the greenhouse, watered every day and fed with liquid fertilizer, a seedling can continue to grow and look good for several weeks after becoming pot-bound. But that seedling will probably wilt when set out unless severely pruned back and/or watered daily for over a week; it will certainly take a week or more for the tangled root system to push out into new soil. With some types of seedlings, especially cauliflower, cabbage, and broccoli, becoming pot-bound can be a disaster. Once their root development is checked, these bras-sicas become irreversibly stunted, and head out or bolt long before they can develop into full-size plants. The result, predetermined from the time the seedlings were six weeks old, is a very small and poor-quality yield.

To have more success when transplanting pot-bound seedlings, clip off half the leaf area, starting at the bottom. This simple action accomplishes two things: It reduces the amount of water that the roots have to supply, and it allows you to bury the root ball deeper. Together these steps eliminate the need for daily watering and avoid exposing the seedling to moisture stress. Even though you have removed half its food-manufacturing ability, the seedling will resume growth much sooner and ultimately grow bigger than if you had not pruned it.

If, upon inspection, many of its root tips are visible but only a few have begun to wrap around the outside of the soil ball, the seedling is just right for transplanting. When it's set out, the soil ball will probably hold together; not having been damaged, the root system will begin expanding into the new soil immediately. The seedling will need no special watering and still is unlikely to wilt if the stem is buried to the first leaf joint and given a drink when first set out. It will take off and grow fast.

A transplant can go from being insufficiently rooted to being pot-bound in a week to ten days. Nurseries often move seedlings from the greenhouse to the point of retail sale several days before they are fully rooted, even sooner if terrific spring weather creates greater demand than anticipated, usually without hardening the seedlings off a bit. The retailer may not discard the seedlings until they've been on the shelf two weeks or more. Both nursery and retailer are usually looking after their own self-interest, often at the expense of the gardener.

The gardener, in response, is best off being a fussy and wary shopper—doing whatever it takes to find transplants that are not quite fully rooted, being prepared to hold them in their pots for at least a week while hardening them off, and then transplanting when the root systems are ready. It's worth this bit of extra trouble. After all, you're investing a lot of soil preparation and valuable space and time in that seedling.

Hard Versus Soft Seedlings

You can easily inspect the readiness of a seedling's root system for transplanting. Hardness is not so easy to learn to gauge. Plants respond to luxurious growth conditions by producing "soft" tissue. When soil fertility is optimum, water abundant, days and nights pleasantly warm, and winds gentle or nonexistent, plants relax and grow very rapidly. Under ideal conditions, plants make larger, water-filled cells with thinner, weaker walls. Their leaves become luxuriant and broad, the stems longer and too flexible to handle wind. Delicate tissue like this needs a greater water supply to keep from wilting. If, on the other hand, the environment is not fully to the plants' liking, they grow "hard," with smaller, tougher leaves; shorter, stockier stems; and a stronger root system. Hard seedlings are much less likely to be damaged by handling, winds, and insects. In this respect, seedling plants and children are very similar.

A soft plant is likely to be shocked when exposed to stresses it has not yet experienced. Shocks can so weaken a soft seedling that it falls prey to disease and insect attacks or, at the very least, stops growing until it adjusts to the more severe conditions. For example, a soft hothouse-grown pepper seedling that has always been held above 60°F at night and is then exposed to a single nighttime low of 50°F will be so shocked that it may not grow for a week. Exposed repeatedly to temperatures below 50°F, it may not grow properly again all season. If that is the case, imagine how tender a pepper might be that has never experienced a temperature below 70°F.

A hard-grown pepper seedling that has already experienced several nights in the mid- to low 50s might not be severely shocked until the nights fall to about 45°F. Cold rains with large, heavy droplets and the battering of wind can also be severe shocks to a hothouse plant. A light frost can stun even a frost-hardy brassica seedling if that seedling has never before experienced temperatures below 50°F. Loss of root hairs, which is inevitable when transplanting, is also a shock. Put yourself in the place of a tender greenhouse-grown seedling that has known only ideal growing conditions and then is relentlessly exposed to wind, rain, root damage, strong direct sunlight, low overnight temperatures, soil diseases, and predatory insects, and it is easy to see why transplanting is so often fatal.

The difference between hard and soft seedlings was powerfully impressed on me one year when I grew a tomato trial in Lorane, Oregon. At an elevation of 900 feet, surprising late frosts are almost to be expected. So when on Memorial Day weekend I'd set out a trial of frost-sensitive seedlings, I'd repot a few plants of each variety in 4-inch individual containers to hold in my cold frame for another ten days or so, just in case. That year, a particularly disappointing frost on June 13 wiped out me out. Unfortunately, I was short a few reserve transplants. Rather than waste the trial ground space already allocated to tomatoes, I went into the local garden center and bought a few tomato seedlings of what I hoped might prove interesting varieties. The difference in appearance between my own cold frame–grown seedlings and the commercial hothouse ones was amazing. Where mine looked stocky, thick stemmed, and tough, the garden center ones were spindly, light-colored, and delicate. Mine started growing as soon as they were set out; the commercial ones went into shock. Mine were untroubled by insects; the others were badly chewed by flea beetles, and I had to dust them with rotenone twice. Although the garden center seedlings did eventually harden off and get growing, my homegrown seedlings ended up much larger, bore more heavily, and generally ripened earlier. Mixing these soft seedlings into a trial with hard ones proved a waste of time and space.

Why, then, do commercial growers not grow harder seedlings? Greenhouse space is valuable, so there is a natural inclination to rush from seed to sellable seedlings as fast as possible. Growers can go from seed to the sales bench in four to five weeks, instead of six or seven, by having a warmer hothouse. More responsible producers transfer seedlings from the hothouse to an unheated greenhouse after two or three weeks, so their growth rate slows and they become harder. I know of one highly ethical transplant grower who uses a third step, moving her seedlings to a windy, open-air cold frame consisting of little more than a plastic roof without sides, to further toughen them up before putting them out for sale. The less protection is offered, the harder the transplant becomes, the slower it grows, and the more costly it becomes to produce.

It's safest to assume that garden store seedlings have not been hardened off and then to check that they're not pot-bound. Plan on giving them at least a week to harden off, gradually introducing seedlings to environmental shocks. Two weeks would be better. You don't need a cold frame to do this, although having one is certainly convenient. If you don't have a frame, the first day put new seedlings outside in bright shade to become accustomed to wind and to light that is unfiltered by glass or plastic, and bring them back indoors before sunset. The next morning, introduce the seedlings to direct morning and/or late-afternoon sun, and bring them in at night. Give them full sun (if there is any) all the third day, and at night put them in an unheated building. Then let them spend all night outside, unless the temperature will be shockingly

How to Transplant

If you follow these directions, you'll almost never have a seedling wilt.

- With a shovel or hand trowel, scoop out a small hole about 4 inches deep. Pour ½ cup of complete organic fertilizer on the bottom, and mix it with your hand, a shovel, or trowel into about a gallon of soil directly below where the seedling will go.

- Fill the hole back in with loose soil.

- Restore capillarity by gently compressing the soil with your fist or by pressing a pint mason jar into the earth so that there is a pint-jar-sized hole.

- Shake out the seedling while supporting the soil with your fingers on either side of the seedling's stem. Set it gently into the hole, atop the compressed soil. The bottom leaves of the seedling should be at about the level the soil will be at when the hole is refilled.

- From a bucket of tepid water, using an old tin can or jar, scoop out a quart of water and gently fill the hole to the top. Do not allow the force of the water to wash soil away from the seedling's roots.

- Immediately, before the water is absorbed by the surrounding soil, begin pushing soil back into the hole, forming a muddy slurry that coats the soil ball and all the exposed rootlets. Keep pushing in small amounts of soil until the seedling is entirely "mudded in."

- If you want that seedling to really leap up and grow, make the bucket of transplanting water a half-strength solution of liquid fertilizer. This is especially helpful for commercial seedlings that have become accustomed to high levels of soluble chemicals. I get slightly better results using Rapid-Gro or Miracle-Gro than I do with liquid fish emulsion.

cold—below 45°F (or 50° for tender species). If frost threatens, bring in even frost-hardy species. After a few more nights outdoors, they'll probably be tough enough to transfer to the garden, with a much higher likelihood of surviving the shocks that delay growth and retard maturity. If you're a working gardener who can't hover over seedlings, you might initially transplant each seedling into a 3- or 4-inch pot before hardening them off, and even keep them where they get only a half-day of sun so they don't have to be watered twice a day.

Growing transplants from garden centers can be very disappointing for other reasons as well. Varieties popular with the bedding-plant raiser are often bred primarily to create hand-some-looking five-week-old seedlings. This is especially true of ornamentals. The transplant raiser cares intensely that stems grow straight, that seedlings appear to be husky even if they're soft, that they look large and mature when only four weeks old instead of five or six, and that the marigold seedlings already have blooming flowers on them when put out for sale. That's profitable. What happens with that variety after it is transplanted is of less concern.

Varieties bred for hothouse operators may be better adapted to more populous regions back east where seed distributors specializing in the bedding-plant trade have a larger market. As long as the seedlings look good, who cares if the broccoli is a variety that reacts to cool nights (common west of the Cascades but rare back east) by bursting apart in yellow flowers before growing large enough? "Well," the growers justify to themselves, "maybe it'll be a warm spring, or maybe most of the customers will plant later in the season when the variety does better." Who cares if all the tasteless cabbages split two days after getting hard? Who cares if the marigolds quit blooming in midsummer? The home gardener is not a critical trade.

Raising Your Own

The most successful gardeners raise their own plants from seed. This may sound glibly insensitive to working families without the luxury of keeping one potential wage-earner at home or to those less dedicated to eating from their gardens than I am. Growing your own does demand a lot of attention, so much that in spring I sometimes feel enslaved to my cold frame.

Raising Transplants Outdoors

Here's how to direct-seed many sorts of vegetables that are usually started as purchased transplants.

■ Mix up some seedling mix/potting soil (described shortly). Take a bucket of it out to the garden. In recently worked soil wherever you'd want to set a transplant, dig out one shovelful of soil (making a little hole about 4 inches deep and 6 inches around). Pour in ½ cup of complete organic fertilizer. Mix the fertilizer into about a quart of soil at the bottom of the hole with your fingers. Then fill the hole back in with the loose earth you just dug out. Take an empty half-pint mason jar and press it into that spot, making a half-pint-jar-sized hole. Doing this also restores capillarity below the spot. Then pour a heaping half-pint of seedling mix into the hole and press it down gently. With your fingertip, make a depression ½ inch deep (or deeper for larger seeds like squash or cucumber) in the middle of that core of seedling mix, and into that little hole count out four seeds, and cover them. Water lightly every few days if the sun shines, every morning when the sun shines strong. You'll be amazed how well this works as the newly sprouted seedlings enjoy growing in greenhouse mix right in the field. The illustration below shows what you will have created.

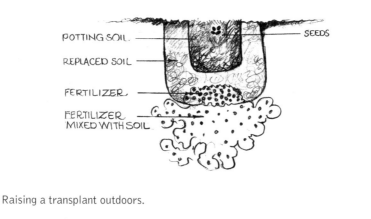

POTTING SOIL — — SEEDS

REPLACED SOIL —

FERTILIZER —

FERTILIZER MIXED WITH SOIL —

Raising a transplant outdoors.

To reduce the need to hover over a cold frame, try direct-seeding broccoli, cabbage, Brussels sprouts, cauliflower, celery, onions, leeks, lettuce, parsley, squash, and cucumber—species that gardeners commonly (and incorrectly) start from purchased transplants.

Raising transplants in little pots is more difficult than directly seeding the same vegetables. In the garden, many growth factors are left to nature, but when raising seedlings, the gardener must take responsibility for light and temperature as well as moisture, soil quality, and fertility. Success will come only to the degree that each of these factors is provided for.

TEMPERATURE

Chapter 6 discusses at length how temperature sensitive the sprouting process is. Some tropical varieties, such as melons, peppers, and eggplants, will not sprout at all below 70°F. Most others sprout best when stably held between 75° and 82°F. I suggest that when germinating seed indoors you aim for 75°F, except with celery and celeriac, which won't sprout well at all above 70°F and do best in the low to mid-60s.

Growth rate is greatly affected by temperature. Tropicals—peppers, eggplants, melons, squash, cucumber—kept at about 70° to 72°F in the daytime grow "hard" and are entirely healthy; higher temperatures make them grow much faster but grow soft. Below 65°F, they grow too slowly. Nighttime temperatures for these should not drop below 55° to 60°F. Cool-weather seedlings—the coles, celery, parsley, and lettuce—become very spindly and weak when grown at temperatures

tropicals would find ideal. These do best at 65°F in the daytime and 45° to 55°F at night; they can handle it a bit warmer if not overfertilized. Tomatoes are intermediate, not quite tropical but not at all frost tolerant. They do best at 70°F in the days and 55° to 60°F nights, but most varieties can learn (if accustomed to it gradually) to tolerate lows down to 45°F without shock and make adequate growth if days are in the mid-60s. Tomatoes become very soft and spindly at temperatures suitable for eggplant.

If you were only producing a single type of seedling, it would be sensible to maintain one range of ideal temperatures. But a compromise is needed if you wish to grow many species at once. Probably the best single temperature range to permit most types of vegetables to thrive and grow fairly close to their best is 68° to 70°F in the daytime and 52° to 60°F at night. These temperatures are easiest to achieve away from the woodstove or other heat source.

SOIL

The seedlings we raise to transplant often have delicate root systems. To promote rapid growth, their potting soil should stay light and loose. And it should be moist—small containers dry out rapidly, but if seedlings wilt, even once, they may not recover properly. Commercial greenhouses use sterilized artificial soil mixes composed of peat moss, vermiculite, perlite, sand, and compost, fertilized with chemicals. You should understand that bagged potting mixes sold in garden centers, even if supposedly prefertilized, contain only enough nutrients to grow plants for a few weeks at most. These two sample commercial formulations will give you an idea of how typical potting mixes are compounded. I'm not suggesting you use these mixes. I am suggesting we observe the intention behind their formulation and then do something better.

University of California Mix

75 percent coarse sand
25 percent sphagnum moss
Add to each cubic yard of mix:
7½ pounds agricultural lime
2½ pounds dolomite lime
3 pounds 10-20-10 chemical fertilizer

Cornell University "Peat-Lite" Mix

11 bushels sphagnum moss
11 bushels horticultural-grade vermiculite or perlite
5 pounds dolomite lime
1 pound superphosphate
12 pounds 5-10-5 chemical fertilizer

Sphagnum moss is usually sterile and has the capacity to absorb ten to twenty times its own weight in water. Moss provides almost no nutrients itself and has a very acid pH, about 3.5. It also contains some natural fungicidal substances that tend to inhibit damping-off diseases. Sphagnum moss is usually sold finely ground and completely dehydrated, though it is often clumpy when it is broken out of compressed bales. You can remove the clumps by sifting it through a ¼-inch mesh screen. Slow to take up water when completely dry, it should be thoroughly remoistened before use.

Vermiculite is made from a naturally occurring clay rock that, when heated, expands until it bursts open like popcorn. Once popped it weighs only 6 to 10 pounds per cubic foot (a cubic foot of solid rock might weigh 150 pounds), has a pH of about 7.0, and is able to absorb three to five times its own weight in water. Vermiculite has a strong ability to attract and hold nutrients, reducing the amount of fertilizer lost when water passes through the pots. Unlike clay, vermiculite remains loose after a wet-dry cycle unless it's compressed when wet. Vermiculite is graded into four horticultural sizes: no. 1 is a bit coarse for bedding plants, no. 2 is the regular horticultural grade, and the very fine nos. 3 and 4 are used in commercial greenhouses as germinating media for extremely small seeds such as petunia or some of the herbs. Vermiculite is usually sterile.

Perlite is a gray-white, pumicelike material mined from lava flows. The rock is crushed and heated so it pops like vermiculite, expanding the particles to small, spongy bits that are very light, weighing 5 to 8 pounds per cubic foot. Perlite will hold three to four times its own weight in water. It has little ability to hold dissolved nutrients the way clay does, has a pH of about 7.0, and is used to lighten and aerate soil mixes.

Compost is a highly variable material available from many garden centers by the sack or from specialized recyclers by the cubic yard and "unit," and often made at home by gardeners. Your ordinary garden recycling should make a much better product than what you'll usually find in the sack (see Chapter 3). If purchased by the sack, it will probably be some well-rotted organic matter blended with larger quantities of partially digested straw, sawdust, or bark and may range in pH from 4.0 to 7.0. Compost has the ability to hold many times its weight in water, and it loosens soil. Sometimes compost is nutrient rich, sometimes not. Composts are not usually sterile, though they can be (odoriferously) baked into sterility.

Gardeners can obtain a better product, grow huskier seedlings, and save money by mixing their own organic potting mix. Here is a formula I've used for many years. It is not sterilized. If I had sandy garden soil, I'd add vermiculite instead of sphagnum moss.

My Own Seedling Mix

Thoroughly blend:

1 part by volume garden soil

½ part by volume finely screened compost

½ part by volume sifted and premoistened sphagnum moss

Blend into each cubic foot (5 gallons) of mix:

2 cups complete organic fertilizer (see pages 34–35)

½ cup agricultural lime (in addition to what is the complete organic fertilizer)

WATERING

Seedlings in small containers usually have to be watered daily. On sunny days in cold frames, they may need watering twice daily— late morning and midafternoon. This makes it essential to use a soil mix that can rapidly reabsorb water after pretty much drying out, and that won't shrink, compact, or crust over. If the soil shrinks away from the sides of the pot, water you add may run down the sides

and out the bottom without really wetting the contents. If the surface crusts over, water uptake may slow so much that the soil looks saturated when it actually is very dry. This is why bedding plant mixes use sphagnum moss, perlite, and vermiculite—they can take up and release water without becoming compacted. However, a strange anomaly occurs with sphagnum moss. Once allowed to dry out fully, moss is very difficult to remoisten and may actually inhibit water uptake. For that reason, I find that about one-third moss is the maximum safe level.

Light, loose soil can be disturbed easily by watering; root systems, especially those of tiny seedlings, may be exposed or damaged if not watered gently. No one system or device is ideal for this purpose. For the home gardener, the gentlest and easiest system I know of is to use a ⅜-inch (internal diameter) plastic or rubber siphon tube draining a gallon jar, plastic milk container, or bucket located 1 to 2 feet above the seedlings. You can easily adjust the water pressure by changing the height of the container. Let the water stand for a few hours to warm up before using it, to avoid shocks to tropical seedlings. Because thin tubing is flexible and light, the water supply can be conveniently located several feet away from the seedlings if necessary. The illustration on the top left of the next page shows this setup.

Outdoors, I water the cold frame seedlings using a 5-gallon bucket and a siphon. I tie one end of the tube to an old broom handle and, to provide pressure, rest the water bucket atop an inverted 5-gallon bucket behind the frame. The broom handle allows me to conveniently

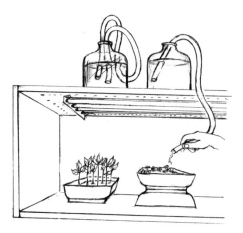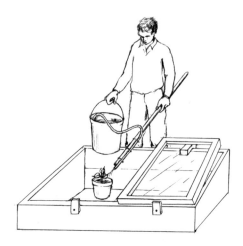

move the hose around in my cold frame. This is pictured in the illustration above, right.

This bucket siphon system is also useful to fertigate smaller plants in the garden. Carry the bucket in one hand and the broomstick in the other. Place the tube near a growing plant, and slowly pour a quart or two of full-strength liquid fertilizer into the root zone of a growing plant. This is shown in the illustration on the next page.

CONTAINERS

Commercial growers seek profit and work their greenhouses full-time, so they use the smallest possible cell or pot size so as to produce the largest number of seedlings per square foot of bench, and then they monitor their seedlings every minute the sun is shining, watering as needed. The home gardener should use containers providing about twice as much soil as the ones you'll see holding bedding plants for sale. This maintains a bigger moisture reserve for the seedlings and takes a lot of pressure off you.

I can't glibly specify any particular size. Many factors can influence the growth rate and ratio of top to root, including light levels, temperatures, species, varieties, and soil mixes. What is most important is to transplant before the seedling becomes pot-bound. Although it's best to transplant straight into the garden, you can move it into a larger pot if conditions outdoors are not welcoming. If repotting, remember that root mass doubles every week to ten days. Generally, about 4 cubic inches of soil (1½ inches by 1½ inches by 1½ inches) will provide adequate room for most small-seeded species from sowing to transplanting. Tropical plants such as peppers, eggplants, and tomatoes produce a lot more ripe fruit if grown a bit bigger and a week or so longer than the minimum time before they are set out; give them at least a 2- by 2- by 2-inch pot. Melons, cucumbers, squash, and beans get big fast and need 2- by 2- by 2-inch pots or cells.

Ordinary household items are easily adapted to serve as pots for bedding plants. Plastic or foam cups, egg cartons, milk carton bottoms, and disposable aluminum cake tins can all be used. However, none of these containers have drainage holes. If water is allowed

Fertigating small plants.

fragile insert sheet nestles in a 10- by 20-inch reusable tray. Tight-fitting, clear plastic covers (called propagation domes) turn these trays into moisture-tight germination chambers that won't need watering until the seeds germinate. (Before I got so well off, I used to put the just-seeded trays into big clear plastic bags to seal in the moisture, and before that, I laid very thin sheets of clear plastic film (from the dry cleaner) over the trays, and before that, I used to water the germinating trays frequently and experienced erratic results.) The domes are used only until the seeds sprout; then they go atop the next batch of seeds to be sprouted. Don't try to grow seedlings under them; it's too humid.

With 2⅜-inch-square cells, I can raise brassicas, tomatoes, and peppers to a very husky, four-true-leaf size without the seedlings becoming pot-bound, and even squash seedlings will hold for nearly a week after sprouting without becoming overcrowded. I've also recycled an assortment of sturdy plastic pots, ranging in size from 2 by 2 inches to 1 gallon.

Some mail-order seed companies sell these modular setups: seedling-raising trays, domes to go over them, and assorted sizes of disposable inserts sheets. However, their prices are far more than double what you'd pay for a full case at a nursery's supply house. If you contact a nursery supply company, say you grow a big garden; you'll almost certainly be welcomed as a potential customer and be sent a most interesting catalog.

I do not recommend using peat pots. It is hard enough to keep transplants watered without also using a container that transpires

to stand in the pot, seedlings will become sickly or die, so punch several quarter-inch holes in the bottom of each container to allow excess water to run out.

I grow a big garden, and I expect to be doing so for many years to come, so I bought a full case of plastic multicell insert sheets, just like those the commercial seedling growers use, from a nursery wholesale distributor. I use the kind that fits inside a sturdy supporting tray. These cell-sheets come in all sorts of sizes and layouts. I personally prefer a husky, oversized seedling, so I use sheets containing only thirty-two cells, each cell 2⅜ inches square by 2¼ inches deep. Most garden centers sell much smaller seedlings, grown in sheets of seventy-two or more cells. Each a lot of water through the sides. The sales pitch for these is that you can plant the pot along with the seedling, reducing shock, and the roots will grow right through the pot. I've never found this to be the case; when I've tried it the seedlings wilt and get pot-bound. A few roots do get through, but many don't.

Sow three or four seeds per pot or cell and then gradually thin out the extra seedlings. This allows for losses from damping-off and removal of any weak seedlings.

Rapidly growing seedlings double the size of their root system every week. When cramped, they increase the density of their root systems and become pot-bound. But any transplanting, no matter how gently done, causes a bit of a shock and setback. So the best container is one that is large enough to accommodate a seedling from sprouting to transplanting size without repotting.

LIGHT

East of the Cascades, there are more spring days when the sun shines brightly than days that are cloudy, so home gardeners often grow transplants in a sunny, south-facing window. However, in the cloudy maritime Northwest, windowsill-grown plants become spindly and weak. This inescapable fact of light means that we must invest a bit to raise healthy, strong transplants.

There are two solutions: indoor grow lights and protected outdoor spaces such as cold frames, hot frames, and greenhouses. By far the cheapest approach for a family-sized garden is fluorescent grow lights used indoors. Light is every bit as essential a growth factor as nutri-

ents or water, and growing healthy plants under artificial light requires some thought.

Light quality and light intensity have profound and immediate effects on growth. Under low light, many plants become spindly and long stemmed. The name for this phenomenon is *etiolation*. You can easily demonstrate etiolation by putting a potted plant in a dark closet for a few weeks. The stems soon become vinelike, and the leaves turn pale and barely develop. In experiments with intense artificial light sources such as halide, sodium, and mercury lamps, great distortions in plant growth have been induced by using lamp combinations that differ in spectral composition from natural sunlight. For example, certain plants flower best under reddish light, a spectral quality that occurs naturally in late summer and early autumn; under bluish lights, their flowers are looser, smaller, and less fragrant.

Creating a workable imitation of sunlight by combining high-intensity lights gets quite expensive, while the huge bulbs are each capable of illuminating large areas. Fortunately, one common and fairly inexpensive light source, the "cool-white" fluorescent tube, does promotes very good vegetative growth in seedlings for their first five to six weeks after germination, just what gardeners need.

Because fluorescent bulbs aren't very bright, they're impractical for growing large plants; however, they will sustain vegetable seedlings when the leaves are very close to the bulbs. These bulbs are commonly available in 4- or 8-foot lengths. The 4-foot tube is the usual choice for home gardeners. Two to six parallel 4-foot-long cool-white tubes suspended over the growing area can produce stocky seedlings indoors at a low cost. You'll need the highest light intensity that fluorescents can create, so place the tubes close together and suspend the array of tubes no more than a few inches above the top leaves. Because you'll need to increase the distance between the lights and the plant trays as the seedlings grow, the lamps must be suspended in such a way that they can be raised and lowered on pulleys, the shelf holding the seedlings must be movable, or individual plant containers must be on props and gradually lowered as the seedlings grow. I generally prefer the last option because at any one time I am growing a mix of seedlings that get tall at different rates. Fluorescents do generate a bit of heat in their immediately vicinity. Setting up the growing area on a sun porch or in a cooler room will probably create the right temperature ranges. See the table below, "Configuring and Using Grow Lights."

Plants need a period of darkness each day to accomplish certain kinds of essential work. Only four hours of darkness per each twenty-four hours can be enough, but when pushed that hard the seedlings experience shock when you put them outdoors into a shorter day length. With some photoperiodic species like brassicas, onions, mustard, and spinach, this shock may trigger seed formation or other undesirable responses. I suggest a stable fourteen-hour illumination period and strongly recommend buying an inexpensive twenty-four-hour timer to keep it regular.

FERTILIZERS

Whenever I've put enough complete organic fertilizer into a soil mix to suffice without any further supplementation, I've reduced or sometimes wrecked seed germination. After many years of trying different approaches, I've come to consider potting soil primarily as a moisture-retaining root development medium providing only background nutrition. I regulate seedling growth with liquid fertilizer.

Unfortunately, this approach is not foolproof either. Liquid organic fertilizers are inevitably phosphorus deficient; fish emulsion is usually 7-2-2 or thereabouts, while seaweed or kelp concentrates are even more unbalanced—0.5-1-1, more or less. With organics I suggest starting with 2 tablespoons of liquid seaweed concentrate per gallon and 1 tablespoonful of fish emulsion, being ready to dilute it further. And if you're going to use liquid organics, for balance consider putting as much

Configuring and Using Grow Lights

Number of Tubes	Maximum Height Above Top of Seedlings	Width of Strongly Illuminated Area	Period of Growth with Sufficient Light
2	2 inches	6 inches	4 weeks
4	3 inches	9 inches	6 weeks
6	4 inches	12 inches	8 weeks

extra bone meal into your potting mix as you do complete organic fertilizer. Not surprisingly, I've gotten far better results using Rapid-Gro or Miracle-Gro, diluted to one-half or even one-quarter the recommended strength. It doesn't take much, either. One small box lasts for several years of transplant raising.

I recommend using below-strength fertilizer because the soil mix already contains some slow-release organic fertilizer. Cautious fertigation controls growth without overstimulation. Too much fertilizer, particularly too much nitrogen fertilizer, tends to result in lush, soft growth and spindly stems, especially when combined with higher growing temperatures. If one feeding of weak liquid fertilizer does not increase the rate of growth, a second feeding can be tried a few days later without danger of salting up the soil. Plants should be fed every ten days to two weeks, or whenever growth slows. Fertilizer can even be routinely supplied with every watering if it's diluted to about one-eighth normal strength. I do this when watering my cold frame, putting a scant tablespoonful of Rapid-Gro into every 5-gallon bucket of water. I think the practice is synergistic in that the more the sun shines, the faster the seedlings grow, and the more they need water and the more fertilizer they take up.

COLD FRAMES

Cold frames for growing seedlings are often put together from recycled planks topped with old window glass or plastic, fiberglass, or polyethylene sheeting. A well-built frame with 2-inch-thick walls and well-fitted windows, caulked and sealed, can hold nighttime temperatures at 10°F warmer than outside air. Even a hastily constructed, drafty frame is capable of holding nighttime temperatures 3° to 5°F warmer than outside, more if a thick blanket is thrown over the frame when frosts threaten. The family gardener will need a cold frame no larger than 3 feet wide by 5 feet long, 18 inches tall at the back and 6 inches high at the front, built very much like the one described in Chapter 4.

Having both a cold frame and grow lights is highly advantageous. By mid-March, the light outside, in the frame, will equal the level inside under the fluorescents. March/April daytime temperatures, regulated by opening or closing the tops, can be kept cooler than indoors (advantageous for cool-season transplants), and with the frame sashes closed, nighttime lows within will not reach the freezing point. This makes the cold frame a fine place to put one- to two-week-old early brassica seedlings that were sprouted and grown for a week or so indoors; after a few weeks of slow, hard growth in the frame, they'll be stocky and strong. By mid-April the frame environment will be comfortable for celery and tomato seedlings. If four- or five-week-old tomato seedlings started under fluorescent lights are transplanted into individual 3- or 4-inch pots and put out in the frame in mid-April, they'll be hard and quite large by the time it's warm enough to put them in the garden. About the time no more frosts are expected and the frame has been emptied of tomato seedlings, it becomes a suitable environment for hardening peppers, eggplants, melons, and cucumbers, which should be held in the frame until really warm, summery weather settles in.

A hot frame is simply a cold frame with heat below it. In the old days, these were called hot beds, made by setting cold frames over pits filled with fresh strong manure that heated naturally. Now most people use thermostatically controlled electric cables. Hot frames are interesting luxury items that permit a gardener to grow tropical plants such as peppers outside after March 1, to germinate heat-demanding seeds outside, and to eliminate the need for fluorescent lights inside, removing gardening clutter from the house. Hot frames are not necessary for successful gardening; however, any serious gardener will eventually want a cold frame.

ENHANCING GERMINATION

In commercial greenhouse operations, fungicide-treated seeds are often sown in sterile vermiculite. Germination trays are sealed with clear, airtight lids, placed on electrically heated benches, and kept at optimum temperatures until the seeds sprout. There will be no damping-off disease. The germination rate will be very close to that of a germination laboratory.

If ordinary garden soil and untreated seed are used, effective germination will drop to somewhere around 50 percent at best. Unprotected by fungicide, a few more seedlings will die from damping-off diseases during their first week. If the variety is open-pollinated, some of these surviving seedlings will probably not be particularly vigorous or desirable. The home transplant raiser should sprout three to five seeds for every seedling ultimately

desired, and cull out the weaker survivors. With this approach, damping-off diseases are an easy way to allow nature to thin disease-susceptible specimens.

To sow seed, first make sure that the planting mix is damp but not wet. Then press a small hole to the proper depth with the blunt end of a pencil (equal to a tool called a dibble when used outdoors), and place three to five seeds in the hole (two or three if big seeds—cucurbits, beans, corn, and so on—are being started). For most species, trays and pots holding germinating seeds can be put on a shelf above the fluorescent light bank, where the heat generated by the lamps and ballasts creates warm conditions. In fact, this place can be a bit too warm if you have a bank of six tubes. In that case, use spacers to create some air flow below the germinating containers. The mantle over a fireplace insert or a shelf near the woodstove is also a good spot. Inside the oven with the lamp turned on can also be quite workable. Atop the hot water tank isn't a good spot, because they're too well insulated these days. Garden centers and mail-order seed companies sell electric heat tapes or pads to put under germinating seedlings.

Maintain the proper moisture level in germinating trays by covering each with a very thin sheet of clear plastic or by sealing them in large, clear plastic bags until the seedlings emerge. When sprouting seeds in a pressed-fiber pot or tray, which tends to lose moisture through its sides, seal the entire pot within a clear poly bag until sprouts emerge.

After germination, thin small-seeded vegetables to about three plants per spot within the first week, and continue to thin as the tray becomes crowded. Don't let plants shade one another or force one another's stems very far off vertical as they compete for light. Thinning is best done with small, sharp scissors, snipping the stem near the soil line. By the time the seedlings have fully developed one true leaf and started the second one, the tray should be completely thinned to one plant per spot. Then they're ready for the cold frame.

How to Grow Transplants

Planting dates in this section are for the Willamette Valley, in Oregon. Gardeners to the south might start seedlings a little earlier; gardeners north of Longview, Washington, might start seedlings a little later. The dates are listed in the sections that follow describing each particular vegetable species and provided in the table on the next page, "A Typical Transplanting Calendar." Chapter 9 gives further tips and information about each species.

Beans About three weeks before the last frost date, sow two seeds per individual 2-inch pot, 1½ inches deep. Sprout at 75° to 85°F. Thin promptly to one plant per pot. Grow under lights for about one week, and then move to a cold frame until one pair of true leaves is fully developed. Transplant outdoors at the same time bean seeds would be sown outdoors. An early start like this is almost

essential to obtain any yield from lima beans. Snap beans will mature abundantly when direct-seeded but may start producing beans two weeks sooner if transplanted.

Beets Grow for transplanting only to have the earliest possible harvest. By mid-April, beets are much easier to direct-seed outdoors. Individual beet seeds usually produce clusters of seedlings. In March, sow two seeds per individual 2-inch pot or cell, ½ inch deep. Sprout at 75° to 85°F. Grow three to four weeks at 60° to 70°F under lights, and then transfer to a cold frame if available. Do not thin unless you end up with more than four plants per pot. Hold in a cold frame until the clumps of four seedlings have well-developed true leaves and are 2 to 4 inches tall. Do not allow clusters of seedlings to become pot-bound. Transplant clusters of seedlings 8 to 12 inches apart in rows 18 inches apart; although crowded, almost every beet in each cluster will form if you harvest gently, one by one. It's best to use a slow-bolting, open-pollinated variety with variable maturation, like Early Wonder.

Broccoli By April, broccoli is much easier to direct-seed, so start only very early broccoli indoors. Earliest broccoli is always a big gamble anyway: Seedlings whose growth is checked by cold conditions at transplanting may not head out well, and the earliest seedlings start sizing up just when root maggots peak. During February or March, sow seeds ½ inch deep, three to five seeds per individual cell or 2-inch individual pot. Broccoli

A Typical Transplanting Calendar

Sow Under Lights	Species	Move to Cold Frame	Transplant in Garden
Feb 1	Autumn leeks	April 1	May 1–31
Feb 1	Bulb onions	March 5–15	April 1–15
Feb 15	Early cabbage, broccoli	March 5	April 1
Feb 15	Celery, celeriac	April 15	May 15
March 1	Cauliflower	March 20	April 10
March 1	Earliest possible lettuce	March 20	April 10
March 15	Tomatoes	April 15	May 1–15
April 1	Peppers, eggplant	May 5	June 1–15
April 15	Squash	April 25	May 1
May 20	Cucumbers, melon	June 1	June 5–10

Note: Dates in this table are for Willamette Valley, Oregon, gardeners. South of Drain, Oregon, these dates may be a week or two too late, even more so in the redwoods. North of Longview, Washington, and at higher elevations in western Oregon, these dates may be a week or two too early.

sprouts fastest at 70° to 85°F. Grow two to three weeks under lights at 60° to 70°F daytime, above 40°F at night. Indoor growing temperatures over 70°F may cause spindly growth. Thin gradually so seedlings don't compete for light, ending up with one plant per pot by the time the first true leaf is totally developed. Transfer at the two-leaf stage to a cold frame, if available. When seedlings have three true leaves (five to six weeks after sowing), they should be well rooted and ready to set out. If transplanting outdoors in March, consider using hot caps made of translucent half-gallon plastic jugs or transplanting into a cloche, as illustrated on the next page.

Brussels Sprouts If transplants are desired, grow like broccoli; however, Brussels sprouts are far less troubled with aphids if scheduled for harvest to begin in mid- to late autumn.

I strongly recommend direct-seeding about June 1.

Cabbage For earliest heads, grow exactly like broccoli. Start seeds during February or March. By April, cabbage can be direct-seeded outdoors. In this earliest season, I recommend only Jersey Wakefield (pointed-head) types, Golden Acre types, or similar extra-early hybrids like Derby Day.

Cauliflower Cauliflower is a little more sensitive to chilly conditions and to root maggots than cabbage or broccoli. Grow for early harvest like broccoli transplants, but do not start seeds before February 20. By April 1, cauliflower is better direct-seeded. For earliest sowings, I recommend only a variety developed especially for early sowing, such as Snow Crown Hybrid. There used to be a great many

Hot cap.

early open-pollinated varieties or, as the Europeans called them, Alpha types. Now very few are left, and most are hybrids.

Celery and Celeriac Between February 15 and March 15, sow clumps of four to five seeds ¼ inch deep in individual 2-inch pots or cells. Seeds will sprout best but slowly at 55° to 70°F, sometimes taking more than two weeks. Thin gradually without permitting competition. Grow at 65° to 75°F during the day, 50° to 60°F at night. Celery requires high moisture and fertility levels and eight to twelve weeks to attain transplanting size. Move to a cold frame for the last two or four weeks, but not before nighttime temperatures in the frame are generally above 50°F. Although celery is somewhat frost hardy, too many hours' exposure to temperatures below 50°F will make seedlings bolt prematurely. I prefer to direct-seed toward the end of April,

when cool, moist conditions are perfect for its germination but nights aren't too cold.

Sweet Corn Handle the fast-growing corn seedlings like beans if earliest possible production is desired. Sow four seeds per 2-inch pot, and thin to three plants per pot. Transplant clumps of three every 30 inches in rows 30 inches apart. Corn will do slightly better grown as single stalks rather far apart in rows rather than in clusters, spaced one plant every 10 inches in rows 30 inches apart.

Cucumbers Because the species is difficult to transplant, especially when seedlings get very big, cucumbers should be started indoors roughly at the time tomato seedlings are transplanted, giving a slight advantage over direct-seeding about two weeks after the tomato seedlings are set out. Raising cucumber transplants makes more sense farther north, as I found out one year at Yelm, Washington.

Sprouting all cucurbits (squash and melons, too) requires warm, only slightly damp conditions to avoid seedling diseases. *Test potting soil moisture carefully.* It should barely form a ball when squeezed hard and should break up easily. If too damp, allow the soil to dry out before using. Sow three seeds in each individual 2- to 3-inch pot, 1 inch deep. To keep moisture even, place pots in sealed, lightweight poly bags such as those found in supermarket produce departments. Keep the pots over 70°F until emergence; the ideal temperature is 80°F. When seedlings appear, remove the poly bags and begin watering. Grow under lights for about one week at 70° to 80°F in the daytime, over 55°F at night. Thin to the best two plants per pot by the time they have developed one true leaf. Transfer to a cold frame for a final week of slight hardening off; it is impossible to make cucumbers (or melons) very hard. Transplant very carefully to avoid root damage. After the transplanted seedlings have become securely established, thin to a single plant per spot or hill.

Eggplants Handle like peppers (discussed later), but note that eggplant seedlings are even more sensitive to temperatures below 50°F.

Kale Kale is grown like broccoli, but it is so vigorous that direct-seeding is better. Kale is also so much better eating in fall that raising transplants to obtain earlier production seems pointless to me. And why fight root maggots for kale?

Kohlrabi Don't. I always direct-seed about April 1 and have all I want. For fall harvest, direct-seed about August 1.

Leeks If summertime harvest is desired, raise transplants like onion seedlings and use faster-growing varieties intended for late summer/autumn harvest. If fall/winter harvest is desired, direct-seed leeks in May and use hardier winter leek varieties. See onions, later in this section.

Lettuce Raise transplants only for earliest harvest, and grow like broccoli; otherwise, direct-seed.

Melons Grow like cucumbers, but note that melons are even more sensitive to low temperatures and damp conditions in the seedling stage. See the section on melons in Chapter 9.

Onions For the largest bulbs and earliest scallions, raise transplants. In February or early March, sow seeds ½ inch deep, eight to twelve seeds per inch, in rows 2½ to 3 inches apart on a 2-inch-deep flat; if using cellular trays, sow eight seeds per 2-inch cell. Sprout seed between 60° and 75°F. Grow at 50° to 70°F in the day, 40° to 50°F at night. Do not thin. With sharp scissors, give the tops a haircut, shearing them back to about 3 inches tall every few weeks to promote thicker stems and better-developed root systems. Indoors, grow onions with at least a fourteen-hour day length to prevent premature bulbing. Harden off in a cold frame, if available, starting in mid-April. Prune the tops again just before transplanting outdoors to reduce stress on the root systems. Transplant when stems are about $\frac{3}{16}$ inch in diameter, or by May 1 at the latest. Onions transplant very easily bare-rooted, so separate the individual seedlings by shaking them apart or washing them in gently running water.

Parsley Slow to germinate, parsley is often transplanted, although it is very easily direct-seeded if sown before things begin to warm up and dry out in the garden. Otherwise, grow it like broccoli, but note that germination can take fourteen to seventeen days at 60°F.

Peppers These heat-loving plants don't readily adapt to climatic conditions north of the Yoncalla Valley. If grown soft, they are often irreversibly shocked by outdoor night-time temperatures below 55°F; if grown as hard as a tender pepper can be grown—which is not very hard if permanent stunting is to be avoided—they can barely handle a 50°F overnight low.

Many gardeners make the mistake of setting peppers out at the same time as tomatoes—right after there is no frost danger. This, however, will almost certainly expose them to overnight temperatures of 45°F or even worse. Any surprisingly cool night during June can shock peppers sufficiently to stop their growth for a time. It is far better to wait two or three weeks more and set out the largest but hardest pepper seedlings possible. Start slow-growing pepper seedlings about six to eight weeks before the last expected frost. In 2- to 3-inch individual pots or 2-inch cells, sow four seeds, ½ inch deep. Sprout this heat-demanding seed at over 70°F (best at 80°). Grow at 65° to 75°F in the day, above 50°F at night. Thin gradually to one plant per pot.

When tomatoes are planted outside, pepper seedlings may be transferred to a cold frame and repotted if they are becoming crowded. Grow in the frame for another two or three weeks, or until summer is really on. If given ample root room in big pots, peppers will make much more growth in a frame that stays above 50°F when nights drop into the 40s than they would if unprotected or even in a cloche.

Squash Raised like cucumbers, squash are equally hard to transplant and need bigger pots since the seedlings are so large. I suggest germinating squash seeds at 75° to 80°F about ten days to two weeks before the last anticipated frost, sowing three seeds per individual 2-inch pot or cell. This avoids the dangers of trying to sprout them in chilly, damp spring soil. Once germinated, thin to two plants per pot, and move them immediately to a cold frame if available. Grow in pots only four to seven days, until the seedlings are sufficiently rooted to hold the soil ball together, and then transplant.

Squash is much more tolerant of cool conditions than its relatives, melons and cucumbers, and is a good gamble when direct-seeded into a cloche about five weeks before the last expected frost date or sprouted indoors and then moved into a cloche about three weeks before the last expected frost date. Most years, the cloche will provide enough frost protection to get the seedlings through unscathed while enhancing early seedling growth, so harvesting will start three or four weeks earlier than if you had direct-seeded. To our family, an extra month of summer squash is worth quite a bit of trouble and the occasional failure.

Tomatoes For the earliest possible harvest, grow the largest possible seedlings, with fruit set on them if possible, before transplanting. I start them about March 1, move them to a cold frame by April 1, and transplant a few weeks later under a large tunnel cloche. Some years I've held the tomatoes in gallon pots in the cold frame until late May, setting out 18-inch-tall seedlings already bearing fruit. Either way, I start eating ripe tomatoes from my earliest varieties by the end of June. Tomato seedlings can be usefully started as late as April 15. Sow four seeds in each 2-inch pot or cell, ½ inch deep. Sprout at 70° to 80°F. Grow under lights at 65° to 75°F in the day, 50° to 60°F at night. Thin gradually to one plant per pot. Move to a cold frame, if available, after three or four weeks indoors. Try to keep nighttime lows in the frame above 40°F.

Chapter 8 Predators

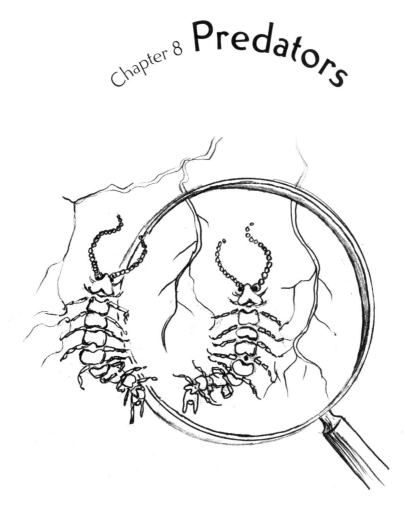

If I keep a green bough in my heart,
the singing bird will come.

—Chinese proverb

The interaction of soil microorganisms with higher plants is very complex and multiform. Depending on the plant cover on the same soil under equal external conditions, the composition of the microflora changes sharply. Plants are a very strong ecological factor, selecting certain species of bacteria, fungi, actinomycetes, and other inhabitants of the soil. As a result of wrong agricultural practices and crop rotation, the soil becomes infested with harmful microbial forms. By use of suitable plants in the crop rotation, one may change the microflora of soil in the desired direction, and eliminate harmful organisms—in other words, restore the health of soil."

N. S. Krasil'nikov,
Soil Microorganisms and Higher Plants

Sir Albert Howard believed that before a plant has noticeable trouble, it is already an unhealthy plant in some respect. He was largely correct. However, in some areas humans have put the environment so out of balance that no plant growing on an organic gardener's postage stamp of land, no matter how ideally fertile the gardener has made the soil, can withstand the insect plagues that develop.

Generally speaking, a healthy plant either will be unattackable or will outgrow insect damage and will not succumb to disease. I've witnessed this time and time again, especially in trials where I've grown many varieties side by side. In a row holding eight plants each of a dozen Brussels sprout varieties, only one poorly adapted variety (that became unhealthy as a consequence) was seriously damaged by aphids, while the others, growing lustily, remained untouched.

Here's another example. The year I first started gardening at Lorane, Oregon, not yet understanding all the benefits of direct-sowing whenever possible, I bought many transplants. After I had planted the entire rototilled area, there still remained three little cabbage seedlings. Rather than waste them, I dug up a small area by hand and planted them, blending in only a little fertilizer but no manure or lime. As the season went on, the difference between the cabbages in the garden and those on the fringe was astonishing. The garden cabbages grew big and healthy without problems. The ones on the fringe grew slowly and were attacked first by flea beetles and then by cabbage worms, both of which I sprayed; I gave them extra fertilizer, but the roots were attacked by maggots, and one wilted. When it was all over, the cabbages in the garden were 8 to 10 pounds each and very fine tasting; the two survivors on the fringe were 1 to 2 pounds at best and were tough and bitter.

Healthy plants are usually safe from attack. If we focus on soil fertility and otherwise create growth conditions that will make our plants thrive, we'll have little trouble with pests or diseases. That's how I've always experienced gardening—generally trouble free.

Occasionally even the best-adapted variety in ideal soil will have trouble. It is important to understand how this can happen, because otherwise organic gardeners can feel betrayed when problems arise that, according to their belief system, should not have occurred. Through human intervention and ecological mismanagement, insect populations occasionally become highly unbalanced, reaching plague levels that no vegetable can outgrow. In Washington's Skagit Valley, too many acres are devoted to brassica seed crops. There's an enormous amount of food available for the cabbage fly, while the poisons used to control it kill its predators as well. But the cabbage fly has become resistant to the pesticides and, consequently, has become so numerous that unless effective controls are used in the home garden, cole crops can hardly be grown in the Skagit district. These controls need not be chemical poisons, however. This chapter offers various natural but effective remedies for the cabbage root maggot.

Here's another example. In some areas the carrot rust fly's maggots riddle carrots and leave them inedible. Yet I had no trouble with rust flies at Lorane, and it was the same at Elkton. I believe that's because both gardens were in marginal agricultural districts where the surrounding pastures are full of wild carrot (Queen Anne's lace). In the Willamette Valley, where intense agriculture allows little room for wild carrot, gardeners do complain of rust fly problems. Large, stable populations of wild carrot mean stable populations of both carrot rust fly and its predators. Wherever there are garden carrots but few wild carrots, the fly, discovering your carrot patch, can quickly breed into a serious plague, unchecked by predation. In the same way, the poorer hay-fields and extensive waste areas around Lorane and Elkton contain lots of wild cabbage and wild radish, which support a stable population of cabbage flies and their predators, tending to limit the cabbage fly population. Urban gardeners and those living in prosperous agricultural districts will probably have much more serious problems with pests than will rural homesteaders on infertile hillsides and in small upland valleys, where a wide variety of plants support balanced ecologies of insect pests and their predators.

Weather too can cause disease or insect problems beyond the responsibility or control of the gardener. One cabbage year there were just too many cloudy, humid, cool days, and a late blight scythed Cascadia's tomatoes, north to south, in a few weeks. Virtually every tomato died except a lucky few that had grown in greenhouses or under the protective eaves of south-facing white-painted walls. This loss was no one's fault. Should we have many unseasonably warm, humid days during the time the peas are forming seeds, we'll have the kinds of pea diseases that are common in the East. We generally escape them because of our low humidity conditions during June.

Certain vegetables are very fussy about the types of soil they will and won't grow in; these species may express their difficultness by appearing to be attacked by insect or disease. When this happens to those gardening in clay, there is little or nothing that can be done short of importing a bed of special soil. This type of problem is especially common with weakly rooting species intolerant of clay soils, such as artichoke, asparagus, celery, celeriac, melons (especially watermelon), and cauliflower.

Pesticide Versus Fertilizer

Before you rush to spray poisons, even natural pesticides, first wonder if perhaps the plant simply is not growing fast enough to overcome the predation. Sometimes infertile soil is the real culprit; sometimes bad weather or, most often, sowing too early retards growth and lowers the health of the plant. Often the best cure to try first is not "killer" but liquid organic fertilizer—a foliar spray of fish emulsion (a double whammy that not only feeds the plant but also disguises its odor from predators that locate their chow by the smell). A chemical foliar spray will often do as well or better. A half-and-half mix of both may be best. If fact, if you are prompted to spray insecticide, try mixing some foliar fertilizer into the brew as well.

In spring, if slow-growing seedlings are being chewed down by slugs or flea beetles, and fertilization doesn't solve the problem, most likely the seeds were sown too early or too sparsely. When weather conditions are unfavorable, if you start many more seeds than the final number of plants ultimately wanted, you can have a relatively benign attitude, as slugs and insects help thin out the weaker seedlings. Sowing again a little later, when soils are warmer and the sun is stronger, allows seedlings to grow faster from the start. As you'll recall from Chapter 1, a late April sowing usually matures only a little earlier than one made five or six weeks earlier. If it's early in the season and you're having to fight for your crop, besides spraying and fertilizing, also try sowing again.

Pesticides may be a short-term springtime solution while you wait for weather to moderate and growth to resume. But bad weather and decreasing light levels at the summer's end can also prompt troubles with diseases and insects on heat-loving crops; these attacks are hardly worth fighting, since the plants' life cycle is virtually over anyway. So don't be upset when spider mites attack your eggplants after mid-September, or when the cucumbers, squash, and melons inevitably succumb to powdery mildew at the same time. You did nothing wrong and can do nothing to help; the season no longer suits the species.

Gardening Aikido

I try to coexist peacefully with nature and often am able to see pests as potential allies who can help me grow a better, more natural garden. One very important step along this road is abandoning what self-help psychologists and some preachers call "poverty consciousness." Instead of planting a garden from which you'll harvest only exactly what you want if everything grows well, plant two or three times as much, so that pests and diseases could wipe out one-third of the garden without threatening your food supply or upsetting you. Plan to grow a garden that allows you to give away buckets of food most years.

Some years just are "cabbage years": The sun doesn't shine often, it rains all summer, the tomatoes get late blight as soon as they start to ripen, melons and cucumbers succumb to powdery mildew, eggplants won't set, peppers don't mature, corn is very late and not very sweet, and snap beans become covered with aphids. If the garden is big enough, you can at least eat a lot of salad greens, scallions, and rutabagas. If the leek patch doesn't grow well one year but you planted twice what you needed, there will still be enough leeks.

Another way to avoid battling nature is to inspect and reject one of our cultural peculiarities—what I call the American Sanitary Model. This belief that food should be "clean" and free of bugs is so prevalent that in our supermarkets no one would buy spinach with a few holes in the leaves or a rutabaga with a few maggot scars on the skin. Imagine finding a blanched cabbage worm in a frozen broccoli packet!

Why not change your attitude about what constitutes acceptable table fare and learn to coexist with insects? Remove as many of them as possible when the food is being washed, and discreetly slide to the side of your plate the one that may occasionally escape the cook's scrutiny. There's a big difference between a plant showing the effects of an occasional insect and one that has been severely damaged. As long as the plant is still growing vigorously, a few (even a few hundred) pinholes in the leaves or a scar on the cucumber's skin doesn't matter. As long as the cook can peel off the damage without wasting too much time, why even bother to oppose the predation? Let commercial farmers fight bugs on behalf of their unrealistic clientele.

Pests: Aphids to Zitherbugs

There are occasions when pests must be fought or too much of the garden will be lost. What follows is a summary of the little I've learned about common garden pests in the maritime Northwest. Fortunately for me, I am the wrong person to write a complete, authoritative statement about poaching animals, insect pests, and plant diseases and their control in and around the garden. I've always made healthy soil and had a positive mental attitude about how my garden was going to grow. So in my garden, only the most ubiquitous and prolific pests make their presence felt at all.

If in the next paragraphs I do not describe your particular plague or show how to lessen its effect on your garden (or on your attitude), or tell how to control it without artificial poisons, you might consider asking your friendly garden center owner or extension agent for advice. The extension service people have a far wider knowledge than I about many garden pests and diseases; your nearest garden center has a wide repertory of remedies certified as safe by the U.S. Government or Agriculture Canada—high-powered poisons that can kill almost anything living in or around the soil, except symphylans (see Chapter 4). The best I can say of these substances is that the ones available to the home gardener are not the kinds that kill humans quickly in tiny doses; how they may affect your body or the environment over the years, I do not wish to speculate about here.

Aphids *(Aphidoidea family)* Often called plant lice, aphids are small, soft-bodied insects that cluster on leaves and stems, sucking plant sap and causing leaves to curl and cup; in large numbers, aphids can weaken or badly stunt a plant, reducing yields. Aphids multiply with amazing rapidity, exploding from nothing to a serious threat in days. They also transport various plant diseases such as pea enation and the potato viruses, although by the time you realize they're present the disease is present, too; belatedly spraying the carrier won't stop the virus.

Aphids often have a close relationship with ants, which "farm" them much as humans graze cows on pasture. Ants place aphids on leaves and then milk a sweet secretion from their livestock. Aphid control often involves eliminating ant nests. Ants creating aphid colonies can be killed safely by setting out ant poison stakes, which contain sugar bait laced with a tiny amount of arsenic. (Arsenic is a natural mineral poison quite acceptable to me as long as it's not broadcast about the environment or left where kids, pets, or livestock can get at it.) The ants carry the poisoned sugar back to feed their larvae and queen, thus neatly wiping out the nest with a minuscule amount of toxin. The bait is protected within a little container.

Aphids already on plant leaves can be sprayed off with a hose and nozzle; once removed, the ones you sprayed will probably not find their way back, though others may if you haven't eliminated the ants farming them (if the ants were the vector). Safer's soap (insecticidal soap made from special fats) is effective and virtually nontoxic to animals and most other types of insects, though it can singe the leaves of delicate plants themselves (especially spinach) if used in strong concentrations. If you're going to use Safer's, test a bit on a single leaf a few days before spraying a whole patch of something. Various preparations of rotenone and pyrethrum are also available; these are neat for people who like to spray, because just about any insect hit with this combination drops dead almost instantly, but the natural poisons decompose in the environment in hours. The trouble with rotenone and pyrethrum is that they also kill bees and beneficial insects. Finally, there's neem, a long-lasting natural oil from a tropical seed that, when emulsified into water and sprayed on leaves, makes them taste disgusting to most insects, including aphids.

Cabbage Maggots (*Hylemya brassicae*) Cabbage maggots are the larvae of an innocent-looking little fly. The sly fly usually waits until the root system of a cabbage family member is extensive enough to support a brood of larvae (when the stem approaches ¼ inch in diameter) before laying its eggs on the surface of the soil near the plant. After hatching, the larvae burrow down and begin to feed on the root system of the host plant.

The gardener suddenly discovers the maggot at work when the weaker-rooted members of the family—cabbage, broccoli, cauliflower, and sometimes Brussels sprouts—wilt and collapse or become stunted and barely grow. The maggots are also found tunneling through turnips, radishes, and the lower portions of Chinese cabbage leaves, though they tend to leave rutabagas alone or at most scar up the thick skin, which is peeled away before cooking.

Growing brassicas in spring without chemical soil pesticides requires encouraging the most rapid possible root development, which can mean paying attention to improving soil tilth as well as fertility. Vigorous root systems can tolerate a good deal of predation without the plant wilting or becoming noticeably stunted. The particular variety you choose has a lot to do with how vigorous the root system will be. That's one reason I always did my brassica trials without any maggot protection. A great trial is one in which eight out of ten varieties are demolished by maggots. All other things being equal, the remaining two varieties are great varieties for the home garden. In the case of radish and turnip crops, the choice of variety has no effect; only timely harvest can get them out of the ground before the maggots have invaded many roots. If maggot predation is totally eliminated, the plant size and ultimate yield of brassicas will be greater.

Gardeners can avoid much trouble simply

by planting after the April/May population peak. By early June, cabbage fly numbers decrease rapidly while the spring maggots are pupating in the soil. So mid-May through July is the easiest time to sow brassicas. Maggot levels increase again in late summer when the pupae hatch out, but by then nonroot brassica crops are usually large enough to withstand considerable predation, while light intensity has dropped so much that even if plants do lose some root, they are not likely to wilt.

Twenty years ago, there were no organic pesticides that were effective in the soil against the root maggot. The late Blair Adams, research horticulturist at the Washington State University Extension Service in Puyallup, did extensive trials on a number of traditional organic remedies for root maggots. He found that dustings of wood ashes—once widely recommended—actually attracted cabbage flies; he speculated that ashes helped despite that fact because in unlimed, acidic, calcium-deficient soils, the calcium-rich wood ashes boost the growth of brassicas enough to compensate for the increased predation the ash caused. Diatomaceous earth, helpful against hard-shelled insects even in the soil, did not kill the soft-skinned maggots. Blair found that careful and persistent hilling of soil around the plants' stems increased the survival rate of seedlings somewhat by burying the root system deeper.

The best control he could come up with was the collar. Gardeners had long used tarpaper collars, cut to fit tightly around the stem, but Blair felt that sawdust was better. A ring of sawdust about 1½ inches thick and 6 to 8 inches in diameter, touching the stem and carefully maintained, will prevent the fly from laying its eggs on the soil's surface. (See the illustration below.) Radish and turnip seed sown on the soil's surface and covered with a 4- to 6-inch-wide band of sawdust 1 inch deep will also be protected, but timely harvest is still essential because the swelling roots push aside the sawdust and expose themselves to the fly.

Since Blair did his work, another organic remedy has become available. Certain species of parasitic nematodes effectively attack root maggots in the ground. If large numbers of

Maggot protection using sawdust.

these microscopic life forms are seeded into the soil surrounding brassica seedlings, the nematodes can live for months and actively knock off maggots as fast as they hatch out, even breeding and maintaining fairly effective population levels for awhile. Parasitic nematodes will also control numerous other pests that may or may not be a problem in the maritime Northwest, including wireworms, onion maggots, carrot weevils, cutworms, rhododendron root weevil larvae, strawberry root weevil larvae, and cucumber beetle larvae.

Parasitic nematodes are easy and cheap to culture by the billions, but not so simple to transport or store out of the culture medium. Nematode cultures are still not suitable for retail sale from a room-temperature store shelf, but better long-term refrigerated storage methods have been developed. Buy them from mail-order seed companies. If the culture is purchased fresh, the gardener can hold it under refrigeration for several months before the nematodes lose viability. Obviously, you shouldn't place your order too many months in advance of anticipated need.

Reemay or other brands of floating row covers effectively prevent cabbage root maggots from reaching plants. These are especially useful for Chinese cabbage and turnips. They are discussed at greater length next, as a technique for controlling carrot rust flies.

Carrot Rust Flies *(Psila rosae)* As I mentioned before, the carrot rust fly is a pest with which I have little personal experience. I know from the literature that the fly begins breeding in late summer and will go through a generation every month, increasing to wildly high numbers by midwinter if the season is not too severe. Carrots started in late May come up after the spring hatch is through and may finish growing relatively unharmed and be harvested by late summer. However, carrots left in the ground after summer ends become increasingly infested.

Nematodes are of little use against this pest because the maggot is most active when soil temperatures are low, while chill renders the nematodes inactive. Covering the bed with well-anchored spun fiber row covers may give a gardener a maggot-free crop. These are very lightweight sheets of semitransparent polyester fabric, much like mosquito netting. The neatest thing about these row covers is that they allow air and water to pass through and are lifted up by the plants as they grow. If carefully anchored with a sprinkling of soil all around the edge, the fabric makes an effective insect barrier as well as a growth-enhancing cloche that doesn't require ventilation or special watering. To deter the rust fly, thin the carrots when the tops are 3 or 4 inches tall, to about 150 percent of their normal spacing (to allow for the slight loss of light through the fabric) and then carefully cover the bed. Gardeners have used homemade solutions similar to this for years, building screened boxes to cover their growing carrot crop and prevent the fly from laying eggs.

Storing carrots during winter by carefully laying sheets of plastic over the carrot tops and a few inches of straw over that for insulation might prevent the fly from gaining access, although it may also make a haven for field mice, who enjoy carrots as much as humans do.

Deer If you share your environment with deer, don't think for a moment that you can grow a garden without an effective fence. I've seen neighbors gardening without deer fencing, and they have inevitably experienced a midnight visit, ending up minus most of the

top two-thirds of their broccoli plants and all of their carrot leaves.

Other neighbors have gardened with jerry-rigged deer fencing, and they too have almost inevitably experienced a midnight visit. Certain acquaintances of mine have reckoned that anything in their unfenced garden was "good groceries"; expert shots with a nearly silent .22 rifle who cared not a whit about hunting season regulations, they kept a freezer filled with venison, but their gardens functioned more as an attraction to the deer than as a source of vegetables. Most of the groceries their garden produced was meat. And those neighbors who got a dog to keep the deer out of the garden have found that the dog often slept through a deer visit.

The Oregon Department of Fish and Wildlife has long subsidized the erection of garden fencing. Perhaps it is the same story in Washington State. Even if their subsidies should evaporate, they'll still give you an information sheet and personal advice about how to make a proper fence. It's worth it.

Flea Beetles (*Phyllotreta striolata*) Flea beetles are tiny, black, hopping insects that chew pinholes in leaves. They primarily affect members of the cabbage family but occasionally feed on other vegetables, including beets and tomato transplants. They particularly like sucking on thick, juicy brassica cotyledons (the first two leaves that emerge after germination), where the seedling stores its remaining food reserves until it develops a true leaf and really gets growing. In large numbers, flea beetles stunt and kill seedlings. Fast-growing, healthy

plants are not seriously stunted, though their leaves may be highly perforated.

Overwintering adult flea beetles migrate to the garden in spring from surrounding fields and begin to feed on newly sprouted or transplanted vegetables. Later in spring, the adults lay eggs in the soil, which quickly hatch out. Flea beetle larvae feed on potato tubers and various roots, usually without doing much more than cosmetic damage. After maturing into adults, the beetles then continue to feed until they hibernate in fall.

You can usually prevent flea beetle problems by raising husky, well-hardened transplants that don't go into shock and stop growing when set out (as cheaply raised commercial seedlings do), or by overseeding and not planting too early, which gives the beetles lots to chew on while leaving the gardener enough survivors to establish a stand. If plants are being too heavily damaged, they're probably not growing fast enough. In that case, the best strategy may be liquid fertilizer and improvement of soil tilth and fertility before the next planting.

Severe infestations can be sprayed with several types of pesticides, the safest being rotenone, which is available as a dust or a powder to mix in water. Rotenone is very, very effective but short-lasting; it must be sprayed every few days until the seedlings are growing well and producing much more new leaf than the beetles are chewing away. Another acceptable organic pesticide is a liquid combination of rotenone and pyrethrum (obtained from a perennial daisy), often combined with a synergist called piperonyl butoxide, an evil-sounding name for a substance actually derived from natural sources that increases the potency of both rotenone and pyrethrum. The pyrethrum probably has little effect on flea beetles.

Imported Cabbageworms *(Pieris rapae)* Cabbageworms are the greenish larvae of a white butterfly often seen fluttering about the garden. Their clusters of small, yellowish, bullet-shaped eggs are laid on cabbage family plants, usually on the undersides of the leaves. A similar pest is the cabbage looper (*Trichoplusia ni*), the slightly smaller larva of a night-flying brown butterfly. Its round, greenish-white eggs are laid singly on the upper surface of leaves. The larvae of both pests hatch out quickly and grow rapidly, feeding on brassica leaves. They can do a great deal of damage in a short time, especially if they begin feeding at critical times, such as during the early formation of cabbage heads, or if their numbers are excessive. Once the larvae reach their full size (1¼ to 1½ inches), they pupate unnoticed.

In a very small garden, hand-picking the larvae and tossing them away from any cabbage family plant can be sufficient control. An extremely effective nontoxic pesticide called *Bacillus thuringiensis* is widely available, marketed as Bt, Dipel, or Thuricide. Bt can be sprayed the day of harvest because it is a bacterial culture lethal only to the cabbageworm, cabbage looper, and a few close relatives. The culture remains active on the leaves for only a few days, but even if sprayed only once, it seems to persist in the garden at a low level, as infection is transmitted from decaying infected worms to healthy worms, greatly reducing their numbers

for the rest of the season. If sprayed every few weeks, Bt can offer control good enough for finicky growers who become grossly offended at the very idea of a cabbageworm appearing in their broccoli or cauliflower heads.

Leaf Miners *(Liromyza species)* Leaf miners are the maggots of a small fly similar to the cabbage fly or carrot rust fly. These larvae most enjoy tunneling through leaves of beets, chard, and spinach, although they'll also mine bean, blackberry, lettuce, and other leaves. I have not had any trouble with leaf miners, but some gardeners to the north do. I know of no organic insecticide that will control leaf miners effectively, because they're protected from sprays by being inside the leaf itself.

I once sent some spun-fiber row cover to a Washington State gardener who complained of leaf miner problems completely ruining every beet crop he planted. The gardener carefully covered most of a beet bed after the seedlings were large enough to thin and weed, and kept the cover in place undisturbed until harvest. His unprotected beets were thoroughly ruined—not one plant survived to make a beet root. Under the cover, there was a fine harvest, though the fabric did drop light levels somewhat so the beets were a bit toppy, with smaller roots than he would have liked. As with carrots, this problem can be eliminated by thinning the beets to a slightly wider-than-normal spacing.

Slugs *(Gastropodae)* More garden damage is done by the small gray slug than by its larger and more noticeable relatives. Slugs eat seedlings

and nestle inside lettuce and cabbage heads. Some gardeners say they can ruin new plantings in a few nights. Never has damage been that severe in my garden, though. They'll also share your fruit, especially ripening tomatoes and strawberries.

Slugs hide and lay eggs under garden debris, so keeping soil bare, putting garden trash carefully in a compost pile, and eliminating daytime hiding places such as boards lying on the soil will reduce their populations. Slugs are a major reason that year-round mulching, so popular with eastern gardeners, is unworkable in the maritime Northwest. Gardeners who find slugs multiplying beyond the minor annoyance level can try switching to later sowings so seedlings grow faster, and sowing more seeds to give the slugs some extras to knock off. Banding a little fertilizer along seedling rows or below transplants might increase growth rates sufficiently that slugs are no longer a serious threat.

Large slug populations can easily be reduced by trapping and/or poisoning. The simplest method is to lay boards on the garden paths. Each morning at sunrise, many slugs will hide under these boards. The gardener can then turn the boards over during the day, hand-pick the slugs, and drop them into a jar of detergent solution, salt water, or gasoline, or sprinkle a bit of salt on them. A friend of mine with a small garden likes to go out at night with a gasoline lantern and a pair of sharp scissors, snipping hundreds of slugs in half. He needs to do this only once or twice a month to keep slug populations manageable.

Slug baits made only with metaldehyde are acceptable to me, but I won't use baits made with fluoride poisons. Metaldehyde is a simple organic substance similar to wood alcohol. It quickly breaks down into harmless components. That is why some baits use other, more durable poisons. Slugs love to intoxicate themselves to death with metaldehyde in the same way they'll happily drown themselves in beer. Bait need not be placed within the garden to eliminate slugs; it can be sprinkled in a 12-inch-wide band or "slug fence" outside of the garden. Slugs travel at random. A foot-wide bait barrier will prevent slugs from entering the garden for several weeks, while those already in the garden will leave, especially if they find little cover in the garden to hide under during daylight hours. Reactivated every few weeks, a bait barrier can quickly reduce garden populations.

Slug bait can be fatally attractive to pets. A more aggressive approach, which completely avoids broadcasting slug bait, is to construct traps out of pie tins and sprinkle bait in the tins. Or you can put some bait into a short length of large-diameter plastic tube or pipe and rest it on the ground so the slugs can easily enter when the sun comes up. To make a flying saucer trap, sink a small pie tin in the soil, its rim flush with the surface; then insert four long supporting nails through the rim and on them suspend a larger, inverted pie tin a few inches above the sunken one to guard the lower one from rain or irrigation. Devoutly organic gardeners can fill the lower pie tin with stale beer. The illustration on the next page shows different types of slug traps.

I was once introduced to a fine Swiss organic

Slug traps.

slug control product. Called Fertosan Slug Destroyer, it consists of a natural but highly stable gelatin containing herbal attractants and some industrial ethyl alcohol. I managed to get a gallon in through customs for trial—it worked fine. A few ounces of gel poured into a small hole in the earth resisted the effects of rain and did not degrade for several weeks; the little hole gradually filled up with dead slugs pickled in gel. However, the patented stuff couldn't be imported from Switzerland for

resale nor could it be manufactured under license in the United States without the same level of EPA and U.S. Department of Agriculture approvals demanded for lethally poisonous pesticides. The Swiss company put me in touch with an American who had obtained a license to manufacture the slug gel on this side of the ocean. He confidently started the approval process but became bogged down in bureaucracy and vanished, probably after losing a lot of money. Thus are we protected by our benevolent government.

To get slugs out of your food, submerge the vegetables in cold water for fifteen minutes or so and then rinse well; slugs suffocate and drop to the bottom of the sink.

Symphylans *(Scutigerella immaculata)* The horrible pests known as symphylans are discussed at length Chapter 4, on pages 115 through 120, because the only known cure is long-term rotation.

Chapter 9 How to Grow It

Since I have given my attention to the cultivation of the soil,
I find I have no competition to fear,
have nothing to apprehend from the success of my neighbor,
and owe no thanks for the purchase of my commodities.
Possessing on my land all the necessaries of life,
I am under no anxiety regarding my daily subsistence.

—JOHN SILLETT,
A New Practical System of Fork and Spade Husbandry

This chapter

is a reference guide, organized by what I think of as vegetable "families." Scientifically trained readers may be mildly amused that I have not followed strict rules of botanical classification. But I believe a system of classification and definition is only useful if it permits a person to do something with it; organizing vegetables into families that grow similarly helps a gardener and encourages experimentation with new vegetables.

These are the groups I use:

Solanums: eggplants, peppers, tomatoes

Legumes: beans, peas

Green manures: clover, field peas, favas, grains

Greens: celery, celeriac, corn salad, endive, lettuce, mustard, parsley, spinach, Swiss chard, rocket, sorrel

Brassicas: broccoli, Brussels sprouts, cabbage, Chinese cabbage, cauliflower, collards, kale, kohlrabi, rutabagas, turnips

Roots: beets, carrots, Belgian endive, chicory, parsley and root parsley, parsnips, potatoes, radishes

Cucurbits: cucumbers, melons, pumpkins, squashes

Alliums: garlic, leeks, shallots, onions

Miscellaneous: asparagus, sweet corn, herbs, horseradish, sunflowers, and other low-demand food crops

How to Use This Chapter

PLANTING DATES

The planting dates I suggest are about right for the Willamette Valley (Oregon) gardener. I target this area because Willamette conditions are about average for our entire region. Readers to the north or south, along the coast, or at higher elevations must make adjustments.

Spring and summer come later north of the Willamette Valley and at higher elevations; gardeners there should plant their spring and summer crops a week or two later than the dates I suggest. Fall comes sooner to northern and higher-elevation gardens; growth rates there slow a bit sooner than they do in the Willamette Valley. Summers are cooler along the coast, which has the same effect. Gardeners there should start their fall/winter and overwintering crops a week or two sooner.

Spring starts earlier along the coast, but summer arrives a bit later and is cooler. Coastal gardeners might start their spring crops a bit earlier, and their summer and winter crops at about the same time as in the Willamette Valley and hope for a warm summer.

Spring and summer arrive markedly earlier south of Drain, Oregon. Gardeners along the southern Oregon coast, in the Yoncalla Valley, along the Umpqua and Rogue Rivers should start their spring and summer plantings a week or two earlier than I suggest. Fortunate gardeners in northern California might start their spring crops as much as three or four weeks earlier. Fall comes later to the south. Gardeners south of Drain should sow their autumn, winter, and overwintering crops a week or two after I suggest for the Willamette Valley. Gardeners in northern California might hold off starting for fall/winter/overwintering as much as three or four weeks. The diagram on the next page, "Local Planting Dates," shows how planting dates vary by region.

Local Planting Dates

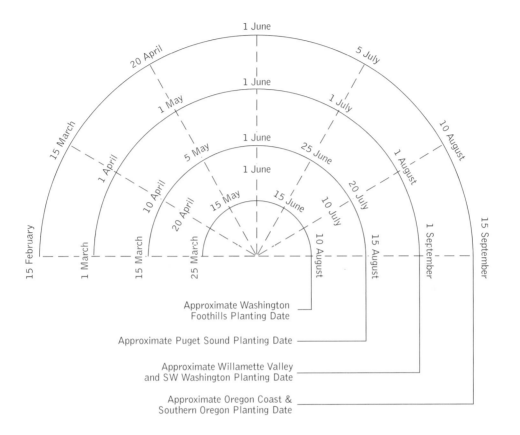

Approximate Washington Foothills Planting Date

Approximate Puget Sound Planting Date

Approximate Willamette Valley and SW Washington Planting Date

Approximate Oregon Coast & Southern Oregon Planting Date

Plant Spacings and General Cultivation Methods

Many of the suggested spacings in this chapter envision semipermanent raised beds, 3½ to 4½ feet wide and as long as you like. When the directions say to sow seeds every so many inches in the row, with the rows so many inches apart, it means to plant in short, parallel rows that run across the width of the bed. For larger plants, the directions will sometimes suggest 18- to 24-inch centers. In this case, what is envisioned is a regularly spaced grid pattern atop a raised bed. Sometimes I suggest sowing in long rows. In this case the rows are to be deeply dug, two or three shovel blades wide, the row centers 4 to 5 feet apart, with narrow footpaths between them, the plants spaced the specified distance apart down the row. Sometimes I suggest planting in hills even farther apart.

The suggested spacings will, in almost every case, grow big, handsome vegetables enjoying abundant irrigation in well-fertilized soil. I assume that the soil moisture in these beds will be kept above 70 percent of capacity at all times and that the plants will experience no shortage of fertility. In southern Oregon or northern California, where heat-loving species grow faster and larger, gardeners might separate these vegetables a bit more. Those to the north could grow their heat lovers a little closer together because they won't get as large. Lovers of giant beets can increase my recommended spacings; those who like little beets harvested sooner can decrease them. The same is true for cabbage heads, which vary a great deal in size according to soil fertility and the amount of space each plant has to grow in.

Of course, there are limits. Increasing plant spacing more than one-third beyond what this book recommends will probably make purposeless gaps. Decreasing plant spacing by more than one-third may be all right for some crops but not at all for others. Lettuce, for example—especially heading types—will not develop properly when crowded. Competing carrots do not make good roots; crowded radishes don't bulb. Densely grown bush beans, on the other hand, will make larger yields of slightly smaller pods.

If you're a novice gardener, try my recommendations without alteration and see what happens. You can always make adjustments next year. At least you'll get a good crop this year.

FERTILIZERS

I recommend mainly organic fertilizers, most frequently the complete organic fertilizer blend given in Chapter 2. It is more than adequate. Fertilizer is best applied twice: a minimal amount broadcast and worked into the growing bed, and additional amounts side-dressed as needed. When I advise broadcasting fertilizer before sowing or transplanting, about 1 gallon of complete organic fertilizer per 100 square feet of growing bed is sufficient unless otherwise stated.

HARVEST QUANTITIES

I can give you only a rough guide as to how much you will harvest from a given planting. Were I to try to say that so much bed or so many plants yield so much, I'd be wrong more often than I'd be right. Yield per area occupied depends on soil, spacing, weather, variety—too much variation to predict. I garden for two vegetableatarian adults plus occasional visitors who are forced to eat vegetableatarian when their feet are placed beneath our table. (A vegetableatarian is someone who mostly eats vegetables most of the time but may eat small quantities of meat or other animal-related products on occasion. The major portion of a vegetableatarian's calories do not come from cereals or other grains.) The quantities and area allocations I suggest suit us at the time I write this book. I am constantly revising the size of my plantings as tastes, desires, and my body's capacity to handle foods changes. You will have to do the same.

VARIETIES

For many kinds of vegetables, I suggest specific varietal choices. Some varieties are widely sold and easily available, and for those no sources are given. Other varieties are rarer. The following abbreviations are used to indicate seed sources:

JSS: Johnny's Selected Seeds
ST: Stokes
TS: Territorial Seed Company
WCO: West Coast Seeds

The address and Web site for each of these companies is given in Chapter 6 on pages 180–182.

The seed business changes rapidly; new varieties are developed, and old ones fall out of favor and disappear. Much of what is available as this is being written (the summer of 1999) may not be sold three years from now. For that reason I also describe how to choose likely candidates from the new varieties to come.

Solanums

Solanums are semitropical or tropical plants. The family is heat loving; in our cool climate, solanums must be aggressively helped or they won't mature much fruit before summer's end. Especially intolerant of cool conditions in the seedling stage, solanums must be pampered and guarded against chill until they have three or four true leaves.

Tomatoes are the hardiest member of the family; eggplant and peppers are much less so. Were you to sow tomato seeds outdoors, germination might not occur until mid- to late May; pepper seeds might not sprout outside until mid-June. Although growth might be rapid after direct-seeding, the first ripe peppers would not appear until the end of summer at best; direct-seeded quick-maturing tomato varieties will ripen a few fruit by late August. Except in the redwoods, what we call "mid-season" tomato varieties would never ripen anything at all if direct-seeded. That's why maritime Northwest Solanaceae are given a six- to eight-week indoor head start on the hot weather and then transplanted outdoors. This way, we can enjoy two to three months of harvest in a climate far to the north of this family's natural range.

Unless the weather is warm and sunny and the nights stay above 55°F, peppers and eggplants grow slowly. Nights below 52°F make them suffer stunting. In the Willamette Valley, nights can't be counted on to be above 52°F until mid-June. The key to success with peppers and eggplants (and melons and cucumbers as well) is to delay transplanting until the weather really suits the crop, because if they don't get stunted as seedlings they'll take off and grow fast. In some cabbage years, "night temperatures regularly above 52°F" does not describe the maritime Northwest summer at all.

Once I saw an amazing demonstration of how poorly these tropical species are adapted to our region. It was the first year I used a superduper, extra-large, thick-walled, tongue-and-groove, solid-cedar-plank hot frame fully equipped with an adjustable thermostatically controlled heating cable and an automatic temperature-sensing exhaust fan. What a toy! I quickly discovered that solanaceous plants grew at an amazing rate if I turned up the soil temperature to 78°F instead of the usual 70°F. My peppers responded by making huge, lush leaves such as I had not seen since I left

California. I planted them out in mid-June as 18-inch-tall bushes in gallon pots, bearing half-sized fruit.

The summer weather was a tad warmer than average that year, but without bottom heat the growth rate immediately dropped, fruit set stopped dead in its tracks, and leaf size declined to a quarter of the size attained in the hot frame! All that changed was that the nighttime lows outdoors were dropping into the 50s; in the bottom-heated frame, air temperature at night had never fallen below 65°F. If the summer had been a cool one, I'm sure those soft beauties would have gone into total shock and died. Grown in a heated greenhouse and given enough root room, peppers will achieve a bushy 4-foot height in one season.

Many gardeners don't fully appreciate this relationship between temperature and growth, and they attempt to cure reticent solanums with more fertilizer. This can be destructive. A plant that can't build new leaf tissue concentrates unneeded fertilizer salts in the vascular system. These can reach toxic levels, further stunting the plant. A wiser response would be to first erect a cloche over struggling solanums and then fertilize after they're growing faster.

Being tropical plants, solanum seedlings can easily be shocked by cold conditions. Minor shocks stop growth for only a day or two. Severe, repeated shocks will stunt plants and prevent rapid growth from ever occurring even if temperatures become virtually ideal. Cold soil can be a shock to newly transplanted seedlings accustomed to greenhouse conditions. Nighttime lows of 40°F shock tomatoes; 50°F shocks peppers and eggplants.

As seedlings get bigger, they can be toughened up to withstand a degree or two more chill. That's all—a degree or two. Raising quality transplants means walking a tightrope between hardening them as fast as possible and not shocking them in the process. It is much better to delay transplanting solanums than to risk severe temperature shocks. Busy gardeners who buy transplants are advised to purchase small pepper and eggplant seedlings in mid-May, set the seedlings in large (4- to 6-inch) pots that will hold enough moisture that they won't need constant tending, harden them off in a crude cold frame, and wait for the pots to fill with roots and the nights to warm up before transplanting.

Solanums will grow fine at any soil pH between 5.5 and 7.0, meaning that if you lime as I recommend in Chapter 2 there is no cause for concern. All are fairly heavy feeders; however, extreme amounts of nitrogen may promote too much vegetative growth while reducing fruit set. One moderate feeding of complete organic fertilizer (½ to 1 cup) worked in below each transplant when they're set out will provide about six weeks of high fertility levels, perfect while the seedlings make rapid growth and begin flowering and fruit set. Additional fertilizer broadcast and tilled into the growing bed before transplanting will provide a healthy background level through the entire summer. If the summer proves a hot one and growth continues very rapidly past mid-July, consider side-dressing.

Solanums are generally self-fertile. Some occasional crossing may occur in peppers and eggplants, but isolation of 20 feet is sufficient to prevent most unwanted crosses. Hybridization of solanums will markedly increase vigor and yield, although open-pollinated tomatoes and peppers will yield adequately in most of the maritime Northwest. In marginal areas where the weather barely suits the species, that extra bit of hybrid vigor can make a considerable difference, particularly with eggplants and peppers.

EGGPLANTS *(Solanum melongena)*

Of all the garden Solanaceae, eggplants are the most temperature sensitive, from sprouting to transplanting. However, once eggplants have four or five true leaves and have hardened off a bit, they will produce more foliage than peppers under poor conditions (but will not set more fruit). Cool nights stop fruiting, so in most areas eggplants demand a black plastic mulch to slightly warm the night air around them. Along the coast and north of Longview, Washington, the use of large cloches or a greenhouse would probably quadruple the yield of even the earliest and most chill-tolerant variety.

Culture Raise transplants like peppers (see Chapter 7). If you watch seedlings respond to weather, you'll soon realize that you have to be a bit more gradual when hardening them off than you do with pepper seedlings. In the Willamette Valley, eggplants may be set out around June 10 most years.

A few weeks before transplanting, dig the bed or row, broadcast complete organic fertilizer, rake it in, and then lay a sheet of black plastic over the entire bed surface, anchoring the edges with soil. Make the black plastic mulch as wide as possible, and take care to leave as much plastic exposed to the sun as possible (keep it free of loose soil on top). Cut small holes (ones you can just put a hand through) in the plastic, spaced about 24 inches apart, and then work about ½ cup complete organic fertilizer into the soil below each hole. The plastic soaks up solar energy, raising soil temperatures a few degrees and increasing the radiation of heat from soil below the plants at night, which creates a slightly warmer microclimate—a little difference that makes all the difference.

If growth slows during August while weather conditions are still sunny and warm, fertigate to provoke renewed growth by saturating the root zone of each plant. (In Chapter 7, I illustrate a quick way to fertigate seedlings using a 5-gallon bucket and a thin plastic siphon tube attached to an old broomstick.) New fruit will be set only while the plant is making vegetative growth.

Garden planning A well-adapted early hybrid variety such as Dusky will produce four to six large fruits in an average Willamette Valley summer. Small-fruited types will produce fifteen to twenty. I usually grow three or four plants because some coolish summers I'm lucky to get one or two fruit per plant. Eggplants follow nicely in succession behind the earliest peas or overwintered green-manure favas.

Insects and disease Healthy eggplants are rarely bothered by anything but low temperatures and lack of nutrients. Attacks after mid-September are probably symptoms of decreasing light intensity and cooler nights, and should be ignored.

Harvest The fruits taste best if picked while slightly immature, before much seed development has occurred—indicated when the fruit has stopped enlarging rapidly but the skin is still shiny and thin. The plants will cease growth and fruit set will stop a week or two before the autumnal equinox. At this time, harvest all well-developed fruit to unburden the weakening plant; the smaller fruits left on the bush may enlarge if sunny, warm temperatures prevail into October.

Saving seed Eggplants are self-pollinated, but an occasional extraordinarily energetic bee does effect crosses. Purity can be ensured by a 20-foot separation between varieties. Seeds mature only after fruits reach full size and after the skin has toughened. Harvest the overmature fruit, crush it into pulp, and wash the heavier seeds free of the lighter pulp. Finally, dry the seeds thoroughly on a newspaper at room temperature. If open-pollinated varieties were productive in our gardens, saving seed would be that simple. However, with the exception of a very few Asian types, only hybrid varieties are vigorous enough to set and ripen fruit west of the Cascades.

Varieties Only a few early hybrid varieties consistently produce much fruit, the best of them being the widely available Dusky. Johnny's has a great interest in eggplant; their varietal offerings change rapidly and are gen-

erally excellent here. Short Tom is an Asian hybrid with very small, traditional, cucumber-shaped fruit. Be quite wary of other varieties unless they come from Territorial, Johnny's, or West Coast. If you want to experiment, make sure the variety matures at least as quickly as the catalog says Dusky will.

Dry-gardening Space 36 inches apart in rows 5 feet apart; fertigate 2 gallons July 1, 4 gallons July 20, 4 gallons August 10, and 3 gallons August 30.

PEPPERS *(Capsicum annuum)*

Climatic variations make quite a difference in pepper varietal performance. South of Drain, Oregon, almost any variety will make at least some fruit. In the Willamette Valley, only early types do well. North of Longview, Washington, and along the coast, only the hardiest pepper varieties will grow in cloches or greenhouses.

Culture See Chapter 7 for raising your own transplants. Nighttime lows below 50°F will shock seedling peppers. Hardening off can improve that by only a degree or two. Though slightly benefited by black plastic mulch, peppers will usually do all right without any forcing if transplanting is delayed until mid-June in the Willamette Valley. In cool summers, I've had much better luck growing peppers under plastic tunnel cloches or under spun-fiber fabric cloches until they start ripening fruit. I'm sure gardeners north of Longview, Washington, will find this to be the case every summer. Transplant on 18- to 24-inch centers, depending on how warm the summers are where you garden. Work ¼ to ½ cup complete organic fertilizer into the soil below each seedling. If growth slows before mid-September and the weather is still warm and sunny, fertigate lightly to see if it will provoke a growth response—if it does, side-dress with a sprinkling of complete organic fertilizer, shallowly raked or hoed into the soil around the plants.

Garden planning In our cool climate, bell types at best produce six large, ripe fruits per plant. Small-fruited varieties make dozens.

Insects and diseases Rarely a problem. Heavy infestations of symphylans may stunt peppers.

Harvest Many varieties change color from green to red or from green to yellow as they ripen, acquiring thicker, juicier walls and a sweeter taste in the process. This is also true of thick-walled hot types such as Jalapeño and Hungarian. If thin-walled hot varieties such as Cayenne and Red Chile, which are intended to be used dried, have not ripened red by summer's end, yank the entire plant, roots and all, before frost or excessive rains rot the fruit, and hang it upside down in a cool, dim place. Some of the mature fruit will ripen and dry simultaneously.

Saving seed Allow the fruit to color up fully (and then some) before harvest to obtain ripe, high-germination seed. Spread the seed on a sheet of paper to dry fully at room temperature before storage. Peppers have a somewhat higher likelihood of crossing than eggplant. Varieties should be given 50 feet of isolation, especially if you're growing sweet and hot types in the garden at the same time.

Varieties There are huge differences in how well varieties can grow and make fruit under cool conditions. *Small-fruited varieties are earlier and more prolific than bell types.* Very tropical sorts such as Serrano will hardly grow vegetatively, much less make fruit; standard California market open-pollinated varieties such as Cal Wonder, Keystone Resistant Giant, and Yolo Wonder will produce plenty of vegetation but be very late to mature fruit and usually yield poorly, although these types do better in southern Oregon and okay in the redwoods.

Golden Bell and Gypsy are large-fruited sweet hybrids that do well and seem to be available from all seed sellers. New hybrid pepper varieties come and go in a flash, and peppers fruit in all sorts of colors and flavors. Pepper lovers should experiment freely, but try only varieties as early as or earlier than the successful bell varieties just mentioned. Stokes has a large selection of early peppers of all sorts but also sells many late varieties that won't make it here. Johnny's, Territorial, and West Coast are safe sources to play around with—nothing in their catalogs will be too late.

Dry-gardening Space 30 inches apart in rows 4 to 5 feet apart; fertigate 2 gallons July 1, 4 gallons July 20, 4 gallons August 10, and 3 gallons August 30.

TOMATOES (*Lycopersicon esculentum*)

Tomatoes are the most cool tolerant of the garden Solanaceae. All varieties are certain to grow vegetatively and set lots of fruit. However, getting that fruit to ripen is not always so certain.

Culture The earlier fruit is set, the sooner the tomatoes will ripen. To encourage early fruit set, transplant a well-hardened seedling so no growth check occurs. See Chapter 7.

Tomato varieties have different growth habits—determinate and indeterminate. This is one distinction that makes a lot of difference.

Determinate types grow as compact bushes that usually set and ripen their first fruit sooner and bear more heavily at first, but the yield and/or the flavor quickly tapers off. These varieties cannot be trellised or pruned and don't benefit much from staking or being put inside wire cages to hold them up, as they have been bred to hold most of their fruit up off the ground. Yes, some tomatoes are lost to slugs and rot or are overlooked by the picker, but these losses are more than offset by earlier ripening and ease of growing. Most determinate types should be spaced on 2- to 3-foot centers, though some of the earliest varieties are smaller and can be more closely spaced. I grow indeterminates for the later harvests, because determinate yields naturally peter out, and because the best-tasting varieties are inevitably indeterminate. So I pack my determinate varieties a little tightly on the bed and am not concerned when they get crowded, because by that time the harvest of my indeterminate varieties is in full swing.

I get the earliest possible harvest by forcing them under a 4-foot-wide tunnel cloche. I set six-week-old tomato seedlings out in the cloche three weeks before the last usual frost date. I keep determinate varieties under plastic until the entire bed is a green mass of vines pushing against the cloche's walls, usually early in July (see the illustration on the next page). Then I remove their cloche, and ripe fruits start appearing almost immediately.

Indeterminate types make ever-expanding vines that, if weather conditions and light intensity permitted, would never stop setting new fruit. These sorts can make quite a tangle if allowed to sprawl on the ground. If you grow them "wild" (I have, and it works fine, though picking is more difficult, fruit size is smaller, and a fraction of them will rot or be eaten by sow bugs), they should be 3 to 4 feet apart in all directions. Indeterminate varieties are often propped up in wire-mesh cages or are grown against trellises of one type or another. These are the sort of tomatoes you see photographs of in magazines, showing a single plant covering the entire wall of a garage (in the southern states.)

My favorite system for controlling indeterminate varieties comes from the English glasshouse trade. I plant seedlings out early under a 4-foot-wide tunnel cloche in two parallel rows, the rows 36 inches apart, the seedlings 18 inches apart in the row. When the bushes are about 18 inches tall (early to mid-June), I remove the cloche. I then erect two parallel horizontal beams (2-by-4s) 7 feet above the two rows of seedlings, supported by an X framework, much like an old-fashioned clothes drying rack. Every 9 inches along the beams, I tie on and drop a length of stout baling twine—two strings for each plant—and tie the twine loosely to the base of each seedling. I then prune the plant back to two leaders, the terminal one and a single vigorous one on the side. As each leader grows, I guide it around and around the twine, and I pinch off new leaders as they appear. This management takes only a few minutes each week. If a vine reaches the top, it is allowed to drape over the beam and return toward earth. (Most years, 6 to 7 feet of vine growth is all I get before the season ends.) Trellising and training (snipping off most side branches) produce slightly earlier ripening, slightly tastier, and much larger blemish-free fruit.

In addition to broadcast-fertilizing the tomato beds, I work in complete organic fertilizer, ¼ to ½ cup, below each seedling when transplanting. When growth slows, I side-dress a little more fertilizer around the plants or fertigate them.

Garden planning
One well-grown 100-square-foot bed, half in early determinate varieties and half in trellised indeterminate varieties, keeps my family, many visitors, and some of our friends overwhelmed with fresh tomatoes during the season. A single tunnel cloche can cover the whole bed at the start, making using the cloche (and enjoying its benefits) very little trouble. If you intend to do extensive canning, in a decent summer another bed of the same size should produce about

250 pounds of ripe processing tomatoes from determinate vines.

Transplant tomatoes into a bed that grew overwintered green manure; when the vines begin to fall apart, pull them, prepare the bed for spring planting (compost), and plant crimson clover or small-seeded favas to establish a winter ground cover.

Insects and diseases
Flea beetles may attack newly transplanted seedlings, although well-hardened transplants are hardly touched. Rotenone/pyrethrum sprayed every two or three days will protect soft seedlings until they harden off, come out of shock, and begin to grow. Tomato hornworms and fruitworms (rarely found west of the Cascades) can be easily killed with Bt.

Most of the diseases tomatoes have been bred to resist are found only in commercial tomato-growing areas and are no cause for concern to us. Tomato late blight, a fungus that killed virtually every maritime Northwest tomato plant in August 1983, gallops through our region when the vines experience too many weeks of cool, damp conditions—which both weaken tomatoes and promote the fungus. Although farmers have chemical fungicides in their *batterie de cuisine* to prevent the disease, there is no cure once late blight strikes. There is no known varietal resistance to the blight, although scattered plants do survive the blight, mostly ones located in very favorable microclimates such as against a white-painted wall under a roof overhang that kept off most of the rains. I'm sure we'll see late blight again in some future cabbage year.

Two problems with tomatoes appear to be diseases but aren't. If large amounts of water are added to very dry soil, tomatoes often respond by curling their leaves, and the blossom ends of fruits may blacken and rot. Tomato leaf curl and blossom-end rot can be prevented by providing a steady moisture supply and liming the soil to make sufficient calcium available. End-rot occurs when moisture fluctuations interfere with calcium uptake. Adding lime to complete organic fertilizer blends will reduce or eliminate blossom-end rot.

Harvest Determinate varieties tend to grossly overbear; thinning, by removing more than half of the flower clusters from determinate tomatoes, lightens the fruit load. This permits the vines to ripen bigger, better-flavored fruit a bit earlier. (Overbearing varieties of apple trees are similarly thinned—if they weren't, the fruit would be tiny and tasteless.)

The proportion of flowers to remove is determined by how leafy the variety is. Some extra-early varieties have very small leaves, show a lot of stem, and set huge quantities of fruit that have next to no flavor. How could they have any, when it is food made by leaves that puts flavor into fruit? These varieties benefit enormously from the heaviest thinning. Toward summer's end the gardener can encourage ripening of the larger fruits already set by removing all the flower clusters and the smaller immature tomatoes, beginning about September 1. This is no loss; the little ones won't mature anyway.

A third trick is to attempt to kill the vines by withholding water, starting in mid- to late August, depending on how water-retentive the soil is. Putting the vines under severe moisture stress causes them to ripen their fruit. However, nature sometimes defeats this strategy by sending late-summer rains, which often cause the vines to fall apart and become diseased.

Green tomatoes, if harvested when full sized, will often ripen in the house. We usually bring in several buckets just before the first frost. These keep us in ripe tomatoes for six to eight more weeks. Although there are many involved methods promising more success with indoor ripening of green fruit, and there are even varieties like Longkeeper and Golden Treasure that produce only green tomatoes especially for ripening over a long period indoors, we've found that if buckets of blemish-free, clean fruit of any slicing variety are kept fairly cool and are checked every few days for coloring up, most of the tomatoes ripen and very few rot.

Saving seed Tomatoes are invariably self-pollinated, with no danger of unwanted crossing. To save seed from open-pollinated varieties, simply remove the pulp from a few fully ripe tomatoes (overripe, slug-eaten ones hiding under thick foliage are ideal), and place the pulp in a drinking glass or mason jar on the kitchen counter. Allow the mash to ferment. After three to five days, the solids rise to the top and the seeds settle to the bottom. Slowly run water into the glass to float off the pulp, leaving the seeds. Pour the seeds into a strainer, wash them thoroughly in cold water, and dry them on a sheet of paper. The only trick to obtaining high-germination seeds is to conduct the fermentation speedily at a temperature over 70°F. Cold ferments lasting more than one week often result in dead seed.

Varieties Any variety described in an eastern seed catalog as needing more than seventy-two days to maturity (or needing longer than Fantastic Hybrid is said to need) will not likely ripen heavily north of Drain, Oregon. Heat-loving eastern beefsteak types and "main season" eastern varieties especially do not do well in the maritime Northwest. This is because cool nights prevent pollination on many heat-loving varieties, causing the early fruit sets to abort; ripening on heat lovers is also retarded by cool nights. There is a considerable varietal difference about what constitutes "too cool." Keep in mind that back east, midsummer nighttime lows average around 68° to 72°F at sunup.

One very interesting group of open-pollinated determinate varieties was developed for maritime conditions by Dr. Jim Baggett at Corvallis, Oregon. Starting with a parthenocarpic Russian variety (parthenocarpic means

that it sets seedless fruit instead of aborting its fruit when cool conditions defeat pollination), Baggett bred a series of bushy little varieties that set and ripen in the Willamette Valley weeks earlier than any other early varieties. These include Oregon 11, Santiam, Gold Nugget, and Oregon Spring. I still consider the best-flavored firm-meated slicer we can grow to be Fantastic Hybrid, though others prefer Pic Red. Other reliable varieties include Early Cascade, Kootenai, and Willamette, although Willamette is also known for all the green tomatoes it leaves at season's end. Popular "mid-season" hybrids such as Celebrity, Floramerica, Big Boy, and Better Boy, though usually billed as "only a few days later" than Fantastic in the East, are much later here and tend to be disappointing. Old eastern standards, the ones with remarkable home-garden flavor, such as Marglobe and Rutgers, never ripened fruit for me despite frequent attempts. Johnny's and Stokes' open-pollinated varieties sometimes don't set fruit well here. The major catalogs present a bewildering assortment. Beware—do small trials on untested varieties except those in Territorial's and West Coast's catalogs (already thoroughly tested in our climate); be doubly wary of any variety listed as later than Fantastic.

Gardeners who make tomato sauce or paste using anything but varieties bred for that purpose may be practicing false economy. Salad or slicing varieties have a high water content: A potful of salad tomatoes cooks down to almost nothing. Canning varieties, which have little juice and a high percentage of solids, cook down rapidly into thick sauce and hold up for whole-pack canning. Standard canners carried by most major seed companies don't ripen nearly as heavily as Baggett's parthenocarpic Oregon Pride or Oregon Star, or Territorial's or West Coast's other saucers.

In the same way that small-fruited peppers grow better here than the fancy large-fruited ones, most cherry varieties are prolific here. Try Jim Baggett's Gold Nuggett (TSC, NIC) for a unique mild flavor and an abundance of early fruit. In fact, Gold Nuggett is usually the first ripe fruit in my garden, year after year. Yellow Pear and Yellow Plum, both old heirlooms and great nibbling, are too late for comfort except south of Drain.

Although Golden Jubilee produces absolutely the most delicious, rich-flavored, big yellow tomatoes you've ever tasted, many summers it fails to ripen much fruit. Golden Delight and Taxi (both determinate) are much earlier and the best of many alternatives, though still not as tasty as Jubilee.

Dry-gardening Best with indeterminates because their root systems are every bit as aggressive as their vines. Space them 5 feet apart in rows 5 feet apart and allow to sprawl without training, staking, or pruning; fertigate 2 gallons July 1, 4 gallons July 20, 5 gallons August 10, and 5 gallons August 30. I've had good results from Fantastic Hybrid and the old Small Red Cherry, the most sprawling of all cherry varieties. Try it with Gold Nuggett (determinate), too, spaced 3 feet apart in rows 5 feet apart. And try it with a tunnel cloche to get them ripening before they're put under moisture stress.

Legumes

Cool-season legumes create nitrates from the air through a process called fixation and, while growing, make abundant organic matter. With hundreds of acres of browned-off pasture grasses around the homestead during winter, the contrast of vibrant green patches of clover and fava beans among the rain-beaten winter garden plants brings me great joy.

Nitrogen-rich fertilizer is not needed for any legumes if the soil has been amended with some organic matter; in fact, concentrated soil nitrate levels force legumes to become nitrate consumers, preventing nitrate fixation. Legumes do feed heavily on the other soil mineral nutrients. There's an old farmers' adage that goes, "Feed your phosphate to your clover, feed your clover to your corn (plow it in), and you can't go wrong." If the plot has been adequately limed, is not grossly deficient in phosphorus, and has had some compost, legumes will usually flourish.

Legumes do not make nitrates from air by themselves but do so in cooperation with certain specialized soil bacteria, which form little pinkish nodules along legume roots. These nodules are visible to the naked eye, often reaching the size of lentils. Without the bacteria, legume roots do not nodulate and the plants become consumers rather than makers of nitrogen. If soil contains a reasonable amount of organic matter (most soils in the maritime Northwest not in commercial row crops contain 4 to 5 percent organic matter), it will also support active populations of all sorts of soil organisms, including those that colonize legume roots. Dead soils, chemically farmed for years, may have had most of their organic matter burned out by nitrogen fertilizers. In that case, even though the gardener adds manure or compost, legumes may not encounter the necessary bacteria and may require inoculation the first time they're grown.

The first thing I'd do when investigating poorly growing legumes in someone else's garden is to pull out a plant and carefully inspect its root system for an abundance of healthy pinkish nodules. This tells me more about the state of the level of organic matter than anything else. Then, regardless of what I found, I'd usually suggest side-dressing with complete organic fertilizer to rescue the existing crop, and I'd probably suggest increasing the organic matter content before growing any other crop. Clay soils, which tend to be airless even when organic matter has been increased somewhat, retard the development of nitrogen around legume roots.

The amount of nitrogen fixed by legumes is not inconsequential, but it is not automatically deposited in the soil for other crops to use, as is commonly believed. Garden beans and peas will fix 60 to 80 pounds of nitrogen per acre, nearly enough to feed themselves. Clovers fix more—up to 100 pounds per acre, though little of these nitrates remain in the root system where they are created. Most nitrates fixed by legumes are translocated by the plant to its leaves. If an entire field of clover—tops and roots—is turned in, that's nearly enough nitrogen to grow a reasonable yield of sweet corn, lettuce, or squash. The most amazing nitrogen fixer of all is the fava bean. Overwintered favas may create more than 200 pounds per acre, often enough to grow a following crop of the more demanding brassicas. If tilled under before the seed is set, legume vegetation is so nitrogen rich and tender that it will rot completely and allow sowing of the succeeding crop within two weeks.

BUSH BEANS (*Phaseolus vulgaris*)

Bush snap beans were bred mostly for the convenience of canneries. They don't need costly trellising and can be harvested mechanically. Their taste (and probably their nutritional content) can't equal that of the pole bean because the crowded leaves on bush beans are layered on top of one another and compete for light; the leaves of pole beans are widely separated so almost every one can gather direct, unfiltered light. It is the effectiveness and amount of the food manufacturing area (the leaf) compared to the amount of pod production that determines how much nutrition (which we usually perceive as flavor) is available to be stored in each pod. In this respect, bush beans are like highly determinate tomato varieties that similarly have little leaf area yet set a huge quantity of relatively tasteless tomatoes. Some varieties of bush beans do have pretty rich flavor, but when I've grown both kinds, the family rarely bothers to eat the bush varieties. That should tell you something.

Culture Like other species from the tropics, *P. vulgaris* beans grow only in warm soils; most varieties will not germinate at all if soil temperatures are below 60°F for long. In the

Willamette Valley, the first sowing can usually be made in early May, although on dark-colored, light-textured loams that heat up fast in spring, it may be possible to sow a little earlier. At frosty Lorane, I had to wait until June 1.

Fertilize each 100-square-foot bed with 1 gallon of complete organic fertilizer. Sow bush beans 1½ inches deep, four to six seeds per foot, in rows 18 inches apart. After the seedlings are established and growing well, thin to 6 or 8 inches apart in the row. Should a spell of chilly or rainy weather follow sowing, the seeds may not germinate; if they do eventually struggle to the surface, the stunned seedlings will be exhausted and won't grow fast for some weeks, even if the sun returns. Weakened bean seedlings are defenseless against the Mexican bean beetle, which can rapidly nibble leaves down to nubbins. When making early sowings, I try to outguess the weather and sow just before a dry, sunny period.

Sometimes the best thing to do when early bean sowings get into trouble is to immediately replant. The later planting may encounter nothing but clear sailing and end up maturing beans as early as the first sowing—while markedly outgrowing and outyielding the earlier attempt.

Garden planning Bush beans are like determinate tomatoes in another respect: They produce intensely for a short time and then quit. If a continuous harvest for the table is desired, make several sowings a few weeks apart. The last one should be made in early July; it will begin yielding in early or mid-September. For earliest harvest, bush beans can be started under a cloche about three weeks earlier than normal and grown under protection for several weeks after the last usual frost date. Follow a cloche-forced bed of earliest possible beans with late brassicas (kale, rutabaga, Chinese cabbage, overwintering broccoli, or cauliflower) or fall-garden salad greens (lettuce, spinach, corn salad, or endive). The harvest from 50 square feet of raised bed provides our family with all the fresh beans we can eat, plus as many as we feel like picking to give away.

Insects and diseases Mexican bean beetles can be controlled with rotenone/pyrethrum, sprayed every few days. If you're still spraying away predation after the plants have a few leaves, broadcast a little complete organic fertilizer around the too-slow-growing bean plants. Beans are sensitive to several diseases that are spread by touching damp plants. Wait until the sun has evaporated the morning dew before handling beans. Most new varieties are disease resistant.

Harvest Bean bushes are brittle and easily damaged by rough handling, so remove the pods gently. (The plants don't thrive in windy locations for the same reason, though they'll handle wind a lot better than pole beans will.) Pick frequently—keeping the plants carefully picked will extend their production period. Once a plant is forming a few seeds, it stops setting as many new pods.

Saving seed Natural crosses between varieties are extremely rare, so isolation is unnecessary. Neither is there much variation in individual plants. Select a few plants with traits you like—more tender, earlier, slower to develop strings and seeds, and so on—and do not harvest these. Allow the pods to form seed, and permit them to mature and begin to dry out. If the seed dries completely on the bush, germination and vigor will be higher, but if the seed plants are located in a part of the garden that gets watered frequently, it's better to remove pods by hand a few at a time just after they have dried to the point that the pod's vascular connection has broken (gets floppy and thin at stem end). Take these pods indoors and allow them to dry before shelling out the seed.

Varieties Green, "blue," yellow, filet, flageo-let, haricot vert, Dutch, English, romano, Guatemalan, purple-mottled, longpod, fat-pod—just about every one of the dozens of varieties of *P. vulgaris* bush snap beans I've grown has yielded well enough, though some are higher yielding than others and some are rather later than the climate will permit. Some pods get tough and fibrous quickly, while others hold on the bush and retain good eating quality quite a bit longer. You can experiment without much risk.

There seems to be little difference in flavor from variety to variety after cooking. The differences are much more noticeable in the flavors of raw pods. I prefer Blue Lake types, of which there are many excellent proprietary strains. Filet beans are European varieties bred for harvesting at half-size or smaller; their pods are very thin and usually round. They're pretty when artfully arrayed on *nouvelle cuisine* platters, but not very different when they get past the eyeballs.

Purple-podded types, which turn green when cooked, are slightly more vigorous sprouters in cool soil and make better growth under cool conditions. They should be considered seriously for under-cloche sowings and in coastal and cooler microclimates. I don't think Royalty Purple Pod is the equal of a new variety called Royal Burgundy. Bush wax beans don't become really waxy the way some old pole wax types did; they're only a different color—same flavor.

Dry-gardening Space 1 foot apart in rows 3 feet apart. Planted this way, they'll go weeks between irrigations. It's better to use pole varieties for dry-gardening; the habits of their root systems match those of the aggressively spreading vines.

POLE SNAP BEANS *(Phaseolus vulgaris)*

Pole beans take a week or so longer to start producing than bush types, but they yield all summer, ultimately producing quite a bit more for the space occupied. In this respect, pole beans are to bush beans as indeterminate tomatoes are to determinate tomatoes. Their vining habit has not been civilized into a compact bush, and their spread-out leaves trap more light and create much more flavorful pods—and likely more nutrition, too.

Culture Pole varieties naturally climb rough poles or go up a trellis, fence, or strings. The commercial trellising method for Willamette Valley Blue Lake pole beans was to zigzag a string every 8 inches up and down between two stout parallel wires, one a few inches above the ground, the other about 7 feet up. The pioneers used skinny rough poles with the bark left on, often set up as tripods lashed together at the top, and grew a few vines up each pole. I've used deer fences (in neighborhoods where deer are rarely seen anymore), and in my trials ground I used plastic "fishnet" hung from a stout steel wire stretched across the top of a row of 2-by-2 poles. Along a trellis, sow the seeds 1½ inches deep, one seed every 4 to 5 inches, and thin to one seedling every 8 to 10 inches, one bean per string. Fertilize with complete organic fertilizer, about 1 gallon per 100 feet of trellis.

Garden planning Only one sowing is required. Fifty row-feet or two parallel rows on a 4-foot by 25-foot raised bed produce more beans than my family can eat fresh. Serious bean fanciers might consider a single early sowing of bush beans to tide the kitchen over until the later pole varieties start bearing.

Insects and diseases Same as bush beans. They're especially touchy about windy sites.

Harvest It is essential to keep pole varieties picked clean. Allowing even a few pods to form seed will greatly reduce further pod set. If gently and completely harvested, most pole varieties will produce until the end of September. Like all snap beans, the pods are better flavored and more tender if picked on the immature side.

Saving seed Use the same process as for bush beans. You're a fool not to.

Varieties Of the traditional varieties, Blue Lake pole has the slowest seed and string development, with longer, fancier pods than the bush varieties—this is the bean that made Willamette Valley canneries famous nationwide. Kentucky Wonder—either strain, brown or white seeded—has a richer, beanier flavor than Blue Lake. The brown-seeded type (sometimes called Old Homestead) has rapid seed development and is the best all-purpose variety for dry-gardening and for snap and shell beans.

I mourn the disappearance of Kentucky Wonder Wax; it had a unique waxy texture and bland flavor—it really *was* a wax bean. Look for it through the seed saver's networks. Oregon Giant (Cascade Giant is an improved version) is an old, early-maturing variety with huge, watery/tender, mild-flavored, mottled purplish-green pods and large, fast-developing seeds good for shell beans. Oregon Giant does tend to quit producing before the summer ends.

Pole beans are still a commercial item in Europe. Dozens and dozens of specialty varieties exist there. My absolute favorite is Musica (TSC, WCO).

Dry-gardening The best variety for dry-gardening is Kentucky Wonder Brown Seeded, not dubbed Old Homestead for nothing. Space 1 foot apart on rows 4 feet apart. Even when allowed to sprawl without poles or trellises (the pods will get curly but will still be quite edible), you'll get a decent yield of delicious dry seed that tastes a lot like pinto beans.

RUNNER BEANS

(Phaseolus multifloris, also known as P. coccineus)

Runner beans are very popular in England, where people think the *P. vulgaris* snap beans we 'mer'cuns prefer do not have much flavor. That's true. Runners produce thick, fuzzy pods that taste very rich and settle satisfyingly in the stomach like beefsteak. Like the Brits, I've come to relish runner beans.

Culture Grow like pole beans. Runner beans tend to mature a bit later but grow better than *P. vulgaris* under cool conditions. The vines are a little more vigorous and run longer distances than *P. vulgaris* pole varieties. Give them a few inches more in-the-row space and be prepared for them to climb back down the trellis after reaching the top. Where there are only a few light winter frosts, *P. multifloris* can be perennial, regrowing in spring from the roots.

Harvest The better culinary varieties are selected for slower seed, string, and fiber development (all these traits are linked together in beans), although the huge pods are still much more tender if picked when three-quarters grown. Varieties with very rapid seed development make better shell beans.

Saving seed Runner beans have some tendency to cross-pollinate, so seed savers should grow only one variety. Some have white flowers, some have red.

Varieties Scarlet Runner is an old variety offered by many U.S. companies, but it tends toward fast seed development and tough, fibrous pods. Scarlet Emperor (TSC, WCO) has much slower seed development; tender pods; a sweet, full-bodied flavor; and showy flowers. Thompson & Morgan offers many varieties, some bred to make extremely long fancy pods, both white and red flowered.

Dry-gardening Runner beans are very suitable for dry-gardening, maybe better than Kentucky Wonder Brown Seeded. Try one seed every 2 feet in rows 5 feet apart. Set a 3-foot-tall rough pole next to the seed. The vines climb to the top and then spread out like an umbrella in moisture-retentive fertile soil, filling in all available row space by summer's end.

FAVA BEANS *(Vicia faba)*

Large-seeded varieties of fava beans are faintly known to some Americans as horse beans and loved by the English as broad beans. Their hardier small-seeded relatives are known to a very few Americans as bell beans and to the English as tic beans if spring sown and as winter beans if fall sown. Canadians with their recent Commonwealth connection are better acquainted with the species. Favas of all sorts will become much better known west of the Cascades because the species is amazingly well adapted to our climate. All of the major field crops of the maritime Northwest are grown over the winter, and favas are the only edible legume that has this potential.

Fava beans can taste pretty good when consumed in the green stage like peas or shell beans; dried favas are extensively used in the Middle East and by South American indigenes for bean soups. But favas can also taste pretty bad, tending toward bitterness; thick, tough skins; bland, mushy centers; and a strong cooking odor, especially the dried seeds. Unfortunately, for many years the only readily available variety in the United States was Windsor—fair eating during its short season as a shell bean but awful when dried and cooked like a dry bean. Windsor is also not winter hardy this far north. There are much better varieties.

Culture

Favas freeze out anywhere from 6° to 20°F, depending on the variety. The hardier ones can be overwintered and will mature dry seed without irrigation—a big advantage in the maritime Northwest. Overwintered varieties are sown between October 1 and November 15 after fall rains moisten the soil—the earlier the better. Enduring the winter as short, stocky plants, they'll tiller (send up numerous stalks from the base) in spring, and can get quite tall. Less hardy sorts are spring sown in late February or March. These do not tiller (that is, they make only one stalk per seed) and consequently don't yield nearly as much as overwintered plants.

Vigorous growers, favas generally don't need fertilizer when given compost-enriched garden soil; as a field crop, their plot should be limed and treated with phosphate rock and perhaps a little fertilizer on poorer, heavy soils.

For spring-sown shell beans, sow on raised garden beds, one seed every 4 inches, 1½ inches deep, in rows 18 inches apart. *For dry beans,* raise overwintering varieties. Sow one seed every 8 inches in rows 42 to 48 inches apart, and keep well weeded from spring until the seeds are drying out.

Garden planning

Shelling favas are finished in June, making their bed a good spot to grow salad greens or brassicas for fall harvest or overwintering. With small-seeded varieties, dry-seed yields without irrigation run as high as 2 tons per acre on fertile soil. Large-seeded varieties don't yield nearly as well.

Insects and diseases

We don't have much experience with favas in North America yet. After growing dozens of fava varieties on humusy soil since 1979, I have noted no disease problems. British books on how to farm organically say that diseases occur only in infertile soils. Bean or pea weevils will chew chunks out of their leaves in spring, but this minor damage causes little loss of yield.

Harvest

Pods form in May and June, with shell beans ready by early June and the pods drying out by early July. Large-seeded varieties tend to fall over from the weight of the forming pods; some gardeners give them support in numerous innovative ways. It may be helpful to pinch the tops of overwintered large-seeded favas at the beginning of spring regrowth, which encourages the plant to bush out from the base and produce a larger number of shorter stalks with less tendency to topple.

Large-seeded varieties grown for dry seed are very forgiving about timely harvest. The seed is held tightly in hard, wrinkled-up pods that don't shatter. The pods of small-seeded varieties are more delicate. Once the seed has dried, some pods will begin to shatter and some seed falls on the ground. These sorts should be harvested as soon as possible.

Spread the mostly dry small-seeded stalks on a large tarp right in the fava patch, piled not more than 10 inches thick; allow the stalks to dry until they're crisp and black. If rain threatens before threshing, cover them with another large tarp. One sunny afternoon after the night's moisture has been baked out and the pods are really crisp, hold a "rain dance" on the stalks, breaking the seed free, or beat them with a flail or pair of thin sticks about the length of a policeman's baton. Winnow in a light breeze or in front of a window fan until the seed is clean. Two energetic adults can thresh and winnow 100 pounds of seed in about two hours.

Saving seed See the Harvest section. Favas do have some tendency to cross—about one in 2,000 seeds may be hybrid if more than one variety is grown. Different varieties should be separated by 100 feet or more.

Large-seeded varieties Almost all U.S. seed companies still offer Windsor, an old large-seeded, bitter-tasting, mealy-centered variety with a tough brown skin that's not hardy enough to overwinter (except perhaps in northern California or along the southern Oregon coast). Aquadulce Claudia (WCO) is a much hardier and better-flavored, light-colored, large-seeded type. Originally from Spain, where it is overwintered, it's hardy to about 12°F and will survive many Willamette Valley or coastal winters.

Another new variety was developed (or discovered) by Ianto Evans when he was with Aprovecho, a nonprofit foundation concerned with ecology in less-developed countries, located near Cottage Grove, Oregon. Aprovecho Select Fava is the best-tasting large-seeded variety I know of. Seeds of Change sells Aprovecho Fava—and a few others that Ianto probably forgot he had a few seeds of in his hip pocket when he came back through customs after assorted travels to Latin America. Thompson & Morgan, typical of a British seed house, lists numerous fava varieties in its catalog.

Small-seeded varieties Banner (TSC, WCO), developed by the British National Variety Research Station (NVRS), is hardy to about 7°F and is used as a green manure crop. The seeds are edible but, as they say in the mushroom books, "not choice." Friedrichs (TSC) is a local variety grown in the Skagit Valley; it costs less but is less hardy than Banner and similarly "edible." Sweet Lorane (TSC, WCO) is a pretty decent-tasting and very hardy variety useful both as green manure and as a survival crop, as it can be eaten with pleasure (after you've learned to season it and your taste buds have become Middle Eastern). I am proud to say that I selected this variety out of a huge gene pool obtained from the USDA Plant Introduction service.

Dry-gardening Not a problem. They totally suit the rainfall pattern.

FIELD BEANS & HORTICULTURAL BEANS

(Phaseolus vulgaris)

Growing enough *P. vulgaris* seed to serve as a food staple is possible but dicey. Late September is harvest time, but that month is rarely reliably dry, making drying the seed very difficult. Even if it doesn't rain there are always heavy dews, so achieving the earliest possible harvest is essential. People south of Drain, Oregon, where summers are hotter and seeds mature faster, have a much easier time with field beans.

Culture Grow like bush beans. *With irrigation,* sow seeds 4 inches apart in rows 24 inches apart. Thin when established to 8 inches in the row. Stop all watering when the first pods start drying out, and absolutely stop irrigating by September 1, regardless. *Without irrigation,* sow seeds 6 inches apart in rows 36 to 48 inches apart. Thin when established to 12 inches in the row. Keep extremely well weeded. Grown without irrigation, beans quickly come under moisture stress, which reduces seed set and prompts earlier drying. This can be helpful but lowers yield. (Consider growing favas.)

Garden planning Irrigated yields run around a ton per acre, or 50 pounds per 1,000 square feet.

Insects and diseases Same as bush beans. Bean seed weevils can be eliminated by hard-freezing sacks immediately after harvest for a few weeks. Don't freeze the seed you're saving to sow next year. The hole that weevils leave after emerging from your planting stock will not reduce germination a bit.

Harvest Ideally, you would harvest when 90 percent of the leaves have yellowed and the pods have dried, but before the pods begin to shatter. You would pull the plants from the dusty, dry earth, pile them on a large tarp, and dry them to a crisp in a few more days before threshing. In most of the maritime Northwest, however, few varieties reach this stage of maturity before conditions deteriorate. Usually the plants have to be bunched and hung or loosely stacked on a porch and carefully turned every few days. (Reconsider growing favas.) Threshing can be done with a flail or by banging the plants (held by the stems at the root end) against the inner wall of a 55-gallon drum. Winnow the seeds by slowly pouring them back and forth between two 5-gallon buckets in a gentle breeze or in front of a window fan.

Saving seed A certain degree of variation develops in all beans. You can maintain higher-quality seed stocks by flagging a few perfect plants each year, harvesting them separately, and then increasing their seed, carefully removing any off-type plants. For the highest possible quality, grow out the progeny of each selected plant in a separate row or section of row (called growing out lines), and then from those rows save seed only from plants that appear perfectly uniform and that have all the desirable traits you're selecting for. Careful purification like this is done each year by the highest-quality bean-seed growers. In the home garden, it might be done once in four or five years if at all.

Varieties Taylor's Horticultural (Speckled Bays) is widely grown west of the Cascades because it is one of the earliest. Black Coco is my favorite dry bean; I always emptied all the unsold packets of Black Coco every September and ate them. Johnny's Selected Seeds carries a wide dry bean assortment; concentrate on earliest maturity.

Dry-gardening Most varieties will work okay. Kentucky Wonder Brown Seeded makes fine dry seed. See the information on dry-gardening in the Pole Beans section.

LIMA BEANS *(Phaseolus limensis)*

I never managed to harvest more than a few seeds by growing heat-loving limas. Jackson Wonder is reputed to be early enough. Good luck! You'll have better luck if you start them as early as possible indoors and transplant; see Chapter 7. The so-called Oregon Lima is not a lima at all but a white-flowered, white-seeded runner bean with rapid seed development, useful primarily as a shell bean.

SOYBEANS *(Glycine max)*

Soybeans are heat lovers. A few chill-tolerant varieties can make enough vegetative growth to yield modestly in the warmer parts of our region, although this is not likely north of Longview or along the cool coasts. Unlike other legume species, soybeans grow vegetatively for a while and then, triggered by decreasing day length, cease growing and set seed. The larger the bush gets before flowering must begin, the more seed will be set. Because we have to sow rather late to get them to germinate, and because vegetative growth is slow under our cool conditions, the bushes tend to be small when flowering starts, so yields are low. For this reason, soybeans aren't a good candidate for our gardens. If you insist on reinventing the wheel, buy seed from Johnny's and grow them like dry beans. Surprisingly, you might get higher yields from the later varieties they sell.

PEAS *(Pisum sativum)*

Almost any pea variety makes tasty and easy-to-grow maritime Northwest garden food *if planted early enough.* Unfortunately, if the variety hasn't been picked before the weather turns hot and sunny, an unavoidable regional pea disease called enation makes it *seem* as though heat has killed the vines. If you think peas are hard to grow for this reason, please think again and read on.

Culture Peas will manage to sprout and can grow weakly in cold soils. But when the soil is cold and they have wet feet, peas are subject to numerous root diseases. Peas start growing fast, even on colder clayey soils, around mid-March, which is usually too late a sowing date to evade enation. Fortunately, there are now enation-resistant varieties. These can be sown later in spring and even in early summer.

Broadcast a gallon of complete organic fertilizer over each 100 square feet of bed. Chop the top few inches of the bed with a strong hoe while blending in the fertilizer, and rake roughly. Sow modern dwarf enation-resistant varieties, several seeds per inch, about 1½ inches deep in rows 18 inches apart. Do not thin. Keep weeded until the pea vines make a solid stand. You may have read in old garden books about giving peas fences to climb up, but most modern varieties are highly dwarfed, and will not climb a trellis even if one is offered.

Garden planning Dwarf varieties are determinate, meaning that they yield for a short period and then quit. A single 50-square-foot bed oversupplies our family's fresh table needs for one to two weeks of intense harvesting. I sow a bed every few weeks from late February through mid-April. By the time the mid-April sowing has been harvested, the bush beans are coming on and we're tired of peas. Indeterminate climbing varieties keep on producing for a longer time, but none of these heirlooms are disease resistant and so must be sown very early to mature before enation burns them.

Peas leave the soil in particularly nice shape when the vines are pulled out. Any bed that has come over the winter bare, or that has held overwintered crops harvested by early April, is a good candidate for peas (or small-seeded favas). Even if the peas aren't needed for food, the vines make good green manures.

Dry soup peas should be grown in an area of the garden where irrigation can be avoided; plant a bit less densely if irrigation is not available at all.

Insects and diseases Pea diseases are numerous—wilts, yellows, mildews, streaks, and enation, to name but a few. Most years only enation will be a problem, but wet, damp, cloudy weather encourages other sorts of disease. There's not much an organic gardener can do about pea diseases except to grow peas in raised beds to enhance soil drainage, fertilize well to boost overall health and vigor, and choose resistant varieties. Pea enation is a virus, spread by the green peach aphid, which hatches out and begins traveling when the weather turns summery. Enation makes the pods look mottled and warty, ends flowering and pod set, and then kills the vine. None of the old home-garden standards are enation resistant, although these can still be grown if sown early enough to mature before June's heat. Gardeners with sandy soil that heats up fast in spring will have the best chance with heirloom pea varieties.

Harvest Shelling peas are best picked on the small side, before the seeds have begun to get tough. Keeping the vines picked clean encourages somewhat longer production. Freezer types tend to form lots of pods that fill out all at once, encouraging a single, overall harvest. Snow peas (edible-pod peas, or *mange-tout*) are usually picked small, before string and seed form, but many varieties don't toughen too rapidly and, if allowed to develop a little string, will also become much sweeter (the strings are easy to strip out right in the field as the pods are picked). Snap peas become much sweeter if allowed to develop seeds and strings.

Saving seed Let some vines mature seed, harvest the vines, fully dry on a tarp, thresh, and store. It's that simple! To simplify drying, you may want to plant peas intended for seed in an area that won't be irrigated.

Varieties Such old standard dwarfs as Little Marvel, Lincoln (small, delicious peas), Dark Skinned Perfection, Early Frosty, Freezonian, and the like need no trellising and may mature if sown early enough to beat enation, which usually means sprouted before March 1st. Enation is not as serious a problem north of Puget Sound. Alderman or Tall Telephone, the very best tasting of the classic old garden peas still available, requires a trellis, the earliest possible sowing, and the fastest possible growth to mature before being wiped out by enation. I wouldn't try Alderman unless I had well-drained, sandy loam soil. Enation-resistant types are much better adapted south of the Sound. Especially good are the "Oregon" varieties developed by Dr. Jim Baggett at Oregon State University (OSU).

Oregon Sugar Pod, a highly enation-resistant OSU variety, became the basis of a snow-pea farming business in the Willamette Valley that now supplies the entire nation when California production falters in the intense heat of their summer. Other similar, newer varieties from OSU include Oregon Giant. These grow well right through our midsummer's heat.

Snap peas are the latest thing, and I like them very much. Sugar Snap is an indeterminate trellised type with the very best flavor (for the same reasons that pole beans and indeterminate tomatoes taste best), but it is often a bit too late to produce a good yield before enation takes it out. Sugar Ann is an earlier-maturing bush variety with a flavor nearly as good as Sugar Snap. Although the stringless Sugar Daddy is touted as being the wonder disease-resistant snap pea, it's relatively flavorless. Watch for newer, improved varieties of this sort of pea.

Alaska is the traditional dry pea for soup.

Capucijners, a traditional Dutch field pea with a unique flattened seed, cooks quickly into a delicious, rich brown gravy. These are hard to find now.

GARBANZO BEANS *(Cicer arietinum)* & LENTILS *(Lens culinaris)*

Garbanzo beans and lentils grow like peas, but they're not quite as frost hardy or as tolerant of cold soil. Their seed dries out in July when the soil naturally dries out; they are best planted in an area of the garden where irrigation can be withheld without harming other crops. Garbanzos are also known as chickpeas, Egyptian peas, and Bengal gram.

Culture Sow in early March to early April—earlier is better because more soil moisture will remain to support the crop, but the sowing date will depend on when your soil becomes warm enough to sprout the seed. Plant about 1 inch deep, three to four seeds per foot, in rows 36 inches apart. A bit of compost chopped into the planting rows should provide adequate nutrition; if more help seems necessary, the best fertilizer is additional bone meal at about 5 to 10 pounds per 100 row-feet, worked in with the compost. Thin seedlings when established: garbanzos to about 8 inches apart in the row, lentils to about 4 inches apart. Keep well weeded, as the seed crop will need all available soil moisture.

Harvest Like dry beans, but harvest will occur in midsummer.

Saving seed When you grow them to eat, you've also saved seed to replant.

Varieties I find the small black garbanzos particularly tasty and tender—300 percent better than the big, tough, yellow ones. Any bag of lentils or garbanzos from the grocery store will probably sprout and grow fine. Iranian, Pakistani, and Indian specialty grocery stores usually have many varieties. There are a number of different varieties of the ordinary large-seeded yellow sorts that Americans eat, although there is no way to know what you're getting when you buy "seed" in the grocery store.

Green Manures & Field Crops

The best sources of seed for common green manures are local feed and grain dealers and better garden centers. You can buy regionally adapted green manures by mail, but shipping costs for these inexpensive species often more than doubles the price. When choosing garden green manures, ease with which the mature vegetation can be handled is the crucial consideration; gardeners usually don't have heavy tractors.

CRIMSON CLOVER (*Trifolium incarnatum*)

Crimson clover is a perfectly adapted legume cover crop for our region. Although it grows rather badly on poorly drained soils and will be disappointing on very acid or infertile ones, crimson clover is easy to sow, reliably winter hardy, and easily eliminated in spring. Plant in late September through October. One pound of broadcast seed covers about 500 square feet. (Farmers use 15 to 25 pounds per acre when precision planting.) Broadcast the seed evenly and rake or rototill it in about 1 inch deep. A thicker stand is a better stand. Crimson clover can be sprinkled into deteriorating beds of melons, cucumbers, or solanums, to sprout and take over by the end of October. Once the fall rains begin in earnest, crimson clover can be scattered in beds of tall-growing winter crops like kale and Brussels sprouts and allowed to sprout on the soil's surface. (However, this method uses two or three times as much seed to establish a thick understory.) Low-growing and noncompetitive until spring, it will take over the beds in March, swallowing the stumps and remains of winter crops.

Regardless of when it is sown, crimson clover flowers in April. Till it in or pull it out as soon as possible after it starts blooming; once seed formation starts, the stems rapidly become tough and woody, take longer to break down, and become harder to handle. On raised beds and small plots, blooming clover can be scythed down, the vegetation raked up and composted, and the root stubble hoed in. The stubble will be rotted and gone within ten days, rapidly leaving the bed ready for a new crop. The clover can also be cut with a powerful lawn mower. Early in spring, while the vegetation is short and very tender, beds of crimson clover can be shallowly and gently hoed in, tops and all. The very succulent small greens rot within days, permitting easy sowings of spring mustard, spinach, peas, and other very early crops without rototilling.

Warning: Beware of other types of clover. Crimson clover has intense crimson flowers, is an annual variety, and is very succulent—easily killed with a hoe or tiller. Perennials such as red, sub, Dutch, and white clover form strong root clumps and underground runners that resist tillage and reestablish themselves. Red clover (pink flowers) can become one of the most difficult weeds to eliminate because it has hard seeds that can lie in the soil for many years before sprouting. I know, because years ago an ignorant or unscrupulous garden store merchant sold me some "crimson clover" that was really red clover. I had clumps of red clover coming up for three years despite persistent hoeing.

AUSTRIAN FIELD PEAS *(Pisum arvense)*

The Austrian field pea is a very small-seeded, winter-hardy pea that can be grown alone or in combination with cereal grains such as winter wheat or barley. When peas are interplanted with grain, the nitrogen fixed by the peas slightly improves the grain's growth, while the grain physically supports the pea vines. A pea/grain combination produces an enormous amount of biomass, but turning under the combination takes a powerful tractor. The combination can also be too slow to break down enough to allow easy planting. Field peas tend to tangle small tillers when the vines have become long. Like other peas, they do leave the beds in fine condition for the next crop. Now that we have reliably winter-hardy, small-seed favas, I no longer recommend field peas.

FAVAS *(Vicia faba)*

Use only small-seeded fava varieties as green manure; these grow much taller than large-seeded types, producing a lot more biomass. Small-seeded favas are low-cost seed with a much higher seed count per pound, requiring far fewer pounds of seed to establish a stand on a given area. In October (and even into early November in southern Oregon or northern California), set seed 1 to 2 inches deep, 2 inches apart, in rows 12 inches apart, or broadcast 5 to 10 pounds per 1,000 square feet (150 to 250 pounds per acre) and till in shallowly. Favas also make excellent green manure sown in early spring—if you can work the ground. Before the seeds start forming (mid- to late May), the stalks are brittle and tender and can be turned under quite rapidly with a walk-behind garden tiller (without tangling), even when the stand is thick and 4 to 5 feet tall. Like clover, fava stalks can also be scythed down, raked up, and composted, the stubble hoed in by hand. Unlike clover, favas are much later to start getting woody, making them better for heavier soils that are ready to till later.

In the east, spring-sown favas are becoming increasingly popular with farmers, but these varieties aren't hardy enough for fall sowing here. One winter-hardy, small-seeded variety available at this time is Banner (TSC). You can also use Sweet Lorane as an excellent green manure. Watch out for "bell beans," spring-sown varieties that will disappoint you by freezing out.

For a symphylan control rotation, consider a three-year fava bean dry fallow/green manure, while moving the vegetable garden to another plot. In autumn of the first year, sow as though raising dry seed without irrigation (see the discussion of fava beans in the earlier section on legumes), but do not harvest the seed. Planting for seed production takes only a few pounds of seed to sow 1,000 square feet. Keep the plot as free of weeds as possible through summer so the soil won't be weedy several years later when it goes back into vegetables. Most of the dry seeds will hold on the tall bushes all summer, protected from sprouting by the pods even if there are a few light rains. Once the fall rains start, even if it is only late September, knock down the plants as you rototill the plot shallowly but thoroughly, setting most of the beans an inch or two down and eliminating any germinating weeds. An amazingly dense stand of favas will appear because there may have been as much as 100 pounds of dry seed standing on every 1,000 square feet.

Allow the favas to grow, overwinter, set seed, and mature the next summer. Weed growth will be strongly suppressed by the dense stand. Though highly overcrowded, enough seed will still set to permit yet another very dense stand of favas to be established in fall (the beginning of year three) when you again till in the bean stalks. The next spring, till in the favas as a green manure as soon in spring as possible, and put the plot back into irrigated vegetables. Symphylan populations should be quite low after three years of favas and no irrigation, while organic matter content will have been maintained and soil nitrogen levels will be quite high.

TYFON *(Brassica napa x)*

There's nothing better than a green manure crop people can eat. Tyfon, a turnip and Chinese cabbage cross, is one. It is hardy to about 10°F, forms deep taproots that break up the soil, and grows mild, edible greens similar to mustard spinach. If the crop was sown late in summer, some plants will form tasty turnips during midwinter.

Tyfon can be sown from May through September at rates of about 1 ounce per 100 square feet or 10 pounds per acre; broadcast the fine seed and rake or hoe it in shallowly. Tyfon sprouts and grows amazingly fast and doesn't flower until late March after overwintering. The unopened flowers make an acceptable sort of "broccoli." I like to sow Tyfon in the fall on beds I'm going to plant early in spring because its long taproots pull out easily by hand from a raised bed, leaving no stubble and a ready-to-plant seedbed. Commercially, the very palatable leaves are used as animal feed; spring sowings may be cut several times in a single season. Tyfon produces more biomass per unit of time than any other green manure crop known.

CORN SALAD *(Valerianella locusta olitoria)*

Discussed later as a salad green, this very hardy plant can also be sown on raised beds more densely than normal, harvested by gradually thinning out the stand through the winter for salad greens, and then allowed to go through rapid spring growth, flowering by April. Even in bloom, the vegetation is very tender and can be easily chopped into the bed with a hoe, creating a very fine seedbed.

As green manure, broadcast and shallowly rake in about 1 ounce of seed per 100 square feet of bed during September after the heat of summer is over. I like to grow one bed each winter. Seed is widely available. For more details, see the discussion of corn salad later in this chapter in the Greens section.

GRAINS *(Grammineae species)*

Any winter cereal—wheat, barley, oats, rye—can be used as a green manure, but they have liabilities as *garden* green manures. They're physically tough, requiring powerful equipment to till in. Cereals also rot slowly, resulting in a late garden if the spring is a wet one. The grain that "yields to the disc" most easily is winter wheat; soft white winter wheat varieties well adapted to maritime conditions can be purchased in feed and seed stores and health food stores. One pound of seed densely covers 100 to 200 square feet. Broadcast seed and till in shallowly in mid-September to mid-October. Be sure to process the vegetation early in spring, before the seed heads form, or the plants will become very woody and tough.

BUCKWHEAT *(Fagopyrum esculentum)*

Buckwheat is the unexcelled summertime green manure. It grows fast on most soils, matures seed without irrigation if you want to grow it as a grain crop, and rapidly forms such a dense cover that it shades out competing weeds and grasses. Buckwheat is not frost hardy and will make rapid growth only from May through July. By August, the decreasing day length forces buckwheat to flower almost as soon as it sprouts. Buckwheat is also one of the best weeds you can have in your garden, being so tender and delicate it is very easily hoed out or tilled in. I've even tilled in hiphigh blooming stands of thick buckwheat with a front-end tiller without tangling. *After being tilled in, buckwheat rots in a few days, leaving behind a fine, loose seedbed.* Beware, though: Once the seeds start forming, the stalks get fibrous and tough, will take a long time to rot, and will tangle tillers.

Buckwheat goes from sprout to full bloom in five to six weeks. I'd suggest using buckwheat as a short-term green manure on bare spots where something will be planted in a month or so. One pound of seed covers 300 to 500 square feet and should be broadcast and tilled or hoed in about 1 inch deep.

Greens

There is no botanical classification called "greens," but every vegetable in this group has similar growing characteristics: They all make fast vegetative growth after germination and are harvested before they have begun to flower. Greens have been bred to produce thick, succulent, and usually sweet leaves and sometimes juicy, tender stalks. Most species will do this only in fertile, moist soil.

As a group, greens require moderate amounts of phosphorus and potassium and fairly high amounts of nitrogen. If I were a chemical fertilizer proponent interested in raising profit by pushing the plants into producing maximum bulk, I'd brew up something like 20-5-10 for growing them. However, I believe the balance in complete organic fertilizer makes a much more nutritious plant.

Breeders frequently shape these varieties for abundant top growth at the expense of root development, so with most it's essential to maintain soil moisture and apply fertilizer close to the seedlings' roots. Once the soil has warmed up well, organic matter breakdown in "built-up" soils may provide barely enough nitrogen, although a bit of complete organic fertilizer in addition to compost will help immensely. Strong fertilizer is essential in spring, and will result in much sweeter and more succulent greens. However, greens sown for fall harvest will be more resistant to cold if they grow less lushly, so fertility should be reduced for crops sown after mid-July.

Rapid growth is essential to harvesting tender, sweet leaves. If you crowd plants, the competition stress slows growth. So give greens lots of room. Once they've "bumped" in the bed or row, either thin them or harvest and use the thinnings so they can keep growing fast. If they've room to grow and aren't growing, side-dress.

CELERY (Apium dulce) & CELERIAC (A. rapaceum)

Celery is the most demandingly difficult crop I know, especially if you wish it to grow to supermarket standards. Celeriac, a root form of celery, is perhaps even more difficult. Throughout this section, just about everything said about celery applies equally to celeriac. The seedlings are delicate, slow-growing, and hard to get established. This species requires more fertilization than any other garden vegetable and amazing amounts of water if it is to make fast, succulent growth. Celery grows best in areas with mild nights and cool days with intense sunlight, which is why commercial crops are produced along the southern California coast close to the sea, where the maritime influence moderates and stabilizes temperatures, yet light levels are intense and dependable.

Starting celery too early is dangerous, for the species has a tendency to bolt prematurely (and most disappointingly, considering how much work must go into the crop) if exposed to temperatures below 50°F for too many hours. I've found it more relaxing to consider garden celery as a crop for late summer, fall, and winter harvest. It certainly will improve a cabbage salad, while celeriac will do more for soups than even celery will.

Celery has a very small lateral root system. If direct-seeded, its carrotlike taproot will extend down 4 feet or more, drawing on subsoil moisture. Feeder roots nearer the surface are few and close to the plant. This affects optimum watering and fertilizer placement. Transplanted celery forms a more fibrous, shallower root system that needs to be watered more frequently. The weak and inefficient root system is poorly adapted to airless conditions, so clayey soils must be especially well and deeply amended with organic matter for this crop. Celery will grow to supermarket standards only in loams or sands, and then only with skillful handling, abundant fertilizer and water, and some good luck.

Culture Slow-growing at all stages, celery transplants can take ten to twelve weeks of patient care. See Chapter 7. Direct-seeding takes much less effort and works enormously better. Sow seed outdoors no sooner than mid-April but no later than the middle of May (earlier is better). Spread 1 gallon of complete organic fertilizer per 100 square feet, and then deeply dig a raised bed that is located near your water source and that also has recently received some compost. On 24-inch centers, dig out a shovelful of soil and set it aside, pour ½ cup more complete organic fertilizer into each small hole, mix it into a few inches of soil with your fingers or a shovel, and refill the hole with loose soil. Push a half-pint mason jar into that spot, compressing the soil and making a half-pint hole. Fill that half-pint hole heaping full with the home gardener's potting mix I describe in Chapter 7. Then press that potting mix down firmly but not so as to make a brick—only enough to restore capillarity. With your fingertip, make a ¼-inch-deep depression in the middle of the potting mix and put in half a dozen celery seeds. Cover the seed with fine compost or more potting mix.

Slow-sprouting celery seed germinates best when on the cool side, taking two weeks or so depending on the temperature. April sowings are usually kept naturally moist by weather conditions; if the soil dries out, gently sprinkle the seeds as needed to keep them moist. After germination, gradually thin the seedlings to one per spot as they establish themselves.

Keep the plants well watered during summer's heat. Hand-water every few days if you think of it, in addition to regular overall garden irrigation. If growth slows, fertigate every two weeks, or side-dress with complete organic fertilizer close to the plants. One side-dressing may last four to eight weeks. It is essential that the plants grow rapidly without check or the stalks will become pithy, stringy, and tough, while celeriac roots that are under moisture stress or that grow slowly for other reasons (such as inappropriate soil conditions or inadequate spacing) lose quality by getting tough, fibrous, and knobby. Stop fertilizing about September 1 so the plants harden off a bit as fall approaches. Grow celeriac exactly like celery but on 18-inch centers unless you want really big roots; do not crowd them.

Garden planning Six or eight healthy celery plants will provide more than enough stalks to spruce up your salads all fall and winter without picking the plants bare. With good management and a little luck regarding winter low temperatures, celery is going to occupy the bed for nearly a year. Mature plants can be protected under a tunnel cloche over the winter, where they'll make more winter growth and have a better chance of surviving frosts.

Our family can go through more than a dozen celeriac roots over a winter. Hilling up a little soil over the root when fall weather checks it will protect celeriac from freezing in frostier areas.

If the celery growth was only average to poor, quite a bit of light will be hitting the soil around the plants; sprinkling a bit of crimson clover seed in the celery or celeriac bed in fall may establish a noncompetitive green manure that will take over in spring. If the bed grew well, even on 24-inch centers it'll be so solid with stalks and leaves that clover won't be able to get established.

Insects and diseases Although there's a whole shelf's worth of books and journal articles about celery diseases (usually found in commercial growing areas), I've had no problems.

Harvest Celery will certainly be harvestable by late summer from direct-seeded plants; beds started from transplants can be picked by midsummer. Do not cut the entire celery plant as market gardeners do. Instead, cut or break off the outer largest stalks as needed. If the winter is mild, celery tolerates continuous light pickings until it bolts and begins seed formation in spring. Even while bolting, the unopened flowers and tender stalks below them are good salad greens. With celeriac, simply dig a root as needed.

Saving seed Celery is a biennial, flowering in its second year unless it freezes out. Too much cold weather in the seedling stages can make celery react as though it had overwintered, so it bolts in summer before it's full grown. Premature bolting is an undesirable genetic trait, so occasional early bolters should be culled by the seed saver, though plants that start flowering in summer are not likely to mature seed in any case. Celery is pollinated by insects and freely crosses with other varieties and with celeriac, so to prevent most crossing, isolate varieties by at least 200 feet. There's no

need to grow celery and celeriac seed in the same year, since the species makes very long-lived seed (seven to ten years with decent storage). Even if the crop freezes out two winters in three, home gardeners should be able to produce their own seed often enough.

In March, before bolting occurs, dig up six to twelve surviving plants (even more would be better), and transplant them where water can be withheld once the seed starts drying out. Because of the species' weak root systems and because you broke their taproots when transplanting, it might not be a bad idea to mulch plants intended for seed. Celery flowers are small, white umbels, similar to those of wild carrot. The seed is easily detached from the drying flowers, so take care when harvesting. Finish drying the seed heads under cover on newspapers to catch shattering seeds.

Varieties All seed companies offer Utah strains in one variant or another. Avoid the Florida selections, which are bred to mature in winter at southern latitudes and day lengths. Pascal types are more resistant to early bolting. Golden or Golden Self-Blanching types have shorter stalks and usually less vigorous growth. I've had bad luck with the weakly growing golden varieties.

Celeriac is grown for its rough, bulbous root, which is peeled and then steamed, fried, or used in soups. It tastes much like celery stalks and is not starchy. We love celeriac slowly butter-fried to a crisp golden-brown atop the woodstove. Celeriac doesn't absorb fat like parsnips or potatoes, so a tiny pat of butter is enough to prevent sticking and flavor a whole skilletful. All mail-order seed companies sell some sort of celeriac. Quality selections are free of big lateral roots and are smoother, cutting down waste.

Dry-gardening No way, José! Unless, that is, you've got a naturally swampy place to put them.

CORN SALAD *(Valerianella locusta olitoria)*

In Europe, small grains like wheat, barley, and oats are called corn. What we call corn in North America, Europeans call maize. Corn salad was once a winter-hardy, wild, edible salad weed that came up in the stubble of harvested grain fields. In recent centuries, the species was bred for increased leaf size and more civilized flavor. It's still pretty wild stuff, and if allowed to go to seed in the garden, it may naturalize into an edible weed. That would be good!

Culture Corn salad grows great on fertilizer remaining in the bed following summer crops. The low-germination seeds will not sprout until soil temperatures have dropped well below their summer peak. Plant during September; earlier in the month is better if it isn't too hot. Sow three seeds per inch, ½ inch deep in rows at least 12 inches apart. Do not thin much until harvesting begins. (See the Green Manures section, earlier in this chapter, for another slant on growing corn salad.)

Garden planning Sow following any crop that finishes up in September—for example, bush beans or lettuce. Fifty row-feet atop a raised bed is enough to fill a big salad bowl full once a week. We prefer to use the tender, mild-flavored leaves to balance tougher greens like finely cut savoy cabbage. Corn salad goes to seed in April; the flowering stalks remain tender for several weeks after flowering begins but get too strong-tasting to eat.

Insects and diseases None known.

Harvest With your fingertips, grip the small leaves in small clumps and cut with a sharp knife an inch or two above the ground; this allows the plants to regrow. Or grow crowded and progressively thin out whole plants through the winter, cutting them off at the soil line. Leaves often contact soil; wash thoroughly.

Saving seed The light, irregularly shaped seeds form in late April and drop to earth or travel a goodly distance in strong winds. As soon as flowering begins, pull every other row to increase between-row spacing to at least 24 inches. Spread a sheet of cardboard under the plants to catch falling seeds, and collect them daily. At best, corn salad seed lives only a year or two; be sure to dry it thoroughly before storage.

Varieties Several varieties are available, but the differences are mostly insignificant. All varieties are hardy enough for the maritime Northwest.

ENDIVE, ESCAROLE *(Cichorium endivia)*, & OTHER CHICORIES

Endive (escarole) makes an essential ingredient in our midwinter salads. Freeze-out for most lettuce varieties is about 21°F; some exceptional strains of lettuce will survive brief exposures to 19°F. Endive has overwintered in my garden, *protected from rain* by a very drafty cold frame, and has survived temperatures below 7°F with no sign of damage. The sweetness of endive increases after very hard frosts have worked the plant over a few times, so if you don't like bitter foods, avoid supermarket endive grown in central or southern California, where frost is rarely seen. Endive is a chicory, and in the last decade or so, many other sorts of chicory have become available. These are all grown very similarly to endive; the differences and distinctions among chicory varieties are briefly discussed in the section on varieties.

Culture Although endive can be grown as a summer vegetable from sowings in spring or early summer, the taste seems too bitter then to suit me. I sow it only for fall and winter harvest. To grow unprotected endive, sow in late July to early September. To fill a cold frame, sowings can be as late as October 1. Broadcast and work in the usual amount of complete organic fertilizer. Sow seeds ½ inch deep, two to four seeds per inch, in rows 18 inches apart. Crowded plants without good air circulation rot more easily, so thin gradually and thoroughly—the plants should never touch one another. Early sowings in fertile soil will grow huge heads if thinned to about 18 inches apart in the row; thin later sowings to about 12 inches. In cloches protected from moisture, endive can be a bit more crowded.

Garden planning Salad greens get mighty scarce some winters, and some endive garnished with a sweet dressing can seem mighty desirable. Unprotected August sowings often hold until spring in good condition in a dry winter; on the other hand, endive may rot by January. Usually it's not the cold that does endive in, but rain and damp-induced mildews and molds, which gradually eat back the beautiful rosette to a stump. Later sowings, which don't head until midwinter, have less tendency to rot and may withstand weather that would destroy bigger plants.

Any cloche or cold frame, or even a sheet of glass that will keep off the damaging rains and increase daytime temperatures a bit, will encourage more growth and prevent rot. Cold frames filled with endive can be started on beds that grew melons, cucumbers, corn, tomatoes, or other hot-weather crops.

Insects and diseases Not a problem if kept dry in winter.

Harvest When harvesting most types of winter salad greens, it is best to cut individual leaves, which permits the plants to continue production. Europeans sometimes blanch endive to make it more mild tasting by tying up the leaves into a tight head for a few weeks before cutting. The maritime Northwest's rainy weather may not permit blanching except in frames. Besides, winter's cold makes the species quite mild without doing this.

Saving seed All chicories, including endive, are self-pollinated biennials. Plants that survive the winter can be dug in March and transplanted to an area where irrigation can be withheld once seed formation begins. I've had good luck dry-gardening seed crops without any irrigation whatsoever, by sowing in late May, spacing the plants 2 feet apart in rows 4 feet apart. After growing through a hot summer without any water, overwintering, and finally bolting, the gnarled stalks will grow 3 feet high or more and will be covered with small chicory-blue flowers that leave behind little rock-hard knobs full of seed.

When the stalks are partly dry, cut and finish under cover, and *dry until brittle.* Milling the seeds out can take a lot of sweat. The best at-home system I ever devised is to spread the stalks out on a concrete walkway or slab and pound them with a flat-bottomed, 3-inch-diameter, 5-foot-long wooden staff until the seeds separate. Then sieve the remains through a large-mesh food strainer to remove the big stuff; the seed will pass through. Winnow the seed from the dust and chaff by pouring it from bucket to bucket in a mild breeze. Endive seed is long-lived. One plant will produce about ½ ounce of seed.

Endive varieties Two basic varieties are grown. Endive (frisée) has deeply cut leaves like Salad Bowl lettuce; the other sort, usually called Batavian endive or escarole, has broad, plain leaves. Large heads of both tend to have semiblanched inner leaves. Many varieties sold in the United States are intended for California or Florida agribusiness and are not necessarily as cold hardy or rain resistant as the species can be. Look for catalog language like "handles bad weather" or "tolerates low temperatures" and Dutch- or French-sounding names. Johnny's concentrates on fancy European selections for summer or early fall harvest, rather than the varieties we need for winter. That's sensible: The winters in Maine, where Johnny's is located, are too severe for the species to survive long.

Chicory varieties Chicory has long been popular in Italian home gardens. Lately it's also become popular with the American *haute cuisine* set. The various sorts are basically just endives and are grown like endive. One heading type is called radicchio. Somewhat slower growing than endive, radicchio is sown during July. Thin in stages just like endive. Most radicchio selections form purple-red colored ball heads. If you cut as high as possible to keep the stump intact, winter regrowth will probably occur, giving leaves to snip for salads. Like endive, radicchio is prone to rots and prefers cloche environments.

My favorite chicory is variously called Sugar Loaf, Sugar Hat, or Zuccerhat. It forms a green, conical head somewhat like romaine. It's prone to rotting in winter, but if the big heads are cut as high as possible and used during November, the regrowth is a lot more rain resistant and good eating. Grumolo sorts are too bitter to eat during autumn, but their tops die back in winter. Very early in spring their regrowth is rapid and very much milder. They'll really help balance a cabbagey salad. After the spring regrowth is cut, more will appear.

Catalogna is like a wild dandelion, an annual whose flowers are supposed to be picked before they open. Perhaps the Italians know what to do with Catalogna—cooked or raw, it seems inedibly bitter to me. But then, so does the tropical bitter melon so loved in Asia. One warning: Only recently have the big primary growers paid any attention to chicory. The varieties tend to be highly variable and may disappoint you with many off-types.

Dry-gardening Start endive and other chicories before the heat of summer, and thin steadily to 24 inches apart. If you make the between-row space 4 feet apart, you probably won't have to water them at all. If they get too rank by the time the rains return, cut off the tops and use the regrowth during winter.

BELGIAN ENDIVE *(See the Roots section.)*

LETTUCE *(Lactuca sativa)*

A moderately frost-hardy annual leafy green, lettuce can easily be harvested from late spring through late fall and sometimes from frames all winter. It is a common misconception among health-conscious people that lettuce is devoid of nutrients. This is true only of crisphead or iceberg types. Full of high-protein chlorophyll, dark green loose-leaf varieties are nutritionally the equal of any other salad green. The popular crispheads are also the most difficult to grow, as they demand ideal soil and weather conditions to head properly.

I grew them when I conducted variety trials for Territorial. Now I never bother with them.

Lettuce needs a fair degree of fertility and abundant soil moisture if it is to grow fast and be sweetly succulent, and most varieties prefer weather on the cool side. The main trick to producing beautiful heads is early and careful thinning. Given ample room and enough water and nutrients to support rapid growth, the rosettes develop beautifully in any soil type. Iceberg and butterhead types given too much nitrogen tend to blow up (form loose, poorly shaped heads) or suffer internal tip burn (have thin blackened edges on interior leaves). Growing head lettuce well takes a bit of experimentation to discover the amount of fertilizer for the crop and your soil.

Lettuce has a dense, delicate root system that breaks down rapidly after harvest, leaving the soil in friable condition. Irrigation must be plentiful. Even though lettuce stores up a lot of water in its core and taproot, survives drought handily, and may not seem to suffer, it needs a lot of moisture to be good eating.

Culture The use of cold frames can extend sowing dates by about one month, both earlier and later. Without protection, sow outdoors from April through mid-August. Iceberg types won't head if sown after mid-July. Broadcast I gallon of complete organic fertilizer per 100 square feet of bed, and work into the soil. In the cold soils of spring, a little extra fertilizer can also be side-dressed right after germination to kick the seedlings into rapid growth. Sprinkle the seeds thinly in the furrows, ½ inch deep, in rows 16 to 18 inches apart.

Ideally about one seedling per inch will emerge.

Thin progressively without permitting any crowding. Eat the thinnings if you wish. When mature, looseleafs should stand about 10 to 14 inches apart; icebergs, Bibbs, and romaines should stand 12 to 16 inches apart, depending on the variety's size at maturity.

Garden planning My household now consists of two adults plus guests. Because we like huge, fresh salads daily, I repeatedly sow lettuce during its season, starting 25 to 50 square feet every three weeks. Sometimes I sow new lettuce between already-growing three- to four-week-old rows, making one continuously harvested bed that lasts all summer. When I do this I make the between-row space about 24 inches. When the plants in the first sowing are 2 to 3 inches in diameter, I seed new rows between the old. The maturing heads are far enough apart that they do not shade out the rows of tiny new seedlings coming up between them. As I cut the big heads, I thin the new ones gradually. By the time the first sowing is all cut, I am harvesting the fastest varieties in the second one. Then I can repeat the cycle by hoeing out the stumps of the first sowing while mixing in a bit of fertilizer and compost and planting new seeds for a third lettuce crop, and so forth. This way, one bed produces lettuce from the first sowing in April through the last harvests of winter.

I start another large bed of the hardiest sorts for fall harvest about mid-August, because growth rates slow as summer fades, and I want to have large pickings as long as possible into winter.

Protected by crude cloches, lettuce can be started about March 1 and as late as October 1. Some varieties are hardy to 19°F and may last out a mild winter, especially if under cloches.

Insects and diseases I've never had any problems, except for having to wash slugs out carefully.

Harvest Cut heads as needed. Many varieties become bitter or bolt very quickly after maturity, so it's wise to grow several different varieties at a time and make successive sowings every three weeks.

Saving seed Lettuce rarely cross-pollinates, so little or no isolation is needed. Lettuce is an annual; commercial seed is produced in California, where a long, mild growing season permits the slowly developing seed to mature.

It is difficult to mature seed in most of the maritime Northwest from spring sowings. But we can grow lettuce seed by sowing it late in summer and overwintering the seedling plants, which are a bit hardier than mature ones. Some mild winters that will happen naturally; sometimes a frame is needed to get the seedlings through the worst of winter, sometimes they freeze out. But lettuce seed lives many years, so it should be possible for this region's gardeners to keep their own seed going by trying every year or so. Another approach is to start plants for seeds indoors very early—say mid-January—and transplant them out about mid-March. This way, seed may mature by September.

Dig up several overwintered plants and transplant to a part of the garden that won't have to be watered with the other vegetable crops. By midsummer, the plants will have bolted, flowered, and be forming seed. With lettuce, the trait of holding in the bed after heading up without bolting or becoming bitter is a good one, so if you're growing enough plants to do some crop improvement, rogue out the first individuals to bolt and taste a leaf on each overly mature head for bitterness, letting the sweetest go on to become the seed crop.

Lettuce seeds are held in small "cups" that tend to shatter quickly, allowing the seed to scatter. When most of the flowers have finished blooming and some seed has shattered, cut the stalks and gently lay them on sheets of newspaper in the shade under cover to finish ripening. Thresh the seed by shaking the thoroughly dry stalks in a drum, or rub the heads between your palms over the newspaper. Winnow the seed by pouring between two buckets in a mild breeze.

Varieties Just about any type of loose-leaf lettuce will grow fine, though in my trials work I've discovered that a few varieties bred for southern latitudes become confused by our day lengths and bolt prematurely. My personal favorites among the common American varieties are Prizehead, Red Sails, Slowbolt (a hardy Grand Rapids strain that I find best for winter cold frames and low light levels), and Buttercrunch. For Boston or Bibb types, I prefer the fancy European market selections. Of the romaines, I find Valmaine the best grower with excellent flavor. Batavians are a new sort from Europe; a romaine-iceberg cross, they are particularly hardy, good tasting, and hold a long time in autumn.

Most varieties have a bad trait from the gardener's viewpoint—they mature uniformly and don't hold long without becoming bitter or bolting. Buttercrunch and Slowbolt hold the longest in highly edible but overmature condition. On my continuous-harvest bed, I mix seed for all the abovementioned varieties into one packet, sow them all together, and thin so that the bed grows a more or less equal percentage of all the varieties, located at random. This spreads out the time of harvest from only ten days or so (for any one variety) to about four weeks. Any odd bit of leftover lettuce seed of any sort except iceberg gets dumped into the "blend" packet.

Salinas seems to grow the best iceberg lettuce.

MUSTARD

(Brassica alba, B. nigra, B. chinensis, B. juncea, B. rapa)
A member of the *Brassica* genus, used for its edible leaves and stalks, mustard is not prone to significant damage by the cabbage root maggot and grows more like lettuce than cabbage. That's why it's included in this section. If not cooked to death, these greens are much more delicious than most North Americans realize. Small quantities of certain milder sorts are good in salads. The ground-up seeds of some types are used for making prepared mustard paste.

Culture Most gardeners have a hard time growing mustard in spring because the plants bolt before they get large enough to reward the gardener. Mustards are actually easy to grow, but only when some basics about the species are understood. Highly photoperiodic, all mustard varieties but one, as far as I know, rapidly go to seed under the influence of lengthening days, and so must be sown very early in spring if they are to grow big before mid-May's long days make them bolt. They can be sown again after mid-July because by then the days have shortened enough that they won't bolt immediately; fall-sown mustards won't bolt until the next spring if they survive the winter. This makes fall mustards easiest to grow; success with spring mustards may require a brief science lesson.

Water has a very high specific heat—much higher than, say, rock powder. "Specific heat" means how much change in the temperature of a substance results from the addition or loss of a certain fixed amount of heat energy. More simply put, it takes many more calories of heat energy to raise the temperature of a given amount of water 1°F than the number of calories it takes to raise the temperature of the same amount of iron or rock 1°F. Thus, water has a higher specific heat than rock—in fact, water has just about the highest specific heat of any substance. That's why when solar home designers want to store heat energy, they frequently use barrels or tanks of water.

Here's how specific heat applies to gardening. Light soils have one-third the water-holding capacity that clay soils have. Thus, sandy soils have a much lower specific heat than clay soils and, consequently, warm up more than clays from absorbing the same amount of solar energy. Heavy soils hold much more water; clay must absorb many more calories of spring solar energy to heat up the same amount. So clay soils can easily be 5°F or more colder than a sandy loam in April or May. This makes a huge difference in the growth of many early crops. I found out to my deep sorrow at Lorane that no matter what you do to improve clay, with respect to spring soil warmup, you can't turn a sow's ear into a silk purse.

Spring mustard must be sown very early, sprout successfully, and grow fast if it is to grow to any size at all before bolting. It's easy to grow spring-sown mustard in warm, loamy soils. But since biological activity, nutrient release, seed sprouting, and root development all go slowly when it's cold, and since heavy soils are cold in spring, growing spring mustard on clays is not so easy. Heavy soil dries out faster in raised beds, and additions of organic matter lighten clay soil a little, helping it to warm up slightly faster and grow mustard better to some degree. Still, on heavy soils, it's best to sow spring mustard in cloches or cold frames.

Sow in early March in furrows about ½ deep, two or three seeds per inch, the rows about 18 inches apart. To grow fast, mustards also need high levels of available nitrogen in spring. So in addition to broadcasting and working in complete organic fertilizer before sowing, immediately after germination sprinkle about 2 tablespoons of blood meal close beside each 4 or 5 feet of row (but not touching the seedlings, as blood meal will burn plants). Thin gradually so plants stand about 6 inches apart when 6 to 8 inches high. Do not thin too rapidly, as some seedlings will succumb to flea beetles, slugs, and generally harsh weather.

For fall and winter harvest, sow in mid-July through mid-August, and separate the rows by 24 inches because the plants will grow much larger. Gradually thin late sowings to 12 inches in the row. Fertilization suitable for other greens will produce excellent fall and winter mustard harvests.

Garden planning Eight to ten row-feet is usually enough in spring; for winter, twice that might not be excessive, and real mustard lovers will want even more. Spring mustard will be done before June, leaving the bed for summer solanums, beans, or other heat lovers. In a mild winter, fall crops will last until April, ideally followed by peas, other greens, or root crops.

Insects and diseases Flea beetles are hard on slow-growing seedlings. The best solutions are lots of extra seedlings, high fertility, cloches, and cold frames to enhance growth. If all else fails, spray with rotenone/pyrethrum or neem.

Harvest In spring, after thinning small seedlings to about 3 inches apart in the row, harvest by repeatedly thinning every other plant, cutting it off at the base, until the in-the-row spacing is 12 inches. Then cut mature plants or pick off large outer leaves as needed. In fall, snip individual leaves through the winter. If garden food is scarce in April, unopened mustard flowers make passable "broccoli," very sweet and tender.

Saving seed Mustards are pollinated by bees. They freely cross with others of their species and sometimes make interspecies crosses (they also cross occasionally with turnips and Chinese cabbage). This can produce many interesting but often not-too-edible progeny, so do not permit more than one variety to form flowers. Mustard seeds often last seven years with good vigor, so the seed saver could keep several varieties going. The clusters of small yellow flowers form pods containing several seeds each. When half of the pods are dry, cut the stalks, finish drying them on a tarp, thresh out the seed by walking on it, and winnow by pouring the seed and chaff between two buckets in a mild breeze. Allowing the flower stalks to fall on the ground will probably result in a self-perpetuating mustard patch that needs only an occasional covering with compost or manure to maintain fertility.

Varieties I suspect that all mustards originated in Asia. Many varieties are amazingly beautiful examples of the plant breeder's art, with frilly leaves on long, graceful stalks. Only three have long been familiar to rural Americans: Green Wave and Southern Giant Curled (both *B. juncea*) are both hot and mustardy; the third, Tendergreen (*B. rapa*), is mild and bland, with uninteresting-looking leaves. Green Wave is slightly slower to bolt in spring, which makes it a better candidate for growth in our spring weather. A much finer mustardy mustard is Miike (Red) Giant (*B. juncea*), with reddish purple leaves and broad, thick stalks. It's not merely hot, but also sweet and flavorful. Miike is also hardier than Green Wave and is thus much more likely to overwinter.

Tendergreen (or Mustard Spinach) is a plain-looking, broad-leaved sort, with virtually no pungency or flavor, and American selections have deteriorated into much variability and earlier bolting. Late Komatsuna (*B. rapa*) is the original slower-bolting Japanese variety that, while still mild, has good flavor and retains uniformity. Tendergreen II is a much more vigorous hybrid Komatsuna.

Many sorts of tai sai and pac choi have become available to North Americans, all of them *B. chinensis* varieties with celerylike stalks, broad green spoon-shaped leaves, and a very pleasant, mild flavor. Pac choi of one sort or another is essential to Asian cookery. There is one strain of pac choi that can be sown later in spring and grown in summer, fall, or winter without bolting immediately. Like tai sai, it has long stems, though not they're not quite as white nor quite as refined. It is given slightly different names by TSC, JSS, and WCO. Read the catalog copy carefully to identify it. Where tai sai's elegant pure-white stalks might suit the Asian restaurant trade, this strain of pac choi is home garden delicious and much more versatile.

Green-in-Snow is from China and is, as its name implies, the hardiest known mustard, suitable only for fall and winter. Mizuna (*B. juncea* 'Japonica') is another sort suitable only for winter because it bolts too fast in spring. Mizuna makes a dense rosette like frilly endive and has a mild flavor. There are some very fancy and elegant hybrid Mizuna varieties.

Although mustards aren't much of a commercial crop in North America, they are still a big item in the Asian diet. Japanese and Chinese seed companies have many interesting varieties that are sometimes available from specialty mail-order companies. Improved hybrid varieties are rapidly being developed for Japanese and Chinese domestic markets. Compared to the open-pollinated sorts, they offer perfect uniformity and amazingly increased vigor.

ASSORTED COOKING GREENS

Some other greens that are generally grown like mustards but are not the same species at all are as follows:

Santoh is a type of nonheading Chinese cabbage, much slower to bolt in spring while handling rain and frosts in fall better than heading sorts. It is best cooked.

Raab (also known as rapa) is a type of turnip grown for its edible greens. The most rapid grower of all greens when spring sown, raab fills the pot before any other new crop can be harvested, but it bolts quickly. The unopened flowers are also very good. Raab is not nearly as choice eating as mustard greens.

Tyfon, mentioned earlier as animal fodder and green manure, has palatable leaves as good as Tendergreen mustard. Being biennial, it won't bolt right away; it can be spring sown and then cut and recut from May through February. Occasional plants make nice turnips, too.

Edible chrysanthemum, actually a small-flowered member of the chrysanthemum family, is used as a stir-fry green in Japanese cookery. It is easy to grow, its culture is like that of mustard, and it can be sown from April through August. Harvest it before the flowers begin to open; after they open, it becomes too spicy to enjoy. For a continuous supply, make successive sowings about three weeks apart.

Don't be afraid to experiment with Asian greens. Once you get the hang of growing them, new sorts will prove no challenge—only opportunities for interesting eating.

PARSLEY

(See the Roots section.)

SPINACH *(Spinacia oleracea)*

Spinach is a natural for the cool maritime Northwest. In fact, the species is so well adapted that much of the world's spinach seed is grown in the Skagit Valley. Spring spinach is grown much like mustard; all the caveats in the mustard section concerning bolting, cold soil, and day length apply here too. About as cold hardy as endive, spinach almost always over-winters under a bit of plastic, sometimes even without protection, although it won't make as much growth as mustard or endive will under low winter light levels. Spinach also demands plenty of nitrogen; in spring, strong fertilizers are essential.

Culture *For spring harvest,* sow early in March. *For summer harvest,* sow bolt-resistant varieties in April through mid-May. *For late summer, fall, and winter harvest,* sow from mid-July through mid-August. Spinach seed germinates well under cool conditions; in fact, hot soils reduce germination. Although a few varieties resist bolting well enough to sow in midsummer, it's more difficult to get summer sowings to sprout very far inland south of Longview, Washington.

Broadcast and work in the usual amount of complete organic fertilizer before planting. Sow seed ½ inch deep, two or three seeds per inch, in rows 14 to 18 inches apart. In spring, side-dress a little additional fertilizer beside the seedlings immediately after germination to enhance rapid growth.

It's a good idea to delay the initial thinning until the seedlings have one true leaf and are growing fast, because there will often be many losses, especially if you have lurking symphylans. Spinach grows fairly well when crowded; however, I strongly suggest you gradually thin seedlings to 3 inches apart in the row by the time the plants are 3 inches in diameter. I thin mine 6 to 8 inches apart in the row and grow handsome giants, quite unlike what you find in the supermarket.

Garden planning The harvest from 50 square feet of fast-growing bed will make all the salads and cooked spring and fall spinach our family can use. Grow spinach in spring following crimson clover green manure. Make another sowing in mid-April of a late-bolting variety for harvest into the summer. For fall, grow a lot more because once the plants size up, they stop growing and will at best hold all winter to be gradually picked. Keep spinach beds well weeded in winter. I realize it is harder to weed in winter, but if the plants aren't swallowed by weeds, and if the fall beds manage to overwinter in good condition, a side-dressing with blood meal in early February will provide a "kick in the pants" that may well result in abundant pickings during March and early April.

Insects and diseases Symphylans seem to prefer spinach over most other species. When they're chewing away down below, even thickly sown stands gradually (and mysteriously) disappear before the seedlings really get established. Organic gardeners can try dealing with symphylans by banding a big handful (per 4 or 5 row-feet) of Perma Guard (insecticidal diatomaceous earth) in a deep furrow below the seeds. This will set the symphylans back enough to permit a decent harvest. When your spinach starts to have problems, it's time to consider a multiyear rotation out of vegetables altogether if you're a country gardener with extra garden land.

Constant moisture, heavy rains, frosts, and low light levels combine to weaken plants in winter, making them susceptible to various molds and other diseases. Newer varieties are a little more resistant to many of these diseases; some will produce new growth during winter and may survive when old standards gradually succumb to mold and rot. For winter harvest, try growing huge individual plants, thinning them much farther apart—8 to 12 inches—so air can move freely around leaves and molds don't form so readily. Simply giving spinach the protection of a leaky cloche or cold frame will keep it drier and raise daytime temperatures enough to let it reliably overwinter.

Saving seed Spring and overwintered sowings bolt and form huge quantities of seed. Plants intended for seed should be located where general garden irrigation won't wet them down. Spinach is wind-pollinated and readily outcrosses; varieties must have at least one mile of isolation to maintain purity. Since varieties are so similar, purity may not matter too much

except when you wish to produce bolt-resistant types for summer growing. The species makes male, female, and hermaphroditic plants; all three put up a stocky central seed stalk. The first bolters may be an undesirable type called dwarf males and should be rogued (weeded out) before they can contribute pollen. Seed stalks on male plants open small pollen sacks; only the females form seed. Males generally bolt first, but early bolting being considered a bad trait, breeders have developed hybrid varieties consisting only of females. I wouldn't hesitate to grow my own seed by crossing hybrid and open-pollinated varieties to gradually develop a reasonably uniform open-pollinated gene pool. The seed stalks ripen unevenly, so delay harvest until the stalks are brown. Cut the stalks, dry fully under cover, and remove the seed from the stalks by rubbing between your palms.

Varieties For spring, Bloomsdale is the classic open-pollinated home garden sort. Its thick, savoyed (crinkly) leaves have the sweetest and richest flavor of any spinach. There are many Bloomsdale strains that vary somewhat as to disease resistance, bolting date, and cold hardiness. Winter Bloomsdale, sometimes called Cold Resistant Savoy, is the best all-around open-pollinated choice for spring or fall. A newer savoy hybrid, Tyee, is quite a bit slower bolting than the Bloomsdales, just about as tasty, and disease-resistant enough to overwinter and make some regrowth during winter.

For late spring sowings, try slow-bolt hybrids like Mazurka (WCO) or my absolute favorite, Steadfast (TSC), an open-pollinated variety that just about refuses to bolt no matter when planted.

Dry-gardening In spring, start a summer variety like Steadfast. Thin gradually and carefully to 1 foot apart in rows 3 feet apart. Give it all the water you can spare. It just may carry you through until next spring. For starting fall/winter spinach, you'll have to irrigate to get it started; delay sowing until early August.

SWISS CHARD (*Beta vulgaris cicla*)

Chard is a beet bred for large, succulent greens instead of root development. It is frost hardy and stands through most winters without freezing out. Chard will produce a lot more leaf if fertilized and irrigated like other greens.

Culture Sow between April and June, eight seeds per foot, seeds ¾ inch deep, in rows at least 18 inches apart. Thin gradually to 10 to 12 inches apart in the row. Earlier sowings (made before spring rains taper off too much) sprout easily. Periodically banding organic fertilizer along the rows will greatly increase the rate of leaf regrowth; if formation of new leaves slows, fertilize again.

Garden planning Ten row-feet sown in March will result in a ten-month oversupply.

Insects and diseases I've had no problems. Symphylans and leaf miners could cause difficulties. See the discussion of beets (in the Roots section) for information on how to handle leaf miners.

Harvest Cut individual leaves as needed. If regrowth is too slow, fertilize.

Saving seed Chard will cross with other beets. The seed-saving procedure is identical. See the discussion of beets in the Roots section.

Varieties Fordhook seems the hardiest of all, but then, most commonly available chard seed is produced in the Skagit Valley by overwintering, so all of the varieties are pretty hardy. Some fancy European varieties don't handle summer heat very well. Ruby or Rhubarb chard tends to bolt prematurely if sown early.

Dry-gardening Swiss chard is an ideal species for dry-gardening. Sow before May; depending on how often you want to water it (maybe never), space as much as 18 inches apart in rows 4 feet apart. If not well watered through the summer, it will still produce a lot of new leaf as soon as the rains return in September and October.

ASSORTED SALAD GREENS

There are numerous minor species of greens that will spice up a salad—especially important during winter when repetitious garden meals can become as confining as the perpetual rains. These greens are basically weeds bred for slightly larger, more succulent leaves. They require little or no extra fertilizer nor special care.

Garden purslane (Portulaca oleracea) is a domesticated version of the ubiquitous low-growing weed found in every garden. The large, succulent leaves and upright thick stalks resemble the "jade" or "money" plant commonly grown as a house plant. It is a summer salad green, not frost tolerant at all. Raw, it has a crunchy, bland taste good in salads in small amounts.

Garden purslane needs no particular care other than thinning and weeding. Start a few plants after the last frost, and snip into salads all summer. Harvest by cutting stalks an inch or so aboveground; the plant will regrow from the base. If seed heads appear, cut them off; these are tough and inedible, and seed development will reduce future leaf growth.

French sorrel is a derivative of the ubiquitous weed sheep's sorrel. It is a perennial and is highly overproductive even if given nothing beyond a bit of compost once a year after it gets started. Sorrel in winter and spring has a lemony taste, and small quantities of the thin, tender leaves make winter and early spring salads far more palatable. I find it too strong tasting to enjoy in summer, but I have other salad leaves in abundance then. Sometimes extremely cold winters will freeze off all of the leaves. This is not a problem; they'll shoot up again in early spring. The first time you grow this plant, sow at least 4 row-feet; this can easily be done with the amount in the smallest garden packet. Sow the tiny seeds in April, sprinkled into a very shallow, freshly scratched furrow and not covered. The seeds fall into cracks and crannies and germinate well in a few weeks so long as the weather is mellow and moist. Thin gradually to about 8 inches apart.

The "varieties" of French sorrel are highly variable; plants that quickly put up seed stalks

should be dug out and destroyed. Periodically, the whole patch will become mainly seed stalks. When this happens, cut off all the vegetation about an inch aboveground, and use the leaves and stalks for mulch, or compost them. Leafy regrowth will start immediately. One year later, try to select a few plants that are the most shy to make seed stalks; these are gems to dig and transplant (and divide). Once you've got a few good plants, you're set for life. Sorrel is so tough that its roots transplant very easily almost anytime.

Arugula (Eruca vesicaria subspecies *sativa)* is a very fast-growing brassica relative with a delicious peppery taste, used to spice up cool-weather salads. Like French sorrel, its flavor is too strong in summer, and the species also bolts much too rapidly to make it worth growing in the long days. I grow it mainly for late summer and through the winter.

Sow one short row every two weeks from mid-July through the end of September. Thinly sprinkle seed in a ½-inch-deep furrow across a raised bed. Thin to an inch or two apart. Pick the leaves as needed. There is no way to keep arugula from going to seed quickly when the days are long. You can cut the plants off an inch aboveground and use the smaller, harder-to-pick regrowth, but after being cut back it'll mainly produce seed stalks. It is almost easier just to start a new row every few weeks. When days are short, however, cutting off seed stalks near the base encourages more winter leaf production. Hopefully, one of your later sowings will survive winter and make seed in pods like other brassicas the next spring. It will not cross with other brassicas.

Spring sowings are usually riddled with flea beetles, grow too slowly, and bolt too quickly.

Brassicas

The brassicas, often called cole crops, thrive in cool weather, are frost hardy—some extremely so—and are dependable producers during those damp, cloudy summers that I have learned to call cabbage years. Brassicas are also very nutritious food; it has been said that the labor that built the Great Wall of China was fueled not by rice but by cabbage. I've also learned that of all the fodder crops, the one that produces the most protein per acre is not, as you might think, alfalfa or some other legume, but kale. Now that's saying something about chlorophyll being an essential food for man or beast.

Included in the brassica family are kale, rutabagas, cabbage, cauliflower, broccoli, Brussels sprouts, collards, and Chinese cabbage, as well as some species I discuss in other parts of this chapter, such as radishes, turnips, mustards, and arugula. Brassicas have a unique potential to be "grotesqued" by the breeder: Terminal buds can be wildly exaggerated into heads of cabbage, axial buds can be swollen into Brussels sprouts, small flower clusters can become giant broccoli and cauliflower, petioles can be elongated into celerylike stalks as found in fancy mustards, stems can be thickened into rutabaga and kohlrabi, and roots can be fattened into turnips and radishes. Unfortunately, the more a single aspect of the species' genetic potential dominates the plant, the less vigor the variety has.

Coarse (more like the wild ancestor) brassicas, such as kale, collards, and Purple Sprouting broccoli, will grow lustily in soil of only moderate fertility. Somewhat more refined ones, like rutabagas and Brussels sprouts, need higher fertility levels, while the intensely inbred coles—cauliflower, kohlrabi, and broccoli—demand the finest soils and lots of fertilizer. The less refined varieties of these types, such as big-framed savoy cabbage and giant kohlrabi (originally grown as animal fodder), are more vigorous than the others and can be considered almost in the same league as kale.

Brassicas require high levels of nitrogen and calcium. Even in soils of fairly neutral pH, additional lime close to seedling roots can markedly improve growth. Not only will a calcium deficiency stunt plants, but in cabbage and Brussels sprouts it will also cause internal browning of the leaf margins or a sort of tip burn.

The cabbage fly, the larvae of which can cause extensive root damage, seems to prefer some types of brassicas over others: Chinese cabbage and turnips seem most attractive to the pest, rutabagas the least interesting. The fly's preferences and the nature of the variety's root system determine how damaging the maggots will be. Cauliflower is usually the most delicate; a little root loss in late spring can be fatal. Brussels sprouts have much more vigorous root systems that can better tolerate predation. Kale, when directly seeded instead of transplanted, is almost never noticeably damaged by the maggot, at least not at the predation levels I have experienced in my gardening.

Neither is the cabbage fly uniformly trouble-some throughout the maritime Northwest. Washington State has a higher level of infestation than Oregon, and the Skagit Valley probably has the worst cabbage fly trouble in the United States. Chapter 8 covers the cabbage maggot as well as a few other brassica pests.

The cole family is also troubled by a soil-borne disease called clubroot. The infected roots swell grotesquely, and root efficiency is inhibited. Mysterious wilting and stunted brassicas with swollen, knobby roots are proof of clubroot. Healthy soil can become infected by soil transported on purchased bedding plants, by compost made from infected plants, and even by the gardener's shoes and tools. If clubroot is present, take care not to spread the disease by composting infected plants; instead, burn them. Clubroot is not easy to eliminate completely; the garden must be kept clear of all brassicas as well as certain host weeds for a period of seven years. However, even three or four years without brassicas will greatly reduce the fungus's effect. The state extension services print a fact sheet (EM 4205) about clubroot that is free for the asking. A few brassica varieties carry resistance to one or more strains of the disease (the seed catalog will proudly let you know about that), but resistance to one strain does not necessarily mean resistance to the strain infecting your particular plot.

Rural gardeners faced with clubroot should think about a multiyear grass fallow that also reduces symphylan levels. In fact, the longer I garden, the more this becomes real to me: *Continuously growing vegetables (even organically)* *inevitably creates unhealthy soil.* Brand-new gardens started from pasture or lawn always grow much better for the first few years.

At any time of year, most brassicas demand and all brassicas respond to abundant fertilization. For all brassicas, a gallon of complete organic fertilizer worked into each 100 square feet of bed before planting would provide minimum nutrition; the more demanding types need additional fertilizer side-dressed around the seedlings as they grow. Brassicas for fall and winter harvest should not be urged to maintain rapid growth after the end of August—they need to toughen up and develop maximum frost resistance. Overwintered crops should not be side-dressed until spring regrowth begins (sometime in February).

Italian broccoli, ordinary cauliflower, and cabbage obey this genetic program: Grow a fixed number of leaves, and then flower or head. They will make their preprogrammed number of leaves at more or less the same rate of speed, in good or bad soil, under high or low fertility. But under good conditions, the plant will have waxed large when the task is done—and the head will match. Under poor conditions, the plant will be stunted and the head, flower, or curd, tiny. Later-maturing varieties produce much larger yields because their genetic program is to make more sets of leaves before flowering or heading.

Overwintering broccoli and overwintering cauliflower are programmed differently—flowering is determined by the increasing day length after exposure to a certain amount of chilling during winter. Still, the larger the plant has grown when flowering commences, the larger the head will be.

Brassicas generally adapt well to transplanting. Most gardeners think that cabbage, cauliflower, broccoli, and Brussels sprouts must be grown from transplants, but this is not so. If vigorous seed is sown outdoors when weather conditions are favorable, and if the planting spot is welcoming to brassica seedlings, direct-seeded plants will always outgrow transplants. Successful direct-seeding demands two basic strategies: following the native habit of the species regarding its establishment by seed in the wild and, for the most refined types, putting the potting soil outdoors rather than in the pot, as I explain shortly.

Brassicas form seed in small pods containing five or six seeds each. The protective pods often retain the seed when they fall off the plant; often, all the seeds in the pod sprout at once. It is very easy for a disease or pest to knock over an individual brassica seedling, just as it's easy for one weak seedling to fail to push past a clod or through a thin crust. They survive all these threats much better when germinating in a little cluster. If the gardener imitates nature in this respect—sowing four or five seeds wherever one plant will be wanted and gradually thinning the seedlings as they become established—success is almost assured.

The more refined brassicas have greatly weakened root systems that demand airy, fertile soil—especially in the seedling stage. Although it's nearly impossible to turn the entire garden into potting soil, the gardener has the ability to put a small quantity of potting soil under each clump of brassica seedlings. This is easier than you might think—in fact, it's the easiest of all methods of starting even the most delicate brassica seedlings (see Chapter 7). All of the cultural directions that follow suggest direct-seeding brassica crops.

Saving seed from fancy, open-pollinated brassicas is not for amateurs, even though our climate is so good for brassicas that it attracts commercial seed growers from around the world. If not carefully selected and sagely rogued (meaning that the off-type or less desirable plants are removed before their genes participate in seed formation), after a few generations refined brassicas rapidly degenerate into a useless hodgepodge of undesirable variation.

Broccoli, cauliflower, cabbage, Brussels sprouts, collards, kohlrabi, and Scottish kale (the type that grows a tall central stalk) all cross with one another. Rutabagas and Siberian kale cross with one another. To prevent most crossing with other flowering brassicas, isolation of ½ mile is required.

Seed for Italian broccoli and ordinary cauliflower—not very hardy compared to other brassicas—is produced in California. We can and do grow overwintering broccoli and overwintering cauliflower for seed in the maritime Northwest. Kale, winter-hardy Brussels sprouts, winter savoy cabbage, and rutabaga are also fairly easy to grow for seed. More difficult but possible are kohlrabi and the sorts of market cabbage that head in late summer.

In early spring, dig up and transplant carefully chosen overwintered mature plants to a part of the garden that won't need to be watered with the rest of the vegetables. Take at least six plants—better several dozen to avoid loss of vigor due to excessive inbreeding. By April, plants that have overwintered will put out seed stalks covered with yellow flowers that mature into small pods, each containing four to six seeds. When the pods first start drying out, cease all irrigation. (I've grown highly vigorous seed without any irrigation at all, although the yields were lower.)

As summer progresses, flowering tapers off and eventually the majority of the pods contain mature, dried seed. At this stage, cut the huge masses of pods, windrow them to dry in the field on tarps (to catch any seed that shatters out of the pod) or dry them under cover, and then thresh, clean, and store the seed. The seed will last four to ten years, depending on its initial vigor and on storage conditions. Each plant will produce over an ounce of seed, sometimes many times that amount.

Hybridization of brassica varieties has become a seed industry standard. Consequently, many of the older, open-pollinated types are no longer quality selections. Hybrid varieties are usually perfectly uniform and much more vigorous. To develop an open-pollinated variety from hybrids, it's best to start with two or more closely similar hybrid varieties and permit them to cross freely. Then, with each succeeding generation, select rigorously for the desired traits.

BROCCOLI *(Brassica oleracea italica)*

There are two basic sorts of broccoli: Italian, which makes large central flowers in a rather short time, and overwintering or sprouting, which *must* overwinter before flowering. Broccoli of any sort is one of the easier brassicas

to grow. It has large, vigorously sprouting seeds. It will produce in clayey soils and those of only moderate fertility, but growing big supermarket-sized heads requires high nitrogen levels and airy soils from sprouting to the initiation of flowering.

Culture Sow broccoli seed in little clumps of four or five, ½ inch deep, over a spot where ½ cup of complete organic fertilizer has been worked into about a gallon of soil. Arrange early varieties on 18-inch centers, late varieties on 24-inch centers. To reduce frequency of irrigation and get enormous flowers, try spacing as much as 24 inches apart in rows 4 feet apart. Thin gradually to the best single plant without permitting competition for light. Thinning should be completed by the time the seedlings have three true leaves.

If growth slows, side-dress the plants. If a side-dressing is given just when the central flower first begins to form, the main head will be only slightly larger, but side-shoot development will be much faster and heavier.

To obtain the hardiest overwintered broccoli in very frosty areas, adjust the sowing date and soil fertility so the plants grow about 12 inches high before November's chill checks further growth. I sow these in mid- to late July. Do not side-dress Purple Sprouting broccoli until after it has overwintered and begun its rapid spring growth (early February) at Elkton. Then provoke the most rapid possible spring growth.

Garden planning Our climate will supply broccoli most of the year, though leaving a few gaps. March-to-May harvests come from overwintering Purple and White Sprouting broccoli. Next come early spring-sown transplants. Seeds can be started indoors as early as February for setting out in mid-March under small paper hot caps or in cold frames. These will flower by June. Outdoor conditions permit direct-seeding or unprotected transplanting in mid-March or April, depending on weather patterns that year. These mature in July. The last sowing of Italian broccoli should be made by mid-July (in more northern areas, perhaps by July 4). The latest sowings mature in October or early November.

Hybrid varieties head all at once. To lengthen the harvest, I sow several different hybrids at one time, producing large, central flowers over four to five weeks, followed by pickings of large side shoots for another three or four weeks. Sowing about six plants of mixed varieties every six weeks from February through July 15 keeps us in broccoli all summer and fall. (Sowing mixes of cauliflower and early cabbage works the same way.) Overwintering broccoli flowers when there is little else to eat; at that time we make whole meals of broccoli stir-fries mixed with scallions or leeks. So I start a dozen or more plants each summer to supply us during spring.

Insects and diseases Italian broccoli is better able to handle predation from symphylans or root maggots than are cabbage and cauliflower. Overwintered broccoli seems nearly as vigorous as kale (and by the look of it, Italian broccoli was probably crossed with kale to create Purple Sprouting broccoli). Direct-

seeding, using lots of fertilizer, and sowing several more seeds than are ultimately wanted handles most insect problems.

Harvest The central head should be cut when the "beads" begin to fatten, but well before they open as yellow flowers. All broccoli varieties put out at least some side shoots after the central head is cut. Slower-maturing, taller varieties make more and larger side shoots. Early varieties are short, bred for once-over mechanical harvest, and usually produce few side shoots. If the side shoots are carefully cut back to where they emerge from the main stalk, the plant will probably make fewer but larger and tastier additional shoots. In mild winters I've had autumn-flowering plants keep making side shoots until spring, although each batch was smaller and more woody than the last.

Purple Sprouting broccoli has been bred to delay opening its blooms, which permits the flower buds to fatten up and sweeten as they swell. The harvest of each flower should be delayed as long as possible.

Saving seed Italian broccoli strains rarely survive winter north of Douglas County, Oregon; the earliest spring sowings won't bloom and then mature seed until very late summer at best, making seed production dicey. Besides, such old, open-pollinated sorts as Waltham 29, DeCicco, and Italian Sprouting aren't much good any longer; they produce smallish variable heads with side shoots often larger than the central head. If broccoli plants do survive an unusually mild winter, they can be dug, transplanted to an area where irrigation won't affect them, and permitted to make seed. Territorial's Umpqua is the only decent Italian open-pollinated Italian variety I know of.

Purple Sprouting and White Sprouting broccoli are very easy to produce seed from. They're usually covered in yellow flowers by May and mature seed nicely in midsummer. These raggedy varieties vary considerably in quality from plant to plant. I'd wait until after the main flowers appear and then select the best plants for seed production, transplanting them to a dry area of the garden.

Varieties Umpqua (TSC), created by a self-educated breeder in southern Oregon named Tim Peters, is the only quality open-pollinated Italian type on the market today. I mention Tim by name because he is active on the fringes of the seed trade and has a unique genius. Anything he is connected with is likely to be very beneficial to our region's home gardeners. Except for the earliest spring harvest, avoid the most rapidly maturing hybrids intended for mechanical harvesting or "close spacing"—these produce fewer side shoots and smaller heads. Go instead for later maturity and taller plants. Some of the better hybrid varieties available in 1999 include Southern Comet, Green Valiant, and Shogun.

Purple Sprouting (probably a kale–Italian broccoli cross) and White Sprouting (a variety that looks like a cauliflower-kale cross) came originally from England. The flower is not as fancy as Italian broccoli, but it tastes as good and is very much appreciated in spring when there's not much else to eat (TSC, WCO). A new winter variety, Rudolph (TSC), has appeared as I write these words. Territorial's description sounds so exciting that I mention it here without having had time for my own trial. It is very slow growing; if it is sown in mid-July, the catalog promises that it will flower around Christmas, filling in a major gap in broccoli production. Rudolph is probably a gamble for most, workable only where or when winter doesn't get too frosty too soon.

Dry-gardening Grow overwintering varieties as though you were dry-gardening kale, starting them late in May, giving them heaps of elbow room, and coaxing them over the summer. It won't matter if they get a bit gnarly by September; once the rains start they'll be restored to health.

BRUSSELS SPROUTS

(Brassica oleracea gemmifera)

A very hardy vegetable, Brussels sprouts have been bred to emphasize the natural brassica tendency to form cabbagelike axial buds. (Cabbages sometimes make "Brussels sprouts" along the base of their stems; Brussels sprouts sometimes form loose heads at the top.) Early-maturing varieties tend to be short, with the sprouts close together. Later ones are bred to be taller, with greater separation between sprouts, which prevents mold. Early varieties seem to initiate bud formation after reaching sufficient height or growing for a certain period; sow them earlier and they'll mature earlier. Sprout formation on late varieties seems to be triggered by decreasing day length. Sown too soon, late varieties may grow very tall and, unless staked up, may fall over in winter; sown too late, they will be short, with fewer leaf axials and hence fewer sprouts. Either way, they form sprouts at much the same time.

Sharp frosts enhance sugar content and increase tenderness, so our locally grown sprouts are much better eating than the ones from California. A special life energy seems to be located in a bud—similar to the concentrated nutrition in a seed. To me, each little Brussels sprout has nearly the same amount of life force as is contained in a big cabbage—a small serving of them is very filling.

Sprouts have lower nutrient requirements and are somewhat less fussy about soil quality than cabbages, broccoli, or cauliflower. In England, this crop was traditionally grown in heavier soils not suitable for the more lucrative brassicas.

Culture Brussels sprouts need a steady supply of nutrients and water to make continuous growth during summer. But too much nitrogen makes them "blow up" (produce loose sprouts) and become less resistant to winter weather. The plants support themselves better on heavier soils; gardeners on lighter loams and sands might consider staking their plants or starting them a few weeks later than normal to keep them shorter. I sow Brussels sprouts about June 1 and don't bother with an early planting. Who wants Brussels sprouts in August when there are tomatoes? Brussels sprouts are even easier to grow from seed than broccoli. Space plants on 24-inch centers and grow like broccoli with a bit less fertilizer.

Garden planning I want to begin eating Brussels sprouts about November and continue through the winter until they bolt in March. Twelve midseason plants and the same number of late plants oversupply my family. Brussels sprouts allow a fair amount of light to filter through to the bed, especially if you first snap off the lower few inches of leaves; a sprinkling of crimson clover gently raked in during early October will take over the bed by March.

Insects and diseases If sprouts are direct-seeded in June, the worst of the cabbage maggot infestation will have passed. In my garden, by the time the fall maggots return, the large, vigorously rooted plants don't seem bothered. Aphids can be troublesome, wrecking the crop by covering and penetrating half-formed sprouts. Colonies can be hosed off frequently, or killed with Safer's soap, but the easiest solution is to concentrate on later varieties that don't form sprouts until both summer and the aphids are gone.

Harvest Brussels sprouts enlarge first at the base of the stem and can be snapped off a few at a time, starting at the bottom and working up over a period of several months. Commercial growers pinch off the growing tip about a month before harvest, encouraging all of the sprouts to fill out simultaneously—not a good idea in the garden. Some gardeners break off the lower leaves a few at a time as they harvest up the stalk, thinking this fattens the sprouts by letting more light in. Doing this also lets enough light strike the ground to grow some clover. Others point out that the leaves form an umbrella that keeps rain off the sprouts, protecting them and enhancing their appearance. Both views are right.

In mid-March, the unopened bolting flowers make a delicious sort of "broccoli."

Saving seed Brussels sprouts are among the hardiest of the brassicas and usually overwinter successfully. Grow seed as for broccoli. Select seed-making plants for large, smooth, compact sprouts with nice green color. The old open-pollinated varieties exhibited considerable variation and could be selected for better taste, later maturity, wider sprout separation, and the ability to retain good harvest quality late in the season. Unfortunately, hybrid varieties are so hugely superior that no open-pollinated varieties of commercial quality remain in existence—late ones especially have deteriorated. Seed savers may have to start with hybrids and patiently develop their own open-pollinated strain from the wildly variable and scantly seeded first generation that hybrids will produce.

Varieties Classic open-pollinated varieties such as Catskill and Long Island have gone the way of Waltham 29 and DeCicco broccoli; besides, these varieties are too early for the maritime Northwest, with poor field-holding qualities. Seeds of Change, Thompson & Morgan, Bountiful Gardens, and Seeds Blum may have open-pollinated varieties.

Magnificent (and very spendy) hybrid varieties are available from Dutch, English, and Japanese seed companies. The Japanese varieties aren't particularly cold hardy, but you'll recognize them because they are more reasonably

priced. The really primo hybrids are Dutch. Be dubious when Stokes or Johnny's says one of their varieties is "late." Buy hybrids from Territorial, West Coast, or Thompson & Morgan.

Dutch and English hybrid seed costs in excess of a dollar a gram wholesale (250 to 300 seeds per gram), but fortunately, nearly every hybrid seed makes an equally good plant. Even if direct-seeded as I suggest, 1 gram can start fifty plants for a few dollars. Because of the seed cost, this is one brassica the gardener might want to start with indoor-raised transplants so as to coax every possible seed into life.

Dry-gardening Possible with late varieties. Direct-seed June 1, 3 feet apart in the row, rows 4 to 5 feet apart. Fertigate as needed through the summer's heat, probably a few gallons per plant every three to four weeks will do it.

CABBAGE *(Brassica oleracea capitata)*

Salad cabbage is one of the most important vegetables I grow, yielding more food per square foot than just about any other vegetable except root crops. Cabbages are nutritious— one can just about live on them, especially when the weather gives us a cabbage year.

Culture There are three basic types of cabbage: (1) early and "midseason" (a slightly slower-maturing early type), (2) late, and (3) overwintering (or spring cabbage, as the British call this type). Each is grown slightly differently.

Early cabbages are fast-growing, smaller types grown on tight spacings. They don't have much cold tolerance compared to the really sturdy late varieties. Early varieties can be set out as transplants in mid-March, at the same time the earliest broccoli goes out; they'll do better during this chilly month when hot caps or cloches are used. From April through the end of June, they can be direct-seeded. Most early varieties are packed close, on about 18-inch centers, and cultured like broccoli. (Mid-season varieties, being larger, are best spaced on 24-inch centers. To water them less often, try spacing them 24 to 30 inches apart in rows 3 to 4 feet apart.) Early varieties tend to be the most delicate of the cabbages, demanding the best soil and the most protection from root-eating insects. Direct-seeded early types take about three months to mature. The cabbages that appear in American supermarkets from November through July are all early varieties, grown in the South. Small red and small savoy cabbages are also early types.

Late cabbages offered in eastern U.S. seed catalogs usually take 120 days or so to mature and are grown either for making kraut or for root-cellar storage. They are intended to be sown in June and harvested about the end of September. Late varieties often grow poorly if sown in spring—the increasing day length makes their heads become pointy instead of round, and they head up too soon and then burst prematurely. Late types are usually grown on 24-inch centers—and for big heads or a few "giant" varieties, 30 inches might be more appropriate. Late varieties bred for eastern North America usually won't hold in the field too long after heading because they're intended for the cellar or immediate sale. Eastern late varieties usually are not for us.

The English and Dutch have developed *very late varieties* suited to their climate—and ours. These must be sown about June 15 to head up from October through December. The latest ones hold in the garden until March and withstand all the frost and rain our climate can usually dish out; some tolerate being frozen solid for a few days and begin growing again after thawing. Late types are also grown like broccoli. If they're to develop maximum hardiness, time the last side-dressing to peter out as soon as the leaves begin to wrap into a ball. Late savoy cabbages are the most vigorous and freeze hardy, the most tolerant of poor soil conditions, and the best for salad—the ideal maritime Northwest garden cabbage. To grow late varieties to maximum size while watering less often, space them 30 to 36 inches apart in rows 4 to 5 feet apart.

Overwintering cabbages are a gambler's crop. Sow seeds in early September without much fertilization (none is usually needed in decent garden soil). The idea is to get the seedlings to grow to their hardiest size—6 to 8 inches in diameter—before winter's chill and low light levels check their growth. In spring, side-dress them heavily. They will go into a growth spurt, and will usually make good heads during April or May without bolting first. Unpredictable variations in fall weather can make big differences in their growth rate—that's why they're a gamble. If they're too small when winter comes, they'll freeze out; if too big, they'll bolt in spring without heading. Generally, overwintering cabbages make small heads at best, so final spacing may be 18 by 18 inches. I had good luck with spring cabbage at frosty Lorane, Oregon, by sowing in October, keeping them protected in cold frames over the winter, and transplanting 8-inch seedlings at about the end of February, side-dressing heavily at that time. Gardeners in northwestern Washington State, where winter freeze-outs are common, might profitably try this type of culture.

Garden planning I depend on cabbage, especially in winter, so I usually begin the year with a dozen overwintering plants started the previous September. That usually supplies us with spring cabbage. A dozen early transplants go outside in mid-March. In warm springs these do fine; in harsh years, they'll be chewed to death or hopelessly stunted and a waste of effort. Early in April, I sow another dozen early cabbages directly in the bed, including a few reds to spice up summer lettuce salads. These always do fine; by June, I'm eating cabbage for sure. I've also got new lettuce by then, so a cabbage supply is not as vital until fall. To avoid wasting cabbage when there's lettuce, I start only a half dozen early types in about mid-June, along with my main sowing of very late varieties for fall and winter harvest. It takes a lot of very late cabbages to keep my family in salad from November through mid-March.

Late savoys, nearly as durable as kale, will make a head in poorer soil than any other sort of cabbage would tolerate, but savoys still appreciate good ground.

Insects and diseases Flea beetles can make hash of direct-seeded seedlings. Sowing five seeds for every plant wanted prevents the need to spray flea beetles most years. Root maggots

especially trouble early varieties before mid-May, though they do less damage to direct-seeded plants. Cabbage worms are easily controlled with a spraying of Bt. Chapter 8 covers all of these pests and describes how to effectively handle them.

Harvest Early varieties tend to burst quickly after heading up. Very late types head up when lower light levels and chilly conditions prevent rapid growth, and they'll usually hold through the winter. If they head up early in October, however, they may burst by Christmas. Thus, late varieties should be sown on the late side—but if sown too late, the heads will be small. You'll have to experiment a bit, seeking the ideal sowing date that matches your microclimate and soil. Sometimes winter cabbage heads will appear to rot; often, however, there's a good head underneath the slimy outer layers.

Saving seed To grow seed for late-maturing winter-hardy varieties, handle like Brussels sprouts. Some tight-headed varieties may need to have their heads cut with a 2-inch-deep X in early March to permit the seed stalks to emerge. Often even the stumps in the field will put up seed stalks. Seed saving from early varieties (which rarely overwinter outdoors) is best accomplished by having them head up in early fall, protecting the plants over the winter, and setting them out again in spring. In Denmark, where winters are too frosty for reliable overwintering, mature plants are sometimes buried under a few inches of soil hilled up over them in October and then exposed in spring to make seed. Before virtually all of the world's cabbage seed was grown in the Skagit Valley, local eastern varieties were produced by digging whole plants, roots and all, keeping them over the winter in root cellars, and transplanting them outdoors when the soil thawed.

Varieties Like other sorts of brassicas, hybrid cabbage varieties have largely replaced the old standard open-pollinated sorts. The remaining early open-pollinated varieties are either pointed-head sorts, such as the Jersey Wakefield, or Golden Acre types, which are small, green, round-headed cabbages, usually with pale yellow-white centers. Hybrid early varieties change fashion so rapidly there's not much point in listing and rating those currently available. When buying early hybrids, look for types that promise to hold in the field without bursting. Beware of the many market early varieties selected primarily for density (Stonehead: does it ever look good—heavy as a rock, round, and as uniform as peas in a pod—and tough as cardboard) and those bred for highest yield per acre (which are likely to be watery and bland).

The savoy cabbage, with thin, crinkly leaves, makes superior salads and slaws and doesn't do badly when cooked or made into sauerkraut— it's far better suited to garden use than the typical market sort. Savoy King is tender and a perennial favorite, though not late enough nor hardy enough to hold all winter.

Red cabbages can be either early or late sorts. The early types won't hold long in the autumn. The late reds can be extremely durable and hold all winter but will be pretty tough chewing.

If you like green supermarket-type cabbage, choosing the right variety for late maturity can be tricky. The English and Dutch have bred smaller, very late, supermarket-sized hybrids that are well protected by wrapper leaves so the interior heads retain good appearance when cut for market after being held in the field for several months (TSC, WCO, T&M). All of these sorts tend to be a bit tough and fibrous—as they must be to withstand frost and contrary conditions. Some varieties, called "storage cabbage" or "wintergreen" by the Dutch, are intended for overwintered storage under climate-controlled conditions similar to those used to keep apples. Stokes sells many of these. When making choices among these sorts, buy the latest maturities available and look for long field-holding ability.

Many seed companies sell special varieties of cabbage for making sauerkraut. Some are poor for home use because they've been bred for the American taste—which means tough enough to withstand boiling and canning after being sliced very thin and fermented—but canning kraut is not necessary when making it at home. The Dutch have bred better sorts for at-home kraut. In fact, decent kraut can be made from any sort of cabbage.

In my opinion, freshly made kraut, eaten before it gets completely sour (and mushy), is far superior to canned; in our region, we can make fresh sour cabbage in small quantities most of the year. Few people realize that sauerkraut is an extremely healthy food when made without salt. All salt does is conveniently wilt the leaves and release the water they contain. If the cabbage is pounded thoroughly with a baseball bat in a 5-gallon bucket before it is crocked and weighted, its juice is rapidly released and the cabbage ferments well. Please try salt-free sauerkraut! Those addicted to salt can add a tiny amount when it is eaten.

For late salads and slaws, European savoys are tougher and hardier; Japanese savoys (like Savoy King) are tender, sweeter, and slightly less hardy. The "late" hybrid savoys you find from Stokes are actually midseason types in the European market; they are tough compared to Savoy King, and not much hardier. For very late savoy cabbage, only Territorial, West Coast, and Thompson & Morgan offer the same slow-growing, superhardy selections used in England for cutting after New Year's. Try January King and Wivoy.

Territorial, West Coast, and Thompson & Morgan are sources for overwintering spring cabbage.

Dry-gardening Winter varieties can be grown like kale.

CHINESE CABBAGE

(Brassica rapa pekinensis, B. rapa chinensis)

In our region, Chinese cabbage is not an easy garden crop at any time of year. Like mustard, its close relative, Chinese cabbage is an annual with a strong tendency to bolt if it experiences increasing day length. Getting it to head in spring before bolting is impossible. Chinese cabbage also bolts readily in summer and fall; it must enlarge rapidly without growth checks if a quality head is to form before seed stalks

begin emerging and before root maggot predation ruins them.

Culture Chinese cabbage requires airy soil that provides high nutrient levels and lots of moisture. Heavy soils must be well amended with thoroughly finished compost. Light soils aren't so fussy. Broadcast and work in the usual amount of complete organic fertilizer. Sow the strongly germinating seeds about one per inch, ½ inch deep, in rows 24 inches apart. As soon as they emerge, side-dress with more fertilizer, about ½ cup per 4 row-feet. Thin seedlings gradually without permitting any crowding, so the plants stand 18 inches apart in the row by the time they're 5 or 6 inches in diameter. Do not try transplanting; Chinese cabbage does much better if its taproot remains intact. Keep the plants well watered; they have very shallow feeder roots and must make very rapid growth to head successfully. Be prepared to side-dress a second time more heavily than the first if growth slows down at all.

Garden planning Early varieties are bred for summer harvest. At best they barely head before bolting. Late varieties, if they grow very rapidly, may stand a month in cooler weather before putting up a seed stalk. Four to six good-sized heads will make a gallon of kimchi, a Korean-style sauerkraut made with hot peppers, garlic, and Chinese cabbage.

Insects and diseases Small gray slugs don't damage the heads, though they do like living in them. Root maggots attack in an unusual way: Instead of invading only the roots, they also tunnel through the bases of the leaves, frequently cutting through the vascular system, which collapses the leaves and causes the head to rot. Some varieties seem to handle maggot infestations better than others; you can always trim off the bottoms of the outer leaves. During the last three weeks of growth, while the heads are forming fast, spraying every few days with rotenone/pyrethrum, making an attempt to get the spray into the head itself, will greatly reduce maggot problems, as may heavy inoculation with predatory nematodes a few weeks after the seeds are sown.

Flea beetles may also chew the leaves badly, slowing the overall increase of the plant. Since the "bolting clock" is ticking away and the plant must be forced to grow as fast as possible, this is one species for which it makes sense to spray flea beetles. Instead of constantly dosing the crop, the organic gardener who is in earnest about growing Chinese cabbage might consider putting the crop under a spun-polyester cloche as soon as the seedlings are thinned to their final spacing, solving both the flea beetle and root maggot problems with one treatment.

Harvest Heads must be cut promptly before they bolt or are overly damaged by root maggots. Bolted heads put up delicious flower stalks excellent in stir-fries and winter salads if cut before the flowers open.

Saving seed As far as I know, there are no longer any reliable open-pollinated strains available, and the seed-making process starts too late in the North to grow seed from plants that have already headed. Chinese cabbage is insect-pollinated, will cross with mustards and turnips, and requires a mile of isolation for reasonable purity.

Varieties High-quality commercial hybrid varieties sold in North America originate from Japanese or Taiwanese seed companies. The hybrids offered change fashion so rapidly that, as with early ballhead market cabbage, there's little point in describing the varieties being sold in 1999. Stokes, Johnny's, West Coast, and Territorial are all reputable sources that do trials and keep up with changes in the market. Early varieties can be sown after May but tend to make small heads; the late types make big yields but must not be sown before mid-July. Sow too late, however, and the plant will not head by fall. I've found August 1 to be about the last workable sowing date.

Dry-gardening Impossible. This delicate species needs the highest possible moisture levels at all times.

CAULIFLOWER (*Brassica oleracea botrytis*)

It took me many years to learn how to grow cauliflower reliably. I made the effort with this difficult vegetable because I especially love to eat it raw dipped into mayonnaise flavored with curry and ginger powders. Really fresh garden cauliflower is much sweeter than that from a supermarket cooler.

Growing cauliflower is a lot like growing Chinese cabbage. Except for very late and overwintering varieties, it must be propelled into the most rapid possible growth from the start, and nothing should slow it down. If a cauliflower has its growth stopped or checked, the plant likely will not form a decent curd later on. If you use garden-store transplants, make sure they aren't pot-bound; set out homegrown seedlings promptly. Because transplants are frequently shocked when set out, I've come to feel it is much easier to direct-seed cauliflower—in fact, when direct-seeded, it becomes a fairly easy-to-grow vegetable if the correct varieties are used.

Culture Cauliflower is grown like a very delicate and very "hungry" cabbage. In spring, sow or transplant a few weeks later than you would for more hardy brassicas. Set out the first transplants in early April; do the earliest outdoor direct-seeding on about April 1; the last sowing of fall-harvested varieties must go in around July 15. Space cauliflower 24 inches apart. Side-dress the plants when they're about 8 inches tall.

Like broccoli, the size of the flower depends on how large the plant has become when it has grown the requisite number of leaves to bloom. If the plant has become big and husky at flowering time, the curd will be, too. If the plant is smallish, the curd will be small and often bitter. If growth was significantly checked, the plant may "button" and produce a tiny curd no matter how big the plant.

Overwintering cauliflower is much easier to grow. The big risk is not a lack of grower skill, but how cold the winter will be. Sow about August 1 and grow like Purple Sprouting broccoli. In spring it demands slightly more side-dressed fertilizer than overwintering broccoli. The 8- to 12-inch tall plants can survive temperatures below 10°F (sometimes below 6°F if they're healthy and tough when summer ends). In spring, as soon as growth resumes (probably mid-February), side-dress each overwintered plant with a tablespoonful of blood meal sprinkled atop the feeder roots and, additionally, scatter a bit of complete organic fertilizer around the plants as you eliminate the weeds.

Garden planning The maritime Northwest has a good climate for a long supply of cauliflower. The harvest begins with overwintered curds in April and May; the earliest spring transplants can be cut in June; direct-seeded varieties are harvested from late June through November and into December during mild winters. Cauliflower has been bred to mature uniformly, so (as with broccoli) sow and grow several varieties with different maturities to permit weeks of cutting from a single sowing date. Overwintered cauliflower is cut at a time when there's not much else going in the garden, so I start about 25 plants of mixed varieties each August.

Insects and diseases Cauliflowers have delicate root systems, easily ruined by the root maggot. Especially delicate are the early varieties, which have to contend with both the worst maggot infestations and the most intense sunlight. Early sowings can be adequately protected from the cabbage root maggot by sawdust collars or parasitic nematodes; direct-seeding works better than transplants because the plants develop huskier root systems. In my garden, later sowings usually grow fine without protection.

Harvest Cut when the curds are just beginning to become "ricey," or separate a bit. This is a trifle later than when commercial crops are cut, but it results in much larger yields. Once the curd starts forming, check the plant almost daily, because it can go from being a nubbin to overblown in a week to ten days. The old varieties used to need blanching, which involved tying the wrapper leaves tightly around the forming curd to protect it from sun. (If the curd gets too much light, its color changes from white to yellowish.) The newer varieties are mostly self-blanching, with large inner leaves that naturally wrap the curd. Sometimes, if I notice that the forming curd is becoming exposed to light, I bend one or two large outer leaves over the curd and snap the central rib to make it lie flat atop the curd.

Saving seed Regular types aren't hardy enough to overwinter this far north. Seed from overwintered cauliflower (which is still mainly open-pollinated) is easily produced here—in fact, it is being grown in the Skagit for Dutch seed companies. Simply permit the finest plants to form seed like any other overwintered brassica.

Varieties Hybrids have now become the industry standard for summer and autumn varieties; only a few open-pollinated sorts are still carefully selected. As with other commercial brassicas, varieties fall in and out of favor so rapidly that there's not much point in suggesting specific ones. Instead, I recommend dealing with quality mail-order suppliers. Do not use cheap seed or you'll grow a lot of bushy green plants without anything much edible for all your effort. Overwintering varieties can be obtained from Territorial, West Coast, and Thompson & Morgan.

"Purple cauliflower" is actually a cauliflower/broccoli cross; it tastes more like broccoli but looks like cauliflower.

Dry-gardening Possible with overwintered varieties with a bit of irrigation and some extra work. Start a few dozen seedlings in a well-watered nursery bed during August and transplant out when the rains come back, or start them in mid-September in a nursery bed, thin to about 12- by 12-inch centers, cover the bed with a cloche in November, grow under a cloche over the winter, and transplant them the very moment in spring that growth resumes, which will probably be early in February.

COLLARDS (*Brassica oleracea capitata*)

Collard greens, called cabbage greens or coleworts in England, are a vigorously growing nonheading sort of cooking cabbage, used for winter harvest. They're grown like kale. Vates is hardier than Georgia. Johnny's has a new Vates selection called Champion, produced and bred in the Skagit Valley.

KALE (*Brassica oleracea acephala, B. napus pabularia*)

Kale, the most vigorous and easiest-to-grow garden brassica, is similar to wild cabbage. The leaves and petioles of most varieties are usually cooked but may be salad quality if cut finely and if they don't dominate the salad. Kale develops more sweetness after some hard frosts but may quickly become tough if not used shortly after cutting. Consequently, the supermarket product from California is doubly inferior.

Culture Grow like Purple Sprouting broccoli. In midsummer, sow a pinch of four of five seeds ½ inch deep on 24-inch centers. Broadcasting some fertilizer into the bed before sowing, keeping the plants watered, and thinning and weeding carefully is more than adequate pampering. If the plants are on a 24-inch spacing and don't bump by November, your soil is quite infertile.

Garden planning Kale is more nutritious by far than cabbage; its dark green leaves are full of high-protein chlorophyll. With each passing year, the garden better educates my dietary habits; I now more enjoy chewy, strong-flavored kale in my salads and less enjoy tender, mild-tasting cabbage. Kale is also a lot easier to grow than cabbage. New gardeners might start with one or two plants. I grow a dozen.

Insects and diseases I've had no problems in my garden.

Harvest Cut individual leaves as needed; the smaller ones are more tender and milder in flavor. Plants don't grow much after mid-November, but spring regrowth starts early. On *B. oleracea* varieties, a lot of that new spring growth will be small side leaves, like Brussels sprouts that aren't making heads. These are especially delicious. A light side-dressing of blood meal in mid-February will produce a lot more spring leaf. The flower stalks make good

"broccoli," though they don't have a broccoli flavor; they appear at the same time Purple Sprouting broccoli is in bloom.

Saving seed Grow plants for seed as you would any other biennial brassica. However, Siberian kales (*B. napa*) cross only with rutabaga; *B. oleracea* varieties, which grow a tall central stalk and are often called Scottish kale, cross freely with other members of the cabbage family.

Varieties Since there's little commercial market for kale in North America, much seed found in catalogs and on seed racks is intended for the home-garden trade—usually called Blue or Green Curled Scotch. There's nothing wrong with these varieties; in fact, they're locally well adapted, having been produced in the Skagit Valley through overwintering. More refined and hardier varieties, often hybrid, come from Holland and England, where kale is a popular market crop. I prefer Winterbor, along with Siberian and Red Russian—a red Siberian.

Dry-gardening Sow before June 1; start little clusters of seeds 3 to 4 feet apart with 5 feet of space between rows. Thin to one plant and weed carefully. Fertigate as often as possible or not at all. If given 5 gallons every four weeks through summer and side-dressed when the rains start, your plants may get enormous—5 feet in diameter and 4 feet tall.

KOHLRABI *(Brassica oleracea caulorapa)*
This peculiar brassica has been grotesqued into

making a sweet-flavored and tender turniplike vegetable, entirely without the characteristic harshness or pungency of the turnip. Kohlrabi is excellent raw. The edible part is held above the soil, where it is impervious to the root maggot.

Culture In hot weather, kohlrabi becomes woody very rapidly, so plan for harvest before mid-June or after the end of September. Sow in April for June harvest and again in mid-July through mid-August for an extended autumn harvest. Sow seeds two per inch, ½ inch deep, in rows 18 inches apart. Thin very carefully as the seedlings become established, so the bulbs stand 3 to 4 inches apart in the row; crowded kohlrabi fails to bulb well. Side-dressing with a little extra fertilizer, in addition to broadcasting it into the beds, makes faster growth and sweeter, more tender bulbs.

Garden planning Because spring sowings mature quickly and won't hold long without losing their good culinary qualities, small sowings are appropriate at that time. If you're a real admirer of the vegetable, consider making the first sowing in a frame in March, with subsequent small sowings every two weeks through April. Fall crops can stand in the field for some time and retain good eating quality, especially if first-class varieties are used and given space to keep growing. I sow more than 50 square feet for fall harvest.

Insects and diseases Fancy kohlrabi varieties tend to have weak root systems; if maggots are thick in spring, it may have trouble. Fortunately, mild infestations affect only the root system, leaving the bulbs untouched—a big advantage over turnips or radishes.

Harvest Keep them growing. If they get crowded, growth slows and the bulbs get woody faster. If you thin out and eat every other plant while supplying lots of water, they'll stay edible longer.

Saving seed Kohlrabi is not as hardy as other biennial brassicas, though it will overwinter in milder years. Hilling up soil over the bulbs (but not the leaves) in November will get them through even a severe winter. A very refined brassica, kohlrabi takes careful selection to prevent a good percentage of the plants from being worthless.

Varieties Cheap U.S.-grown varieties are produced strictly for the home garden trade and contain a high percentage of plants that fail to make decent bulbs. They're usually called Purple Vienna or White Vienna. The popular and high-quality Japanese hybrid, Grand Duke, is not so well adapted to our northern latitudes; Winner FI is much better. There's no significant eating difference between purple- and green-skinned types. I'd buy my seed from a quality supplier to be sure of getting the best European selections. Superschmeltz is a remarkable Swiss variety, a giant kohlrabi that, when grown for autumn harvest, holds good culinary qualities through the entire winter, as it gets ever larger. Space Superschmeltz as though growing medium-sized cabbages—2 feet apart in rows 4 feet apart.

Dry-gardening Try starting Superschmeltz in mid-June, spaced 3 feet apart in rows 5 feet apart. Fertigate at least once a month. You'll get kohlrabi, each one of which is the size of a giant cabbage, that will be good eating into the winter. They don't start getting woody unless they can't grow any more.

RUTABAGAS *(Brassica napus rapifera)*

There are a multitude of reasons to put a big rutabaga patch in a self-sufficient garden. Rutabagas, or Swedish turnips, hold in the soil all winter. They're easy to grow and are as vigorous as kale. They resist damage by brassica pests. Rutabagas produce amazing yields of flavorful roots that are less starchy, and nearly as satisfying, as the potato. And certain home-garden varieties have a wonderful sweet flavor far superior to the supermarket stuff.

Culture Highly vigorous, rutabagas usually grow well enough in soils that have had recent additions of manure or compost: however, broadcasting fertilizer into the bed before sowing plus normal garden practice (thin, weed, water) will ensure a big crop. Sow the seed during July, before mid-month. Sprinkle it thinly in ½-inch-deep furrows, the rows 24 to 36 inches apart, depending on how big you want the rutabagas to get. Thin gradually to 8 inches to a foot apart in the row. Careful thinning is essential; crowded rutabagas don't form big roots. If you want them big *and* would prefer to not water them too frequently, space them 18 inches apart in rows 4 to 5 feet apart.

Garden planning Rutabagas yield abundantly. A true fancier or someone really trying for winter self-sufficiency might try a 100-square-foot bed for starters. When the crop is done, the bed is a good place for spring peas or lettuce; rutabagas grow very well when they follow a pea crop or fava bean green manure.

Insects and diseases In my garden, the root maggot seems relatively uninterested in rutabagas. Although it sometimes tunnels through the skin, it rarely goes into the bulb. Slugs like to dig cavities; so do mice in wintertime. Then the bulbs rot. Those with even less pleasant experiences might consider digging the crop and storing it in the garage or root cellar, as was traditionally done in the North.

Harvest In mild, coastal Douglas County, Oregon, with no special handling whatsoever, the roots hold in the field in acceptable condition until March, when they start going to seed. Most damage from insects and other critters is minor and can be peeled away. If your winter often turns freezing cold, even for only a few short days, the roots, which sit mostly on top of the ground, may freeze solid and then rot afterward if not protected. So during November, consider covering the bed with flakes of straw, or perhaps better, burying the roots under 3 inches or so of soil or compost. This is enough protection to get past a three- to five-day cold snap of 10°F weather. Commercial storage (and home storage in the East) is done in cellars. Rutabagas in storage keep better if they're washed and then coated with paraffin before storage. The waxy coating peels off with the skin.

Saving seed After overwintering, rutabagas go to seed like other biennial brassicas. Rutabagas cross with Siberian kales.

Varieties Most Purple Top or Laurentian selections available in American seed catalogs will produce decent roots. Check out Thompson & Morgan, a company primarily supplying the British home gardener, where rutabagas are a major winter crop and are called Swedes or Swedish turnips. Stokes used to carry a dozen varieties but no longer. I guess Swedes are no longer as popular with increasingly properous Canadian householders. Territorial has Marion, a good-eating, clubroot-resistant variety; Johnny's has York, another unique variety.

Dry-gardening I speculate that dry-gardened Swedes might work around Puget Sound if you could get the seed to germinate (by using fluid drilling, described in Chapter 6) in mid-July. If the area for them was kept scrupulously bare of all vegetation since April and was fertilized in March, enough soil moisture will remain to grow a crop, while the fertility will have been leached into the root zone. I'd make a furrow deep enough to find that moist soil (4 to 5 inches if necessary in a dry summer), and sow the presprouted seed there.

TURNIPS *(Brassica rapa rapifera)*

Turnips are biennial brassicas that behave like radishes (an annual) but require more fertile soil than radishes. In the maritime Northwest, organic turnips are much easier to grow as pot greens than for roots, although sometimes the root maggots leave the gardener a few turnips that have not been completely ruined. See also the description of radishes in the Roots section.

Culture Turnips need fertile, airy soil and plenty of moisture to grow fast enough to outrun the cabbage root maggot. The roots swell amazingly fast if supplied with all the necessaries. If they develop quickly enough, the maggots will have barely hatched out before the roots are plucked from their grasp.

Turnips can be started from April through August. In fertilized soil, below each 5 feet of furrow, band an additional ¼ to ½ cup of complete organic fertilizer. Sow the tiny seed thinly, ½ inch deep, in rows 24 inches apart. When the seedlings are established, thin carefully to 3 inches apart in the row. Water a lot.

Garden planning Because turnips must be harvested promptly in our climate, frequent small sowings are in order. Turnips grow quickly, and they can be followed by other crops.

Insects and diseases Chapter 7 discusses systems for managing root maggots, including nematodes, sawdust mulches, and protective row covers. Flea beetles can slow down growth and give the maggots time to invade; spraying them may be in order if the leaves are becoming badly pin-cushioned.

Harvest Turnips will grow 6 to 8 inches in diameter (like huge rutabagas) if given the space and time, but they are much better picked on the small side, both for milder flavor and less pithy texture, and to avoid the root maggot.

Saving seed Like rutabagas, most turnips are biennial, though less hardy than rutabagas, and may require careful mulching to get over the winter. Some varieties are annual (Crawford and Shogoin) and are spring-sown for seed production. Turnips may cross freely with mustards and Chinese cabbage.

Varieties Purple Top White Globe and its hybrid variants are slightly less attractive to the maggot than the many tasty, milder-flavored, all-white hybrid varieties that originate in Japan. For greens, any variety is edible, but Shogoin was specially bred for this purpose.

Roots

Roots are easy to grow but hard to grow well. To grow biennial roots well (beets, carrots, parsnips, parsley root), you need to appreciate the survival strategy of these plants.

Most root vegetables are biennials that thrust a food-storing taproot farther down than competing annuals can reach—deep into subsoil moisture and nutrient reserves. The subsoil root systems of most root crops can become enormous. Given good conditions, a single carrot will sink a slender, unbranched taproot 3 feet down and then continue down another 3 feet with a wide network of feeder roots that will fill an area of subsoil the size of a 55-gallon drum. Each plant will do this if it can. Beets, parsnips, chicory, burdock, and parsley will do about the same.

Root-crop species intend to dominate relatively infertile soils. For example, wild carrot (Queen Anne's lace) is a nuisance weed in poor pastures; it is smothered out by grasses in rich soil. The basic survival strategy of biennial root crops is, over one season, to slowly bank a large energy reserve in the form of starch or sugar. Then, the following spring, instead of having to grow with the current supply of light, water, and nutrients the way their shallow-rooted competition does, biennials can draw down their savings to outgrow annuals while making seed.

Although their wild relatives are capable of surviving in infertile soil, root crops will not necessarily make succulent food for a lazy gardener. If the soil is soft and friable, and abundant moisture supplies remain available, the storage area swells up uniformly, producing shapely and tasty vegetables. But if the surface layer of soil becomes hard and compacted, or if the plants are densely spaced and the moisture supply fluctuates radically, the tops may look okay, but the edible parts of the plants will develop irregularly and may be tough and bitter. Potatoes and radishes (annual species) are equally sensitive to soil compaction and, especially radishes, to soil moisture levels.

On clayey soils, roots demand deeply dug and especially humusy raised beds. But do not encourage these species with too much fertility or you may see too much top and, at harvest, find too little bottom. Instead, maintain moderate nutrient levels and concentrate on creating loose, moist soil. Softening up clay soils by incorporating massive amounts of manure or compost can also provide too much nitrogen for proper root development. One solution on clay can be to prepare a heavily composted root bed a year in advance, growing highly demanding species there the first year and then using next year's remnants of fertility for root crops. Another solution for root crops grown in clay soil is to bring in a cubic yard or two of sandy loam, creating a special 8-inch-deep bed for carrots, beets, parsley root, and parsnips. A bed like this would also be a good idea for celery and melons; you could work out a rotation especially for this sandy bed.

Early and careful thinning is vital; when crowded, few individuals develop to their potential. Having lots of moisture is also vital, but you can reduce (or virtually eliminate) the need for irrigation by increasing plant spacing. Envision spacing plants so widely that each root can draw up that "barrel" of soil moisture banked in the soil below it.

Hybrid beet and carrot seed is available these days. Although hybridization doesn't seem to increase vigor much, it does produce more uniformity. This is particularly true of carrot varieties, in which hybrids are becoming commercial market standards and the old varieties are deteriorating into home-gardener-only selections.

It is possible to grow biennials (beets, carrots, parsley root or leaf parsley, and parsnips) like "field crops" without any irrigation on loam soils. You must sow early enough that the seed will still sprout, probably by the end of May. Prepare their growing rows a week or two before sowing. With a spade, dig out a shovel-blade-wide trench I foot deep, and neatly pile the soil to the side. To enhance the rapid penetration of taproots, sprinkle I gallon of complete organic fertilizer per 100 row-feet down the bottom of this trench and then, using the spade, thoroughly mix it into the next foot of soil down. It's like double digging without adding all the compost. Then sprinkle another gallon of complete organic fertilizer atop the soil you removed from the trench, so that when the trench is refilled the top foot will also be fertile enough to provoke rapid seedling development. If your soil is a bit on the heavy side, add a bit of compost to the soil going back into the upper part of the trench. Make the rows 42 to 48 inches apart.

Thin carefully; by the time the seedlings are 4 or 5 inches tall, they should stand 4 to 6 inches apart. Keep well weeded through the summer. Starting in mid-July, harvest by thinning every other plant. The remaining roots, standing nearly a foot apart, will grow amazingly large and may well hold in the soil until next spring. In frosty areas, hill up a little soil over the crowns in late October to prevent freezing (and then rotting) should winter turn harsh. Do not use Nantes-type carrots for this; they don't have enough internal fiber to get big without splitting. Early Wonder Tall Top beets, parsnips, and parsley root are also excellent grown this way.

BEETS (Beta vulgaris)

Beets like fertility but are not so fussy about soil type, because the edible part develops at the surface. Nearly any soil type will grow acceptable beets—even clays, as long as they are deep and made permeable—but the finest roots develop in fertile loams. Beets grow best when temperatures are moderate and soils warm, although most varieties can be started earlier. Spells of cold weather or periods of heat-induced moisture stress result in "zoning"—white rings that don't affect the flavor much, though they are of concern to the commercial grower.

Culture

Since beets form on the surface, it is rarely necessary to work the soil deeply when growing them in permanent raised beds. Beets have a low to moderate nutrient requirement; broadcasting and tilling in a gallon of complete organic fertilizer per 100 square feet of bed that received a dose of compost last year is sufficient for a good crop.

Sow from April through July. Make early sowings ½ inch deep; make later ones ¾ inch deep and sow a little more seed. Each beet seed is actually a fruit containing several embryos, but because the germination rate is often low and seed is cheap, it's best to sow two seeds per inch, in rows 18 inches apart. When the seedlings stand about 3 inches tall, thin carefully so the plants stand as far apart as you'll want the diameter of mature roots. For baby beets, that's about 1 inch apart; canners (uniform selections for once-over harvest) should initially be thinned to 3 to 4 inches apart; winter storage varieties can grow 6 inches around. For table use, I always grow Early Wonder, which varies considerably in vigor from seedling to seedling. After thinning Early Wonder to about 2 inches apart, I harvest roots as they enlarge. Smaller, weaker ones will fill in the row spaces as the large beets are pulled.

Garden planning

Home-garden-quality table beet selections harvested by thinning can yield tender (and ever-larger) roots for a long time. I've found that a few rows across a raised bed keep our family in all the table beets we want all summer. For winter use, being (spiritually) a closet Russian and borscht lover, I sow about 50 square feet of bed around July 1.

Insects and diseases

Bean beetles may chew on slow-growing seedlings in spring. The non-spray solution is to plant lots of seed or wait until the soil warms up a bit before starting the beet patch. Leaf miners may attack beets; for organic handling, see Chapter 8.

Harvest

If beets can't keep growing larger, they'll get woody and loose sweetness. Winter-keepers, Early Wonder, and some Detroit selections develop thick, protective skins and hold outdoors from October to March, retaining good eating quality throughout the winter.

Protect overwintering beets with a 2- or 3-inch-thick straw mulch, or hill up some soil over them. If they freeze, they'll rot immediately. In those areas where winters are too severe or mice, slugs, and rain combine to ruin beets left in the garden, they can be dug like potatoes and kept in a cellar, shed, or pumphouse.

Saving seed

Beets are wind-pollinated biennials. Their light pollen can carry a mile or more downwind. Beets also freely cross with chard (which is a beet bred for edible leaves). Since beet seed can easily last four or five years, and since those parts of the region with cool, dry summers produce the world's most vigorous beet seed, you can produce different varieties in alternate years. Harvest seed-roots in early November. Choose ones with small, tight crowns, fine taproots, perfect shape, and deep color. Transplant selected roots to a part of the garden that won't be irrigated next summer. Keep as many leaves intact as possible. Bury each root so that the crown is at the soil line, roots 12 inches apart in rows about 4 feet apart. Then hill several inches of soil over the crown to protect it during winter, leaving the leaves sticking up through the soil. When the worst of winter is past, uncover the crown and wait. The roots will put forth new leaves, and then seed stalks, which bloom and make seed. All the gardener must do is keep the patch clean of weeds, thus reserving all available soil moisture for the beets. When half the seed is dry, cut the stalks and finish drying under cover on a tarp or sheets of newspaper. Strip the seed from the stalks by hand; clean the dusty seed by pouring it between two buckets in a mild breeze. Six plants will produce over a pound of seed. If harsh conditions make outdoor survival of overwintered roots unlikely, root-cellar them like potatoes and plant them outdoors again about March 1.

Varieties Early Wonder is the single best variety for the garden. Most Early Wonder selections have tall, tasty tops and vary in size and vigor from plant to plant so you can harvest a patch over a long time. Early Wonder

types also make better growth in cool weather than most canners, which are usually Detroit types selected for uniformity of size at maturity. The hybrid varieties are mainly Detroit types. "Baby" varieties are bred for dense plantings, making small, perfectly round roots. They are usually very tender and sweet. Cylindrical beets such as Formanova, Cylindra, and Forono are bred for those canneries preferring a shape that can be conveniently sliced into uniform rings. They are also fast-cooking, a trait that saves canneries time and money. Growing deeper into the ground, more like carrots than beets, cylindrical varieties develop better in light soils.

Winterkeepers (often called Lutz) grow very large roots that tend to be irregularly shaped, thick skinned, and very sweet, and are bred especially to hold through the winter in the home garden. They are best sown about July 1 to mature in October. Feel free to experiment with any beet variety, including white, yellow, sugar beet crosses, and monogerm. I've never had a variety-linked failure with beets.

Dry-gardening See the introductory paragraphs to this section for information on dry-gardening with root crops in general.

CARROTS *(Daucus carota sativa)*
Carrots have many potential problems, all of which can be handled without unreasonable effort by anyone who really wants a crop of near-perfect roots.

Culture Carrot seed germinates slowly, often taking twelve to fourteen days to sprout, yet the small seeds must be shallowly sown. The shoots are weak and cannot force their way through crusts, compacted clay, or puddled soil. Plantings started before the heat of summer usually germinate well enough because the soil stays moist and crust free naturally. However, sowings made after mid-May are dicier. To retain moisture and prevent crusting, either rake a bit of sphagnum moss or well-finished compost into the inch of soil atop the carrot bed before sowing or fill the furrow with sifted compost atop the seeds. Either of these techniques will result in very good germination. This technique is also useful for parsnip seed; in fact, it is a good practice for any midsummer sowing.

During the first three to five weeks after sprouting, the seedling puts down a taproot. If that root does not encounter compacted soil, impenetrable clods, or zones of high nitrogen concentration (such as might come from pieces of undecomposed fresh manure or chemical fertilizer granules), it will grow straight without forking or crooking. If the surface 6 to 8 inches of soil then continue to remain fairly soft and the roots don't overly compete with each other or with weeds, the taproot will swell with stored food. To grow decent carrots in heavy soil, spread the bed thickly with ruminant manure or compost and work it in the previous year. If you must increase the organic matter content immediately before sowing, use very old (not rich, not strong) compost.

In all but sandy soil, the bed must be well and deeply fluffed up immediately before sowing carrots. But tilled soil tends to slump back into its native level of compaction within a few weeks of tilling, so it's essential to make the seedlings initially grow very fast—to "outrace" the hardening earth. Once they've made a straight taproot and have started storing food, carrots are able to push much more strongly against gradually compacting soil.

To make sure my carrots do not lack any usable nutrition, I first broadcast about two-thirds of a gallon of complete organic fertilizer over each 100 square feet of bed. Then I deeply break up the soil, using a 12-inch spading fork. I push the fork into the soil to the hilt every 3 or 4 inches, then pull back on the handle to pop the soil loose a foot down. If I could find a 14- or 16-inch spading fork, I'd use that. When one is available, I run a rototiller over the bed several times until it is thoroughly pulverized 8 inches deep. If I did not have a tiller, I'd break up the soil by repetitively turning it over and chopping it with the fork. This may seem like a lot of work, but in finely tilled soil, the carrot yield may be two or three times higher. Besides all this tilling, growing carrots takes a lot of picky, time-consuming thinning. Still, you'll harvest more carrots per unit of effort expended if you take the trouble to do it right.

In early April, in order to have *some* new, fresh carrots as soon as possible, I usually start a small patch of Nantes types in roughly worked soil, even though the majority of these won't develop properly. But I wait until the soil has dried out to exactly the ideal tilling point before making serious sowings—usually at about the same time I start beans, unless we're gifted with a sunny spring. A last sowing before July 10 still has enough growing time in front of it to yield big roots before autumn checks further development. Sow in furrows ½ inch deep, and seed thinly, two seeds per inch. Make the rows about 18 inches apart across raised beds. In hot weather, cover the seed with sifted compost or aged sifted manure. Thin gradually but carefully and thoroughly, so that by the time the seedlings stand 2 to 3 inches tall, they're as far apart in the row as the mature roots will be in diameter—generally about 1 to 1½ inches apart. Keep the bed weeded carefully. Sudden increases in soil moisture after periods of moisture stress can cause many varieties (especially those with less fiber, the more tender kinds) to split and then rot.

When carrot seed is sprinkled into the furrow by hand, the almost inevitable result is a tangle of crowded seedlings. This makes for unnecessarily time-consuming and painstaking work; it can easily take over an hour to correct an overseeded 100-square-foot raised bed. No matter how long it takes, thinning carrots is well worth the trouble, but let me suggest a shortcut. Depending on the size of the seed and its germination percentage, a heaping ¼ teaspoon of carrot seed can uniformly sow 25 to 50 row-feet to more or less the correct density. Instead of trying to distribute that tiny pinch of seed by hand, thoroughly mix the seed into about a gallon of finely sifted compost, and then distribute the mixture equally along the bottom of the furrow. Cover the seed with a little more sifted compost. The result will be a very high germination percentage and uniformly spaced seedlings that require very little thinning.

Garden planning One well-grown, 100-square-foot bed of carrots sown in spring (about 50 row-feet) keeps my family supplied through summer and fall. One more sown about July 1 finishes sizing up in October and is consumed during winter. If I wanted to juice carrots, I'd grow five times that amount.

Insects and diseases Rust fly maggots and wireworms burrow into carrots, causing rot and leaving a bad flavor around their tracks. Chapter 8 discusses how to handle maggots. I cannot offer any remedy for wireworm damage, except to comment that it is minor in my garden (although it does increase through winter the longer the roots are in the soil). The occasional "trail" can be cut away before the carrot is eaten. If damage is too severe, consider digging your carrots in late October and storing them in a root cellar. The traditional method is to fill a barrel with alternating layers of carrots and damp, coarse sand.

Harvest Carrots hold all winter in the ground without serious damage in my garden. At frosty Lorane, Oregon, I covered the carrots with a few inches of straw in November to protect the crowns from freezing in the event of a severe cold snap. (If they freeze, they'll rot.) Covering the mulch with a sheet of plastic increases the protection by keeping the bed dry, but may make a haven for field mice that eat the roots. Covering with soil also works and is much less inviting to mice.

Saving seed Carrot flowers are bee-pollinated and need isolation of 1 mile to grow fairly pure seed. It would be easy to grow strong seed in our climate but for the presence of wild carrots everywhere. Wild carrot crosses result in whitish, dry, fibrous roots with little sweetness. Tim Peters, a talented amateur plant breeder who has lived for decades around Myrtle Creek, Oregon, says he has grown high-quality carrot seed by transplanting carefully selected roots 12 inches by 24 inches apart in March, covering the seed plants with a 5-foot-tall screened box to keep out all insects, and locating the carrot bed where there is an active ant hill. The ants pollinate enough flowers for a decent seed yield.

Varieties Almost any variety of carrot will grow in our climate. The long Imperator types preferred by the supermarket trade require deep, coarse-textured soils to develop well-shaped roots. Imperators were developed strictly for looks and other commercial considerations and don't make good garden carrots, in my opinion. Cylindrical-shaped Nantes varieties have the highest sugar content and are best for earlier sowings and summer eating; they also have the lowest fiber content and so are tender. But without strong fiber, the Nantes tend to split easily when large, and they don't stand up to winter too well. Danvers types (or Flakkee types, as the Europeans call them) make pointed roots 6 to 7 inches long with higher fiber content that hold well in the ground during winter. These are what I sow in July. The short, broad Chantenay varieties develop better in clayey soils than any other sort. Thompson & Morgan also offers an Autumn King variety—

huge carrots bred expressly for in-the-ground winter storage. I don't like the coarse, horse-treat flavor of Autumn King types. Flavor and tenderness vary greatly with variety, so you should experiment.

On the Continent, the old names like Flakkee and Nantes are disappearing, as European primary growers increasingly compete with proprietary patented or hybrid varieties whose appellations do not evoke anything reminiscent of Nantes or Amsterdam Forcing. Buy winter storage carrots from Territorial, Thompson & Morgan, or West Coast.

BELGIAN ENDIVE *(Cichorium intybus)*

All of the various forms of chicory are biennials used for their edible tops. They grow in relatively infertile soils. There are great differences between varieties. Some grow like lettuce and are cut for salad greens; some must go dormant and regrow in spring before the leaves lose enough bitterness to be edible. The most refined types are dug in fall when the tops die back and the plants are then forced to resprout under controlled conditions, making Belgian endive, a very pricey gourmet specialty.

Culture Belgian endive roots are sown in June or early July for fall and winter harvest and are very easy to grow. Plant seeds ½ inch deep in rows 18 inches apart; thin gradually to 8 to 12 inches apart in the row. Fertilizer is not usually needed in garden soil. However, roots should be carefully thinned, grown with all the formalities required for premium carrots. Thin carefully to 6 to 8 inches apart. Overly dense stands produce too-small roots.

Stands spaced too loosely produce overly thick, coarse roots. Excessive nitrogen makes plants too leafy, with thick crowns, undesirable for forcing.

Ideally, roots should be 6 to 8 inches long when mature. The roots are dug from September to December and will last in cold storage until spring. If the tops are still green at harvest, dig the roots and lay them in rows outside for several days; then cut off the tops, leaving about a ½ inch of stalk above the shoulder to avoid damaging the growing point.

Take the roots from cold storage, trim them minimally at the bottom so the upright crowns are all on one level, and pack them tightly into a wooden box about 16 inches deep. Fill the spaces between them with fine, slightly moist, light soil. Then cover the crowns with 8 more inches of fine soil. To retain moisture, cover the soil with straw. Commercial growers heat the box to 65°F (precisely) to force the *chicons* to sprout. Lower sprouting temperatures make the process too slow for the profit-conscious; higher temperatures make tough, bitter heads. At home, a big wooden box in an unheated room in the low 60s would probably be adequate. In about three weeks, Belgian endive is ready for harvest.

Garden planning This is not a vegetable most average gardeners are going to want to devote much space to, unless they adore Belgian endive.

Insects and diseases None known to me yet.

Saving seed Same as endive.

Varieties As North Americans become increasingly interested in this vegetable, more and more European selections appear in our seed catalogs. However, Thompson & Morgan may be best. There are huge differences in the uniformity of selections.

Dry-gardening As suitable for dry-gardening as carrots and grown just like them.

PARSLEY & PARSLEY ROOT

(Petroselinum crispum)

Most people unnecessarily buy parsley transplants. This salad garnish is easy to direct-seed if it's started early. And most people do not know that the best aspect of parsley may not be the leaf but its delicious edible root.

Culture Parsley seed germinates slowly, best under cooler conditions. If sown in April, naturally cool, damp soils enhance germination without attention from the gardener, but if sown in May, germinating parsley must be guarded against drying out for nearly three weeks. Once sprouted, however, parsley is a vigorous grower and highly drought-resistant.

To grow leaf parsley: In April, sow seed thinly, ½ inch deep, in rows 18 inches apart. Thin gradually to 2 or 3 inches apart in the row. If leaf production falters, side-dress with fertilizer and/or irrigate.

To grow root parsley: Culture like carrots, taking extra pains to work the soil deeply, and thin to 3 inches apart in the row. It's best to sow in May, so the soil will be workable to excellent friability, and then do whatever is necessary to get the seed to sprout; I recommend presprout-ing before sowing. Parsley root is less tolerant of heavy soil than most types of carrot but more tolerant than parsnip.

Garden planning One 4-foot row of leaf parsley across a raised bed sown in April produces all the garnishes and seasonings we can use from July until the next spring. Root parsley is similar in flavor to parsnips, although it grows somewhat better in heavier or shallower soil than parsnips will tolerate. Root parsley also holds in the ground all winter.

Insects and diseases None known.

Harvest Snip leaves as needed. In mild winters, the leaves are available all winter; in colder areas, they die back. If mulched so the crowns don't freeze, leaf parsley will resprout in spring for a second short round of cutting before flowering. Dig root parsley from September to March. Cover the roots with a few inches of soil to prevent freezing.

Saving seed Parsley is an insect-pollinated biennial, grown like carrots for a seed crop. Leaf varieties do not require digging, selection, and replanting, because there is little reason to be concerned about root shape or other minor variations. Overwinter the plants and allow them to make seed. Seed for root varieties should be grown only from carefully hand-selected roots, dug in October and replanted like carrots.

Varieties I've done critical varietal trials and have found that there are subtle flavor differences among curly-leaf varieties. Some have longer stems; some are more or less curled. Be a parsley gourmet if you wish. Flat-leaf or "plain" types are more flavorful, good for drying into flakes or for cooking. Buyer beware: The root varieties offered in North American seed catalogs might be high-quality, uniform European selections (where parsley root is a commercial crop) or cheap stuff grown for the domestic garden seed trade without careful selection. Most root varieties are fairly long and need deeply worked soil.

Dry-gardening Grow like carrots.

PARSNIPS (*Pastinaca sativa*)

Very similar to carrots in habit, parsnips are much more prone to hairiness in strong soils than carrots are, and demand deep, loose beds if well-formed, straight roots are to be produced.

Culture Work the bed deeply and finely with a spading fork—to 12 inches at least. Fertilize the bed only if the soil is very poor, and then use only half as much as you would for any other crop. If you add compost, make sure it is mellow—has been well-ripened. Sow the seeds from May through mid-July. Early sowings sprout more easily but produce overly large roots; July sowings produce supermarket-sized, slightly better keepers, but germination is touchy in hot weather.

Sow seeds ¾ inch deep, three or four seeds per inch, in rows 18 inches apart. In hot weather, cover the seeds with sifted organic matter and keep moist until sprouted. Thin the seedlings carefully: Space early sowings at least 4 inches apart; thin July sowings to about 2 inches.

Garden planning Early sowings mature in summer and may keep getting bigger if you gently and delicately dig every other root while avoiding breaking the taproot of those remaining in the row. July sowings mature in fall. Either way the roots will probably hold in the soil all winter.

Insects and diseases Parsnips seem invulnerable to everything except field mice, who prefer its sweet roots to carrots.

Harvest Protect the crowns from freezing by hilling up a little soil over them or layering some straw over the bed. Dig as wanted until spring, when they resprout. Parsnip leaves taste like tough celery and in small quantities will round out winter salads.

Saving seed Treat like carrots. Dig and replant a dozen or two carefully selected roots. The seed tends to shatter easily when ripe, something like dill, so harvest promptly and dry fully under cover. Parsnip seed tends to be short-lived, lasting at best two years with high vigor. It also tends to have a low germination rate.

Varieties The U.S. commercial market for parsnips is not large, and most garden seed is rather raggedy. To grow uniform crops, look for seed that is represented to be grown from painstakingly hand-selected roots. Caveat emptor. Here's one vegetable you should really consider growing your own seed for.

Dry-gardening Treat like carrots.

POTATOES *(Solanum tuberosum)*

Potatoes are solanums, like tomatoes, but they demand far less in the way of nutrients than the other solanums, and they prefer cool weather. Soil texture is as critical for their development as it is for carrots. For all these reasons, potatoes find their home in the root "family."

You might not think that potatoes, being so inexpensive, are worth the trouble they'll take and the space they'll occupy. However, not only are homegrown varieties free of sprays and sprout-inhibiting chemicals but, grown without excessive irrigation and without chemical fertilizers, the flavor and nutritional content of your own crop will be far superior to commercial stuff. And there are home garden varieties that make supermarket potatoes taste like a sad excuse for food. Home garden potato varieties are, in fact, a health food that doesn't need to be deep-fried or slathered in butter, sour cream, vinegar, salt, pepper, or ketchup. They won't leave a bitter taste in your mouth.

Culture The spud grower's most important concern is maintaining loose soil around the forming tubers so they can expand easily and prolifically. Commercially, potatoes are raised in types of loam that will stay loose after planting, while everything after planting is done with the intention of avoiding soil compaction. Home gardeners can easily apply even more effective anticompaction practices that would be commercially unaffordable.

I am well aware that home gardeners grow

spuds in old barrels, in rubber tire stacks, in raised beds, under mulch, and in trenches that are filled up with various things as the vines grow. I have tried most of these ways. Some of these methods only appear to work well because the potato is so prolific and so easy to grow anyway that it will make some yield under almost any circumstance. Sometimes an unusual method may be a really good solution for someone. And some gardeners get evangelically partisan about their favorite method. But rather than do a poor job trying to describe a great many approaches, and at the risk of slighting the sense of righteousness held by some evangelical potato partisans, I am going to advise only one method, chosen by me after long personal experience, on the basis of pounds harvested for effort expended. However, all the others will work to one extent or another. If you get interested in the spud, whole books have been written on its culture, and every other garden magazine issue contains yet another bit of lore.

When to plant: Potato vines are not frost hardy. If they are frosted, they'll "burn" back to the soil's surface and start growing again. If this happens, the final yield will be reduced because some of the food reserve in the seed will already have been used up making that first set of leaves. So we should avoid planting early when frost is still a danger, except for a ceremony that all potato growers absolutely must perform or risk the wrath of the spirits and the saints. On St. Patrick's Day, March 17, plant a spud or two, even if it's just a few sprouters from last year's harvest, and do this no matter what the weather or soil conditions.

Throw a little fertilizer on the earth, wiggle a few single drops into the mud, and cover them an inch deep with compost or what-have-you.

If you are seriously aiming for early potatoes, gamble on planting a few well-chitted tubers ("chitted" and "single drops" are explained in a few paragraphs) of an early variety two weeks before the earliest possible last frost date. If you are *really* aiming for the earliest possible potatoes, plant a chitted early variety under a clear-plastic (or spun-fiber) tunnel cloche about five or six weeks before the last usual frost date, and be prepared to remove the cloche a few times to hill them up. For this planting you might want to have prepared the soil the previous autumn. Why not bless this gamble by sowing on St. Patrick's Day?

Plant the main crop between May 15 and June 1. Sowing later than this will greatly reduce the yield; sowing earlier, even if frosts don't get them, will tend to make the vines dry out too soon, making it harder to store your crop over the winter. (See the Harvest section.)

Spacing: I do not recommend that home gardeners grow potatoes on raised beds. If you do so, you'll probably end up with too many green tubers and won't harvest nearly as many potatoes as you could. This is because in an already raised bed it is much more difficult to hill up enough loose soil to cover them deeply. Instead, plant the seeds in rows 4 feet apart; drop seeds 1 foot apart in the row.

Preparing the soil: Everything suggested here is done to achieve this result: reasonably open, fertile, moist soil below the growing row and very loose, airy, dryish soil above and around the forming tubers. With almost all varieties, the new tubers form along the lower few inches of growing green vines, just above the seed piece. If you bury the seed in a deep trench and then cover it with soil, the soil atop the seed settles and gets compacted, and yield drops a lot. This also happens if you use raised beds with deep trenches dug down their middle. Instead, I suggest that you barely cover the seed pieces with well-tilled, fertile soil and then gradually hill up a mixture of soil, compost, and decaying vegetation over the growing vines. The covering mix remains loose until harvest time, and the yields are enormous. Digging the potatoes out of this above-ground fluff is also a lot easier. And while hilling up soil, you also keep the area well weeded.

The best place for the potato crop is where a healthy stand of fava beans has overwintered. If you have a rototiller, in mid- to late May till in the favas shallowly, so that much of their stalks still lie exposed. If working by hand, pull the plants or cut them close to ground level; cut the stalks into roughly foot-long pieces with a machete, corn knife, scythe, or sickle; rake them into rough windrows, one windrow between each pair of rows of potatoes; and leave them for later use. Don't worry about the stubble.

If the potatoes are going into a somewhat weedy garden site that went over the winter without an intentional cover crop, don't worry much about getting rid of every weed unless you've got huge clumps of grass forming tough sod; your later cultivation will eliminate weeds. If the potato patch will go where there was sod—and most farmers will tell you that a potato crop is about the finest way possible to get rid of sod and the jillions of weed seeds it leaves behind—start rototilling it in March (if possible) so most of it is gone by May. Or, far easier, spray the grass with Roundup (wear rubber boots) on a windless morning in March so it will be largely decomposed by planting time. Even better, spray or till the previous October.

At planting time, sprinkle complete organic fertilizer in a 12-inch-wide band down each row-to-be. Use 2 gallons per 100 row-feet. Using a long-handled combination shovel or a long-handled spading fork, and/or a narrow rototiller, break up the row, ideally a foot deep and a foot wide if you're willing to work that hard. The row centers will be at least 4 feet apart.

If you have any compost to contribute to the crop, broadcast about a ½-inch layer of it in 1- to 1½-foot-wide bands, a band on each side of the just-worked row. Do not till it in deeply; barely mix it into the top inch of soil. Eventually, all this compost and the soil it is mixed in will be pulled up over the growing vines. Do not bother putting compost as well as complete organic fertilizer into the planting row unless you're working clay. Potato plants are quite tough and will root into fairly solid earth, finding nutrition and water; but they won't make many tubers below the seed piece, whatever you do. Now you're ready to plant.

Seed: Seed potatoes should be more than just potatoes; they should be certified to be virtually virus free. (Certification is explained in a few paragraphs.) The very best seeds are *single drops,* small potatoes weighing about 2 ounces each. Single drops aren't cut. Larger potatoes are usually cut into sections weighing 2 to 4 ounces each prior to planting. Each cut piece must contain at least two eyes. Three eyes might be better. There's a lot of lore about how and when to cut seed. Some do it a week or two before planting and put the pieces out in bright light to both let the cuts heal over and encourage the pieces to begin sprouting. Some treat the cuts with fungicide or other organic rot suppressants. Some feel that fungicide treatment or even time for the cuts to heal is rarely needed, while if the cut seed is left in the air, it may dry out a lot, greatly reducing its vigor. I am of this last school. I believe that if you want to let the just-cut seed "heal," this should be done for no more than 24 hours. And I believe this is an unnecessary bother.

Many times more useful than healing cuts or treating cuts to protect cut seed from rotting is *chitting*. Chitting means encouraging the seed potatoes begin to sprout before they are planted. Chitted seed gets growing right away, long before it has time to begin rotting. Commercial growers can't chit their seed very well because the sprouts are delicate, and once sprouting has initiated, the seed needs gentler handling than machine planting can allow for. You are not planting by machine; you are going to gently plant by hand. You should chit your seed potatoes.

To accomplish this, get the seeds at least three to four weeks before you're going to plant them, and spread them out one layer thick in bright light (not direct sun) where it is cool but not cold (55° to 60°F). They'll begin to turn green, and the shoots will begin growing. At this stage, gently carry the seed to

the garden and plant it. Cut big potatoes just before planting. Do not break off the sprouts! To maximize yield, you want to encourage every possible bit of vine growth to occur before flowering commences.

From the just-tilled row, scoop out a little hollow with your hand, and gently place each seed piece so the top of it is about 1 inch below the soil's surface. Set one piece every 12 inches down the row (or every 18 inches if water will be scarce during the growing season). If the eyes are shooting in a direction, set them so the sprouts are growing up. If the shoots are rather long, be extra gentle and don't break them off. Get them covered, if only a bit under the surface.

Hilling and weeding: In short order the vines will appear and, because of the fertilizer you worked in below them, will grow very rapidly. When they are about 4 inches tall, they should be hilled up for the first time. With an ordinary sharp hoe, stand on one side of the row, reach across it, and scrape up a little soil atop the vines. You can weed between the rows and in the row at the same time. Pull the weed tops up around the vines. If you left fava bean trash between the rows, pull up some of this too and mix it into the soil. If you scattered some compost between the rows, a bit of this will come up too. The loose soil you're hilling up comes from the very surface; it will be fairly dry and filled with organic matter.

About once a week for the first two months, walk the potato rows with a hoe and hill up some more. Never cover the bases of the emerging vines with more than an inch or two of new soil with each hilling. By midsummer the hills should be continuous mounds about a foot high at the top center and about 18 inches wide at the base. The vines should be falling across the mounds and getting into the footpaths between them. The mounds will be so high that you can't easily hill them any more, and the now-prostrate vines will prevent further additions of soil. If you haven't pulled up enough soil by the time the vines fall over and begin covering the paths, some tubers will form on the surface and you'll get a few green potatoes.

From this point, it gets easier. For the rest of the crop cycle, if you see any big weeds showing above the vines, hand-pull them if necessary. Otherwise, to avoid unnecessary soil compaction, admire the crop from a distance.

The crop cycle: First the crop grows vines. Then it begins to make tubers. When tuber formation starts, the vines also begin to bloom. With blooming, new vine growth slows, then ceases. The tubers are gradually filled with starch and other nutritional elements manufactured by the leaves. All things being equal, we get only as much tuber formation as we have enabled the plant to make leaves first. Thus, we have to encourage the young vines to grow as much as possible before blooming. If growth seems a bit slower than you'd like, you can try foliar feeding of the vines from emergence until they begin blossoming. Once vine growth stops, there is little left to do but wait and perhaps irrigate. And perhaps *not* irrigate.

Watering: First, *grow* the vines. The plants should get more than adequate fertility from the complete organic fertilizer in the soil below them. Plants making vegetative growth use lots of water. At this stage, think of your potato crop as being like lettuce. Once tuber formation starts, however, you'll do better to taper off the watering. The consequence will be somewhat smaller potatoes, but they will contain more concentrated nutrition. Being less watery, they'll also have a much richer flavor. Additionally, potatoes that finish dry end up with tougher skins that store much longer.

Garden planning Depending on variety and season, a 100-foot-long row may yield 200 to 300 pounds; 100 row-feet with little or no irrigation on deep soil still yields about 100 pounds.

Insects and diseases Flea beetles may chew on leaves, and their larvae are supposed to damage the tuber's skins, although I've had no noticeable trouble in this respect. Scab is a disease that attacks the potato's skin. Scab decreases storage life, making tough patches that have to be cut away before cooking. This disease is said to be promoted by higher soil pH, and liming is supposed to be verboten in the potato bed. But I've never considered this warning to be significant and have grown potatoes in limed soils without scab.

Virus diseases *are* a serious matter. There are about two dozen of them. Most don't make their presence extremely obvious; you can have disease-riddled potatoes and not know it. The diseases are spread by aphids and transmitted from year to year by the seed potatoes. They don't affect the flavor, only the yield. A lot. Diseased potatoes may yield only a quarter as much as disease-free stock. Each year you carry over your own seed, the number of virus diseases in the seed increases and the yield decreases. You might do all right starting with certified seed the first year and then using your own harvest for seed the next year. After that, however, you'll really pay the price in a lower yield. Considering how much work you'll do to grow your row, it is far cheaper to buy certified virus-free planting seed. (Please disregard the ignorant advice I gave about using your own seed in earlier editions of this book. I did not then understand virus diseases and their implications.)

Harvest Begin digging earliest potatoes after blossoming is over, taking a plant or two at a time as needed. When the vines first begin to deteriorate, withhold all water to dry the soil and toughen the skins, enhancing storage potential. September rain may foil you. Ideally, dig the row when the vines are completely dead and the soil completely dried out. (Obviously, this idealized harvest schedule rarely works in the maritime Northwest.) Keep stored potatoes dark, damp, and cold but protected from freezing. I store my potatoes in buckets or cardboard boxes in the dark pumphouse until March, when they naturally begin to resprout, just in time for the St. Patrick's Day ritual. Ideal storage would be quite humid, the temperature a few degrees above freezing, with good air circulation. Books on root cellaring have lots of information about this subject.

The vines of early-maturing varieties will dry out before September; these sorts tend to resprout a bit in the ground before they are dug and cooled down, and they don't last as long in storage. However, without refrigeration they'll probably keep better if left in the field and dug in October than they will if dug while it is still hot.

Saving seed Although you can save potato seed, you shouldn't unless you start from mini-tubers (explained shortly). Certified seed potatoes for a least a few common varieties can be had cheaply from almost every garden center. If you are interested in experiencing other than the most common varieties, buy your certified seed by mail.

Varieties Garden centers usually offer four choices: a red-skinned type, a tasteless baker, Yellow Finns, and a white, thin-skinned poor keeper (usually White Rose, which is more suited to early crops in the South). I prefer to provide the kitchen with something better than a tasteless ball of starch filled with too much water. Of the commonly available varieties, I suggest tasty Yellow Finns. Sometimes you'll find Nooksack Cascadian, an Idaho-type baker bred to make high starch contents in our climate, and it is prolific. Making enough starch gives the spuds a flaky, dry texture when cooked.

Territorial and Johnny's are now selling seed potatoes. A few of their varieties that I prefer are Red Gold, with flaky, rich yellow flesh inside a red wrapper, and Caribe, a purple-skinned, white-fleshed, very crumbly baker that usually makes huge yields and keeps very well. Kennebec is a good all-purpose spud. Canadians are very fortunate because many varieties of very high-quality certified seed are available to them. They will find Warba, also known as Pinkeye in some places, Bintje, and many others from The Pure Seed Company.

Because of shipping costs and space considerations, Territorial offers certified first-generation mini-tubers that at first glance might seem outrageously expensive. However, when you consider what you're getting, these mini-tubers don't turn out to be a bad deal. To raise ordinary certified seed, the grower starts with virus-free single cells sliced by microsurgery from a growing shoot in a tissue culture lab. These are placed in sterile test tubes and, when they have grown to tiny seedlings, are transferred to an aphid-proof greenhouse or screenhouse to produce the first generation of seeds, called mini-tubers. Mini-tubers are usually the size of a quail's egg but, being perfectly virus-free, are many times more productive than later generations. These are what Territorial is selling.

To produce ordinary seed potatoes, the grower plants the mini-tubers outdoors the next season in regions that are virtually free of both aphids and potato virus diseases, usually in the far North or at high elevations. Then, because second-generation tubers would still be too expensive for commercial seed purposes, this second generation is again increased in the isolated region, making a third generation, still nearly free of virus infection. The general rule is that the earlier the generation of seed is, the less virus infection it carries and the higher the yield will be. To be certified, the seed must still contain very little virus and be no more than four generations away from the tissue culture lab.

When you purchase mini-tubers, you are getting first-generation seed, with the option of using your own seed for a few more generations. Virus infection will become apparent because yield and tuber size will both decreased markedly.

U. S. sources:
Wood Prairie Farm, 49 Kinney Rd., Bridgewater, Maine 04735. www.woodprairie.com

The Pure Seed Company, address below, can ship to the United States only by Canada post—a bit more expensive than UPS.

Canadian sources for certified seed:
Becker's Seed Potatoes, RR 1, Trout Creek, ON P0H 2L0

The Pure Seed Company, Mail Bag 6227, Fort St. John, BC V1J 4H7

Dry-gardening Potatoes originated in the Andes, a very dry, cool mountain climate. They are quite able to forage for water if given elbow room. Once many acres were dry-farmed in parts of the West where yearly rainfall was far less than 20 inches. Without irrigation the yields will be lower. For main-season dry-farmed crops, make the rows 5 feet apart and space the seeds 18 inches apart. Very early varieties that will form tubers before the soil gets too dry might be more densely spaced.

RADISHES (Raphanus sativus)
Radishes need soft, humusy soil and a great deal of water to grow properly, but they have little use for high nutrient levels.

Culture Rapid growth is the single most important aspect of producing quality radishes.

The plants' shallow root systems are poorly adapted to bulbing in heavy soil. Although the species stores a lot of water and can survive in droughty soil, radishes make sweet and tender bulbs only with abundant, ever-present moisture. However, the lighter soils radishes prefer don't hold a lot of moisture reserves. Although most other crops will not suffer overly much until soil moisture drops to 60 percent of capacity, radishes need soil held well above 70 percent of capacity at all times; for really succulent radishes, 80 percent of capacity would be ideal. This can be a problem, but it is easily solved.

Broadcast and work in about a gallon of complete organic fertilizer per 100 square feet of bed, and be prepared to water the radish bed every other day in hot weather. Sow from March through August; spring radishes stay naturally moist, so they may prove most successful, if they escape the maggot. Summer crops may be disappointing in very hot weather no matter how much you water unless you can provide about 50 percent shade from 11 A.M. until 3 P.M.

Sow radish seed ½ inch deep in rows 12 inches apart. The seed is rather large and has a high germination rate; carefully placing one seed per inch is easier than thinning. Radishes will not bulb when crowded. By the time the seedlings are developing a true leaf, they should stand 1 to 2 inches apart.

Garden planning Bulbs will form within a month of sowing and, because of the root maggot, must be harvested immediately. A single sowing should be picked over ten days at most. Radishes are a good crop to sow between rows of other crops; they'll be harvested and gone before the other species begins to need the room. I've found that interplanting between rows of onions tends to deter flea beetles, making for quicker bulbing, which lets me yank the bulbs from the jaws of hungry root maggots in the nick of time.

Insects and diseases Two predators make radishes hard to produce. Flea beetles seem to prefer radishes to most other chow, and they chew so many holes in radish leaves that growth is slowed and root formation is retarded. But slowly grown bulbs become hot and woody. Worse, the slower they grow, the longer the bulbs remain in the soil and the more likely they are to become the prey of the root maggot. When flea beetles are thick, spray every few days with rotenone. Another approach is to use tall-topped varieties, which produce enough leaf area to tolerate some predation. Commercial growers often prefer short tops, which permit closer plant spacing, higher yields, and more profits. Of course, the market gardeners' arsenal includes more potent and longer-lasting pesticides than rotenone.

Maggot infestations can be reduced by harvesting promptly before the fly larvae have a chance to invade, along with a number of other techniques discussed in Chapter 8. Radish crops are a natural candidate for protection under spun fabrics, which handle both flea beetles and cabbage flies simultaneously. Lay the fabrics down carefully about ten days after sowing, after the seedlings have been thinned and weeded.

Harvest Do so promptly! Even if effectively protected from root maggots, the small varieties popular with North Americans rapidly usually become pithy, split, or get hot when allowed to grow too large. Besides the bulb, two other parts of the radish are edible. The tops make acceptable stir-fry or soup greens, especially in spring after one of those rare Arctic winters has wrecked the entire winter garden. The seed pods that form after bolting are also tender, with a mild, radishy flavor if picked before seed formation is too far along. The pods are excellent in salads, and severe maggot infestation does not affect seed pod production.

Saving seed Ordinary radishes are annuals, and seed production is easy. Simply allow early sowings to bolt and make seed. Harvest the stalks when most of the seed has dried out, thresh, and clean. Seed produced this simply is best used for growing edible sprouts. Quality seed production is not so easy if you want your homegrown seed to yield a good percentage of decent bulbs. While you're picking the radishes for the table, select the most ideal roots for seed production. Choose the most perfectly red, round, thin-skinned roots with single fine, hair-like taproots and tight, small crowns. Pinch off half of the (larger) leaves to reduce moisture stress, and transplant the bulbs about 12 inches apart in rows about 24 inches apart. For most varieties, I'd select only one absolutely perfect bulb from a dozen acceptable ones. If I started with junk (home-garden quality) radish seed, I'd be lucky if one plant in five or six even bulbed, much less made a perfectly shaped bulb.

Situate the radish seed patch in a section of the garden where water can be withheld while the seeds are drying. Radish varieties cross freely with one another; varieties must be isolated by ½ mile. Radish seed remains vigorous for up to seven years.

Varieties Most small-bulbed varieties grow well from spring through late summer, unless temperatures are very high during bulb formation, but most have the tendency to become pithy when large. Champion is the best for early spring and late summer sowing because it'll get very large without becoming pithy, but it will not bulb in the long summer days. Red Beret (JSS) is an improved Champion. The novel, multicolored Easter Egg is derived from Champion.

Avoid short-top varieties unless you're prepared to spray for flea beetles frequently. Sora (JSS) is usually perfectly uniform and has rather substantial tops; it may be the best variety available right now. Stokes does a big business supplying commercial radish growers—if in doubt, I'd buy taller-topped varieties from Stokes, stick to their commercial varieties, and believe what the catalog says about planting seasons.

I've had difficulties with White Icicles becoming very hot. Also avoid the larger white Asian radishes. Slow to form, these inevitably are riddled with maggots unless screened or heavily dosed with pesticides. However, I really love Black Spanish, a big, long-keeping, black-skinned, semi-pungent winter radish that I grate with fresh raw onion and slather with olive oil and black pepper. I will fight for Black Spanish, sowing some about August I under very perfectly laid spun fabric and keeping it under that fabric during fall and as long into winter as possible.

Dry-gardening It's not possible to grow radishes by dry-gardening.

Cucurbits

The Cucurbitaceae family consists of annual fruiting vines: cucumbers, melons, pumpkins, and squashes. All are incapable of handling frost and are poorly adapted to cool, damp weather. The family originated from desert plants growing where there was subsoil moisture—many cucurbits still develop deep, water-seeking taproots and for this reason do better when not transplanted, which breaks their taproot. When exposed to high humidity, especially combined with cool weather, cucurbits fall prey to powdery mildew, a parasite that covers their leaves with a whitish "dust," preventing photosynthesis and rapidly killing the plant.

Listed in decreasing order of hardiness, the cucurbits are squash (with *C. pepo* being the most hardy of the squashes), cucumber, cantaloupe, and watermelon. Squash will make vigorous vegetative growth even in the cooler parts of the maritime Northwest, except in the most humid, chilly areas directly adjacent to the coast. Cucumbers (the right varieties) can be nearly as hardy but are more touchy about having warm germinating conditions, so they need to be sown a little later than squash. Fortunately, cucumbers are fast-maturing and will form plenty of fruit, even when sown in mid-June. Cantaloupe can be grown throughout the Willamette Valley and along the Columbia to Longview, Washington; if mollycoddled and grown like eggplant, they can be raised at higher elevations in western Oregon such as Lorane. North of Longview they usually need cloches. Watermelon will produce only scantily in the warmer parts of the Willamette Valley most years but is fairly reliable in southern Oregon.

Getting cucurbit seed to sprout outdoors requires an understanding of their family—and, most years, a little persistence. Seedlings are more susceptible to powdery mildew than adult vines are, and they're especially vulnerable while germinating. To sprout, cucurbit seeds need warmer soil than most species. Ideally, after the soil gets warm enough, the large seeds are planted deeply and not watered after sowing. This way, the emerging roots find adequate moisture deep in the bed, while the shoot comes up through dry soil and doesn't succumb to mildew before it even opens leaves to the sun. The gardener must hope it won't rain after sowing. Rain also drops soil temperature, which slows the rate of sprouting, further weakening the seedling and making it even more vulnerable to disease. Gardeners who try to help cucurbit seed sprout by watering it frequently experience poor germination. Only sandy soils—which dry out very rapidly—may have to be watered during sprouting. Perhaps. After being watered, sandy soils dry out and heat back up very rapidly.

It's a sound practice when sprouting cucurbit

seed outdoors to immediately resow adjacent to the first sowing if it rains or if it becomes chilly for a few days before emergence. If both sowings sprout, the earlier one may emerge with mildew and fail to grow well; it can always be hoed out if the second sowing proves to grow better. Some years I've made three sowings a week apart before the weather had really settled. When summer weather seems to arrive really late, I prefer to sprout cucurbit seeds indoors in small pots so I can control soil moisture and temperature. (See Chapter 7.) Once the seeds are sprouted, I harden the small pots off in the cold frame for a few days while the containers fill sufficiently with roots, and then I carefully transplant the seedlings.

All cucurbits make separate male and female flowers, alternating on the same vine. Male blooms appear as a simple flower containing only stamens. The female flower is easily recognized because it forms at the end of an ovary resembling a miniature fruit. The seedling's genetic program first requires the formation of a certain number of leaves before flowering begins—often as many as ten leaves. Then the first flowers form. These are usually male flowers; often five or more male blooms appear before the first ovary is produced. I consider this period of the plant's cycle "early vine growth." Once female flowers are produced and pollinated, I've noticed that the vine begins growing more rapidly and alternates male and female flowers throughout the rest of its life.

In the cooler districts of the maritime Northwest, obtaining ripe melons and fully mature winter squashes demands the earliest possible fruit set. So early vine growth must be encouraged as much as possible. This is not always simple to accomplish, because early vine growth is greatly retarded by the kind of cool, damp conditions we frequently have in early summer. In cooler areas, the gardener should consider raising transplants and/or using black plastic mulches or cloches to create a more optimum environment.

Cucurbits make vegetative growth, setting new fruit as they go, as long as weather and soil conditions permit. So growing vines have a continuous need for fertilization and unoccupied growing room to invade. The best encouragement is to side-dress the sprawling vines, sprinkling a bit of fertilizer over the area where they are about to grow. When the sprawling vines have covered the fertilizer last applied, it is time to side-dress again. Each side-dressing must cover a bit more area and so takes a bit more fertilizer than the previous one. Another way to side-dress cucurbits is to fertigate every two to three weeks, as shown in the illustration on page 153.

Most garden books say that cucurbits naturally wilt during midafternoon heat. Viewing this as "natural" is incorrect; I believe temporary wilting is an unnecessary stress the gardener should plan to avoid. Cucurbits' root systems seem completely adequate to support the leaf load only when there is no competition for soil moisture. The common practice of growing two plants per spot or per hill seems wrong to me. When only one plant totally controls a growing area, it gets through scorching afternoons in much better condition, doesn't temporarily wilt, and continues growing more vigorously. Fruit set doesn't stop, and harvesting continues at a high rate. Give them lots of unoccupied room to grow into, and don't make them compete with each other.

Pollination is done by bees and other insects. If seed is to be produced on a commercial scale, intercrossable varieties must be separated by a mile or more. Gardeners who want to produce their own seed by bee pollination could limit themselves to only one variety of each type. Fortunately, it is easy to hand-pollinate cucurbits, and a few such pollinations produces all the seed a gardener could ever want. Here's how to do it. Early in the morning, before the bees become active, remove a freshly opened male flower from one plant, locate a newly opened female bloom on another plant, insert the male stamen into the female flower, and brush it against the pollen receptors in the time-honored manner used by many of Earth's species. This effects pollination.

Then, to prevent further unintentional pollination, protect the female bloom from insects for a few days. Squash, with their huge blossoms, are simple to protect from bees: Shut the flower by twisting the tip and secure it with a thin string or wire twist-tie. Eventually, the squash flower will fall off naturally. The tiny blooms on cucumbers and melons must be slipped inside a small paper bag after pollination, with the bag tied tightly behind the ovary. Remove the bag in a few days to let the fruit develop. Mark the intentionally pollinated ovary by loosely tying a brightly colored piece of yarn or strip of cloth to the stem, and permit this individual fruit to become part of your seed supply. Be sure to transfer pollen between several different plants to prevent depression of vigor from inbreeding.

CUCUMBERS *(Cucumis sativus)*

Patience is the key to success with cucumbers; wait until conditions outdoors are favorable before sowing seeds. In the Willamette Valley, summer comes "for real" after June I most years and occasionally a week or more later; cucumber seed rarely germinates well before this date, nor will unprotected transplants grow. In fact, seedlings set out before nights stay warm enough usually die rapidly from mildews. (Planting on dark-colored light loams that heat up faster, or starting seeds or transplanting under cloches, may permit slightly earlier starts.) However, once seeds are up and growing, the vines develop rapidly. I can usually harvest cukes from late July until nearly the end of September, at which time the vines inevitably break down as the weather cools and becomes wetter. That's a long enough season to become thoroughly tired of them until next year.

Culture Gamble on your first sowing of cucumber seeds at about the same time you set out tomato seedlings. Broadcast and work in I gallon of complete organic fertilizer per 100 square feet of raised bed. Every 2 to 3 feet down the center of the bed, pour ½ cup of additional fertilizer in a little pile and, with a shovel, work it into a gallon of soil, making a low "hill" about 18 inches in diameter. More or less in the center, press down with your fist to make a 1½-inch-deep depression; this restores capillarity to that spot. Place four or five seeds on the bottom and cover with fine soil. If all goes well, they'll sprout quickly.

If the weather turns cool or it rains—which is what often happens—resow immediately after the weather settles. Be resigned in advance to making additional sowings around the outside of the same hill; do this weekly until one sprouts fast and takes off. To keep track, I make the second sowing at 3 o'clock toward the outside of the hill, and a third sowing, if necessary, at 6 o'clock. Once the seedlings are up, water the bed as needed. When the seedlings have their first true leaf and are growing rapidly, thin each hill to the single best plant.

Garden planning I usually grow about four hills. During August we pick half a bucketful every few days. The vines will be falling apart by late September, making the bed available for an overwintering green manure.

Insects and diseases Other than powdery mildew, I've had no troubles. The vines will inevitably succumb to mildew as soon as summer weather begins to fall apart. Although some varieties are "resistant," all this means is that they'll grow a few days longer under bad conditions before breaking down.

Harvest If seeds are allowed to develop, new fruit set slows; if enough fruits on a plant are forming mature seed, additional fruit set stops until that seed is mature. Keeping the vines picked makes them more productive. Large cukes make good chicken food or compost; they're not prime table fare. Often I merely toss overgrown cucumbers in the row next to their bed.

Saving seed Cucumbers do not cross with other cucurbits, but they do cross with all other cucumbers. Different varieties must be hand-pollinated or isolated by at least 1,000 feet for fair purity. The seeds are mature when the fruit is over-mature and has turned yellow. Remove the seeds and pulp around them and ferment them in a bowl at room temperature (warm), stirring daily. After three to six days, the pulp will liquefy. Pour it off, wash the seeds, and dry completely at room temperature on a newspaper.

Varieties The best open-pollinated types for our region are Marketmore (slicer) and SMR 58 (pickler). Unfortunately for the seed saver, any burpless variety early enough to mature here is a hybrid. Burpless types originated in Asia, tend to mature later, and are intolerant of cool weather—choose the earliest hybrid burpless varieties for success. Hybrids, both slicers and picklers, grow slightly better and yield sooner than open-pollinated varieties.

Some hybrids are gynoecious, meaning they make only female flowers; pollination is accomplished by having a small percentage of the seed in the packet produce another similar variety that does make male flowers. Since the first five or so flowers on normal varieties are male, all-female flowers means earlier harvesting. Tiny gardens growing only a single variety should not risk gynoecious hybrids—there may be no male flowers available and then no fruit will set. Another sort of cucumber is the "greenhouse" type; it also produces only female flowers. However, these must not be pollinated at all or the fruit becomes an inedible gourd. That works in a bee-free greenhouse, not outdoors.

Apple or Lemon are old home garden varieties that make lemon-sized fruit with deep green or white flesh and a remarkably sweet, crisp texture like some exotic tropical fruit. In my opinion the best one of all is the Middle Eastern cucumber—a smaller, thin-skinned, better-flavored fruit popular in Lebanon, Syria, and Israel. It tends to be a bit late; the earliest hybrids will produce admirably here. Get them from TSC or WCO to be safe. The Giant Armenian or Serpent cucumber is actually a melon of some sort. Keep that in mind if you save seed from this type.

Dry-gardening Although these watery fruit are not the most likely seeming drought-resistant candidate, if the hills are placed 5 feet apart in all directions, thinned to one plant per hill, and the vines given some fertigation, they'll surprise you. Especially good is Apple/Lemon, which has a very sprawly vine (and root system).

MELONS *(Cucumis melo, Citrullus lantatus)*

Muskmelons and cantaloupes are so poorly adapted to cool, humid conditions that they won't produce outside of cloches north of Longview, Washington, or on the coast. Watermelons are even dicier—they'll grow only in the hotter parts of the Willamette Valley on the lightest, warmest soils, and in the banana belts of southern Oregon. Be very selective about choosing only the earliest varieties.

Culture Melons strongly prefer light soils that warm up quickly and encourage their delicate root systems. Heavy soils may grow the crop if amended with organic matter, but they may require black plastic mulches (as for eggplant) or cloches to attain sufficient heat by sowing time. Even on dark-colored loams, a black plastic mulch might not be a bad idea. Sugar production in melons is closely related to the amount of magnesium available; using dolomitic lime in their complete organic fertilizer is wise.

About May 25, start seedlings indoors (see Chapter 7), and at the same time prepare a bed as though for cucumbers, with fertilized hills every 2 feet up the center of the bed. Lay a sheet of black plastic over the whole bed and anchor the edges with soil. To warm the soil as much as possible, leave as much plastic exposed to the sun as possible. A few weeks later, when the seedlings are ready to go outside, cut out a 6-inch hole over each hill to receive them. Under the black plastic, the soil will have heated up considerably. Transplant the seedlings about mid-June. In southern Oregon, melons can be direct-seeded like cucumbers, although a black plastic mulch might still be useful. North of Longview, put a wide tunnel cloche over the entire bed, and consider using black plastic too.

Garden planning I never ripened a watermelon at chilly Lorane, Oregon, nor did the sparsely set unripe fruit ever get bigger than a grapefruit. I did grow fine cantaloupes, about ten to the vine in a good summer. Elkton, though, was melon paradise! In this banana belt, a 100-square-foot bed of mixed melons overwhelmed us with the sugary fruit for about a month. Even the watermelons grew great. When the beds fell apart in mid-September, I scattered clover seed over them and raked it in a bit; the clover takes over during autumn.

Insects and diseases Even disease-resistant varieties might come down with powdery mildew during a short spell of unsettled weather during summer, but by September, the lessened light, cooler nights, and heavier dews combine to weaken all varieties. Once September weather turns rainy, the season's over—the leaves mildew, all ripening ceases, and the immature fruit rots.

Harvest Cantaloupes and muskmelons slip the vine (detach) with slight pressure from one finger when ripe. They do not ripen after harvest! They'll ripen only while the leaves are putting sugars into the fruit. Supermarket cantaloupes have been brilliantly bred to mimic the appearance of a ripe melon when picked unripe. But they're never the equal of a real ripe cantaloupe. If left on the counter, supermarket stuff softens up, but it cannot become sweeter or tastier, only rottier. Once you learn what a truly ripe one tastes like, you'll never buy them again.

Very occasionally, industrial food system honeydews from the supermarket are genuinely ripe. Ripe ones can be selected only by persons armed with sensitive nonsmoker's noses, who don't mind making a spectacle of themselves as they poke through the pile sniffing out a rare ball of perfume. The ones that

smell fruity but that slosh when you shake them aren't really ripe, only old and beginning to fall apart inside, and they don't really smell like ripe melons—more like decaying ones. But you can sniff at the stem scars on dozens and dozens of cantaloupes without ever finding one that smells really fragrant. That's because truly ripe cantaloupe are too soft to ship and go bad too quickly.

Watermelons do not improve after harvest either and must be knowledgeably thumped by the gardener to judge ripeness. I regret I can't explain watermelon thumping in words.

Saving seed Generally, the procedure for saving melon seed is like that for cucumbers. Cantaloupes, which have netted skins, may or may not cross with such muskmelons as honeydew, which have smooth skins; certainly neither crosses with watermelons. When the fruit is dead ripe, the seeds are mature. If I lived in California, I'd certainly know in which pollination group to assign all the exotic melons like Crenshaw and Santa Claus.

Varieties A few locally well-adapted, open-pollinated cantaloupe varieties, like the famous Spear Melon, are still preserved by home gardeners, though the seed is not readily available. Hybrids, with their increased vigor, are much more successful, with yields that are double those of open-pollinated varieties, but even so, only a few of the earliest hybrids do well. I'd stick to varieties from TSC or WCO. During cool summers, I've seen dozens of hybrid "early" cantaloupe varieties fail to ripen anything, even on dark-colored, light loam soils at the OSU Vegetable Crops Research Farm outside Corvallis.

Some watermelon varieties that will produce (as well as watermelons can produce) are Crimson Sweet, Sugar Baby, Sweet Meat Hybrid, and Yellow Doll. Especially Yellow Doll. Yum!

Dry-gardening Treat like cucumbers.

SQUASHES & PUMPKINS

(Cucurbita species)

Almost any maritime Northwest garden can produce summer squash; however, in cooler microclimates some care is required to get winter squash fully ripe—winter squash ripens only on those sunny days when the temperature is above 70°F. Although our frost-free growing season may be long, it may not include as many warm, sunny days as squash would like.

Culture The other hard part about growing squash is getting the seed to sprout. Like the rest of the cucurbits, squash will not germinate in cold, wet soil. Once they're up and growing, however, squash will tolerate harsh conditions that would immediately ruin melons and cucumbers. Whereas cucumber seeds need soils that remain at temperatures above 65°F and melons need soil above 70°F to sprout, squash will sprout at 60°F if the soil is not too wet (but squash does much better when soil is well above 60°F).

Sow the seed at the beginning of a long spell of sunny weather; accomplish this by ESP. To avoid lowering the soil temperature,

don't water until germination. And if weather conditions worsen, resow weekly until one sowing both sprouts and begins growing strongly. Winter squash needs every available day to fully ripen its fruit. In cooler areas, a second sowing might fail to mature; in the northern third of our bioregion, I would consider starting slow-ripening winter varieties indoors and transplanting the seedlings outside a few days after they sprout. This can give the vines another week to ten days of growing compared to direct-seeding.

Prepare the beds as though for cucumbers. With a few exceptions, winter squash are highly vigorous vining types; space their hills 4 to 5 feet apart down the center of the bed or down the row, and be prepared to find the vines crossing the paths and getting into neighboring beds and then some. I often locate my winter varieties on an edge of the garden where the vines can go harmlessly through the deer fence. Summer squash can be spaced 2 to 3 feet apart in rows about 4 feet apart, or 2 to 3 feet apart down the center of a 4-foot-wide raised bed. Don't crowd them, as advised in other garden books. If you do, they'll quit yielding when they start competing. If, later in the summer, the bushes "bump," yank every other plant. The ones remaining will yield a lot more because they'll keep growing actively. For both summer and winter varieties, sow four to six seeds per spot, 1½ inches deep; *thin both kinds of squash to one seedling per hill or per spot.*

Garden planning Four summer squash plants will provide most families with more than they want to eat. Winter squash vines usually produce 50 pounds or more per hill— large-fruited varieties yield three to five squash of 10 to 15 pounds each; small-fruited varieties yield ten to fifteen squash of 3 to 5 pounds each.

Insects and diseases Like other cucurbits, squash gets powdery mildew when the weather becomes too cool and humid to suit it. When mildew ends the ripening process on winter varieties, it's time to harvest, ripe or not. Mildewed seedlings at the very beginning of summer rarely recover to resume proper growth. Be resigned in advance to planting again at the first sign of this disease; if it gets rainy and chilly during the sprouting period, it's best to sow again before the emergence of the first lot and thin to one plant from the sowing that grows best. Replanting at the slightest doubt is cheap insurance.

Harvest *Summer squash* are best harvested on the small side, while they still have tender skins and a delicate flavor. Permitting large summer squash to remain on the bush initiates seed formation and reduces set of new fruit. *Winter squash* usually need every possible growing day to fully ripen. Unripe squash have light-colored, flavorless meat and thin, light seeds that sprout poorly. When really mature, the meat is usually deep orange and the seeds are fat and dense after drying. A totally mature winter squash has a shriveled, brown stem that no longer transports nutrients into the fruit. You won't see this degree of finish often west of the Cascades, except in

southern Oregon and the redwood country. One trick to enhance ripening is to begin removing all existing very small squash and all new squash from the vine on about September 1, letting the plant put everything it has into ripening its larger fruit. Allowing winter squash to remain in the field long after powdery mildew has killed off the leaves, or very many days after the first light frost has burned back the leaf cover, only lowers storage potential. To enjoy the longest possible shelf life, sponge off the skin of winter varieties with a disinfecting bleach solution, or fill the kitchen sink with it and roll the squash around in disinfectant for a few moments. This kills mold spores that may later rot the squash. Then cure the skins by drying them at room temperature for a week or so. This makes a beautiful display in the house somewhere. Squashes store best at 55°F and low humidity, with air freely moving around them. I've successfully kept ours in a cool back bedroom closet and also under far less ideal conditions—under the sink in the kitchen where temperatures were warmer. Some varieties will last until late April without rotting.

Saving seed There are four squash species: *Cucurbita pepo, C. maxima, C. mixta,* and *C. moschata.* Each family will cross freely with other members of the same family as well as outcross with other families in most cases. Fortunately for the seed saver, *C. pepo,* the most ubiquitous group, will not cross with *C. maxima,* the other main garden group. *C. moschata* will cross with both *C. pepo* and *C. maxima. C. mixta* is a tropical sort primarily containing the cushaw squashes and cushaw pumpkins, not usually attempted in the North.

C. pepo includes all the summer squashes, most pumpkins, and certain winter squashes such as Acorn, Delicata, Vegetable Gourd (often called Sweet Dumpling), Vegetable Spaghetti, and Gem (or Rôlet). *C. pepo* varieties can usually be recognized by their smaller seeds. These are also the fastest to mature, usually requiring about ninety warm, sunny days. Unfortunately, these are also the winter squash with the poorest storage potential. Gardeners in cooler areas can pretty much count on getting fat, vigorous seed and really ripe fruit from *C. pepo* types, and in fact should concentrate on these for their winter squash supply.

C. maxima varieties include the large, hard-shelled winter squash such as Sweet Meat, Buttercup, Delicious, the various Japanese hybrids, and the numerous Hubbards. Their seeds are much bigger than those of the *C. pepo* varieties, require slightly more heat to sprout, and, most important, taste better—making the best edible "pumpkin seeds." I particularly like munching seeds from Sweet Meat. *C. maxima* needs about 120 warm, sunny days after emergence to fully mature seed and flesh. Most summers in the Willamette Valley, Oregon, 120 warm, sunny growing days are all we get at best. Seed from immature fruit have a low germination rate and low vigor, and the flavor of the flesh is less than ideal.

C. moschata varieties are the Butternuts. They are even longer growing, requiring 120 to 130 days for full maturity of fruit and seed and may need a little more heat. Except in the southern banana belts, gardeners will have trouble getting fully ripe Butternuts.

The laziest route for the seed-saving gardener is to choose only one type of *C. pepo* and one *C. maxima*, or to hand-pollinate selected flowers. For the first, I'd take Yellow Crookneck (summer squash) or Gem if you can find any seed (Gem produces summer squash that, if allowed to mature, develop a hard skin and deep-orange, sweet flesh, making very acceptable winter squash), and Buttercup or one of the Japanese Kuris for my *C. maxima* variety because they're relatively small and keep well. Isolation is very important when growing cucurbit seed; for urban gardeners who can't control what grows in neighboring gardens, hand-pollination is essential. Remove the seed from the mature fruit, wash it free of pulp by rubbing it in water, and then dry it fully. With dry, cool storage, the storage life of fat, well-filled seed is more than seven years.

Varieties Hybrid varieties are beginning to appear for all types of squash in all families because they're more uniform and considerably more vigorous. Many old standard open-pollinated summer varieties have disappeared or have become disappointingly ragged. Most summer squash varieties taste much the same when cooked, though we've noticed that yellow-skinned ones tend to cook down into a thicker, starchier, richer-flavored mash than green-skinned ones. The very best flavor is found with the sprawly, late-maturing heirloom, Yellow Crookneck, which hasn't been trained into a bush habit. Butterstick is a hybrid summer squash with an interesting and useful trait: Its first flowers are female, not male, and when its fruit is not pollinated it still sets. This can make Butterstick a week to ten days earlier than any other variety. For some years, I've grown three or four Buttersticks to act as "gap stuffers," tiding us over until the more delicious Yellow Crooknecks come on. One year when the garden was crowded, I just yanked out the Buttersticks when the Crooknecks began ripening and used the space to sow a winter crop.

In my opinion, Delicata has the richest flavor of all the winter varieties, with the added advantage of small size and quick *C. pepo* maturity. They're also better keepers than the popular Acorn types but still don't store as well as *C. maxima* types.

Dry-gardening Space squash that you plan to dry-garden farther apart: summer squash 5 to 6 feet apart in rows 6 feet apart, winter squash in big, deeply dug hills on an 8-by-8-foot or even a 10-by-10-foot grid. Fertigate about 5 gallons at a time, as often as possible. By summer's end, in fertile, open soil, Yellow Crookneck will sprawl 7 or 8 feet in diameter, both above and below ground, yielding more heavily with each passing week.

ALLIUMS

The alliums include leeks, shallots, scallions, onions, and garlic. All are frost hardy; some, to our great good fortune, are remarkably hardy. By careful planning, we can produce a superior year-round supply of fresh, sweet, salad-quality alliums (though not necessarily bulb onions) all year; the poor eastern gardener must depend on sacks of hot, pungent,

keeping onions to get through winter and spring.

Highly photoperiodic, like mustards and spinach, alliums will bulb or bolt when day length dictates, regardless of sowing date. Many respond to decreasing days; others bulb or make seed only after experiencing winter and then an increasing day length. In another respect, bulbing alliums are much like cauliflower, broccoli, and cabbage: The size the plant has already attained when bulbing starts determines the ultimate size of the onion or garlic. This means that bulbing varieties have to be urged to grow vegetatively as fast as possible. Alliums need abundant nutrients, but only while making vegetative growth. Once bulbing starts, they have little use for more fertilizer— in fact, at that stage any further nutrients the plant needs are drawn down from the leaves, which gradually wither as the bulb matures.

Alliums have small, coarsely textured, shallow root systems, poorly adapted to clayey soils. On the light soils they prefer, careful attention must be paid to keeping soil moisture levels up (without leaching). Slow-release organic fertilizer placed close to the plants will provide nearly ideal nutrient supplies and provoke the fastest possible growth. At Lorane, Oregon, where I gardened on clayey soil, if I had any really well-ripened compost, I'd use it for the onion patch. And no matter how painstaking my efforts, the onions I grew on that clay were never half as large as the ones easily grown by others on light loam soils.

The difficulty of getting seeds of the allium family to sprout and initially grow has discouraged many gardeners. Consequently, growing bulb onions from easy-to-plant sets has become popular, even though set-grown onions are usually of very poor quality compared to those started from seed. You're much better off buying bundles of southern-grown seedlings instead of using sets. But it is actually quite easy to sprout allium seeds in spring, when the weather is usually mild and the soil stays naturally moist. Because onion seed is small and sown shallowly, germinating seed must be kept moist during spells of hot weather, and because the shoots are weak, the soil above the seeds must not form a crust.

Later sowings of scallions and overwintering bulb onions usually germinate well enough if made on raised beds with high surface humus content or covered with sifted compost and watered daily during sunny weather.

Once their stalks have reached pencil size, alliums transplant very readily, even when the roots are completely bare. This makes it easy to reduce the hazards of direct-seeding by starting alliums in a nursery bed right in the garden: A few row-feet sown in very humusy ground near a handy sprinkler can be coaxed into life, grown for a couple of months, and then dug, shaken apart, their tops trimmed back to prevent transpiration shock, and transplanted.

Insects are rarely a problem. Mildews will form on allium leaves during winter when the plants have poor air circulation. Giving winter alliums a little extra elbow room will usually prevent this.

Some alliums have been propagated from bulbs for so long that their seed has become infertile or nonexistent. Included in this group are garlic, some shallots, and certain nonbulbing onions that don't set seed but create top bulblets. Allium flowers are insect-pollinated; varieties have to be isolated by at least several hundred feet for fair purity (commercial seed fields are separated by a mile or so). The seed is lightweight and short-lived—two to three years at best. Getting high-vigor seed with longer storage potential is also dicey. High temperatures during seed formation can kill the embryo, as can molds and various diseases of the seed head. Crop failures or seed that is too weak to sell are typical setbacks in the onion seed business. But seed prices are high, making this high-risk venture a bonanza affair.

GARLIC *(Allium sativum)*
& SHALLOTS *(A. cepa)*

Garlic and shallots are admirably adapted to our climate and make big yields here. These species store excellently because they form bulbs during the dryness of our midsummer, when their skins cure well. The delicious aroma of fresh drying garlic in the kitchen is a treat we anticipate each July.

Culture Garlic bulbs form underground late in spring after they've been planted and have overwintered. For good bulb formation, the soil cannot become compacted, but the crop must overwinter while the soil growing it is being pounded by heavy rains for months. So amend the surface few inches of clayey soils with plenty of compost before planting. Shallots form on or just below the soil's surface and aren't quite so fussy.

To plant garlic, break a head into separate

cloves; with shallots, plant the entire bulb. Sow them from September through mid-October, 1 inch deep, root side down, 3 to 4 inches apart in the row, spacing the rows at least 18 inches apart. In rich garden soil, use no fertilizer at sowing; in poor ground, side-dress about ⅔ gallon of complete organic fertilizer per 100 row-feet close to the cloves after the shoots appear. To end up with really large garlic or shallot bulbs, side-dress the overwintered plants late in February with 2 or 3 tablespoonfuls of blood meal per 5 row-feet. To harvest the largest bulbs, side-dress again about April 1 with complete organic fertilizer. All side-dressing must be done close to the plants. (The root system's effective lateral spread will not exceed 1 foot from the plant.)

Garden planning Remember that the bulbs won't mature until summer. One garlic clove multiplies to one head; one shallot bulb becomes five to eight shallots.

Insects and diseases I've had no problems. There are virus diseases that carry over from year to year in the cloves. Try to get reputable seed to start with.

Harvest Some types of garlic put up a seed stalk; their bulbs have a central core or stalk surrounded with cloves. When the seed is mature, so are the cloves—although the seed is almost never viable. Some varieties brown off at the top and wither like bulb onions; the cloves have no central core/stalk. These sorts tend to be better keepers but have milder flavor.

Some varieties, locally called Italian Silverskin (or Rocambole), although this name may be misapplied to any number of similar varieties, make miniature bulblets on top, each of which will grow a separate garlic head. I've found it optimal to remove this bulblet cluster before much development occurs, to redirect the plant's energies toward making a larger below-ground bulb.

The cleanest garlic is dug before the outer skins dry out. The dirty outer layers are peeled away and the head is allowed to dry indoors in a braid, or clumps of stalks are tied together and hung. If allowed to remain in the ground too long, the bulbs split open and soil enters between the cloves, especially with the type having a central core and flower stalk.

Shallots usually brown off like onion tops and are ready to harvest when fully dried out.

Saving seed To harvest the largest bulbs, plant only the larger cloves. Varieties of garlic do not cross, nor do they make viable seed. Some types of shallots do make good seed, though these are still best propagated from bulbs.

Varieties At one time the only way to get interesting varieties was to haunt Italian, Greek, and Korean grocery stores. Now the major and regional seed companies are offering many interesting kinds of both garlic and shallots.

Dry-gardening Garlic is one crop that is very suited to growing without irrigation: for dryland garlic, plant cloves 6 to 8 inches apart, immediately after the first rains moisten the ground, in rows spaced about 3 feet apart. With careful weeding and a little mulching late in April, the crop will mature on field moisture.

LEEKS (*Allium porrum*)

I manage to keep the kitchen in onions or onion substitutes all year round. Overwintering bulb onions are very easy to grow, even in clayey soils. They have the finest culinary qualities of any bulb onion and mature in June, rounding out all that sweet summer garden food. Unfortunately, even when they're cured to the max, I've never had any overwintered onions left past Thanksgiving. What to do from November to May? Leeks!

Pungent bulb onions that can keep from late summer until late spring are commonly grown in the East. They can be raised here too, especially on light soils. But the storage onions we grow rarely store very well; late-summer humidity is not conducive to curing bulb onions. Winter leeks eliminate all problems of curing and storage—they can be harvested fresh from October until April. On heavy soil where an onion would barely bulb at all, leeks grow fine. Leeks are much milder than storage onions and far better in salads, and, as any gourmet can tell you, they are superior for cooking. For all these reasons, I no longer struggle to produce winter storage onions.

Culture Leeks grown on clayey soil do a lot better if their root zone has been heavily amended with organic matter. Not only do their root systems have the same limited vigor as those of the other alliums, but loose soil permits their shafts to enlarge more readily. Light soil also makes them much easier to dig. To get really big, leeks also need a goodly amount of fertilizer.

Leeks are very slow growing. They are best started as seedlings and transplanted. The transplanting itself is easy when you actually do it but can seem complex when explained in writing. *Autumn leeks* will be big by September and may become absolutely gigantic during autumn. They are sown indoors very early in spring (February) and are grown first under lights and then in a cold frame and transplanted outside in May. Chapter 7 explains the initial production stages for autumn leeks. *Winter leeks* are much easier because they're direct-seeded outdoors in mid-April through May. This is ideal weather for germinating allium seed outside. Winter leeks can be grown without transplanting, like big scallions, but their culinary quality is far better if they are sown in a nursery bed and transplanted a few months later.

The following directions assume that you want to grow enough winter leeks to replace several sacks of storage onions. Prepare the nursery bed by deeply hoeing about an inch of well-aged compost and a pint of complete organic fertilizer into a 4-foot by 4-foot section of raised bed. If you've got any, work in an additional inch of sphagnum moss. Hoe and rake the nursery bed until it is virtually clodless. In other words, make a 4-foot square of 4- or 5-inch-deep potting soil outdoors. Make three ½-inch-deep furrows across the bed, about 12 inches apart, and sow about ten seeds per inch. Cover with loose soil. If the sowing date is closer to the end of May than to the middle of April, cover the seed with finely sifted compost or aged manure to prevent it from drying out before sprouting. Thin the seedlings only if grossly overcrowded; try to end up with about four seedlings per inch—after all, you're raising transplants, and with this species you want them to compete a bit to get leggy. Three short rows like this, only 12 row-feet, will make enough seedlings to fill well over 100 linear feet of trench in a few months. At transplanting time I usually have so many extras that I give some novice gardener a big bundle of seedlings.

Transplant leek seedlings into the bottom of deep trenches, because the most edible portion of the plant is the blanched (white) stem. The deeper the leek is buried, the longer the white part will be. However, do not cover the seedlings deeper than the first leaf joint, or soil will get into the stem itself and may still be there when the leek is cooked. Instead, gradually fill in the trench as the newly transplanted seedlings grow. That's why tall, leggy transplants with a lot of distance between their roots and the first leaf joint are highly desirable. They'll get leggy if they grow crowded.

When autumn leeks are raised in transplant trays, it's hard to get the seedlings more than $\frac{3}{16}$ inch in diameter or very tall before they must be transplanted. Winter leeks raised in crowded nursery beds under a fair degree of competition will be as thick as a pencil and quite leggy in a few months—a big advantage for raising a fancy product.

Dig winter leek transplants very gently from the nursery bed so as to keep as much of their root system intact as possible. Separate the tangled roots without tearing them off by washing the soil from the roots under a gentle flow of water from a hose or standpipe. Autumn leeks, grown in shallow trays, separate more easily.

Make a handful-sized bundle of the seedlings, carefully arranging the bases of the plants in alignment, and then cut off half the leaf area with sharp scissors. This reduces the amount of water the plants need to take up, greatly improving the seedlings' chances of survival. With less transplanting shock, they'll resume growing rapidly and will easily overcome the loss of leaf area. Even if you're going to transplant in a few minutes, put the clipped seedlings in a small bucket, pot, or plastic bag to keep the roots moist. Do not let them dry out at all before transplanting.

For winter leeks, it's wise to delay digging and transplanting until midsummer, by which time the seedlings will have become quite crowded and overcompetition will have begun to slow their growth. At this time they will be the tallest and leggiest they can rapidly become and will be quite husky. You'll shock the seedlings less if you can manage to transplant winter leeks during a spell of cloudy weather (if there is one in midsummer).

The steps needed to prepare the row for transplanting sound more difficult than they actually are. Once you've done it the first time, you'll realize it's a snap. It's easier to do this using an "old-style" long row layout than on raised beds. If your whole garden is in raised beds, this is the one occasion when the planting direction on those beds is reversed and the rows are made the long way, with two rows of leeks per 4-foot-wide raised bed.

Your aim in this process is to end up with a 6- to 8-inch-deep trench with well-worked fertilized soil below it. With this aim in mind, double-dig the leek row. Starting at one end of the bed or row, excavate a trench (or a parallel pair of them on a raised bed) at least 8 inches deep and a shovel blade wide. Carefully place the soil taken from the trench to one side; on a raised bed, heap most of it carefully in the center of the bed with a trench on either side. What gets into the paths adjoining a raised bed will go back into the trench immediately after transplanting.

Sprinkle 1 gallon of complete organic fertilizer down the bottom of each 50 feet of trench. Using a hoe, work the fertilizer into the soil. If the soil at the bottom of the trench is compacted or heavy, you will be wise also to toss in an inch of compost and spade it up thoroughly, creating 8 inches of loose, fertilized soil at the bottom of a trench that, because you fluffed up the bottom, will now be about 5 or 6 inches deep. Loosening the subsoil with compost is worth the effort.

Take a handful of transplants, kneel in the path, lean over the trench, and set the leeks in the bottom down the center, spacing the seedlings about 2 inches apart, spreading the roots out flat as much as possible, and standing the leeks up as straight as possible while leaning against one wall of the trench. Then, by hand, push enough soil back into the trench to cover the roots about an inch deep. Go down the row again and stand each seedling perfectly upright by gently tugging on it, at the same time patting the soil down around the roots to hold them in place. Immediately sprinkle a side-dressing of complete organic fertilizer in the trench (about 1 gallon per 100 trench feet) and then, using the loose soil dug from the trench, carefully and gently

fill in the trench partway. Remember, for clean leeks, do not fill the trench deeper than the first leaf joint of the seedlings.

You're finished. If you've done it right, the leeks will be buried as deeply as possible, the trench will not be completely filled up, the leeks will be 2 inches apart in a straight row, and the first leaf joint of the seedlings will be just above the soil partially filling the trench. Hand-water the trenches, being careful not to wash much soil back into the bottom (keep those leaf notches soil free). If the weather turns particularly hot during the next week, water every few days. Then let the bed grow.

Sound like a lot of work? It takes me about two hours to dig and prepare transplants, trench, and replant about 50 feet of row. For this effort we have many more leeks than we can use all winter. It is easily worth two hours. What would 100 pounds of organically grown storage onions cost? And besides, the leeks are much better in salads or soups or for all the purposes you'd use onions.

In such a perfect environment, the leeks quickly resume rapid growth, and as they do, the weeds will also reappear. Hoe the weeds in such a way that you pull a little soil down into the trench each time. As before, take care not to get soil into the leaf notches. As the leeks grow, completely fill in the trenches and then begin to hill up soil against the leeks. By October the soil will be piled several inches higher around the stems; the leeks will also be so leafy that you won't be able to hill up any more soil. If you dug sufficiently deep trenches to start with, the leeks will be deeply buried. When you harvest them, they will have long white stalks.

Garden planning I rarely grow autumn leeks. The bother of raising slow-growing seedlings in trays and transplanting such delicate seedlings is not worth an allium crop that matures when I've still got a supply of over-wintered bulb onions and lots of fresh scallions left. Winter leeks are, in contrast, easy to start, transplant rapidly, and come on as the sweet overwintered bulb onions run out. I usually grow at least 50 row-feet of them. I try to transplant winter leeks into soil that grew early salad greens or my last harvest of peas.

Insects and diseases I've grown leeks for 25 years and have had no insect problems. I've also never had winter mildew trouble. In areas with very wet or very frosty winters, I'd try spacing them a bit further apart in the row for better air circulation.

Harvest Leeks will grow slowly during winter warm spells, going dormant when the weather gets really frosty or when it rains for long periods. Certain very late varieties are bred to be slow bolting; if they have not grown large enough to suit you by the end of February, consider a side-dressing of blood meal to spur additional spring growth before seed stalks emerge in April. Otherwise, dig them as needed.

Saving seed Leeks bolt in spring, sending up a seed head that does not cross with other alliums. In early spring, select vigorous plants with long shafts between the roots and the first leaf joint that do not have bulbous bottoms (an undesirable trait); dig them and transplant to a section of the garden where the leeks will not have to be watered with the rest of the garden. The root systems on mature plants don't develop very well after transplanting, and so they demand a fair amount of summer irrigation. However, sprinkling the seed heads induces molds that destroy the seed. It is wise to mulch seed-making plants. Around September, the balloon-shaped flowers will show the black seeds they contain. Cut off the flowers with about a foot of stem and dry them under cover, with the seed heads laid out on sheets of newspaper to catch the shattering seed. When fully dry, rub the heads between your hands to thresh out the rest of the seed.

Autumn leek varieties Autumn leeks are bred to be fast growing, tender, and mild tasting. However, they aren't extremely hardy and won't survive freezing very well. In Europe, where leeks are very popular, autumn varieties are intended for use late in summer or early in autumn. Some autumn varieties are bred for market gardeners who dig their fall harvest all at once and hold it in refrigerated storage, like apples. Autumn leeks are popular in North American seed catalogs because winter survival of leeks is not possible in the North (except west of the Cascades).

Winter leek varieties Winter leeks are bred for ultimate hardiness, so they're more fibrous, tougher, and a little more pungent than autumn leeks. Johnny's sensibly sells no winter leeks to people gardening where the soil freezes solid by November. Then there are "spring" leeks, winter-hardy varieties intended for spring harvest because they're very late bolting. I prefer this sort myself, and grow Durabel (TSC, WCO).

Dry-gardening It is possible to dry-garden leeks. Start a nursery bed of "spring" leeks as late as possible, say, the end of May. Give the seedlings a bit more growing space because you'll hold them in the nursery longer, placing rows 18 inches apart and thinning to ½ inch apart in the row. Give the nursery enough water to keep them healthy over the summer. Dig trenches and transplant in early October, using a bit of irrigation when doing this. You'll have big leeks by the end of January.

ONIONS & SCALLIONS (*Allium cepa*)

It is said of knowledgeable people that they "know their onions." This old saw has a lot of truth to it because growing bulb onions is tricky. Overwintered bulb onions are easier to raise than those grown over the summer. Scallions are even easier.

Bulb onions can be grown from seed, seedlings, or sets. I have always encouraged people to use seeds or seedlings because set-started onions are rarely long-keeping varieties, and the percentage of bolters and doubles harvested from sets is high. Sets do solve one problem many gardeners find overwhelming: getting onion seed to sprout and become established. Yet I've never experienced a field germination failure when I planted onion (or scallion) seed that would sprout well in a laboratory. Sowing it in fertile raised beds and covering the seed with pure, sifted humus (if sowing after the spring sprinkles stop) ensures good germination. If you buy southern-grown seedlings to transplant in spring (or if you grow your own), clip half the leaf area before putting them out, if it hasn't been done already by the grower; this will help guarantee transplanting success.

Keep in the forefront of your mind that the size of the bulb will be only as large as the tops grew before bulbing started. Bulbing stops further top growth. Bulbing is initiated by change of day length and will happen when the genes of that particular variety program bulbing to occur. It will occur regardless of how large or how puny the tops have become. To grow big bulbs, you must do everything possible to encourage top growth because the photosynthesis that occurs after bulbing begins makes the food that gets stored in the bulb. The onion plant stores only a little food in its leaves. At first it uses all the surplus food it can make to build even more leaf. Then it uses all of the surplus food the leaves make to store in a bulb. When the bulb is largely completed, the tops wither away, and as they do so the last remnants of nutrients held in the leaves are translocated into the bulb, making it get a bit bigger.

I really want you to know your onions. In North America, we grow three types of bulb onions and three sorts of scallions. Each requires different handling.

Bulb onions: Sweet Spanish onions are large, long-growing bulbing types best adapted to the day lengths occurring where they're grown commercially—Utah, northern New Mexico, and central California. (They're often called *intermediate-day-length* varieties. Like the long-day varieties better suited to our more northerly latitudes, intermediate-day-length varieties grow vegetatively on lengthening days and then bulb when days shorten at the end of summer. However, they are best adapted to day-length conditions found further south of us, where the extremes of long and short day length are less pronounced.) Intermediate-day-length bulbs tend to be sweet and soft, with thick, tender rings and little pungency.

In our latitudes, intermediate-day-length varieties begin to bulb rather too late to mature properly; bulbing usually initiates late in August. In that season, bulb development is limited by rapidly weakening sunlight, and the humid, cool conditions of late September complicate curing. Even the earliest of the sweet Spanish varieties won't top down (as the withering of the leaves is called) before mid-September in our latitudes. If sweet Spanish bulbs don't grow big, they'll be as pungent as any ordinary long-day storage onion, so these sorts are best started indoors and set out in the garden as sizable seedlings. Buying bunches of large, husky, southern-grown seedlings for transplanting is a good idea. Make sure, if you buy seedlings, that they were started from quality (hybrid) seed. At best, they have a limited storage potential; sweet Spanish bulbs rarely hold in the pantry much past New Year's.

Storage onions grow faster and are bred for our latitudes. They're often called *long-day* varieties because they grow vegetatively during the long days of summer and bulb when the days shorten. To enhance their storage potential, breeders often select for considerable pun-

gency: hard, tough, thin rings and thick, strong skins. I've had early storage varieties that topped down by late August, cured, and went into storage in early September when conditions were dry. Heavier-yielding varieties top down later and can be as difficult to cure as sweet Spanish onions, although it is precisely these late varieties that have the most potential to keep from fall until late spring, if properly cured.

If you want the largest bulbs, start storage onions indoors like sweet Spanish onions, and transplant them out; if you sow them later in spring and grow them on tighter spacing, the yield from a bed of the same size can be just about as high, but the bulbs will be smaller.

Overwintered bulb onions have been raised commercially for a long time in California and the most southerly parts of New Mexico and Texas. They're usually called *short-day* varieties because they grow vegetatively during the seasons when day lengths are shorter and bulb when the days lengthen. These delicious, usually flat-topped summer onions show up in the supermarket starting in May and disappear from commercial trade by August, when the first storage onions begin to appear. Before the European Union, Northern Europeans were not fortunate enough to have winter growing regions like the Rio Grande Valley, so they developed varieties of these onions hardy enough to overwinter reliably in Holland and England—and places like western Oregon and Washington.

Short-day varieties for the North are sown in late summer, overwinter, and mature in June. (Those bred for the South are sown in

October or early November and are harvested in May.) Overwintering bulb onions are the easiest of all bulbing types to grow, though care has to be taken to obtain good germination when sowing onion seed in the heat of August. These varieties are usually not long keepers because they're tender, soft, and often extremely sweet, with hardly a hint of pungency—the best possible eating. Occasionally, I've had well-cured overwintered onions of the more pungent sorts keep until mid-November. (There's a genetic linkage between pungency and storage potential.)

Scallions: Sweet Spanish derivatives are very late-bulbing varieties of Spanish onions that are harvested and used as scallions before bulbing begins. These have been bred for a thin, translucent outer skin, for sweetness, and for tenderness (although they tend to be rather pungent). If sown in spring, they'll reach useful size by midsummer and can be harvested until October, when they bulb and go dormant. This sort is most useful to the commercial grower who is going to harvest the crop once and be done with it.

Overwintering scallions don't bulb during the decreasing day length of late summer. This is an advantage for the gardener, because a single sowing can be picked for months and months. Lisbons are tender, sweet, nonpungent scallions that go dormant or make seed in late spring after overwintering. They can be sown any time from spring through midsummer, and they last until the next spring. Welsh onions (*A. fistulosum*) are pungent, rather tough-textured, and far hardier than Lisbons (hardy enough, in fact, to survive a freezing winter in the East). Welsh onions bolt in March or April. Depending on the variety, both Lisbon and Welsh onions may divide and multiply during a maritime Northwest winter if sown early enough to achieve a good size.

Culture *Sweet Spanish onions* should be started very early in spring indoors and transplanted outdoors in late April to early May (see Chapter 7). Broadcast the usual complete organic fertilizer and work the bed. Set out transplants 3 or 4 inches apart in rows at least 18 inches apart. Side-dress ¼ to ½ cup complete organic fertilizer beside each 4 to 5 row-feet of seedlings.

Storage onions, when sown outside too early, may be stunted by harsh spring weather. Spring rains can also make careful soil preparation impossible. If you want the largest onions, start transplants before March 1, or direct-seed outdoors during April. May sowings produce smallish bulbs; gardeners with heavy, late-tilling soil should raise or buy transplants. Broadcast and work in 1 gallon of complete organic fertilizer per 100 square feet. Contribute some compost at the same time. Sow the seed ½ inch deep, three or four seeds per inch, in rows 18 inches apart. Side-dress additional fertilizer beside the seeds after they sprout. Thin gradually so the seedlings stand 2 to 4 inches apart; the final spacing depends on how large the bulbs will grow and can be judged only from prior experience. Yields will be slightly larger if the bulbs are a bit crowded, but bulb size will be smaller. I suggest 4 inches the first time you try storage onions. Onions transplant so easily that thinnings yanked from the ground can often be used to start new beds.

Overwintered onions should be sown around mid-August; choosing the best date is tricky and essential. Overwintering seedlings must become about pencil sized before cold weather checks their growth, but whatever you do, don't plant too early! If seedlings get too big during winter, they'll likely go to seed in spring rather than form bulbs. Fertilize only moderately when sowing to keep the size down. At frosty Lorane, Oregon, I preferred to sow on August I; at Elkton, where it is warmer in winter, I found September I to be best. The first time you grow overwintering onions I suggest three sowings between August I and September I. Then you'll know.

Late in February, when regrowth begins (usually the crocuses come up at the same time), carefully weed the bed, thin the onions to 4 inches apart in the row, and side-dress with blood meal and/or complete organic fertilizer. Thinnings can be transplanted at that time into any gaps, used to establish new beds, given to grateful gardening friends to teach them the wonders of overwintered onions, or replanted densely for spring scallions. Side-dress again late in March with complete organic fertilizer; should March be especially rainy and leach out your bed, consider another scanty side-dressing late in April. Bulbing begins mid-May, and once that occurs, there's little point in additional fertilization.

Scallions are sown like storage onions, from April through July, depending on the variety. When well established, thin to about ½ inch apart in the row. Do not fertilize late sowings intended for overwintering as heavily as spring sowings, and separate them a little wider than summer scallions to enhance air circulation, which helps avoid molds and other diseases.

Garden planning One row-foot of well-grown bulb onions yields a pound or two. Fall storage onions rarely hold well because they rarely cure properly. Besides, I prefer the flavor of leeks. So I grow only overwintering bulb onions, which can cure well if you locate their bed where irrigation can be withheld during the month that bulbs are forming. I sow a small bed of scallions in April for summer but, as good as they are in salads, sweet and tender overwintered bulb onions are better. I make my major scallion sowing in July for winter salads. Scallions are also delicious in winter stir-fries.

Insects and diseases I've had no insect problems. Onion diseases can be a nuisance during harsh, rainy winters when the beds are overcrowded. The only preventive measure is better air circulation, achieved by more open plantings.

Harvest When bulbing starts, stop watering. If the plant divides into two separate parts (called "doubles" by onion growers), these will not keep long before rotting. Cure and bag them, but eat any doubles first. Onions that put up a seed stalk (bolters) will not bulb properly. When the flower stalk first appears, the plant should be pulled immediately and can be eaten as a giant scallion. Even under the best of circumstances a small percentage of overwintered onions will bolt and double;

sown too early, the majority may bolt.

When half the stalks have naturally fallen over, break over the remaining tops, wait a week or so, and then dig the onions and shake all soil from their roots. Lay them out in the sun to dry, covering them at night to protect them from dews. If it should rain much, gather them up and finish drying them under cover. After the bulbs are thoroughly dry, keep them in onion sacks. If not well ventilated, they may rot, so hang the sacks to allow free air circulation. Bulb onions store best in dry, cool conditions.

Harvest scallions by gradually thinning out the bed, permitting the remaining onions to grow bigger. Some varieties will multiply when large, refilling the bed. During winter the plants can look pretty ratty, but you'll be amazed at how good they look once the tops are cut back to about two-thirds their length and the outer skins are peeled off.

Saving seed

The general procedure for growing your own onion seed is similar to that described for leeks. With overwintered onions, the primary difference between a seed crop and a bulb crop is how large the plant has become when it experiences a period of cold weather. If the plant reaches much larger than pencil size by December, it will probably bolt. Top-quality sweet Spanish and storage onion seed is grown from carefully selected mature bulbs that are overwintered in storage and planted back out very early in spring to resprout, bolt, and make seed the next summer. To make top-quality seed from short-day overwintered onions, bulbs are planted back out in late fall, then they resprout, overwinter again, and make seed the next summer.

In either case, for seed production I'd select only perfect bulbs with narrow necks (these are better keepers, usually) that were the last to sprout in the sack. Incidentally, the sweetest onions also tend to be the flattest ones; round, globe-shaped bulbs tend to be the most pungent. Remember that when selecting onions for seed-making; it's also a helpful guide for selecting sweeter onions in the supermarket. Onions that double or bolt before bulbing should not be allowed to make seed; if you use their seed, soon all your onions will have the same bad traits.

Long-day and intermediate-day-length varieties

Open-pollinated sweet Spanish types are out of commercial vogue, so the open-pollinated varieties are usually pretty ragged. The same is true of storage onions. To stand a chance of getting decent open-pollinated seed, buy onion seed only from quality companies. Hybrid varieties are almost always of good commercial uniformity no matter who is the final retailer, but germination may vary depending on the ethics of your seed source.

There are also hybrid sweet Spanish/storage crosses that combine the milder flavor of the Spanish onion with the earlier maturity and longer storage potential of the storage type. These varieties are so numerous and change so rapidly that there is little point in listing them by name. Always choose the earliest maturities.

Red onions are usually pungent long-day storage types with red skins. Pickling onions are early-maturing Spanish types bred for thin, tender, translucent skins that don't require peeling. They are planted on very dense spacings so they don't grow large. Because they're used small, picklers or "pearl onions" can be direct-seeded. One warning: Many commercial onions bred for peat bog soils have root systems poorly adapted to "upland" or "mineral" soils, which is what almost all gardeners have. Stokes has the widest assortment of quality onion varieties of any catalog, but watch out for the company's "muck" varieties.

Overwintered varieties Although most people around here know of Walla Walla, it is no longer a well-selected, uniform variety. Territorial Seed is very interested in overwintering bulb onions and now sells several. West Coast also has them. Avoid overwintering varieties bred for southern latitudes, often called Grano or Granex. They bulb too soon in spring and aren't hardy enough to overwinter reliably. Incidentally, overwintering onions can also be started very early in spring and transplanted out like sweet Spanish types. They'll start bulbing several weeks later than if they had overwintered, will top down in July, and will end up somewhat smaller than if they'd overwintered but will still be quite sweet.

Scallion varieties Scallions with Japanese names are probably Welsh onions. Lisbon onions aren't hardy enough to handle eastern winters and aren't often found in eastern seed catalogs. Lisbons seem to come in many variations (or maybe many seed vendors sell mislabeled lots). Some bulb in summer and immediately resprout; some bulb in spring only after overwintering; all tend to multiply. I prefer Lisbon strains that don't form summer bulbs. Either way, I've always had good luck with mid-July sowings for fall, winter, and spring.

Dry-gardening Possible with overwintering onions; start them in a well-watered nursery bed and transplant them out at their final spacing in early November. If allowed to overwinter crowded in a nursery bed, they'll probably succumb to mildews.

MISCELLANEOUS ONIONS

(Allium cepa proliferum, A. cepa aggregatum)

Top-setting onions are perennial varieties that are used like scallions, grow in ever-enlarging clumps, and make bulblets atop the stalks instead of seed. Their bulblets aggressively self-sow and can become a nuisance. They're quite cold hardy and can seem invaluable after a bad winter freeze. The two varieties—Catawissa and Egyptian Walking—are not very different. They both "walk" because the tops become overweighted with maturing bulblets and fall over, and the bulblets then sow a few feet away from the central clump. Put them in the same sort of place you'd grow other aggressively spreading perennials, like horseradish.

Potato onions are a sort of easy-to-grow shallot with tops that taste good enough to be used as scallions. The bulbs aren't bad eating, either.

Miscellaneous Vegetables

ASPARAGUS *(Asparagus officinalis)*

Asparagus is a perennial that stores food in its root system. Early in spring, it rapidly converts those reserves into succulent shoots that grow several inches a day. Asparagus must have grown lushly the previous year (and have stored up lots of reserve food) if its spring spears are to be fat, tender, and abundant. Asparagus roots don't like wet, airless soil. Commercial production of asparagus is done on very well-drained, deep soils in regions where the soil stays dry in winter. On our side of the mountains, keeping an asparagus patch alive over the winter is virtually impossible on heavy, slow-draining soils. In drier microclimates and on deep, light loam soils, asparagus may not be too difficult. Perhaps.

Culture Asparagus can be started most cheaply from seed, but this economy adds two years to the time one has to wait until the first harvest. Most gardeners buy two-year-old roots from a garden center. In early spring, before the roots sprout, make trenches about 12 inches wide and at least 8 inches deep, spacing the trenches 4 to 6 feet apart. Pile the soil from each trench carefully along one side. Put a couple of inches of well-aged manure or compost into the bottom of the trench. Sprinkle a pint of regular lime and the same amount of dolomite lime, a quart of phosphate rock (or bone meal), and a gallon of complete organic fertilizer into each 50 to 100 trench-feet. Stand in the trench with a shovel or spading fork and work the organic matter, limes, and fertilizers in as deeply as possible, trying to break up the soil an additional 12 inches down. Then spread the same amount of organic matter over the mound of soil removed from the trench. It will blend in when the trench is filled.

Carefully spread out each root and lay it on the soil in the trench, with the crown up. Plant one root per foot; cover the roots about 1 inch deep by pulling some soil back down into the trench. The roots sprout in March. As shoots emerge, gradually fill in the trench, leaving only the tip of the shoot exposed. The trench will be completely filled by May.

In fall, when the tops turn brown, cut them down and compost them, then mulch the bed with an inch of manure or ½ inch of compost. Every spring after the crop has been harvested, sprinkle a gallon or two of complete organic fertilizer over each 100 row-feet of bed. Keep the bed very well weeded and deeply irrigated in summer. Encourage the ferns to grow as much as possible. The root system naturally goes down more than 4 feet. "Weeds" include any little asparagus plants that start from seed—if not pulled out, these will gradually crowd out the big roots and reduce the size of your spears.

To grow your own roots, make a humusy nursery bed. Sow the seed ½ inch deep, thinly, in rows about 2 feet apart. Do this in late April or early May. Thin the seedlings to about 4 inches apart in the row, fertilize well, keep weeded, and grow them for two years. Then dig the roots and transplant.

One sure solution for shallow or slow-draining soil is to build a box of treated (Cuprinol is the only nonphytotoxic preservative) marine plywood, 4 feet high, 4 feet wide, and 8 feet long, to sit atop your native dirt; fill it with highly enriched sandy loam; and grow your asparagus crop in that. Cover the box with a plastic sheet in winter to keep the rains out and the roots dry.

Another way to improve drainage is to plant the crowns right on the soil's surface after tilling, and to gradually hill up soil over the root crowns as though hilling potatoes. If this is done on flat ground, you'll have to bring in the soil to hill up with so the paths don't become water-filled canals during winter. Drainage should be better this way. In our region we certainly don't have to be concerned about burying asparagus crowns deeply to keep them from freezing.

Garden planning The asparagus bed may last indefinitely if fertility is maintained, if weeds are carefully controlled, if little asparagus seedlings are weeded out, and, most importantly, if drainage is good enough that the roots don't die from various soil diseases brought on by winter wetness. The hassle of establishing a bed may seem a lot of trouble, but unless heavy freezing or canning is intended, only 25 row-feet will supply an average family.

Insects and diseases Well-drained soil will prevent most losses from moisture-related diseases. Some years asparagus beetles may defoliate ferns. Spray with rotenone and/or neem;

defoliated ferns can't recharge the crowns for next year.

Harvest There will be no harvest the first year that two-year-old roots are transplanted. Only one spindly shoot (or, rarely, a couple of shoots) per crown will emerge. If these grow well, and if the bed survives the winter, the next year there will be many more shoots of larger size; harvest the largest spears for only one week. You need to exercise self-control and allow the roots to create an abundance of strong foliage, developing big food reserves. However, the year after that the bed should be thick with good-sized spears, and you can cut these for up to three weeks or until the size of the shoots begins to decrease, at which time you should allow the bed to develop ferns and recharge its underground food reserves. Old, really fertile beds that are not overcrowded can be cut for a month or longer every spring.

Saving seed Asparagus is wind-pollinated, and, like spinach, the plants are either male or female. Female plants develop red seed balls, and making seed is a great effort, leaving them less energy to direct into food storage, so females produce fewer, smaller spears. Male plants release pollen from small sacks and then, without the burden of seed making, store more food and produce larger, more abundant spears. Gather seeds when the pods are dry, but before they shatter.

To establish the highest-yielding bed that won't become overcrowded with seedlings, try this trick after the bed has proved to you that it will survive the winter. Dig and remove all female crowns, when their sex can be determined, and replace them with new crowns, or let the surrounding males gradually spread out and take over the area. Do this every year until there are no more females. The goal is a non-seed-producing bed.

Varieties Well-drained fertile soil is more important than varietal choices, but variety can be very important too. European seed companies have recently developed hybrid all-male varieties similar to all-female types of spinach. These combine highest yield with hybrid vigor. The seed is quite expensive. Territorial has a sandy loam trials ground and consequently has been able to do a lot of work with asparagus. These two suppliers address our main problem, which is winter soil moisture. The eastern seed houses are more concerned with ability to resist frozen soil through a harsh winter.

Dry-gardening If the bed survives dry-gardening, it will not thrive. It's not likely to be worth the trouble.

SWEET CORN *(Zea mays)*

Corn is easy to grow if properly fertilized and will make vegetative growth on almost any soil type. However, it won't always mature in time. Formation of ears is not controlled by how large the plant has grown, nor usually by day length (though a few day-length-sensitive corn varieties exist that are used in the far North). The change from vegetative growth to seed making (when the tassel appears) happens after the plant has experienced enough

heat. Plant breeders have developed a measurement called the "heat unit" to accurately quantify the conditions leading to maturity. After the last killing frost of spring, heat units are computed by adding up the number of hours during each 24-hour period that the temperature is above 50°F and multiplying this figure by the number of degrees the temperature is above 50°F.

In seed catalogs intended primarily for other companies in the seed trade, varieties of corn are not described as taking any specific number of days to maturity, but are listed according the number of heat units (HU) they require. The earliest maturing sweet corn varieties need about 1,300 HU to ripen; later types can require more than 2,200 HU. A very early variety like Earlivee is listed by Stokes at fifty-five days and by Johnny's at sixty-nine. What they're really saying is that at their particular trial grounds, that number of days is, on the average, how long it takes to accumulate 1,350 HU— the number Earlivee needs. A later variety like Jubilee, which takes eighty-four days at Stokes and eighty-seven days at Johnny's, needs about 1,750 HU. I tentatively conclude from the information in Stokes' and Johnny's catalogs that early summer is quite a bit warmer in Ontario than in Maine. Johnny's tomato and pepper varieties are, for that reason, also likely to serve us better than those from Stokes.

The Willamette Valley usually receives about 2,000 HU over the entire summer. At higher elevations in Oregon (like Lorane), average total accumulation might be 1,800 HU; to the north, around Puget Sound, there might be only 1,500 HU. Southern Oregon banana belts might receive about 2,400 HU. So that you can make a comparison, Umatilla, along the Columbia River in eastern Oregon, might get 3,000 HU. So a Umatilla gardener might grow two successive crops of early corn on the same plot in one summer, while a gardener in the foothills of northwestern Washington might be lucky to ripen any early corn at all in a cool year.

Culture Corn pollen is wind-blown; if the silks are not thoroughly pollinated, the ears do not fill. To achieve thorough pollination, corn is usually planted in blocks at least four rows wide by at least 10 feet long. For this reason, corn does not lend itself to raised-bed culture. Rain will also reduce pollination, so avoid overhead watering when the tassels are releasing pollen. *Do not space corn so densely that it can't go through a week of hot weather (while releasing pollen) without being irrigated.* The seed does not germinate in soil much below 60°F, although it is slightly more tolerant of cold, damp conditions than bean seed is. Corn is also sensitive to frost, so it should be sown no earlier than a few days before the last anticipated frost date. In the Willamette Valley, corn is sown about May I; at frosty Lorane, I planted it on June I, though it would have sprouted earlier most years (and then been frosted out).

Broadcast and work in I gallon of complete organic fertilizer per 100 square feet of growing area, spreading it evenly over the entire plot. Then make at least four parallel furrows about I to I½ inches deep and 30 inches apart. A good way to do this is by rolling the front wheel of a wheelbarrow or the parallel wheels of a garden cart down the just-rototilled area. This compresses the soil below the seeds. Or use a hoe or furrowing tool. Drop about four seeds per foot and cover them.

To avoid lowering soil temperature, do not water after sowing if at all possible. Hope for warm weather and quick sprouting. After germination, side-dress the seedlings with about I gallon of complete organic fertilizer per 100 row-feet. Within a couple of weeks of germination, thin the rows so the seedlings stand 8 inches apart in the row. Keep the weeds thoroughly hoed until the corn is knee-high, and then stay out of the patch to avoid compacting the soil. Keep the patch well watered except for when the tassels release pollen.

Garden planning Hybrid varieties mature uniformly; their ears remain in good eating condition for ten days at best. Simultaneously sowing separate blocks of three hybrid varieties that mature at ten-day intervals can create a five- to six-week harvest. The corn patch always seems to grow a fine stand of favas or clover when the crop's done; scatter the seed late in September and till it and the standing cornstalks in shallowly.

Insects and diseases Earworms (rare in our region) can be handled with Bt, sprayed when the tassels first drop pollen and again about ten days later.

Harvest Each variety has slightly different indicators of maturity. The ears may be ripe when the wrapper tips are browning off slightly; sometimes the ears will lean out when ready for picking. If you're growing a new-to-you variety, you may have to gingerly strip back the wrappers an inch from the end and peek to determine readiness.

Saving seed *(and growing field corn)* Five hundred feet of isolation will prevent most crossing, especially if the seed crop is upwind of any other corn. The appearance and flavor of the seed is partially determined by the genes of the seed, not only of the parent plant; so if, for example, you grow field corn such as a multicolored "Indian" corn near a patch of yellow corn, every ear of sweet corn in the patch that was pollinated at the same time that the Indian corn was releasing pollen will have occasional kernels of different colors, textures, and flavors. For this same reason, it is a good idea not to grow field corn and sweet corn in close proximity if they have similar maturities. The nature of corn seed is determined as much by the pollen that fertilized it as by the plant holding the ear, and field corn seeds are not particularly sweet, nor have they been bred for tenderness or for holding good eating quality for a long time after harvest.

Open-pollinated sweet corn varieties produce at best half the yield obtained from much more vigorous hybrids, so only a few open-pollinated varieties survive today. One way to keep up the seed quality of open-pollinated sweet corn is to shuck the ear and examine it right when picking it to eat; if it is a highly desirable ear, do not knock over the plant with your foot. Seeds can then be saved from the smaller second ears on selected plants that have been allowed to remain standing.

Harvest seed corn when the wrappers have browned completely and the seed is dry and shriveled. If it has not reached that point by the time late summer rains or dews stop the drying process, cut the whole plant close to the ground, tie them in bunches of ten or so, and hang the bunches upside down to finish drying under cover. Only the earliest varieties of both sweet and field corn will mature corn seed in the maritime Northwest, except in the southern parts of our region. Save seed for planting next year from many of the best ears.

Varieties Open-pollinated sweet corn is hardly worth growing unless you're against hybrids on principle. The few open-pollinated varieties left in existence are low yielding and far from the best eating, although Hooker's Sweet Indian (TSC) is a pretty tasty local legend; in fact, Territorial is to be commended for keeping this variety in its catalog.

For decades now, Jubilee has been the most popular main-season hybrid in the Willamette Valley (and the entire United States). It will just barely mature in warmer microclimates around Puget Sound, and it's a very unlikely variety for Whatcom County or British Columbia. Jubilee is found in virtually every seed catalog, so consider it a benchmark. Except in southern Oregon or northern California, I would not attempt any variety listed in a seed catalog as taking longer than Jubilee, and I would not hesitate to try any variety listed as earlier than Jubilee.

In western Washington and British Columbia, I'd choose an earlier variety to be my main crop. Earlier corns can't simultaneously be as high yielding as Jubilee and as fine tasting. It's one or the other. Here's why: Early varieties don't have as much growing time to store up massive food reserves before drawing them down to make seed. Before tasseling, the plant stores sugar in the stalk. Once corn pollinates, it rapidly begins translocating its food reserves into the fast-developing ear. (For a demonstration of this, chew on the sugary pith of a corn stalk before the tassel drops pollen. If you wanted to make corn syrup, you'd boil down juice squeezed from the pith. After the ear has filled, however, the pith is no longer sweet.) Many early varieties have been bred with the farmers' profits in mind and are geared toward harvesting the biggest possible ears from plants that occupy a valuable field for the shortest period of time.

But there ain't no free lunch on Earth. The kernels of a big-eared early variety are mainly fiber, water, and fluff at the expense of flavor. For my early varieties, I prefer smaller ears that have rich flavor. I've found that the Seneca series of sweet corn varieties are generally bred for taste. With early corn varieties you can't always tell which you're getting unless you can read between the lines, and even then a person can be fooled by a sharp catalog writer.

Variations in corn make interesting eating

and have the advantage of being varieties not intended for the commercial trade. I like bicolor varieties; they're no more difficult to produce than yellows. White corn tends to be too late; Silver Queen, the standard of white corn quality much in the same way that Jubilee is the standard of yellow sweet corn, barely matures in the Willamette Valley.

Some of the supersweets are not worth the bother in my opinion; they're very late, they require isolation from regular corn (or else those kernels pollinated by regular corn taste like field corn), and the very shrunken seeds germinate poorly under less-than-perfect conditions. How do you wait until the soil is really warm before sowing and then mature a very late variety in our climate? I also don't like how they taste—it's more like eating sugar than eating corn. However, SE (sugar-enhanced) supersweets are only a little sweeter than normal; retain a rich, corny flavor; and are as easy to grow as regular corn.

Dry-gardening To grow field corn without irrigation, sow as early as possible. Space the stand, two plants per clump, 3 feet apart, in rows 3 feet apart. Keep thoroughly weeded throughout the summer.

Annotated Bibliography

I prefer to learn from those who originated a body of knowledge, because those who follow in the founders' footsteps are followers, not trail blazers of equivalent depth. Even when the earliest works in a field contain factual errors in light of more recent information, the founders' books still contain enormous wisdom.

However, academia tends to cause the foundations of knowledge to be lost in obscurity. Scholarship continuously brings a large flow of new Ph.Ds on-line, all needing to publish or perish, all needing to invalidate the old so that their contribution seems important. The publishing industry, always looking for something "new" to sell, also contributes to this trend.

The disappearance of the old books would be okay if the new stuff were better and wiser, but usually the opposite is the case. I have observed this tendency in every area of study I've taken up seriously. As the sort of person Sir Albert Howard called "the laboratory hermit . . . someone who knows more and more about less and less" increasingly comes to dominate ever-wider areas of scholarship, the focus of scholarship gets ever narrower and less wise.

Here's an example. Despite the recent advances of so-called "scientific" agriculture, the nutritional qualities of our basic foodstuffs have been declining during this century. That's largely because most agronomists focus on bulk yield and profitability of the crop while knowing next to nothing about animal/human nutrition.

Industrial agriculture has also devastated the self-sufficient, independent lifestyles enjoyed by so many Americans as recently as one century ago. In 1870, most North Americans lived free and clear on farms or in tiny villages. As a consequence, they enjoyed enormously greater personal liberty than we do today. The current decline in personal rights in the United States and Canada is *not* the result of more people dividing up a fixed and limited amount of total possible liberty into smaller and smaller slices. It is a consequence of financial insecurity, financial dependence, and wage slavery. Only free persons can forthrightly demand their liberties.

Since 1870, as the industrial food system has become ever more "efficient," the price of basic agricultural commodities has become lower and lower. Consequently, most Americans rejected their self-sufficient-farm birthright for a paying job in town, and they soon became wage-enslaved. Wage slaves, like all other kinds of slaves, feel insecure and tend to think that they have to shuck and jive in order to survive.

The focus of the industrial system is on efficiency in all areas, including farming, but the apparent cheapness of economically rational agriculture does not reflect a true accounting of its costs. Despite the statistical increase in average lifespan, our average state of health and feelings of wellness have been declining. Consider as an example the large proportion of your neighbors whose mental awareness seems wrapped in fat. Americans especially are disdained worldwide for being hugely obese. Americans spend ever-larger portions of their productivity on the treatment and cure of disease, much of which is caused by their diets. This whole area of "health" care is not a productive use of effort; it really constitutes enormous waste, pain, and suffering, whose source is almost entirely unappreciated.

One would expect that young people would be the most vigorous, stronger and resilient. But older people typically have a much stronger constitution. What's been happening is that each generation has gotten a poorer "start" than the one before it as each generation has built the foundation of its health on foods produced on ever-more-degraded soils grown ever more scientifically, and more and more consisting of processed, denatured fodder. For a good discussion of the concept of "start," read Wrench's *Wheel of Health,* currently in print in paperback and also on-line in the Soil and Health Library at http://www.soilandhealth.org/.

Maybe someone will write and tell me who the sage was that so wisely quipped, "If they can stop you from asking the right questions, you'll never come up with the right answers." I've observed that modern higher education points people's attention away from the Truth and toward an ever-increasing confusion created by too much data. In consequence, many can no longer even recognize barefaced evil when it is in front of their eyes. I hope you will spend time with these key books written by amazing individuals, books that offer major illumination to those who can already see, books that speak the truth to those who can already hear.

WHERE TO FIND THEM

Most of the titles in this bibliography are out of print. Few libraries have them in their stacks, either. Make friends with your inter-library loan librarian. For a small fee, this service will place in your hands most of the books in this list, drawn from libraries around the United States and Canada.

One other resource is the on-line Soil and Health Library, a free public library on the World Wide Web that focuses on this area of study. Find it at http://www.soilandhealth.org/.

Albrecht, William A. *The Albrecht Papers.* Edited by Charles Walters Jr., 4 vols. Kansas City: Acres U.S.A., 1975.
> Albrecht's animal/soil/health studies and his tireless promotion of better farming gave his work significant impact from the 1940s through the 1960s. Perhaps no single individual did more to combine the rigors and legitimacy of academic science with the outlook of the agricultural radical. Unfortunately, Albrecht's willingness to consider nutrients as nutrients without making moral distinctions regarding "organic" versus chemical put him out of favor with J. I. Rodale, and thus placed Albrecht somewhat beyond the ken of contemporary organic gardeners and homesteaders. *The Albrecht Papers* is a collection of articles and lectures appearing in forums ranging from academic journals to dental convention proceedings to health magazines. Volume 2, a reprint of a connected and cohesive series of magazine articles, may be the best introduction.

Appelhof, Mary. *Worms Eat My Garbage.* Kalamazoo, Mich.: Flower Press, 1982.
> A delightful, slim, easy-to-read, and totally positive book offering enthusiastic encouragement to take advantage of vermicomposting.

Balfour, Lady Eve B. *The Living Soil.* London: Faber & Faber, 1943.
> Balfour sets out to muster all scientifically reputable evidence that organically raised food is especially health promoting. Balfour also outlines the beginnings of an experimental farm run on completely acceptable scientific standards to absolutely prove

her contentions. Donald Hopkins's book points out many flaws in Balfour's experiments.

Barrett, Dr. Thomas J. *Harnessing the Earthworm.* Boston: The Wedgewood Press, 1959.

A thorough work.

Bennett, Hugh H. *Soil Erosion: A National Menace.* USDA Circular No. 33. Washington, D.C.: U.S. Government Printing Office, 1928.

The clarion call for a massive effort to handle the problem of soil erosion before the agricultural base of American civilization was lost forever. Clear, concise, powerful writing. Bennett's efforts led to the crusade that founded the Soil and Conservation Service.

Borsodi, Ralph. *Flight from the City.* New York: Harper & Row, 1933.

Chronicles the Borsodi family's journey from job-in-the-city dependency to self-sufficient country independence. Borsodi was far-sighted enough to accomplish this move during the prosperity of the 1920s; his books served as guideposts for many anguished wage slaves who saw them as a means toward financial security, even survival, during the Great Depression. More, Ralph Borsodi was an amazingly intelligent social critic whose view cut to the very heart of the contradictions and problems of industrial civilization. Also see his books *The Distribution Age* (New York: Harper & Brothers, 1925) and *This Ugly Civilization* (New York: Harper & Brothers, 1929).

Bovill, E. W. *English Country Life 1780–1830.* London: Oxford University Press, 1962.

Social history at its most readable. The enclosures in rural England happened during the period this book addresses; this painfully harsh change set the stage for the modernization of English agriculture. Bovill's book helps the reader appreciate the background against which those first creators of scientific agriculture were operating. It covers the social and cultural conditions of the small holders, the cottagers, and the squires, as well as their economic and technical milieu.

Brink, Wellington. *Big Hugh: The Father of Soil Conservation.* New York: Macmillan Company, 1951.

Brink worked for Hugh Bennett's Soil and Conservation Service (SCS). His book stresses not only the magnitude of the SCS's accomplishments, but especially Bennett's democratic vision of voluntary farmer cooperation inspired and led by the SCS.

Bromfield, Louis. *Malibar Farm.* New York: Harper & Brothers, 1947.

Toward the end of his life, Bromfield, a popular American fiction author, indulged his deep interest in agriculture and alternative lifestyles by developing a cooperative farm on several hundred worn-out Ohio acres. There, he worked out a New American Farming that incorporated the thoughts of Howard, Bennett, Albrecht, and Leibig. He felt comfortable with chemical fertilizers, crop rotations, lime, organic pesticides whenever possible, and building organic matter. His writing is passionate and intelligent, and his book makes a most understandable case for the New Farming. His farm was a mecca for the agriculturally aware; his acquaintances included the major figures of radical and more standard agriculture. A sensitive anthology of Bromfield's agricultural writings that was compiled by Charles Little, with the assistance of Wendell Berry and Bromfield's publisher, is in print, titled *Louis Bromfield at Malibar* (Baltimore: John Hopkins University Press, 1988).

Campbell, Stu. *Let It Rot.* Pownal, Vt.: Storey Communications, 1975.

Probably the best guide to at-home composting.

Carson, Rachel. *Silent Spring.* Boston: Houghton Mifflin, 1962.

At the time of its publication, concerns about the concentration of pesticide residues through the food chain, resistances being developed to insecticides, and the serious health hazards from pesticide use were novel and frightening ideas. This book first made the American public aware of these dangers.

Carter, Vernon Gill, and Tom Dale. *Topsoil and Civilization.* Norman: University of Oklahoma Press, 1974 (first ed., 1954).

A historical review showing, region by region and civilization by civilization, a repeated pattern of ecological degradation leading to the shattering loss of productive capacity and inevitable decline and collapse. No civilization has lasted more than 1,500 or so years except Egypt. Egypt persisted because Egypt's ecology was remarkably resistant to destruction—although the Aswan high dam and the African population explosion seem to have finally broken that ecology down as well. Europe's soils are more resistant to destruction than the lands of earlier civilizations, but Europe may be approaching the saturation point in terms of population and land use intensity, and decisions will have to be implemented to save its productive base. The question is, will it decide intelligently or go the way of other earlier systems? As for the United States, it is losing its soil faster than any civilization in history.

Cleveland, David A., and Daniela Soleri. *Food from Dryland Gardens: An Ecological, Nutritional and Social Approach to Small-Scale Household Food Production.* Tucson: Center for People, Food and Environment, 1991.

A survey, made in the spirit of world consciousness,

of low-tech food production systems for semi-arid regions.

Colebrook, Binda. *Winter Gardening in the Maritime Northwest.* Seattle: Sasquatch Books, 1998.

> A major revelation when first published. The original was issued in 1977; it was revised in 1984 and again in 1998. Binda discusses the potentials and perils of winter gardening in detail. The latest edition contains updated source lists for winter varieties.

Darwin, Charles R. *The Formation of Vegetable Mould Through the Action of Worms with Observations on their Habits.* London: John Murray & Co., 1881.

> The trailblazing work in the area, by none less than Darwin. Still well worth reading.

Ernle, Lord (Prothero). *English Farming Past and Present.* 6th ed. First published in 1912. Chicago: Quadrangle Books, 1962.

> A perennial classic in any edition the reader can find, this is history at its most readable. The work lives on because of the quality of its narrative. Though focused on mere agriculture, Ernle demonstrates a philosophical understanding of life that is the equal of Gibbon, Beard, Parkman, and Braudel. Ernle, a farmer himself, understands the significances of technological innovation and the interactions between the cultivator, weather, and soil. He brings to life British agricultural experience and the individuals that shaped it. Worth reading by anyone interested in better farming.

Faulkner, Edward H. *Plowman's Folly.* Norman: University of Oklahoma Press, 1943.

> This book created quite a controversy during the 1940s. Though full of mistakes and shallow generalizations based on insufficient experience, the book will effectively make the reader aware of capillary water movements and how to enhance or inhibit them. Plowing tends to stop this essential flow of subsoil water.

Golueke, Clarence G., Ph.D. *Composting: A Study of the Process and Its Principles.* Emmaus, Pa.: Rodale Press, 1972.

> Golueke, writing in "scientific" jargon, can say more about composting in fewer pages using words three times as long as anyone else. He is American's undisputed authority on the subject.

Hall, Bolton. *Three Acres and Liberty.* First published in 1907. New York: Macmillan, 1922.

> A passionate plea for independence and self-sufficiency on small, intensively worked acreages. With a broad sense of history that would do justice to someone of our own era, Hall observes the social forces propelling people into city poverty when they could live with simple liberty and plenty in the country.

Many similar and far less intelligently stated pleas have followed *Three Acres and Liberty*, culminating in the *Mother Earth News* generation of the 1970s.

Hamaker, John D. *The Survival of Civilization.* Annotated by Donald A. Weaver. Lansing, Mich.: Hamaker-Weaver Publishers, 1982.

> A broad-ranging and imaginative impending-doom prophecy involving soil demineralization, human health, the rise and fall of planetary civilization, glaciations, and so on, containing a remarkable bibliography overlapping much contained in this annotated list.

Head, William. *Gardening Under Cover: A Northwest Guide to Solar Greenhouses, Cold Frames, and Cloches.* Seattle: Sasquatch Books, 1989.

> A comprehensive rundown of all of the tricks and strategies; very useful for someone who wants to extend every production possibility to the maximum.

Hopkins, Cyril G. "Bread from Stones." Agricultural Experiment Station, Circular #168. Urbana: University of Illinois, 1913.

> Hopkins was a crusader for the use of unaltered, natural rock flour fertilizers. Rock phosphate was then widely considered useless unless treated to make it soluble; Hopkins dove into the controversy with many pamphlets, speeches, and so on.

————. *Soil Fertility and Permanent Agriculture.* Boston: Ginn and Company, 1910.

> Hopkins's magnum opus points out that chemically treated nutrient substances cost more than the actual cash benefit they produce while having dubious effects on long-term yield; manure, phosphate rock, lime, occasional potassium supplements, and careful recycling of organic wastes result in a stable, lasting system of high yields and health. This is also a complete manual of soil and plant science as of its date of publication; later compendiums by others may benefit from more data but evidence far less wisdom.

————. *The Story of the Soil.* Boston: Richard G. Badger, 1910.

> *Warning:* This book expresses views on race that in its day were considered acceptable, but that in our day are seen as quite incorrect, perhaps even shocking. Those who cannot view such expressions as historical curiosities should not read *The Story of the Soil.* However, the book has redeeming value. This is one of the best "made-simple" soil manuals ever written, all wrapped up as a romance about a bright young man with a solid ag-school education, going out to buy a farm and falling in love.

Hopkins, Donald P. *Chemicals, Humus and the Soil.* Brooklyn, N.Y.: Chemical Publishing Company, 1948.

Hopkins thoroughly and undeniably makes the point that chemical fertilizers are effective and positive to the degree that humus remains in the soil; the real problem with chemicals, he states, has been with those who suggest that chemicals can replace farmyard manure. He takes on the Howardites point by point and demolishes many of their positions. The book's arguments are cogent and largely correct, although Hopkins's "scientific" biases distort his objectivity in areas relating to human health. This book should be carefully read by those who consider themselves "organic."

Hoppe, Henry. *What Every Gardener Should Know About Earthworms.* Charlotte, Vt.: Garden Way Publishing, 1973.

Hoppe was the world's recognized expert on the earthworm. His book is also a delight and really does contain what every gardener should know.

Howard, Sir Albert. *An Agricultural Testament.* New York: Oxford University Press, 1943.

A profound summation of a brilliant life's work. Howard explains how the failure to protect the soil's health leads to a certain decline in crop health and vigor, to disease and predation, and to poor health for those who consume the produce grown on sick soil—culminating, perhaps, in the irreversible decline of the civilization itself. It is filled with examples of how restoring soil organic matter has returned plantations, crops, and districts to health, and it also covers the manufacture of "manure" through composting. It contains a scathing criticism of our agricultural research system, with its fragmentation and various disciplines; a smart, educated farmer working on a problem on the land itself, he says, is more likely to work out sustainable systems. See also his last work, *The Soil and Health* (New York: Devin-Adair, 1947).

Howard, Sir Albert, and Yeshwant D. Wad. *The Waste Products of AgriCulture: Their Utilization as Humus.* New York: Oxford University Press, 1931.

Organic gardeners often have the impression that Howard was the sole creator of the Indore process and that he, virtually alone, discovered scientific composting. Actually, a number of investigators were actively publishing in the area at the time. Selman Waksman, the great soil microbiologist, was perhaps the most significant. This book outlines the research at Indore, provides a most detailed explanation of the various considerations relating to composting versus sheet composting and green manuring, and explains how and why the compost pile is the most thrifty way to preserve and increase biologically accumulated nitrogen. This is Howard at his best.

Howard, Louise E. *The Earth's Green Carpet.* Emmaus, Pa.: Rodale Press, 1947.

Albert Howard was devastated by the death of his first wife, Gabrielle. His second partner, Louise (Gabrielle's younger sister), herein beautifully summarizes, in simple language for the nonspecialist, Howard's life's work and the movement he founded. Her very well-written book will be particularly valuable to those who need an introduction to the entire realm of organic gardening and farming, as she covers all of the basics quite thoroughly. See also *Sir Albert Howard in India* (Emmaus, Pa.: Rodale Press, 1954) for a thorough biography of Howard's research career and the development of his unique and holistic understanding.

Jackson, Wes. *New Roots for Agriculture.* San Francisco: Friends of the Earth, 1980.

Following in the footsteps of J. Russell Smith, Jackson draws a most interesting distinction between trying to solve problems in agriculture, which is what most radical agriculturalists do, and solving the problem of agriculture itself. The problem of agriculture is that on most soils the plow causes more erosion than natural soil replacement, resulting in temporary civilizations. The planet has now run out of undegraded places to start new civilizations. Jackson's focus is on his native, eroded Kansas, where sod was destroyed to grow wheat and huge amounts of soil were lost. His solution is perennial grains. The book contains a most thorough and readable brief review of American radical agricultural history.

Jeavons, John. *How to Grow More Vegetables Than You Ever Thought Possible on Less Land Than You Can Imagine.* Berkeley: Ten Speed Press, 1982.

The original statement of French intensive biodynamic gardening.

Jenny, Hans. *Factors of Soil Formation: A System of Quantitative Pedology.* First published in 1941. New York: Dover Press, 1994.

These days, academic agricultural scientists conceal the basic simplicity of their knowledge by unnecessarily wrapping their views up in polysyllabic verbiage and higher mathematics. In Jenny's time it was not considered demeaning if an intelligent layman could read and understand the writings of a scientist or scholar. Any serious gardener who wants to understand the wide differences in soil should read this book. The paperback reprint is available and affordable. Thanks, Dover!

Kevan, D. Keith. *Soil Animals.* London: H. F. & G. Witherby, 1962.

Soil zoology for otherwise well-schooled lay readers. Very good.

King, F. H. *Farmers of Forty Centuries, or Permanent Agriculture in China, Korea and Japan.* Emmaus, Pa.: Rodale Press, 1911.

A survey of permanent organic agricultural systems as well as a fascinating description of far away and strange places at a time long ago. King, a sharp agricultural observer, traveled through Asia and photographed and reported on his travels. A classic, constantly referred to by Howard in his earlier works as a source of inspiration.

Koepf, H. H., B. D. Petterson, and W. Shaumann. *Bio-Dynamic AgriCulture, An Introduction.* Spring Valley, N.Y.: Anthroposophic Press, 1976.

A full exposition of the biodynamic school's ideas as they relate to mixed farming, showing how biodynamic techniques increase organic matter and make for a healthy farm. Stresses the closed system idealized in biodynamic agriculture. Perhaps the best I've read about the subject.

Kourick, Robert. *Drip Irrigation for Every Landscape and All Climates.* Santa Rosa, Calif.: Metamorphic Press, 1992.

A thorough manual of drip technology full of design information.

Krasil'nikov, N. A. *Soil Microorganisms and Higher Plants.* Translated by Y. A. Halperin. Jerusalem: Israel Program for Scientific Translations, 1961.

The key (and as yet unproven) assertion of the organic mindset is that food raised on humus or compost is more nutritious and health providing than chemically raised stuff. Here, in the magnum opus of a world-class Russian soil microbiologist, is assembled all data as of 1958, when the book was published by the Academy of Sciences of the USSR, correlating humus, microlife fertility, and food quality. Krasil'nikov pointedly asserts and demonstrates that soil fertility is the microbe and that plants require the "phytamins" produced by microbes to make the vitamins they and we need. Anyone wanting to be able to cogently argue the truth of the organic viewpoint has first to become fully acquainted with this book.

Kèuhnelt, Wilhelm. *Soil Biology: With Special Reference to the Animal Kingdom.* East Lansing: Michigan State University Press, 1976.

Soil zoology, written at a level that assumes that readers have university-level biology, zoology, and microbiology under their hats. It's still very interesting to a well-read lay person not intimidated by Latin taxonomy.

Logsdon, Gene. *Small Scale Grain Raising.* Emmaus, Pa.: Rodale, 1977.

The number of books about how to raise cabbages and apples and basil at home or on the homestead is virtually infinite. This is the only book I know of that guides nonfarmers toward the production of their own cereal crops.

Lord, Russell. *To Hold This Soil.* Miscellaneous Publication No. 321. Washington, D.C.: United States Department of Agriculture, 1938.

A beautifully made, designed, and illustrated book by and for the Soil and Conservation Service (SCS). Lord passionately and poetically outlines American agricultural destructiveness and the cures being instituted by the SCS. It seems surprising, in light of the nature of our recent national administrations, that a government publication would evidence such fine and humane writing or that any government bureau could attract people of such quality as Russell Lord.

Lord, Russell, and Kate Lord. *Forever the Land.* New York: Harper & Brothers, 1950.

The Lords became deeply involved with the Friends of the Land movement and its magazine/journal *The Land.* This book introduces the milieu and the persona of the 1940s—a most energetic and hopeful time in America—when it seemed that our farm problems could be solved by the efforts of right-thinking, intelligent men and women. Here one meets Hugh Bennett, Louis Bromfield, J. Russell Smith, Aldo Leopold, Paul Sears, and even John Dos Passos.

Loudermilk, Walter C. *Palestine: Land of Promise.* New York: Harper & Brothers, 1944.

Loudermilk, a prime mover in the Soil and Conservation Service, toured Palestine just prior to World War II. He was most impressed with the creative force of Jewish settlement and documented the state of the country, both in socioeconomic and in agricultural/ecological areas. The book also tells the sad story of the destruction of an ecosystem through erosion and the hopeful story of Palestine's rehabilitation by its returning Jewish settlers.

Lundberg, Ferdinand. *The Rich and the Super Rich.* New York: Lyle Stuart, 1968.

Anyone contemplating social change or concerned about the problems of our farming and health systems has to consider the actual nature of our political system. This book is a powerful and wryly funny exposé of who really rules America or, at least, who really ruled it in 1968. The cast of ruling characters has changed slightly since that time, but the method and system of their rule seem identical today. There was another, more popular book (popular because its contention was more acceptable to academia) called *Who Rules America.* Don't confuse them. *Who Rules America* concludes that about one-tenth of I percent of the population is an effective ruling class and describes the nature and concerns of that upper class. That number—amounting to perhaps 300,000 people—is a very thin slice of the whole population of a country that pretends to be a democracy. But Lundberg's analysis proves that the real rulers are more like a big roomful consisting virtually entirely of men. Maybe a hundred or so. And Lundberg shows exactly how they rule.

McCarrison, Sir Robert. *The Work of Sir Robert McCarrison.* Edited by H. M. Sinclair. London: Faber & Faber, 1953.

The organic farming movement rested on the work of two men, Albert Howard and Robert McCarrison. While Howard's thoughts attained the permanency of books and consequently are still widely available today, McCarrison's writings vanished into the dusty back shelves of old journal holdings. This book resurrects McCarrison's papers of the 1920s, provides a complete McCarrison bibliography, and introduces the reader to an unadulterated telling of his experiments at Coonoor, where he created extraordinary health and miserable illness in rat populations by feeding them the national diets of various Indian and European races. This book will also be of great interest to anyone concerned with natural health. See also McCarrison's *Nutrition and Health* (London: Faber & Faber, 1936). It's hard to find in print but is available on-line at http://www.soilandhealth.org/.

Minnich, Jerry. *The Earthworm Book: How to Raise and Use Earthworms for Your Farm and Garden.* Emmaus, Pa.: Rodale Press, 1977.

A thorough, comprehensive, and encyclopedic survey of the subject.

Minnich, Jerry, and Marjorie Hunt. *The Rodale Guide to Composting.* Emmaus, Pa.: Rodale Press, 1979.

A complete survey of composting: at home, on the farm, and for municipalities. There are numerous later editions, but in my opinion, the original 1979 edition is the best of the lot. It is more cohesive and sounds less as though it was compiled by a committee. *Organic Gardening and Farming* magazine may have been at its best during part of the 1970s, when Minnich was its senior editor.

Nabhan, Gary. *The Desert Smells Like Rain: A Naturalist in Papago Indian Country.* San Francisco: North Point Press, 1987.

Describes Native American dry-gardening techniques that can be applied to the maritime Northwest. This is also a beautiful and sensitive journal of inner adventure.

Nearing, Helen, and Scott Nearing. *Living the Good Life: How to Live Sanely and Simply in a Troubled World.* First published in 1950. Reprint, New York: Schoken Books, 1970.

The original is out of print, but a Nearing anthology is available. The Nearings were among the most philosophically intelligent Americans ever to make the change from urban to rural, from family to intentional community, from a cash-labor economy to voluntary simplicity. Their classic book has been a profound influence on the several cadres of back-to-the-landers, including me. The book describes how and why the Nearings decided to move from New York City to a Vermont farm, how they built using native materials, and how they developed sustainable food production systems and a domestic economy that required very little cash, yet produced a maximum of free time and enjoyment. It also discusses their understanding of health, its derivation from good nutrition, and the treatment of disease conditions by natural methods. Incidentally, Scott Nearing remained active and alert until his 100th birthday, when he made a decision that he'd had enough, went to his bed, and departed this life a few days later.

Orr, Sir John B. *Minerals in Pastures and Their Relation to Animal Nutrition.* London: H. K. Lewis & Co., 1929.

Albrecht derived much of his inspiration from Orr's works. This very readable book is a complete data review (as of 1929) linking soil fertility with grass/pasture mineralization with animal health. Here is incontrovertible proof that soil fertility equals health, at least for cows.

Parnes, Robert. *Fertile Soil: A Grower's Guide to Organic and Inorganic Fertilizers.* Originally published as *Organic and Inorganic Fertilizers.* Mt. Vernon, Maine: Woods End Agricultural Institute, 1986. Reprint, Davis, Calif.: AgAccess, 1990.

A practical book, one intermediate in complexity between a garden book and a university-level ag-school text on soil. Parnes asks the right questions. He is neither "organic" nor "chemical" but transcends this conflict and arrives at some pretty universal understandings.

Pfeiffer, E. E. *The Earth's Face and Human Destiny.* Emmaus, Pa.: Rodale, 1947.

A survey of proper land use and man's proper attitude to the land, complete with photos and poetic imagery. This small work is Pfeiffer's least "biodynamic" and perhaps most acceptable to the general reader.

————. *Biodynamic Farming and Gardening.* New York: Anthroposophic Press, 1938.

Without a doubt his best work. Avoids the abstruse verbiage used by Rudolph Steiner, founder of the biodynamic system, and presents a basic organic message, covering a complete method for farm and garden.

Picton, Dr. Lionel James. *Nutrition and the Soil: Thoughts on Feeding.* New York: Devin-Adair, 1949.

Why are whole wheat bread, dairy, fruits, and vegetables that are produced on healthy soil the staff of life? Dr. Picton demonstrates through his own patient files and the animal studies of other researchers how the body needs what is in wheat germ and wheat bran to properly use the rest. Picton, in alignment with his friend and much-admired associate Albert Howard, also asserts that chemically fertilized food is not health producing. However, this vital portion of the book is weakly documented. Contains the "Medical Testament" as a single chapter, a much-referred-to document critical of the state of British public health that shook up Britain after World War II.

Pottenger, Francis M. Jr., M.D. *Pottenger's Cats.* Edited by Elaine Pottenger with Robert T. Pottenger Jr., M.D. La Mesa, Calif.: Price-Pottenger Nutritional Foundation, 1983.

These simple studies in cat nutrition have profound implications for human nutrition and health, implications that modern medical science has done an excellent job of totally ignoring. Cats, naturally consumers of raw mice, other small mammals and birds, insects, and so on, are genetically unable to properly digest cooked foods. By a simple alteration from raw to cooked foods, Pottenger caused cats to grossly deteriorate over several generations until they could no longer breed. Manifestations of degeneration included antisocial behavior, emotional unbalance, immune system deterioration, poor dental development, and alterations in facial appearance due to improper skeletal formation, very similar to the gross problems affecting Americans today. If the degeneration was turned around with proper diet before total infertility occurred, the population could begin to recover, and after several generations with correct diet, the cats reassumed healthy form and vigor.

Price, Weston A. *Nutrition and Physical Degeneration.* First published in 1939. Reprint, La Mesa, Calif.: Price-Pottenger Nutrition Foundation, 1970.

Price, a prosperous 1920s dentist, was frustrated with his researches into preventive dentistry. He suspected that his studies were inconclusive because no control group of healthy humans was available. Price set out to discover whether there remained on Earth any groups of people with excellent teeth—and he found them of every race and on every continent. In every case, they were so isolated that there was no store selling "civilized" food. In addition, these people lived either by the sea and made seafoods a significant portion of their diet, or were organic agriculturists. In both cases, their food supply was maximally nutritious. The book is full of photos showing good versus poor dental/facial development. A great classic of nutrition/health literature that should be read by all. After reading this book, you'll never look at your neighbors' facial structures and body types the same way. G. T. Wrench's *The Wheel of Health* is the perfect complement to this book.

Rodale, J. I. *Pay Dirt.* Emmaus, Pa.: Rodale Press, 1945.

Albert Howard commented in his introduction to this book that Rodale was audacious to plunge so enthusiastically into a new field and educate himself. Rodale was more than audacious; his desire to oversimplify has shaped the prejudices of organic gardeners ever since. This book is a good review of all of Rodale's ideas and the sources that shaped his conceptions. It is clear that he had a compulsive dislike for chemical fertilizers and would overly condemn them on shallow grounds as well as solid ones; and that he had little sense of agricultural macroeconomics. Well worth reading for those who are unfamiliar with the antagonistic stance found in the older *Organic Gardening and Farming* magazines. See also *The Healthy Hunzas* (Emmaus, Pa.: Rodale, 1948).

————. *The Organic Front.* Emmaus, Pa.: Rodale Press, 1948.

An intensely ideological statement of the basic organic faith. Rodale's views, limitations, and preferences have largely defined the meaning of the word "organic" ever since.

Russell, Sir E. John. *Soil Conditions and Plant Growth.* 8th ed. New York: Longmans, Green & Co., 1950.

The soils science manual of England since 1913, taken through numerous revisions until 1943 by Sir E. John (for many years director of Rothamstead). Later editions and revisions were carried on by his son. Even the 1950 edition is readable and generally understandable without an advanced background in science, focusing on the relations between soil conditions and the responses of plants to them. Especially good is the first chapter, a review of the history and development of agricultural chemistry. This book should be carefully studied by anyone who really wants to intelligently relate to their plants. The very disappointing eleventh edition has been recently rewritten by a committee of experts and has consequently lost most of the elegant simplicity and beauty of earlier efforts.

Schaller, Fredrich. *Soil Animals.* Ann Arbor: University of Michigan Press, 1968.

Soil zoology without the big words, written for readers without an extensive scientific background. Shaler was Kèuhnelt's student. A very useful introduction for the ordinary reader.

Schuphan, Werner. *Nutritional Values in Crops and Plants.* London: Faber & Faber, 1965.

Every radical agriculturist is certain that organically raised food is more nutritious. Schuphan probes this belief and, after much experimentation, proves that there actually are differences in food quality. Unfortunately for the organic faithful, he contests that food raised with manure/compost and then additional chemical fertilizers is the best of all. Schuphan also carefully defines the parameters of "quality" and considers other aspects of growing, harvesting, and preserving quality. A most useful book.

Shaler, Nathaniel Southgate. *Man and the Earth.* 1905. Reprint, New York: Johnson Reprint Corp., 1971.

The first overall consideration of man as a part of earth's ecology and our effect on our ecosystem and resource base, with an emphasis on soil erosion that well anticipated the work of the SCS. Also good, readable writing.

Smith, J. Russell. *Tree Crops: A Permanent Agriculture.* First published in 1929. Reprint, Old Greenwich, Conn.: Devon-Adair.

Anticipating the dust bowls and urgent movement toward soil conservation of the 1930s, anticipating *Topsoil and Civilization* by two decades, anticipating Wes Jackson's grassland permaculture thrust by five decades, Smith's plea was that the only responsible system to use on uplands is a system of permaculture tree crops—chestnut, oak, filbert, various tropical legumes, and so on. The book suggests that tree forage crops yield as much meat per acre as good grass pastures and that tree farming is much less work; it also gently asserts that certain nuts might be better human food than meat. Although energy usage and the cost in energy per calorie produced was not one of Smith's concerns, certainly tree crops require virtually no machinery and little or no use of oil or other chemicals. Readers interested in the development of Smith's unique vision might see also his book *The World's Food Resources* (New York: Henry Holt, 1919).

Solomon, Steve. *Water-Wise Vegetables.* Seattle: Sasquatch Books, 1993.

This is a guide to growing food without dependence on irrigation. It was written entirely from personal observations and original research between 1979 and 1993, all in western Oregon, a climate that has virtually no rainfall from June through September, a guaranteed four months of drought every year. It has broad applications anywhere that the rains can't be depended upon and to anyone who is using a well or is off the grid. There's another facet to this book too. The current gardening trend is intensive, postage-stamp, high-yield raised beds. This book explains the dynamics behind the absolute opposite of what everyone else is doing: extensive, low-yield, low-maintenance gardening.

Stout, Ruth. *Gardening Without Work: For the Aging, the Busy, and the Indolent.* Old Greenwich, Conn.: Devin-Adair, 1961.

The original statement of perennial mulching. This book, though inapplicable to the maritime Northwest vegetable garden, is still a delight to read. It almost makes me wish I could live back east, where the snow covers the fields for months on end. Richard Clemence, her disciple, published several books in the late 1970s that develop the method further.

Sykes, Friend. *Humus and the Farmer.* Emmaus, Pa.: Rodale Press, 1949.

A collection of essays, magazine pieces, and various ramblings, some very readable, some pretty stuffy, that have inspired many. Sykes was an active British farmer, lecturer, and writer of farmers' magazine pieces. An acquaintance had purchased a worn-out though potentially rich farm atop a limestone-derived soil body and, through natural methods, without fertilizer, resuscitated it. Sykes was so impressed that he sold his rich farm and purchased 750 worn-out acres atop a chalk bed and proceeded to restore the place through subsoiling, deep-rooted semi-permanent pastures, and composting. Sykes was closely involved with Albert Howard, Eve Balfour, and so on. See also *Food, Farming and the Future* (Emmaus, Pa.: Rodale, 1951).

Tompkins, Peter, and Christopher Bird. *The Secret Life of Plants.* London: Lane, 1974.

What is a plant? What is the nature of the living system we are all part of? Those who think they know the answer to these questions or who would like to explore them further should read this most interesting book. See also *Secrets of the Soil* (Anchorage: Earthpulse Press, 1998).

Turner, Frank Newman. *Fertility, Pastures and Cover Crops Based on Nature's Own Balanced Organic Pasture Feeds.* First published in 1955. Reprint, San Diego: Rateaver, 1975.

Turner was at the forefront of the English natural farming movement during the 1940s and 1950s. This book demonstrates how a smart farmer can figure out natural systems that work. His main thesis is that conventional dairying operations, depending on purchased food concentrates, fertilizer, and medicines, are much less profitable than low-input systems where soil fertility builds itself and the health of the animals as well. His definition of fertility is based not on bulk yield but on biological assay, measuring food quality by measuring the health of the animals living from the land itself. Turner made use of deeply rooting herbal/grass pasture mixes, including numerous species that access nutrients below the topsoil; long rotations with many years in grass/herbal mixtures, all parts of the rotation but the hay grazed in place; and a simple in-field silage production and feeding system that greatly improves feed value compared to hay made too late. See also *Fertility Farming.*

U.S. *Dept. of Agriculture. Soils & Men: Yearbook of Agriculture, 1938.* Washington, D.C.: Government Printing Office, 1938.

From the viewpoint of the natural farmer/gardener, this particular yearbook represents the USDA's best. It came out when Washington was concerned with devastating soil erosion and declines in agricultural productivity and prosperity, and the "new agriculture" promoted by the Friends of the Land was enthusiastically going forward. In the volume are articles by Albrecht on organic matter and conservation and a definitive survey of soil erosion by Hugh Bennett and Walter Loudermilk, as well as general reviews of most aspects of soil science. It also contains a very complete bibliography.

Voisin, André. *Soil, Grass and Cancer.* New York: Philosophical Library, 1959.

The key unanswered questions of radical agriculture are proving that better soil makes better food and thus healthier people. Though flawed and only partial, here is that proof, primarily through relating variations in soil fertility to the laboratory and biological assays of food quality. A wide-ranging, openminded book. Voisin is better known for his works on pasture management, but this effort is probably his most significant. See also *Grass Productivity* (London: Crosby Lockwood and Sons, 1959), *Better Grassland Sward* (London: Crosby Lockwood and Sons, 1960, which contains a thorough survey of the role of the earthworm in soil fertility), and *Grass Tetany* (London: Crosby Lockwood and Sons, 1963).

Waksman, Selman A. *Humus: Origin, Chemical Composition and Importance in Nature.* Baltimore: The Williams & Wilkins Company, 1938.

The comprehensive text on the subject by the master of research.

Widtsoe, John. *Dry Farming: A System of Agriculture for Countries Under Low Rainfall.* New York: Macmillan, 1920.

Between the lines one can read how farmers' lack of ethics and greed led them to ignore Widtsoe's warnings, making the Great Plains dustbowls inevitable. I also found the dry-gardening insights here to research my own book *Water-wise Vegetables.* There are lots of clues for someone seeking to reduce their dependence on the water pump and grow their own food strictly on natural rainfall.

Williams, Roger J. *Nutrition Against Disease.* New York: Pitmann, 1971.

A thorough and very readable introduction for the reader who feels uncertain about the connections between health and nutrition. Williams was a university medical researcher more interested in the cellular-level nutritional causes of disease than in inventing drugs to "cure" diseases.

Whorton, James. *Before Silent Spring: Pesticides and Public Health in Pre-DDT America.* Princeton, NJ: Princeton University Press, 1974.

DDT was by no means the beginning of the poisoning of America; Arsenic/ lead insecticides were far more dangerous than organophosphates and were used nearly as widely as DDT later came to be depended on. Whorton shows the development of pesticide use and the early attempts to limit their damage. The horrors in this book really stick with the reader.

Wrench, G. T., M.D. *The Restoration of the Peasantries, with especial reference to that of India.* London: C. W. Daniel Co., Ltd., 1939.

Through a review of history and world conditions, including unique looks at Rome, China, Japan, India, and Java, Wrench persuasively makes the case that capitalistic farming leads only to destruction of the soil, loss of health and degradation of humans, while peasant farming systems are perpetual and health-producing. Wrench has a fresh outlook that unfortunately has not remained of contemporary interest. See also *The Wheel of Health* (below) and *Reconstruction by Way of the Soil* (London: Faber & Faber, 1946).

————. *The Wheel of Health.* First published in 1938. Reprint, Lee Foundation for Nutritional Research, 1960; Escondido, Calif.: Bernard Jensen International, 1990. Currently available on-line by permission of C. W. Daniels Company in the Soil and Health Library, http://www.soilandhealth.org/.

One of the first expositions of how soil fertility and diet create human health. A health classic that should be read by all.

Index

Boldface type denotes charts, illustrations, or tables.

Growth regulators, 45
"Gumbo," 67

H

Hardening-off, 129, 131, 194–95
Harvest
    extension with plant spacing, 121–22, 158
    extension with variety mixtures, 121
    yields, 130–31, 232
    See also specific vegetables
Hay
    carbon-nitrogen ratio, **84**, 91
    from clay soil, 61–62
    contribution to organic content, 50, **51**, 52
    nutrient quality of, as feed, 27, 30, 42–43
Heat unit, 335
Herbicides
    in cottonseed meal, 36
    glyphosate, 57
    root exudates as, 114
    for sod elimination, 57
Herbs, 120–21
Hoes
    how to make, 20–21
    how to sharpen, 18–20, **20**
    importance of, 9, 47
    onion, **20**
    with stilettolike blade, **20**
    weeding technique with, 8, 17–18, **18**, **19**
Horse beans. *See* Fava beans
Horticultural beans (*Phaseolus vulgaris*), 249–51
Hot cap, **208**
Hot frame, 205
How to Grow More Vegetables Than You Ever Thought Possible on Less Than You Can Imagine, 137
Humidity and seed storage, 184–85
Humus, 33–34
    carbon-nitrogen ratio, 78
    definition of, 72
    effects of cropping pattern, 50, **51**, 52
    effects of fertilizer, 79
    effects of gardening, 52–53
    importance of, 44–45
    regional variation in, 48
    role in soil tilth, 46–47, 49
    water absorption by, 61, 159
Hybridization, 6–7, 186–87
Hydroponics, 45

I-J

Indeterminate growth habit, 238, 252
Inoculants, role in composting, 91–93
Insects
    coexistence with, 218–19
    companion planting, 111
    crop rotation and, 115–20
    local ecology and abundance, 216–17
    See also Pesticides; *specific vegetables*
Intensive gardening, 7, 60, 151
Irrigation. *See* Sprinklers; Watering
Jeavons, John, 60, 150
Johnny's Selected Seeds, 180–81

K-L

Kale (*Brassica oleracea acephala; B. napa; B. napus pabularia*), 254, 288–90
    how to grow transplants, **207**, 209
    nutrients in, 274, 289
    sugar production in, 128
Kelp meal, 35, 36, 131–32
Kohlrabi (*Brassica oleracea caulorapa*), 122, 209, 290–91
Leaching, 27, 32, 138, 139
Leaf miners (*Liromyza species*), 224, 272, 295
Leeks (*Allium porrum*), 209, 323–27
Legumes, 230
    as cover crops, 55, 254–56
    for eating, 242–54
Lentils (*Lens culinaris*), 253–54
Lettuce (*Lactuca sativa*), 264–66
    cold frames for, 125, **128**, **207**, 209, 264–65
    growth rate and planting schedule, 15–17, **16**, **16**, 131
Light, 12–17
    fertilization and intensity of, 37
    fluorescent grow lights, 202–3, **203**
    illumination period. *See* Photoperiod
    intensive gardening and, 60
    number of sunny days per month, 124
    seasonal changes in intensity, **15**
Lima beans (*Phaseolus limensis*), 251
Lime, 31–33, 34
    application of, 53
    for asparagus, 333
    in complete organic fertilizer, 35
    enhancement of clay soil, 63, 64
    enhancement of sandy soil, 66
    for melons, 315
Limestone, 32
Loam, 64, 66–67
Long-term rotations, 115–20

M

Magic in the garden, 111–14
Magnesium, 31–32
    in liquid fertilizer, 39
    for melons, 315
    selective leaching of, 27, 32
Mail-order seed companies, 180–83
Manure
    carbon-nitrogen ratios, **84**
    chicken, 40–42, 43, 79, 86, 91
    compost from, 90–91
    as fertilizer, 39, 40–43
    green. *See* Green manure
    horse, 90–91
    Northwest, poor quality of, 26, 27, 30–31, 34, 42–43
    sawdust in, 43, 90
    tillage as, 47
Manure tea, 39
Melons (*Citrullus lantatus; Cucumis melo*), **128**, 209, 315–17
Mendel, Gregor, 7
Metaldehyde, 225
Mexican bean beetle, 244
Mice, 34, 291, 295, 302
Microirrigation, 148
Microorganisms in the soil
    diurnal migration of, 56

harvest of 2 1/2 months a year, 99–101
harvest of 12 months a year, 101–7, **128**
of light, 12–14
number of sunny days, 124
of pest control, 56
sugar production after a frost, 128, 280, 289
Seed business, economics of the, 174–80
Seed companies, reputable, 179–83, 233
Seed meal, 79
carbon-nitrogen ratio, **84**
in complete organic fertilizer, 35
in compost, 86
pricing of, 35
Seed racks, 179–80
Seed saving, 185–87. *See also specific vegetables*
Seeds, 163–87
effects of high temperatures, 80
germination factors, 168–74
how to sprout, 173
planting techniques, 170–71
reputable companies for, 179–83, 233
storage tips, 106–7
variety mixtures of, 121
vigor of, 164–68
Seeds of Change, 249
Self-fertilization, 234–35, 236, 240
Semitropical plants. *See* Solanums
Shallots (*Allium cepa*), 321–22
Sheet-composting, 79–80
Short-term rotation, 110–14
Shovels, 21, 58
Shredder/grinder, 84
Side-dressing fertilization, 38–39, **39**, 131
Silt and silty soil, 61, 62, 64, 66–67
Slug gel, 226
Slug traps, 225, **226**
Slugs (*Gastropodae*)
how to remove from food, 226
in mulch, 56, 225
on vegetables, 224–26, 268, 285–86, 291
Snap beans. *See* Bush beans; Pole snap beans
Snow peas, 252, 253
Sod, elimination of, 56–57
Soil
clay. *See* Clay soil
color of, 172, 244, 313, 315
depth of, 159
Eastern, 27
ideal, composition of, 64
initial preparation of, **28**, 32, 53, 59, 109–10
leaching of minerals from, 27, 32, 138
microorganisms in. *See* Microorganisms in the soil
optimum NPK ratio, 35
Pacific Northwest, poor quality of, 26–27, 36
pH, 31, 34
"resting" of the. *See* Fallow techniques
role in composting, 88
sandy. *See* Sand and sandy soil
seedling/potting, 169–71, 197–99
silt. *See* Silt and silty soil
testing of, 31, 62–63, 65, 140
water absorption by, 137–38.
See also Moisture in the soil
Soil Conservation Service (SCS), 65, 130

Soil ecology, 44–46, 49–50, 52, 56, 73
Soil management, **28–29**, 30–31
Soil Microorganisms and Higher Plants, 45, 71
Soil texture
air and, 46, 47, 56, 61
effects of compaction, 57–58
effects on potatoes, 302–3, 304
the quality of tilth, 46–47
Soil thermometer, 172
Soil type, 65–67
effects on alliums, 320, 332
effects on root vegetables, 293–94
leaching and, 32–33
specific heat and, 267
watering and, 137, **138**
Solanums, 230, 233–42
Solar greenhouses, 123–24
Sorrel, 273
Sow bugs, 56
Soybeans (*Glycine max*), 251
Spacing. *See* Plant spacing
Specific heat of water, 267
Sphagnum moss, 198, 199
Spinach (*Spinacia oleracea*), **128**, 270–72
Sprinklers
high- *vs.* low-application rate, **141**, 141–42
stands for, **147**, 148
system design, 142–48, **145**, **155**
testing of, 139–40
water distribution patterns, 140, 142–44, **143**
Sprouting medium, 169–71
Squashes and pumpkins (*Cucurbita maxima; C. mixta; C. moschata; C. pepo*), **128**, 165, 210, 311, 317–20
Stokes Seeds, 181
Storage tips
alliums, 322, 331
Belgian endive, 300
carrots, 222, 298
fertilizer, 34
potatoes, 307
rutabagas, 292
seeds, 106–7, 184–85
winter squash, 318
Streaks, 252
Subsoil, 64, 97
Succession of crops, annual, 105–6
Sugar production, 13, 128, 280, 289
Summer squash. *See* Squashes and pumpkins
Sweet corn (*Zea mays*), 335–38
heat units of, 335
how to grow transplants, 208
sugar production in, 338
supersweets, 338
Swiss chard (*Beta vulgaris cicla*), **128**, 272
Symphylans (*Scutigerella immaculata*), **213**
on broccoli, 278
crop rotation and, 115–20, 256
description of, 116
on spinach, 270, 271
on Swiss chard, 272

T

Tai sai, 269
Temperature

SPECIAL OFFER
Get Growing!

Sasquatch Books has arranged with Territorial Seed Company of Lorane, Oregon, to provide you with a sample packet of seed for your Northwest garden.

Choose one of the three vegetables listed below; then fill out and send the form at the bottom of the page. Your sample seeds will be sent with a full catalog from Territorial Seed Co., offering dozens of vegetable varieties ideally suited for home gardens west of the Cascades.

Buttercrunch Lettuce

Similar to bibb types, but with thick, juicy, sweet leaves and tight, small heads. When the weather turns hot, Buttercrunch doesn't become bitter. It stands well into fall and makes good growth when used in spring cold frames.

Santiam Tomatoes

A delicious determinate variety remarkably adapted to our summer's cool nights. Developed by Dr. Baggett at OSU, Santiam produces fruit especially early because blossoms don't drop when nights fall below 50 degrees. Later, when nights warm up, the tomatoes have seed. Determinate habitat; parthenocarpic fruit; very good flavor.

Sweet Meat Winter Squash

Extra-hard, thick, slate-gray skin protects round, 10-15 lb. squash all winter. Its excellent keeping quality and flavor have made it a favorite west of the Cascades, though it is virtually unknown in the rest of the United States.

ORDER FORM

☐ Please send me a sample packet of (choose one of the vegetables listed above):

Name
_____

Address
_____

City/State/Zip
_____

☐ Please send me a complete catalog of Sasquatch Books.

Return this coupon to:

Territorial Seed Company

P.O. Box 27; 80030 Territorial Road; Lorane, Oregon 97451; 503/942-9547

11/05